# TRAPS

for Michael and Sue

in support of

enlightened Black

manhood

in friendship
Merry Xmas
[signature]

# AFRICAN AMERICAN MEN ON GENDER AND SEXUALITY

Edited by Rudolph P. Byrd and Beverly Guy-Sheftall

INDIANA UNIVERSITY PRESS BLOOMINGTON & INDIANAPOLIS

This book is a publication of

Indiana University Press
601 North Morton Street
Bloomington, IN 47404-3797 USA

http://iupress.indiana.edu

*Telephone orders*   800-842-6796
*Fax orders*   812-855-7931
*Orders by e-mail*   iuporder@indiana.edu

© 2001 by Indiana University Press

The paper used in this publication meets the minimum
requirements of American National Standard for Information
Sciences—Permanence of Paper for Printed Library Materials,
ANSI Z39.48-1984.

Manufactured in the United States of America

**Library of Congress Cataloging-in-Publication Data**

Traps : African American men on gender and sexuality / edited by
Rudolph P. Byrd and Beverly Guy-Sheftall.
p.   cm.
Includes bibliographical references and index.
ISBN 0-253-33901-4 (cloth : alk. paper) —
ISBN 0-253-21448-3 (pbk. : alk. paper)
1. Afro-American men—Attitudes. 2. Afro-American men—Sexual
behavior. 3. Afro-American men—Psychology. 4. Masculinity—
United States. 5. Homophobia—United States. 6. Afro-Americans—
Race identity. 7. Man-woman relationships—United States. 8. Sex
role—United States. 9. Afro-American women—Social conditions.
10. Feminism—United States.   I. Byrd, Rudolph P.
II. Guy-Sheftall, Beverly.

E185.86 .T72 2001
305.38'896073—dc21
00-053539
1  2  3  4  5   06  05  04  03  02  01

FOR

JEFFREY B. LEAK

AND

VANESSA DARLENE SANDERSON

The emotions were not at issue here—each had its essence, but feeling was something else again: a process plainly metaphysical, with its own grammar. What grammar was this? All the more urgent, then, was it for me to know, in this age of sexual warfare, my heart, make it my meditation, and be forever creating some meaning for what it meant to be male, though with what real satisfaction, and with how much resemblance to the promise of my gender, I did not know.

—CHARLES JOHNSON, *Oxherding Tale*

# CONTENTS

**PART THREE: MEDITATIONS FROM THE HEART**
**Making Meaning Out of Masculinity**

# PREFACE

*Traps* is the first anthology that historicizes the writings by African American men who have examined the meanings of the overlapping categories of race, gender, and sexuality, and who have theorized these categories in the most expansive and progressive terms. *Traps* contains the landmark speeches, essays, letters, and a manifesto by nineteenth- and twentieth-century African American men who have examined the complex terrain of gender and sexuality within the historical and cultural matrix of the United States.

Within the parameters of *Traps*, the selections on gender in Parts one and two reveal the longstanding commitment of African American men to ending sexism. In these pioneering profeminist viewpoints and in the critiques of the subordinate social, economic, and political position of African American women, one finds commentary on the historical basis for the oppression of African American women, and the radix for Black male feminism. The selections in Parts one and two also offer an analysis of the social, cultural, and historical forces which shape the construction of gender, as well as the manner in which sexism defines public and private relationships between Black men and Black women. The selections on sexuality in Parts three and four offer an analysis of the taboos and myths in which Black sexuality is enmeshed. They also stress the importance of rejecting homophobia, along with the necessity to contest the predominance of a heterosexist paradigm. Monolithic constructions of gender and sexuality whose potency is derived, respectively, from a strong identification with the practices of sexism and historically sanctioned homophobia are the *traps* into which we all have fallen. The deconstruction and dismantlement of these ideological traps, which are both internally and externally imposed, are a matter of considerable urgency to us all.

Spanning a century and a half of thought by African American men whose viewpoints constitute the expanding floor of a progressive engagement with antisexist and antihomophobic practices, *Traps* contains selections from the following periods: the antebellum and post-bellum periods which marked the second period of the American anti-slavery movement and the first wave of American feminism; the period of a heightened national sense of collective Black self-assertion preceding and following World War I; the Black Arts Movement and the Black Power Movement of the 1960s and the 1970s which were characterized in large part by a narrow cultural nationalism producing profound consequences for an analysis of gender and sexuality; and the period following the emergence of the second wave of American feminism of the 1970s and 1980s which would provide new paradigms for conceptualizing difference.

Containing headings that reflect an organizational scheme that is thematic as well as chronological, a particular strength of *Traps* is the kinship of positions which emerges within and between sections. Whether the subject is the rights and education of women, the position of gays and lesbians *vis-à-vis* the Black liberation struggle, the necessity of becoming an anti-rapist, the spectrum of Black sexualities, new modes of Black masculinity, assessments of the O. J. Simpson trial and the Million Man March, the points of view represented in *Traps* are progressive and complex. Provocative in its constellation of interests, *Traps* maps the evolution of thought among African American men whose viewpoints may serve as the foundation for the emergence of a new politics as well as new theories on gender and sexuality.

*Traps* is a collaboration between two scholars in Women's Studies, American Studies, and African American Studies. The anthology functions as a model for the kind of scholarship which will stimulate greater dialogue among scholars working in these fields. As a collaborative project, *Traps* has its genesis in three imperatives.

The first imperative is to contest and dispel the notion that African American men have not supported nor have had any engagement with feminism. This misreading of American history is reflected in Alice Jardine and Paul Smith's *Men in Feminism* (New York: Methuen, 1987), a text which lacks a sufficiently broad historical trajectory, and consequently omits the progressive perspectives on women's rights by Frederick Douglass, Alexander Crummell, and W. E. B. Du Bois. As an intervention against erasure and selective reconstructions of history which would posit that only such Euro-American men as William Lloyd Garrison, Theodore Parker, Wendell Phillips, and Parker Pillsbury were the earliest supporters of American feminism, *Traps* seeks to address certain glaring omissions in the contemporary scholarship in Men's Studies and Gender Studies. Let us be clear: Of the 32 men present, Frederick Douglass was the only man to "play a prominent part in the proceedings" of the first Women's Rights Convention in Seneca Falls, New York, in 1848. Concerned about the passage of the ninth resolution which asserted that it was the "duty of the women of this country to secure to themselves their sacred right to the elective franchise," Elizabeth Cady Stanton, undeterred by the reluctance of Lucretia Mott to argue for this resolution, appealed to Douglass to address the delegates on this vital matter of the franchise for women. Without hesitation Douglass rose to address the delegates in Wesleyan Chapel and argued forcefully and eloquently that the elective franchise was essential to the political equality of women. As a result of the effective alliance between Stanton and Douglass, the delegates adopted the ninth resolution but only by a small majority.[1] In his pioneering

PREFACE xv

collection *Frederick Douglass on Women's Rights* (1976), Eric Foner writes that "when American women who led the early [women's] movement were asked later in their lives to suggest the names of men who should be placed on an honor roll of male supporters, the list was invariably headed by [Douglass]."[2] In one sense, *Traps* calls all American men, and specifically African American men, to reclaim this radical tradition of male feminism.

The second imperative of *Traps* is to chart the progressive engagement of African American men on the crucial and divisive issue of homophobia. The heterosexist rhetoric of Black nationalism and Afrocentrism, as well as the powerful influence of the Black church and other religious institutions have legitimized homophobia in many areas of Black life. As editors of this anthology, we wish to offer a critique of this toxic strain of Black fundamentalism through the voices and writings of African American men who argue for alternative modes of masculinity and femininity. Further, our intention is not only to contest the divisive consequences of homophobia, but also to reveal the progressive dialogue on sexuality which is growing in force and significance in various African American communities, a dialogue which may have escaped the attention of scholars and activists in Gay and Lesbian Studies as well as in Queer Theory.

The third imperative of *Traps* is to acknowledge and address a tragedy in our own city of Atlanta, a tragedy which occurs far too frequently in cities across this nation. In February 1998, Vanessa Darlene Sanderson, an employee of Spelman College, was shot and killed by James F. Jeffries, Jr., her former companion and the father of one of her two sons. Unwilling to accept Ms. Sanderson's decision to terminate an abusive relationship, Mr. Jeffries forcibly entered her apartment and shot Ms. Sanderson who died of two gunshot wounds to the head. At the time of the murder, one of her sons, a five-year-old, was asleep in the bedroom where the murder occurred. Fortunately, the children were not *physically* harmed during the murder. In October 1998, Mr. Jeffries was found guilty of murder, burglary, and possession of a firearm. He received a life sentence for murder, ten years for burglary, and five years for the possession of a firearm in the commitment of a felony.

*Traps* emerges out of our unwavering opposition to the most blatant forms of sexism: violence against women and misogyny. As scholars we are not interested merely in grammar, as some critics of the academy mistakenly suppose, but in a scholarship that seeks to address and influence lived experiences in our communities. It is at this vital juncture that activism and scholarship converge. Trapped in the ideology of misogyny, in emasculating forms of masculinity, Mr. Jeffries stalked and killed Ms. Sanderson. It is our strong belief that scholarship is not merely a collection of abstractions, but at its best also provides tools for living. *Traps* constitutes, in part, an intervention into the zone of violence which degrades our communities. This anthology is dedicated, in part, to the memory of Vanessa Sanderson, and to the potentiality of her two young sons who, we hope, will make radically different choices from Mr. Jeffries *vis-à-vis* women, and bravely experiment with alternative modes of masculinity.

Containing canonical as well as new selections, *Traps* is evidence that African American men have been engaged in an analysis of the politics of sexism and homophobia for far longer than many realize. As editors of this timely anthology, we hope that the historical trajectory, the theoretical positions, and the nature and range of the voices represented in *Traps* will expand the discourse on gender and sexuality in African American communities and in the wider society.

The Editors

**NOTES**

1. Philip Foner, *Frederick Douglass* (New York: Citadel Press, 1969), 104.
2. Eric Foner, *Frederick Douglass on Women's Rights* (Westport, Conn.: Greenwood Press, 1976), ix.

# ACKNOWLEDGMENTS

Permission to reprint the following selections is gratefully acknowledged:

"The Rights of Women" by Frederick Douglass from *The Life and Writings of Frederick Douglass* (International Publishers, 1950) edited by Philip S. Foner.

"Give Women Fair Play" by Frederick Douglass from *The Frederick Douglass Papers* Vol. 5 (Yale University Press, 1992) edited by John W. Blassingame and John R. McKivigan.

"I Am a Radical Woman Suffrage Man" by Frederick Douglass from *The Frederick Douglass Papers* Vol. 5 (Yale University Press, 1992) edited by John W. Blassingame and John R. McKivigan.

"The Black Woman of the South" by Alexander Crummell reprinted from *Destiny and Race: Selected Writings, 1840–1898 / Alexander Crummell*, edited by Wilson Jeremiah Moses (University of Massachusetts Press, 1992), copyright © 1992 by Wilson Jeremiah Moses.

"The Damnation of Women" by W. E. B. DuBois from *W. E. B Du Bois: A Reader* (Henry Holt, 1995) edited by David Levering Lewis.

"In the Days of My Youth" by Benjamin E. Mays from *Born to Rebel* (University of Georgia Press, 1971; 1987), copyright © 1987 by Benjamin E. Mays.

"Feminism and Equality" by Bayard Rustin from *Down the Line* (Quadrangle Books, 1971).

"Women's Rights are Human Rights" by Kalamu ya Salaam first published in the *Black Scholar* 10.6/7, copyright © by Kalamu ya Salaam. Used by permission of the author.

"Groundings with My Sisters: Patriarchy and the Exploitation of Black Women" by Manning Marable from *How Capitalism Underdeveloped Black America* (South End Press, 1983).

"Breaking Silences" by Calvin Hernton from *Court of Appeal* (Ballantine Books, 1992) edited by Robert Chrisman and Robert L. Allen.

"On Becoming Anti-Rapist" by Haki R. Madhubuti from *Claiming Earth: Race, Rage, Rape, Redemption* (1994).

"The Sexual Diversion: The Black Man/Black Woman Debate in Context" by Derrick Bell from *Speak My Name: Black Men on Masculinity and the American Dream* (Beacon Press, 1995) edited by Don Belton.

"A Black Man's Place in Black Feminist Criticism" by Michael Awkward from *Negotiating Difference: Race, Gender, and the Politics of Positionality* (University of Chicago Press, 1995).

"Men: We Just Don't Get It" by Nathan McCall from *What's Going On: Personal Essays* (Random House, 1997).

"Here Be Dragons" was originally published as "Freaks and the American Ideal of Manhood" in *Playboy*, January 1985. Copyright © by James Baldwin. Collected in *The Price of the Ticket*, published by St. Martin's Press. Reprinted by arrangement with the James Baldwin Estate.

"In the Limelight" by Arthur J. Robinson, Jr., from *Essence* (July 1990).

"The Sexist in Me" by Kevin Powell from *Essence* (September 1992).

"A Phenomenology of the Black Body" by Charles Johnson from *Michigan Quarterly Review* (Fall 1993).

"Thirteen Ways of Looking at a Black Man" by Henry Louis Gates, Jr., from *Thirteen Ways of Looking at a Black Man* (Vintage, 1997).

"Mike's Brilliant Career" by Gerald Early from *Transition* issue 71.

"It's Raining Men" by Robert Reid-Pharr from *Transition* issue 69.

"Dear Minister Farrakhan" by Men Stopping Violence, a letter dated August 24, 1995 (2000).

"A Letter from Huey to the Revolutionary Brothers and Sisters about the Women's Liberation and Gay Liberation Movements" by Huey P. Newton from *Gay Flames Pamphlet*, no. 7, 1970.

"Brother to Brother: Words from the Heart" by Joseph Beam from *In the Life: A Black Gay Anthology* (Alyson Publications, 1986).

"Black Macho Revisited: Reflections of a SNAP! Queen" by Marlon Riggs from *Brother to Brother: New Writings by Black Gay Men* (Alyson Publications, 1991).

"Does Your Mama Know about Me?" by Essex Hemphill from *Ceremonies: Prose and Poetry* (Plume Books, 1992).

"Black Sexuality: The Taboo Subject" by Cornel West from *Race Matters* (Beacon Press, 1993).

"When You Divide Body and Soul, Problems Multiply: The Black Church and Sex" by Michael Eric Dyson from *Race Rules: Navigating the Color Line* (Vintage, 1996).

"'Ain't Nothin' Like the Real Thing': Black Masculinity, Gay Sexuality, and the Jargon of Authenticity" by Kendall Thomas from *The House that Race Built: Black Americans, U.S. Terrain* (Pantheon Books, 1997) edited by Wahneema Lubiano.

*Traps*, a collage by Ronald Lockett (1990), reproduced on the cover by permission of William Arnett.

As co-editor of this volume, I would like to acknowledge the work and example of colleagues who have supported me in my efforts to bring what I hope will be a useful work of scholarship to the public. I am indebted most especially to Valerie Boyd, John F. Callahan, Johnnetta B. Cole, Sonia Sanchez, Frances Smith Foster, Mark A. Sanders, Alice Walker, Kimberly

Wallace-Sanders, and Nagueyalti Warren for their advice, support, and example. I also have been encouraged by the engagement of students who are committed to eradicating sexism and homophobia, most especially Omar Freilla, Keron Williams, Mark Joseph, Anasa Troutman, and Seitu of Morehouse College. I value this first of many collaborations with my friend and colleague Beverly Guy-Sheftall. I owe a special thanks to Meardis Byrd Lund, my mother and the first feminist I had the privilege to meet.

—R.P.B.


I want to remember the men in my family from whom I learned early on that men can certainly *choose* to be humane, and there's no excuse for cruelty to women and children—not racism, not poverty, not anger. I am thankful for my grandparents and parents who, more than anything else, were kind and decent, and encouraged my dreams. If I had a son, I would wish that he were like Rudolph. From him I have learned how precious is a male friend. And, finally, for my cousin Levi, on whom I know I can always depend.

—B.G.-S.

# TRAPS

# PROLOGUE
## The Tradition of John:
## A Mode of Black Masculinity

RUDOLPH P. BYRD

**In the tradition of John:**

1. From *High John the Conqueror:* A mode of masculinity for Black men who are committed to the liberation and survival whole of Black people. Inspired by a trickster figure in African American folklore also known as Jack who is the human analogue of Brer Rabbit. As a slave, John is a redemptive, transgressive, and resourceful figure who achieves advantages over "Old Massa" through motherwit, laughter, and song. He lives in the slaves' quarters of plantations and in the conjure root that bears his name.

2. *Also:* A man of courage who routinely "beats the unbeatable." A man who laughs at himself and also understands the many uses of laughter. As the hope-bringer, a man who's been "down so long that down don't bother" him. Unflappable. Responsible, as in: "Takes care of business" or "On the case." Traditionally capable, as in: "able to make a way out of no way and can hit a straight lick with a crooked stick." A man of strength possessing confidence and a durable constitution, as in: "Ain't no hammer in dis lan strikes like mine." Admirable and honorable, as in: "You de man." (Opposite of trifling, jive, half-stepping, irresponsible, player, not serious).

3. In his youth: mannish. From the Black folk expression of elders to male children: "You acting mannish," i.e., like a man. Often referring to bodacious, defiant, willful, and risky behavior, as in: "He's smelling himself" or "You trying to be grown." Evincing a premature interest in adult activities and privileges.

4. Loves the Spirit. Loves men (sexually and/or nonsexually) and the society of men. Loves women (sexually and/or nonsexually) and the society of women. Loves children. Loves his ancestors. Loves difference. Loves creativity, song, and dance. Loves the beautiful/ugly. Loved by others: as in, "My main man" or "Show me some love." Loves movement: as in, "Gotta highball thru some country." Loves himself. *Irregardless.*

5. Free, as in "I ain't worried about that." Spunky. Crazy but got good sense. Regular. Committed to coalitions, but capable of independent action. Nonviolent, but capable of self-defense. Persevering and enduring, as in "Keep a-inchin' along lak a po' inch worm." A man who flourishes in the "Be class," as in: "*Be* here when the ruthless man comes and *be* here when he is gone." Cool.

6. "A bottom fish," as in values knowledge, truth, and wisdom. Values process and improvisation. Values collective work and solitude. Values dialogue, listening, and harmony. Values tenderness. Values the strength in feelings and tears. Values freedom and its responsibilities. Values justice. Values peace.

7. A mode of masculinity for Black men who are committed to the abolition of emasculating forms of masculinity; a mode of masculinity for Black men who are committed to the abolition of racism, sexism, homophobia, and other ideological traps.

## I

"Yeah, Ah'm de King. Don't you like it, don't you take it. Here's mah collar, come and shake it."

—JOHN in conversation with Brer Lion, "How the Lion Met the King of the World," *Mules and Men*

"Of course, High John de Conquer got plenty power."

—ZORA NEALE HURSTON, "High John De Conquer"

This is the urgency: Live!
and have your blooming in the noise of the whirlwind.

—GWENDOLYN BROOKS, "The Second Sermon on the Warpland"

I wish to summon a power that will make the rulers of empires quake, that will inspire in them the deepest regret and shame, and that will, above all, vanquish and outlast them. More specifically, I wish to summon a power that may serve as the foundation for a new mode of Black masculinity. Such a manifestation of Black male agency speaks to the many possibilities of Black men. It also potentially poses the greatest danger to empires, in whatever form and in whatever place, as well as to the fossilized notions of Black masculinity they have spawned and that presently confound, sadly, so many of us.

Where might such a power reside? In what figures? In what traditions? In what texts? I would like to suggest that one domain for such a power is African American folklore. So much of what a people know about themselves is revealed in the stories they tell about themselves. When we wish to know who we are and what we might become we consult and investigate many sources, and chief among them is the oral tradition—storytelling. It is out of this rich field of Black expression that we have fashioned not only a theory of the African American literary tradition (signifying) as well as a theory of Black feminism (womanism), but also many of the art forms and life-sustaining traditions of African American culture.[1] It also is in this fecund field that we initially apprehended the panoply of Black or diasporic identities, now visible and still in process, that extends far beyond the center of what many of us have come to imagine as the Black Atlantic world.[2]

And precisely where, in which body of Black folk tales, might we discover the most desirable and efficacious clustering of attributes and potentialities to advance this effort to forge a new mode of Black masculinity? In the tales of John Henry? In the legendary transgressions of Stagolee? In the allegorical world of Brer Rabbit? Where, in our briar patch of possibilities, might we turn? While I admire the strength and perseverance of the railroad man John Henry, as well as the bravado of the outlaw Stagolee, I believe High John the Conqueror is the figure in whom exists the various elements that in their totality may serve as a new mode of Black masculinity, and as an alternative to normative modes of masculinity. It is in the figure of John, who is sometimes called Jack and who is the human analogue of the irrepressible Brer Rabbit, that such a mode of Black masculinity might assume significance and, I hope, a certain instrumentality.

Folklorists and anthropologists have preserved and documented the many tales of High John the Conqueror.[3] In the tales of John we encounter a slave who bodies forth power, resourcefulness, and resilience. In African American folklore, John is a trickster figure whose chief weapons in the daily struggle with "Old Massa" to assert and affirm the humanity of his fellow slaves are motherwit, laughter, and song. As a figure of resistance who confounds and thwarts "Old Massa," John is also one of the central pillars in the slaves' psychic sanctuary. He is the secular analogue to the promise of transcendence, hope, love, and deliverance found in the sacred songs and Black folk religion. As the "great human culture hero in Negro folk-lore" and "the wish-fulfillment hero of the race," John symbolizes the capacity of Black people to resist, endure, and prevail with our humanity intact.[4]

While there is a compelling portrait of John that emerges from the totality of Black folk tales, there is yet another portrait of this mythical slave in the folkloric writings of Zora Neale Hurston, anthropologist and novelist. Neither as widely known nor referenced to the extent that it deserves, Hurston's "High John De Conquer" is a poetic distillation of the principal attributes of John celebrated in the tales in which he emerges as a redemptive and transgressive figure. While "High John De Conquer" is an essay of marked creativity that describes the origins, attributes, and significance of John in the folk imagination, I would like to advance a different reading of it. I propose to read Hurston's "High John De Conquer" as a meditation on Black masculinity. In the tales of John and in Hurston's essay we discover the elements from which we may construct a new mode of Black masculinity, one which conjures the many interesting possibilities of Black men, and one which some of us may wish to embrace in this vibrant period of a marked interrogation of masculinities. Although located in the realm of myth, this is a mode of masculinity that is stained with the shadings of human aspirations, of *male* aspirations and potentialities. Together with the tales, Hurston's portrait of John may serve, I believe, as an excellent foundation for the creation of a new mode of Black masculinity in an era in which many of us are contesting the rigid and toxic forms of Black masculinity everywhere in circulation.[5]

Hurston writes that before John assumed the form of a man, before he became as she tells us "a man in full" or a "natural man," that he was a "whisper, a will to hope, a wish to find something worthy of laughter and song."[6] An invisible presence who walked out of Africa "on the waves of sound," John could "beat the unbeatable" (70). A figure of courage, he was daunted by neither danger nor sorrow. "He could beat it all," writes Hurston, "and what made it so cool, finish it off with a laugh" (70). The laughter of John is a phenomenon of considerable complexity. As Hurston reminds us, in the many tales of John, laughter was sometimes "at the expense of the slave" (75). It was laughter that asserted: "We are just as ridiculous as anybody else. We can be wrong, too" (75). It also was laughter that functioned as an antidote to hysteria and nihilism. Above all, it was laughter which acknowledged the absurdities and contradictions of chattel slavery in a democratic republic, affirmed the humanity of Black people, and functioned as a bulwark against the inevitability of the psychic and physical assaults, from so many quarters, upon that humanity.[7]

As a figure over whom "distance and the impossible had no power," John also is remembered, according to Hurston, as the "hope-bringer" (70). These particular attributes of John—courage, laughter, and hope—are reflected in a tale embedded within Hurston's beautifully rendered meditation. Hurston recounts the tale in which John leads a group of slaves on a journey through hell, heaven, and back to earth on the sheltering body of a great black crow "so big that one wing rested on the morning, while the other dusted off the evening star" (76). While in heaven, Hurston tells us that John and his fellow slaves visited "Old Maker . . . [who] made them a tune and put it in their mouths. It had no words. It was a tune that you could bend and shape in most any way you wanted to fit the words and feelings that you had. They learned it and began to sing" (77). Returning to the plantation after this spiritual odyssey, John counsels his fellow travelers to ignore the carping of "Old Massa": "Don't pay what he say no mind" (77). John also urges them to hold in secret the rich interior life he has revealed to them. "Don't tell [Old Massa] nothing," asserts John. "Nobody don't have to know where us get our pleasure from" (77–78). After this transforming journey and these loving, bracing words, Hurston writes that the slaves returned to the fields changed: "The day didn't seem hot like it had before. Their gift song came back into their memories in pieces, and they sang about glittering new robes and harps, and the work flew" (78).

As the "hope-bringer" and the embodiment of a self-forgetting love, John is the spiritual intermediary between "Old Maker" and these now transfigured slaves. He is the vehicle through which they discover the hidden dimension of the spirit and its transformative, regenerative powers. In this tale, he also is the intermediary through which the slaves discover and are given the "gift song"—the sacred songs, the spirituals—that becomes a vital means of resistance, a song "that would whip," asserts John, "Old Massa's earlaps down" (76). In addition to being a source of resistance, the "gift song," as we have seen, is the mode of transport between the world of the plantation and the worlds beyond it. In fine, the "gift song" is a means to a transcendent reality. To sing, as the poet Michael S. Harper tells us, is to speak of the transcendent.[8] As an example of courage, hope, the regenerative powers of song, love, and the spirit, John is a powerful figure who symbolizes the potentialities of Black people and the potentialities of a liberated and liberating Black masculinity. It is in such a figure that we discover the essential elements in this new mode of Black masculinity which I shall call the tradition of John.

What would it mean for Black men to be in the tradition of John? If we choose to reclaim this tradition and adapt it to meet our very modern circumstances, how might our lives, the lives of others, and the communities we share with others be transformed? What would it mean for us to choose this mode of masculinity, to be in the tradition? With John as our example, are there particular values and principles which would shape our actions and decisions? In the tradition of John there is a value placed upon motherwit, laughter, courage, hope, as well as the regenerative powers of song, love, and the spirit. Existing alongside a full apprehension of the bleakest actualities, these are the values and knowledge that enabled John and his spiritual descendants to make, as Hurston observes, "a way out of no way, . . . [to hit] a straight lick with a crooked stick" (70). In this mode of Black masculinity, there also is a value placed upon the development of inner strength and inner resources. The objective is to prevail in the "mighty battle" of life "without outside-showing force," to pair courage with self-possession, thus enabling John to win, as Hurston writes, the war "from

within" (70). If we prevail against the masters in the world as well as those
mastering presences within us, then we win in a "permanent way," asserts
Hurston, with "the soul of the black man whole and free" (70–71). Hurston's
decision to masculinize this process of self-assertion and self-actualization
does not diminish the significance of John as a dynamic presence in the lives
of Black women. Rather the androcentric phrase—"the soul of the black
man"—makes this process specific. While John functions as a metonym for
the emancipative actualities and potentialities of Black people, he also
functions as a metonym for these properties within Black men, properties
central to this mode of Black masculinity which I have termed the tradition
of John.

If we continue to select and identify the attributes of John, attributes that
will endow this mode of Black masculinity with additional weight and heft,
we also discover that John, to return to Hurston's metaphorical language,
"was a bottom fish" (71). By this Hurston means that he "was deep. He had,"
as she boasts, "the wisdom tooth of the East in his head" (71). John's "deep"
knowledge was of himself and the changing structures of the worlds he
altered and through which he moved. It was a knowledge of actualities and
potentialities which he combined in his struggle against the sweeping powers of "Old Massa." It also was a knowledge infused with a profound awareness of life as improvisation and process. "He who wins from within" or who
possesses, as Hurston implies, the knowledge of things in their right constellation, "is in the 'Be' class. *Be* here when the ruthless man comes and *be* here
when he is gone" (71). To exist in the "Be class" is not only to endure but also
to affirm that life is *process*: an unbroken cycle of becoming and perishing,
of change and transformation.[9] Perhaps above all, it means that even when
one is most vulnerable to stasis and exploitation that one also finds the
capacity for renewal through self-examination and self-assertion. To be sure,
this capacity for renewal is strengthened by the conviction that life is a
process through which one journeys toward an illusive but nevertheless
actual unity.

"There is no established picture," notes Hurston, "of what sort of looking-
man this John de Conquer was. To some, he was a big, physical-looking man
like John Henry. To others, he was a little, hammered-down, low-built man
like the Devil's doll-baby" (71). Hurston provides us with only rather general
information regarding the facts of John's human form: Black with male
characteristics. Beyond these obvious facts of race and sex she is uncertain
and John, ever the figure of legend, disappears into his name and the
talismanic root with which he is associated. As a protean figure who possesses the power to assume both animal—Brer Rabbit—and human form,
John is as malleable as the "gift song" of "Old Maker," the "tune that you
could bend and shape in most any way you wanted to fit the words and
feelings that you had" (77). What does John look like? What is the color of
his eyes? In whose image do we see him now reflected? As a figure of infinite
suppleness who exists in the "Be class" and who thus symbolizes the most

fundamental and creative processes of the Black world, John resembles, to identify one collective visage that bears his imprint, every Black man who has ever drawn breath and struggled for dignity and freedom in this American republic. Hurston's vagueness regarding John's physicality is both logical and desirable because as a mythic figure and racial concept he is expansive enough to hold and carry the forms of all Black men, as well as express our most fundamental yearnings and aspirations. In one sense, John's physical characteristics are irrelevant. What is relevant are his deeds, values, and function in the Black imagination.

And just as there is a necessary ambiguity regarding John's physical characteristics, so too is there ambiguity regarding his sexuality. In her essay, Hurston makes no allusions to John's sexuality. Desire for John is sometimes expressed or manifested in heterosexual terms, I am thinking of such tales as "How Jack Beat the Devil" and "John Outruns the Lord." More often in the folk tales he is a compelling figure wholly unto himself.[10] As he exists in the "Be class" or rather on the shifting and complex plane of all human desire, John is the embodiment of all sexualities and none. Ultimately, he is not a man, but a principle of Black self-assertion with male characteristics. What is the color of his eyes? Irrelevant. What form does desire assume for him? Again, irrelevant. What are his deeds, values, and function in the Black imagination? These vital matters are reflected both in the tales and in Hurston's essay, both of which are the foundation for this new mode of Black masculinity.

Committed to the overthrow of slavery and the ideology of white supremacy, John is the supreme antagonist of "Old Massa" and the various hegemonic structures he and his descendants have created and, most disheartening, many of them predictably still cherish. In John's various acts of resistance are reflected his most exemplary values and attributes: motherwit, the power of laughter and song, self-assertion, self-examination, self-knowledge, a belief that life is process grounded in the fertile field of improvisation, hope, and, most importantly, love. And his aspirations? Nothing less than the full and complete emancipation of Black people from every species of slavery. These are the constitutive elements and aspirations that together comprise the tradition of John. In these days of so many hours, it is a mode of Black masculinity grounded in enduring principles that possesses, I believe, a broad and vital instrumentality.

Why is such a mode of Black masculinity needed now? What forces and processes would it counter? Is there a particular kind of intellectual labor the tradition of John is expected to perform? Such a progressive mode of Black masculinity is needed to counter what is nothing less than the new species of slavery that shackles so many of us. And what slavery is this? The slavery of calcified and even toxic constructions of Black masculinity that possess only the dimensions of a television screen and, tragically in far too many instances, the depth of the barrel of a gun. Such a masculinity is mired in the slavery of misogyny that prizes the outmoded but still powerful values of

patriarchy. Such a masculinity also is enmeshed in the slavery of homophobia and is scornful, fearful of any sexuality that does not present itself within
the trappings of a heterosexual ideal. Such a masculinity legitimizes the
reduction of human beings into targets. It reduces men and women stained
with an undesirable shade of difference to the category of pariah. And prey.
Like all forms of slavery, such a masculinity is, above all, emasculating as
much of its power emanates from the darkest zone of Blackness: a region
where the denigration of difference is commonplace, a region where vision
and the angle of ascent are not determined by the horizon, but instead by the
tunnel. The maze.

Not losing sight of the ongoing struggle against racism and white supremacy, these are the ideological traps—sexism and homophobia—into
which many of us have fallen. These are the varieties of slavery for which
the tradition of John may function as an intervention and a catalyst for the
creation of a new politics whose purpose is to transform and further radicalize the political consciousness of African American men trapped in
emasculating forms of masculinity, by which I mean a masculinity which
achieves its power and legitimacy through the denigration of others. A
dramatic alteration in political consciousness and the rigorous interrogation
of the prevailing paradigms of a strangely emasculating masculinity constitutes the first steps toward a new freedom to imagine Black male agency in
the broadest possible terms. Emerging from within the dynamic context of
cultural, social, and political change, this is the kind of intellectual labor the
tradition of John is meant to perform: why not this? In this transitional period between one age and the next, a period which is distinguished by an
unprecedented inquiry into the meanings of masculinity, it is imperative
that we reclaim our progressive traditions, as well as imagine new and alternative modes of masculinity for Black men. It is time to move to the next
level of difficulty and possibility.

I believe it is important to stress that the tradition of John is not to be
confused with Iron John, a mode of masculinity fully described in Robert
Bly's *Iron John* (1990). An early and influential text in what is regarded now
as Men's Studies, Bly's chief concerns in *Iron John* are with male initiation
and the urgent need to restore such practices to contemporary American life
in order to counter the continued growth of what he terms the "dark side of
men." According to Bly, the deleterious effects of the "dark side of men"
manifest themselves in a variety of ways including the "mad exploitation of
earth resources, devaluation and humiliation of women and obsession with
tribal warfare."[11] Further, in *Iron John* Bly maintains that male initiation
may counter the growth of the phenomena of what he terms the "fifties
male" and the "soft male" of the 1970s. Emerging from but not confined to
this decade of the 1950s, Bly describes the "fifties male" as one who "got to
work early, labored responsibly, supported his wife and children and admired discipline. . . . Many of his qualities were strong and positive," he

maintains "but underneath the charm and bluff there was, and there remain, much isolation, deprivation, and passivity. Unless he has an enemy, he isn't sure that he is alive." Bly suggests that Ronald Reagan is a "sort of mummified version of this dogged type." [12]

In contrast, the "soft male," as defined by Bly, is a product of the negative consequences of the Vietnam War and the positive encounter with feminism as it emerged within the political and social context of the second wave of American feminism in the 1970s. He describes the "soft male" as "more thoughtful, more gentle," and "not interested in harming the earth or starting wars." [13] Paradoxically, "many of these men," argues Bly, "are not happy." Lacking energy, the "soft male" is "life-preserving but not exactly life-giving." [14]

Judging the "fifties male" and the "soft male" as problematic modes of masculinity, Bly believes that there is a "third possibility" or "mode" for men in Iron John: a central figure in a European folk tale recorded by Jacob and Wilhelm Grimm in 1820. Bly reads the folk tale of "Iron John" or "Iron Haus" as a metaphor of male initiation in eight stages. According to Bly, the primary purpose of this particular tale of initiation is to place contemporary American men in contact with the Wild Man: the mysterious and powerful figure at the tale's center whose attributes include "love of spontaneity, association with wilderness, honoring grief and respect for riskiness." [15] Bly is careful to stress that the Wild Man is a part of what he terms a "company or a community in a man's psyche" which includes the King, the Warrior, the Lover, the Trickster, the Cook and the Grief Man." By way of conclusion, he insists that the objective of contemporary men "is not to *be* the Wild Man, but to be *in touch with the Wild Man.*" [16]

There is much that I admire about Bly's *Iron John*. First, I value his use of folklore in order to address what Charles Johnson has aptly termed "the crisis in the male spirit." [17] Bly's insightful reading of the European folktale "Iron John" is confirmation of my own belief in the value of reclaiming and adapting the stories of High John the Conqueror to address the "crisis of the male spirit" in the lives of contemporary African American men. An additional value of *Iron John* is Bly's critique of machoism and his thoughtful examination of the tragic consequences of the expanding gulf between fathers and sons. Third and finally, as a landmark text in the emerging field of Men's Studies, through *Iron John* Bly has contributed much to our collective understanding of the several factors that constitute the "crisis of the male spirit" as well as the manner in which these factors might be productively addressed.

Having outlined the concerns and objectives of Bly's *Iron John*, I would like to stress that the concerns and objectives of the tradition of John as well as the other parts of the totality of *Traps* are not a call for the restoration of male rites of initiation, nor an attempt to place Black men in touch with the "Wild Man." Rather, the tradition of John is a mode of Black masculinity that possesses several distinct but complementary functions *vis-à-vis* Iron John. First, such a mode of Black masculinity is meant to function as a catalyst for the creation of a politics that will further radicalize African American men in our commitment to progressive social change. Second, such a mode of Black masculinity is an affirmation and reclamation of a set of extant radical values and traditions that should inform the choices and actions of African American men in our struggle among ourselves and in coalition with others against emasculating forms of masculinity. Third and above all, the tradition of John functions as an alternative mode of Black masculinity which possesses the potentiality to emancipate African American men from the network of traps—sexism and homophobia—that have blocked our collective growth and liberation for far too long. This, then, is the function of this new mode of Black masculinity which I have termed the tradition of John. Like the story of Iron John, this new mode of Black masculinity does not stand in opposition to the progressive goals of feminism and the rapidly developing field of queer theory. Like Iron John, the tradition of John is a mode of masculinity useful to men across many different racial, class, and sexual lines, but I have conceived the tradition of John as a mode of masculinity designed to address the historical and contemporary conditions of men of African descent. This new mode of Black masculinity is meant to underscore the urgency of African American men to reclaim the progressive traditions in Black political, cultural, and social thought which would support us in our efforts to practice the most advanced forms of democratic politics. This, then, is the intellectual labor the tradition of John is meant to perform: again, why not this? We have sanctioned for too long, even during the most progressive periods of Black self-assertion, the most doctrinaire and retrograde constructions of gender and sexuality. As I say, it is time to move to the next level of difficulty and possibility.

## II

Our doctrine is that "right is of no sex."

—FREDERICK DOUGLASS, *The North Star*

You judge a woman
by the length of her skirt,
by the way she walks,
talks, looks, and acts;
by the color of her skin you judge
and will call her "bitch!"
"Black bitch"
if she doesn't answer your:
"Hey baby, watcha gonna say
to a man."

—ESSEX HEMPHILL, XXI from *Conditions*

I have always, I think, opposed the stereotypic definitions of "masculine" and "feminine," not only because I thought it was a lot of merchandising nonsense, but rather because I always found the either/or implicit in those definitions antithetical to what I was all about—and what revolution for self is all about—the whole person.

—TONI CADE BAMBARA, "On the Issue
of Roles" from *The Black Woman*

In the writings of Angela Davis and Elaine P. Brown we find a record of sexism that belies the radical objectives of the Black freedom struggle of the 1960s and the 1970s.[18] Before joining the Communist Party USA in July 1968, Angela Davis searched for an organization through which she might make a contribution to revolutionary politics that would lead to the liberation of Black men and women from all forms of oppression. "When one commits oneself to struggle," writes Davis in her autobiography, "it must be for a lifetime."[19] Serious and deeply committed, Davis's search for a revolutionary political organization led her first to the San Diego Black Conference, a coalition of community organizations led by Ron Karenga's US (United Slaves) Organization. For a period of time, Davis allied herself with the San Diego Black Conference in its work to support Ed Lynn, a Black seaman who "was challenging racial discrimination at the Balboa Naval Base." With others, Davis planned a rally in San Diego in order to publicize the case of Ed Lynn. It was within the context of political struggle in southern California in the 1960s that Davis would encounter what she describes as a "constant problem in my political life":

> I was criticized very heavily, especially by male members of Karenga's organization, for doing "a man's job." Women should not play leadership roles, they insisted. A woman was supposed to "inspire" her man and educate his children. The irony of their complaint was that much of what I was doing had fallen to me by default. The arrangements for the publicity rally, for instance, had been in a man's hands, but because his work left much to be desired, I began to do it simply to make sure that it got done. It was also ironical that precisely those who criticized me most did the least to ensure the success of the rally.
>
> I became acquainted very early with the widespread presence of an unfortunate syndrome among some Black male activists—namely to confuse their political activity with an assertion of their maleness. They saw—and some continue to see—Black manhood as something separate from Black womanhood. These men view Black women as a threat to their attainment of manhood—especially those Black women who take initiative and work to become leaders in their own right. The constant harangue by the US men was that I needed to redirect my energies and use them to give my man strength and inspiration so that he might more effectively contribute his talents to the struggle for Black liberation.[20]

The "harangue by the US men" surfaced some time later within the context of LA SNCC (Los Angeles Student Nonviolent Coordinating Committee).

Davis describes with a legitimate sense of pride the important work of LA SNCC in such areas as police brutality as well as the organization and education of youth. She recalls that the Liberation School, "which was under my charge, drew scores of people each time it convened."[21]

Predictably, it would not be long before some of the men of LA SNCC began to express their opposition to the leadership of Davis and other women in the organization. While unwavering in her commitment to revolutionary struggle, Davis recalls her growing sense of disappointment in the divisive politics of staff meetings where the opposition of some male members to female leadership was openly expressed:

> Some of the brothers came around only for staff meetings (sometimes), and whenever we women were involved in something important, they began to talk about "women taking over the organization"—calling it a matriarchal coup d'état. All the myths about Black women surfaced. . . . By playing such a leading role in the organization, some of them insisted, we were aiding and abetting the enemy, who wanted to see Black men weak and unable to hold their own. This condemnation was especially bitter because we were one of the few organizations on the Black Liberation Front in Los Angeles, and probably in the country, where women did play a leading role. It was a period in which one of the unfortunate hallmarks of some nationalist groups was their determination to push women into the background. The brothers opposing us leaned heavily on the male supremacist trends which were winding their way through the movement, although I am sure that some of them were politically mature enough to understand the reactionary nature of these trends. . . .[22]

While Davis was understandably disappointed in the sexism of some of her so-called fellow revolutionaries, their reactionary positions did not dissuade her from her commitment to revolutionary struggle. On the contrary, she displayed remarkable resilience in the face of such emasculating forms of masculinity. We can only speculate about how much more Davis and the other women of LA SNCC and the San Diego Black Conference would have been able to contribute to the Black freedom struggle if they had not had to expend so much of their considerable collective energy countering such conservative views concerning the so-called "place" of women in revolutionary struggle.

In *A Taste of Power* (1992), Elaine Brown describes a similar pattern of sexism in the ranks of the Black Panther Party. In the opening chapter of her riveting memoir, she enunciates the framework and terms of her struggle against sexism concomitant with her struggle against racism, capitalism, and imperialism as the chairman of the Black Panther Party:

> I have all the guns and all the money. I can withstand challenge from without and from within. . . .
>   I repeat, I have control over all the guns and all the money of this party. There will be no external or internal opposition I will not resist and put down. I will deal resolutely with anyone or anything that stands in the way. So if you don't like it, if you don't like the fact that I am a woman, if you don't like what

we're going to do, here is your chance to leave. You'd better leave because you won't be tolerated![23]

In this bold assertion of her powers as chairman of a paramilitary organization, Brown acknowledges the existence of sexism in the party, as well as the resentment of both men and women to her carefully plotted ascendancy to the chairmanship. Later in her memoir, she describes the manner in which sexism emerged in the northern chapter of the Black Panther Party, ironically the site of her ascendancy to the chairmanship, and the manner in which she and other female members of the Black Panther Party chose to address it. Brown recalls attending a strategy meeting of the Black Panther Party in northern California at which she found herself after a meal in the kitchen with several other women washing the dirty dishes. Cognizant of this insult to the leadership of women in a revolutionary organization, Brown offers the following critique:

> We knew the Brothers dragged their old habits into the party. We all did. The party's role, however, was not limited to external revolution but incorporated the revolutionizing of its ranks. If, however, the very leadership of a male-dominated organization was bent on clinging to old habits about women, we had a problem. We would have to fight for the right to fight for freedom.
>
> Our [Joan Kelly, Ericka Huggins, Evon Carter, and Gwen Goodloe] collective posture emerged, and we became known as "the clique." As the Brothers in Southern California began to feel the changes in our consciousness, they whined that we had "bad attitude."
>
> The reputation of the clique spread. Brothers throughout the many chapters that had emerged all over the country were mumbling about the clique in L.A., we learned. "Smart bitches" like us, they were saying, needed to be silenced. But we would silence them in the end by our hard work and dedication; and by the specter of the fierce Brothers who supported us, the leadership of Southern California, Geronimo and Masai [Hewitt].[24]

Brown's "hard work and dedication" against emasculating forms of masculinity yielded historic results as she emerged as the leader of the Black Panther Party, which was committed to advancing the Black freedom struggle. Significantly, the Student Nonviolent Coordinating Committee (SNCC), the Congress of Racial Equality, US Organization, and the Southern Christian Leadership Conference (SCLC) were and remained male-dominated organizations.

Five years after Elaine Brown's rise to the chairmanship of the Black Panther Party, the debate over sexism in African American communities would assume, for the first time, a far more public form. In 1979, the editors of *The Black Scholar* devoted a special issue to what they termed and what we now recall as "the black sexism debate." At the center of this firestorm was an essay by sociologist Robert Staples entitled "The Myth of the Black Macho." Strongly objecting to the representation of Black men in Ntozake Shange's *For Colored Girls Who Have Considered Suicide When the Rainbow Is Enuf* (1974) and the charge of Black male sexism in Michelle Wallace's *Black*

*Macho and the Myth of the Superwoman* (1978), Staples was both critical
and dismissive of the efforts of Shange and Wallace to critique the sexism of
Black men.

According to Beverly Guy-Sheftall, the Black sexism debate published in
the pages of *The Black Scholar* was the first public debate of sexism in
African American communities during the second wave of American feminism. While this historic debate served to reveal the contradictory positions
on gender equality which were well known in Black communities, this
debate among Black intellectuals did not prepare us for the debate and
analysis of Black sexism which would emerge with such regularity in the
landmark events of the 1980s and the 1990s, events within which race and
gender collided and emerged as an unmixable mix.

Of the several critiques of Staples's problematic reading of the work of
Shange and Wallace, perhaps the most eloquent and searching among them
was that by Audre Lorde. In an essay entitled "The Great American Disease," Lorde examines the interlocking nature of the oppressive ideologies of
racism, sexism, misogyny, and, prophetically, homophobia, and calls for the
further radicalization of the political consciousness of Staples and other
African American men who share his views on gender:

> [The] black male consciousness must be raised so that he realizes that sexism
> and woman-hating are critically dysfunctional to his liberation as a black man,
> because they rise out of the same constellation that engenders racism and
> homophobia, a constellation of intolerance for difference serving a profit
> motivation. And until this is done, black men like Staples will view sexism and
> the destruction of black women only as tangential to the cause of black
> liberation, rather than as central to that struggle. So long as this occurs, we will
> never be able to embark upon that dialogue between black women and black
> men that is so essential to our survival as a people. And this continued blind-
> ness between us can only serve the oppressive system within which we live.[25]

In her critique of Staples, Lorde places the Black sexism debate within a
necessarily broad but highly specific political, social, and economic framework. In doing so, she provides us with a template for apprehending the
workings of power in their right constellation, as well as the foundation for
the practice of emasculating forms of masculinity. As a Black lesbian feminist, Lorde was keenly aware of the operations of certain powers upon her
own life, specifically the interlocking ideologies of capitalism, racism, sexism, and homophobia, and she powerfully resisted these ideologies every
day of her life. Like Angela Davis and Elaine Brown, Lorde understood that
within the context of the Black freedom struggle Black women, to recall the
words of Brown, "had to fight for the right to fight for freedom."[26]

In the lives of Angela Davis and Elaine Brown, as well as in the issues
which emerged within Lorde's critique of Staples, we find disturbing evidence of an orthodoxy that confines Black women to only the most traditional roles.[27] Such an orthodoxy further polarizes discussions of gender in
various African American communities as they emerge within such public

spectacles as the controversy surrounding Alice Walker's *The Color Purple* (1982) (the novel and the film), the confirmation hearings of Supreme Court Justice Clarence Thomas, the trial and conviction of Mike Tyson, the verdicts in the criminal and civil trials of O. J. Simpson, the contested goals and objectives of Minister Louis Farrakhan's Million Man March, and the case of Reverend Henry Lyons and the Convention of Southern Baptists. In the unmixable mix of these events, the legitimate issues of sexual harassment, misogyny, rape, domestic violence, and the centrality of African American women in the liberation of African Americans were all subordinated, again and wrongly, to the ideal of loyalty to the race and Black patriarchy. It is time to abandon the unhelpful and terribly oversimplified position of "either/or" in the analysis and interpretation of landmark events in which the historic maladies of the nation assume enlarged significance through the lives of its Black citizens. Our objective should be always to seek an engagement with only the most advanced formulations of gender equality and radical democratic politics. Nothing else will serve Black communities. Nothing else is worth the trouble and the work. Nothing else will make us free and whole.

## III

> Once when I walked into a room
> my eyes would seek out the one or two black faces
> for contact or reassurance or a sign
> I was not alone
> now walking into rooms full of black faces
> that would destroy me for any difference
> where shall my eyes look?
> Once it was easy to know
> who were my people.
>
> —AUDRE LORDE, "Between Ourselves"
> from *The Black Unicorn*

> I am angry because of the treatment I am afforded as a Black man. That fiery anger is stoked additionally with the fuels of contempt and despisal shown me by my community because I am gay. *I cannot go home as who I am.*
>
> —JOSEPH BEAM, *In the Life*

Turning now from gender to the question of sexuality, in other words from sexism to homophobia, we are confronted with as many if not more disturbing orthodoxies, that is to say, with the practice of emasculating forms of masculinity within the context of the Black freedom struggle. Public and published attacks by African Americans upon other African Americans centering upon their sexuality is a relatively recent shame. This rupture in Black public discourse begins with the publication of Eldridge Cleaver's *Soul on Ice* (1968).[28] After taking James Baldwin to task for what he terms his self-hatred in such texts as *Notes of a Native Son*, Cleaver makes the following sweeping statement about Black gays: "The case of James Baldwin aside for the moment, it seems that many Negro homosexuals, acquiescing in this racial death-wish, are outraged and frustrated because in their sickness they are unable to have a baby by a white man." Near the conclusion of this tendentious assessment of what he perceives as Baldwin's failings as a writer, Cleaver offers this patronizing and conventional view of homosexuality, a view which makes it impossible for him to imagine Baldwin as anything other than a perversion of Black manhood: "Homosexuality is a sickness, just as are baby-rape or wanting to become the head of General Motors."[29] Cleaver's vicious attacks upon Baldwin's sexuality marked a dramatic shift in the Black freedom struggle as it legitimized homophobia in Black public discourse beyond the domain of the Black church. In the public debates between such figures as Frederick Douglass and Ida B. Wells, W. E. B. Du Bois and Booker T. Washington, Marcus Garvey and Du Bois, the exchanges were very often acrimonious, but public attacks upon the sexuality of one's opponent never occurred. Indeed, such attacks were regarded as simply unimaginable.

Of course, this taboo, enforced by a latent Victorianism, did not preclude the existence of the most sordid but veiled political contests in which the expanding floor for such exertions was homophobia. In *Bayard Rustin: Troubles I've Seen* (1997), Jervis Anderson describes such a political contest involving Adam Clayton Powell, Bayard Rustin, Martin Luther King, Jr., and A. Phillip Randolph. Concerned that the demonstrations planned by King and Rustin for the Democratic National Convention in Los Angeles in 1960 would jeopardize the candidacy of John F. Kennedy for president, Powell threatened to announce that King and Rustin were involved in a homosexual relationship. Powell promised not to publicize this lie on the condition that King dismiss Rustin from his position in the Southern Christian Leadership Conference as well as cancel the demonstrations. A. Phillip Randolph urged King not to capitulate to Powell's blackmail. In spite of the principled objections of Randolph who supported and admired Rustin, King dismissed—through an intermediary—Rustin who had provided him with loyal service and inspired tactical advice since the Montgomery Bus Boycott of 1956. Neither wishing to discredit King's leadership nor the objectives of SCLC, an organization he had conceived and for which he had drafted the mission statement, Rustin resigned. According to Baldwin, King "lost much moral credit" in sacrificing Rustin to the unscrupulous politics of the former reverend, now congressman, Powell.[30]

Preferring to conceal the weapon in the billowing sleeve of his clerical robe, Powell, in contrast to Cleaver, wielded the knife of division in sub-rosa fashion. As Powell was to discover in his bitter disputes with the Dixiecrats, such a knife cuts both ways. As I say, Cleaver's attack upon Baldwin's sexuality eight years later in *Soul on Ice* marked a dramatic shift in Black public discourse, one which has brought us to the pit out of which issues the fulminations of such a person as Minister Khalil Muhammad who also specializes in the double-edged politics of division. By positing homosexuality as a discredited sexuality incompatible with Black manhood and corrosive of the goals of Black revolution, Cleaver traduced Baldwin and legitimized homophobia in Black public discourse. Like Powell, he also exhibited an emasculating masculinity, by which I mean a masculinity which achieves its power and legitimacy through the denigration of others. In such a masculinity, the deepest wounds are often self-inflicted. The supreme irony is that like Rustin, Baldwin had demonstrated, in words, deeds, and texts, that homosexuality is not incompatible with Black self-assertion in politics or any other arena. Huey P. Newton, Cleaver's leader in the Black Panther Party, formulated a radically different position regarding the role of gays and lesbians in revolutionary struggle.[31] Newton rejected Cleaver's homophobia and asserted that the gay and lesbian liberation movement was not antithetical to the Black liberation movement as conceptualized by the Black Panther Party. Rejecting the tyranny of compulsory heterosexuality, Newton went so far as to assert that when compared with other revolutionaries of whatever stripe that perhaps the "homosexual could be the most revolutionary."[32] As the debate between Newton and Cleaver makes plain, within the context of the Black freedom struggle, African American gays and lesbians, like African American women, would have to fight for the right, to recall the words of Elaine Brown, to fight for freedom.

The worlds-apart positions of Cleaver and Newton on the political question of sexuality is emblematic of the almost schizophrenic position of Black leaders and Black organizations on sexuality: radical in the advocacy of political reform for African Americans as a group; and silent, ambivalent, or condemnatory in the advocacy of reform for African American gays and lesbians. To the credit of Newton, Cleaver, and Brown, the Black Panther Party was the first Black organization to openly debate the role of Black gays and lesbians in the struggle for Black liberation, and also to publish something approaching the seriousness of a position paper on this contested subject. One searches in vain for a similar public debate in such organizations as the National Association for the Advancement of Colored People, the Urban League, the Southern Christian Leadership Conference, and the National Council of Negro Women. While these organizations have collectively achieved historic and far-reaching transformations of political systems at the municipal, state, and federal levels, there is much work that awaits the leadership in these organizations in the political domain of sexuality. The reluctance and slowness of the leadership in these organizations to publicly and systematically address homophobia, to link the struggle against homophobia with the Black freedom struggle is in part based upon the conservatism of the Black church and other religious institutions which have legitimized homophobia (and sexism) through the affirmation of what the leadership of these institutions regard as God-ordained practices. Additionally, the reluctance of the leadership of Black secular institutions and organizations to publicly denounce homophobia is predicated upon the belief that sexuality is a private matter, a personal matter. But the personal, as feminists have proven beyond all doubt, is political. For those who contest this truism, I invite them to ponder the political implications and consequences of the sodomy laws, the homophobic legislation adopted by the legislature of Colorado, and the bankrupt policy concerning gays and lesbians in the U.S. military. Sexuality, then, as these examples make astoundingly clear, is both personal and political.

In *One More River to Cross: Black and Gay in America* (1996) Keith Boykin writes that "black leaders such as Coretta Scott King, the Reverend Jesse Jackson and Benjamin Chavis" have supported the lesbian and gay movement.[33] Boykin is correct and I would add Angela Davis and the poet and educator Sonia Sanchez to this list of Black leaders. But these individuals, while influential, constitute only a small number of a powerful elite. As Boykin is careful to point out, within this Black elite General Colin Powell has emerged as the most outspoken opponent to the gay and lesbian movement. Powell and other African American leaders would do well to emulate the example of Nelson Mandella, Winnie Mandella, Archbishop Desmond Tutu, Mamphela Ramphele, and the leadership of the African National Congress who concretized in the founding documents of post-apartheid South Africa clear prohibitions against discrimination of South African citizens on the grounds of gender and sexuality.

Homophobia in the modern Black freedom struggle is reflected not only in the writings of Cleaver and in the unmerited devaluation of such figures as Baldwin and Rustin, but also in the work of yet another Black radical from this period: Amiri Baraka. In such texts as "Babylon Revisited" and *The Toilet* (1963), to name only two, Baraka posits the "faggot" as a symbol of decadence and impotence. Strangely but predictably, Baraka, like Cleaver, remains silent on lesbianism. In this silence we discover another species of sexism which posits that only male sexuality is deserving of this degree of policing and scrutiny. In their view, lesbianism is a trivial matter, outside certain orders of high discourse and, therefore, undeserving of commentary. As Johnnetta B. Cole has observed, when lesbianism does emerge within Black public discourse it is used as a term of opprobrium often by Black men to discredit the progressive work of Black women who are committed to the politics of feminism or womanism.[34] The loaded charge of lesbian or dyke becomes then a weapon, a tool of sexism. In "Transferences and Confluences: Black Poetries, the Black Arts Movement, and Black Lesbian-Feminism," Cheryl Clarke masterfully documents the manner in which the introduction of lesbian themes in the reading of Black texts was a *cause célèbre* at the Black Writers Conference at Howard University in 1978. On a panel chaired by June Jordan and which included Acklyn Lynch and Sonia Sanchez, Barbara Smith posited that Toni Morrison's *Sula* was a "lesbian novel" in the sense that the central characters have "pivotal relationships with one another." Clarke writes that a "visceral collective groan resonated throughout the room when Smith said the words 'lesbian novel.' We witnessed extreme reactions from a number of well-known figures of the black cultural world—nationalists and nonnationalists—in response to Smith's lesbian reading. The emphatic hostility astounded both Smith and Jordan.[35] Here, as in other landmark events of this period, race and discredited forms of sexuality collide and emerge as an unmixable mix.

Slaves to the tyranny of compulsory heterosexuality, the homophobic positions of Cleaver, Baraka, and others have been embraced by one of the major figures in Afrocentrism: Molefi Asante. Just as Cleaver and Baraka argue that homosexuality is incompatible with Black manhood and Black liberation, Asante argues in *Afrocentricity* (1988) that homosexuality "is a deviation from Afrocentric thought. . . ."[36] In this absurd pronouncement, essentialism, homophobia, and distorted racial reasoning assume their most toxic form. In the writings of Cleaver, Baraka, and Asante, along with those by Frances Cress Welsing, and in some of the public pronouncements of Minister Louis Farrakhan, we discover not only a recycling of orthodox conceptions of sexuality which have been contested and refuted, but also a deep and abiding anxiety about Black manhood.[37] The collective silence on the mystery and range of Black female sexuality makes this anxiety even more visible and contradictory. Why is the sexuality of women less worthy of commentary than the sexuality of men? Again, there is sexism here, the tendency to conflate Black liberation with Black manhood, the insistence that heterosexuality is the *sine qua non* of Blackness, and a marked degree of fear and hostility toward any conception of male sexuality that does not conform to a heterosexual ideal.

The homophobia of Cleaver, Baraka, Asante, and others has deeply compromised their advocacy of Black liberation. In the body of their work, the very palpable anxiety concerning homosexuality reveals an acceptance of normative modes of masculinity, and a devotion to only the most rigid constructions of Black masculinity. Further, there also is a refusal in their work to acknowledge the mystery and range within human sexuality for, just as there is an authentic, pure, and uncontaminated Black self, or so goes the narrow essentialist, fundamentalist argument of many nationalists and Afrocentrists, there also is an authentic, pure, and uncontaminated Black sexuality which is predictably heterosexual.

Along with the failure to acknowledge the spectrum of femininities and masculinities, in the pronouncements of many nationalists and Afrocentrists there is also the failure to question all orthodoxies. When slaves and free Blacks in antebellum America heard the biblical justifications for slavery, they were skeptical and quickly apprehended the lie and bitter usurpation of power the sweet language of the Old and New Testaments concealed. On this vital point, David Walker, Maria Stewart, and Frederick Douglass were clear. They were neither duped nor confused. With the example of these fearless and questioning figures plainly before them and with so much more knowledge, why have Cleaver, Baraka, Asante, Welsing, and others failed to exercise the same degree of skepticism and disdain in the presence of an orthodoxy that possesses, in many ways, the same compromised objectives? Do their positions on sexuality repose upon fear, expediency, conventions, or reasoned conclusions? Why have they insisted upon a uniformity in the shifting domain of sexuality that is closer to slavery than freedom, and that leads to a monotony of consciousness that *disprepares* one for revolutionary politics and struggle? In fine, why have they attempted to rob the Black world of the richness that is the Black world? Of course, these are questions that only they can fully answer. And I hope they will respond to these questions as their retrograde positions on sexuality and their valorization of emasculating forms of masculinity have deeply compromised their roles in the Black freedom struggle and alienated many African Americans in whom we find the full spectrum of human sexuality.

## IV

Look out, Rayfield! Move over, Gabriel! You better stand way back, Jesus! Ah'm fixin to throw.

> —JACK, in a triumphant contest of strength with the Devil, in "Strength Test Between Jack and the Devil," *Mules and Men*

High John de Conquer came to be a man, and a mighty man at that.

> —ZORA NEALE HURSTON, from "High John de Conquer"

Resistance is the secret of joy.

> —ALICE WALKER, *Possessing the Secret of Joy*

The uncritical acceptance of orthodox conceptions of gender and sexuality and the attending practice of emasculating forms of masculinity are our new traps. They are, to conjure another familiar image in African American folklore, the new tar baby to which we have been stuck for far too long. Many African American men have been uncritical in our acceptance of certain male and heterosexual privileges. This lack of a deeper political consciousness, this failure to critique and contest apparently widely held assumptions that foster the growth of the traps of sexism and homophobia have produced injuries, both psychic and physical, among those of us who are not only excluded from the attainment of these privileges, but who also recognize that these privileges are potential traps. The tradition of John is a new mode of Black masculinity that constitutes a radical rejection of the divisive politics of sexism and homophobia, as well as the repudiation of the practice of emasculating forms of masculinity. If African American men are to continue to have a credible voice in the historic struggle against white supremacy, we must be disloyal to the ideologies of sexism and homophobia. Equally as important, we must reclaim the progressive tradition of political, cultural, and social thought of Black men who have stood bravely in opposition to sexism and homophobia. This progressive tradition begins in the writings of Frederick Douglass and it grows in force and power in the writings of Alexander Crummel, W. E. B. Du Bois, Bayard Rustin, Huey P. Newton, James Baldwin, Essex Hemphill, Michael Eric Dyson, and others. The reclamation of this progressive tradition of activists and intellectuals, and the enactment of the principles of this new mode of Black masculinity I have termed the tradition of John—by *living into it*—constitute the first radical steps in the collective liberation of African American men from the traps of sexism and homophobia.[38]

This essay began with the invocation of a power that would make the rulers of empires and the political systems that guarantee their hegemony, quake. I attempted to summon a power that would vanquish and outlast princes and principalities. Was this a vain, naive, even preposterous gesture? Some might dismiss it as such. I have, however, unwavering faith in the value of individual acts of agency and self-assertion, in the ability of a concept to grow in force, meaning, and significance. Is it possible that this new mode of Black masculinity, the tradition of John, possesses the necessary force and depth to accomplish a goal so ambitious and far-reaching as the overthrow of empires? Only indirectly. The reformation of political systems occurs through the process of political struggle. While this is true, there also is a powerful dialectic between political consciousness and political struggle. A political consciousness is born of and shaped by a multitude of powerful factors and chief among them is culture, along with its artifacts and traditions. The tradition of John is a new and alternative mode of Black masculinity that emerges from one of the most progressive and transgressive traditions in African American culture: the tradition of Black folklore. I offer this gift in language and ideas grounded in the lore of Black people in a spirit of solidarity. The tradition of John is a mode of masculinity that may serve as the foundation for the creation of a new politics that will transform and empower African American men to begin the work of dismantling two of the central pillars in the temple of the American empire: sexism and homophobia. Moreover, the tradition of John may serve as the theoretical space within which African American men may recapture ourselves in history, in our collective past, and remake, reimagine ourselves as purposeful, transgressive, and progressive subjects for the future. It is in this continuum I position myself and offer this alternative mode of masculinity to the normative modes of masculinity that beset us all. I do so fully cognizant of the fact that the tradition of John is a mode of Black masculinity that does not transcend, like other theoretical models, the process of ideological recuperation. As the stories of John empowered and sustained us as a people through the abolition of chattel slavery, can we now reclaim and adapt these powerful and instructive tales to assist us in creating radical strategies and emancipative models to abolish sexism, homophobia, and other species of slavery? Again, why not this?

Fully cognizant of our historic struggle against racism and white supremacy, let us recommit ourselves to the struggles that exist simultaneously on other fronts. Casting aside emasculating forms of masculinity, let us begin this difficult work of teaching and dialogue, of communion and reclamation, of imagining new possibilities of Black male agency with the tradition of John as our lodestar and talisman. As an example of resistance who embodies the potentiality of a liberated and liberating Black masculinity, John has been asleep in the soil of the South, as Hurston tells us, for long enough. It is time to awaken John. It is time to reclaim and emulate this mythic slave's example of principled self-assertion, and adapt it to meet the exigencies of the modern forms of slavery by which many of us are trapped. It is time to begin the joyful work of resistance, work that changes consciousness, work that changes behavior, work that saves lives, work that transforms communities and institutions.

And what, now, is the work for Black men? It must be to discover and actualize the value of being a good man, and to reject the temptation (and the excuse) of merely being good at being a man. And also this: to honor the deep masculine that is not macho, but human. And above all this: to continue our brave walk through the whirlwind, ever toward Jerusalem, in the tradition of John.

## NOTES

1. The Black folk tale of the signifying monkey is the foundation for Henry Louis Gates, Jr.'s, theory of African American literature, signifying, set forth in *The Signifying Monkey*. Alice Walker's theory of womanism or Black feminism defined in *In Search of Our Mothers' Gardens: Womanist Prose*, is based upon the Black folk expression "womanish."

2. The argument that Black folklore is the expanding floor for the development of Black identities is illustrated in the lobotomy episode in Ralph Ellison's *Invisible Man*. More recently this argument has received treatment in such texts as Toni Morrison's "Rootedness: The Ancestor as Foundation" in *Black Women Writers*, edited by Mari Evans; Lawrence Levine's *Black Folklore, Black Consciousness*; and Alice Walker's "The Dummy in the Window" in *Living by the Word*. The concept of the Black Atlantic world is a theory of the African diaspora developed in Paul Gilroy's *The Black Atlantic World*.

3. For tales of John, consult Zora Neale Hurston's *Mules and Men*; Langston Hughes and Arna Bontemps's *Book of Negro Folklore*, *The Negro Caravan*, edited by Sterling A. Brown, Arthur P. Davis, and Ulysses Lee; and Roger Abraham's *Afro-American Folktales: Stories from Black Traditions in the New World*.

4. Zora Neale Hurston, "Glossary," *Mules and Men* (New York: Harper and Row, 1935; 1970), 305.

5. The central works that explore paradigms of Black masculinity include Robert Staples's *Black Masculinity; Black Male: Representations of Masculinity in Contemporary American Art,* edited by Thelma Golden; *Representing Black Men,* edited by Marcelleus Blount and George P. Cunningham; *Speak My Name,* edited by Don Belton; *In the Life,* edited by Joseph Beam; *Brother to Brother,* edited by Essex Hemphill; *Welcome to the Jungle* by Kobena Mercer; *What Is Cool: Understanding Black Manhood in America* by Marlene Connor; *Black Noise* by Tricia Rose; and Phillip Brian Harper's *Are We Not Men? Masculine Anxiety and the Problems of African American Identity.*

6. Zora Neale Hurston, "High John De Conquer," *The Sanctified Church: The Folklore Writings of Zora Neale Hurston* (Berkeley: Turtle Island Foundation, 1981), 69. All further references to this edition will appear in parentheses.

7. For a thorough analysis of the function of Black humor, consult Mel Watkins's *In the Real Side: Laughing and Signifying — The Underground Tradition of African American Humor that Transformed American Culture from Slavery to Richard Pryor.*

8. Michael S. Harper, *Images of Kin: New and Selected Poems* (Urbana: University of Illinois Press, 1988), 113.

9. This concept of process as becoming and perishing bears the imprint of the thinking found in Alfred North Whitehead's essay "Adventure" in *Adventures of Ideas* (New York: Free Press, 1933; 1967) and Charles Johnson's *The Sorcerer's Apprentice: Tales and Conjurations* (New York: Plume Books, 1994).

10. "How Jack Beat the Devil" appears in Zora Neale Hurston's *Mules and Men* (New York: Harper and Row, 1935; 1970); "John Outruns the Lord" appears in Roger D. Abrahms's *Afro-American Folk Tales* (New York: Pantheon, 1985).

11. Robert Bly, *Iron John* (Reading, Mass.: Addison-Wesley Publishing Company, 1990), x.

12. Ibid., 1.

13. Ibid., 2.

14. Ibid., 3.

15. Ibid., 226.

16. Ibid., 227–228.

17. Charles Johnson, *Oxherding Tale* (1982; reprint, with a new introduction by the author, New York: Plume/Penguin Books, 1995).

18. See Angela Davis's *Autobiography* and Elaine P. Brown's *A Taste of Power.*

19. Angela Davis, *The Autobiography of Angela Davis* (New York: Random House, 1974), 162.

20. Angela Davis, *An Autobiography* (New York: Random House, 1974), 161.

21. Ibid., 181.

22. Ibid., 181–182.

23. Elaine Brown, *A Taste of Power* (New York: Anchor Books, 1992), 3–5.

24. Ibid., 191–192.

25. Audre Lorde, "The Great American Disease," *The Black Scholar* (May–June 1979), 19.

26. Brown, 191.

27. For one response to Robert Staples's "The Myth of Black Macho: A Response to Angry Black Feminists," consult Alice Walker's "To the Black Scholar" in *In Search of Our Mothers' Gardens.*

28. See Cleaver's chapter "Notes on a Native Son," in *Soul on Ice* (New York: McGraw Hill, 1968).

29. Eldridge Cleaver, *Soul on Ice* (New York: McGraw Hill, 1968), 102–110.

30. Jervis Anderson, *Bayard Rustin: Troubles I've Seen* (New York: Harper Collins, 1997), 229–231.

31. Consult Huey P. Newton's "A Letter from Huey to the Revolutionary Brothers and Sisters about the Women's Liberation and Gay Liberation Movements" reprinted here in *Traps.*

32. Ibid. For the term and concept of compulsory heterosexuality, I am indebted to Adrienne Rich's "Compulsory Heterosexuality and Lesbian Existence," in *The Lesbian*

*and Gay Studies Reader,* edited by Henry Abelove, Michele Aina Barale, and David M. Halperin (New York: Routledge, 1993).

33. Keith Boykin, *One More River to Cross: Black and Gay in America* (New York: Anchor Books, 1996), 31.

34. Johnnetta B. Cole, "Epilogue," *Words of Fire: An Anthology of African-American Feminist Thought,* edited by Beverly Guy-Sheftall, (New York: New Press, 1995), 549–551.

35. Cheryl Clarke, "Transferences and Confluences: Black Poetries, the Black Arts Movement, and Black Lesbian-Feminism," in *Dangerous Liaisons: Blacks, Gays and the Struggle for Equality,* edited by Eric Brandt (New York: Free Press, 1999), 196.

36. Molefi Kete Asante, *Afrocentricity* (Trenton, N.J.: Africa World Press, 1988), 57.

37. For an overview of Black homophobic literature, consult Ron Simmons's "Some Thoughts on the Challenges Facing Black Gay Intellectuals" in *Brother to Brother: New Writings by Black Gay Men,* edited by Essex Hemphill. For a critique of the biblical injunctions against homosexuality, consult Peter Gomes's *The Good Book: Reading the Bible with Mind and Heart* (New York: Morrow, 1996).

38. I am indebted to Anna Julia Cooper for the vibrant phrase *living into it* which appears in her essay "What Are We Worth" in *A Voice from the South* (1892; reprint, New York: Oxford University Press, 1988).

# PART 1

## REMEMBERING OUR FOREFATHERS
### Pioneering Perspectives on
### the Rights and Education of Women

# 1 THE RIGHTS OF WOMEN

*[appeared in* The North Star, *July 28, 1848]*

FREDERICK DOUGLASS

One of the most interesting events of the past week, was the holding of what is technically styled a Woman's Rights Convention at Seneca Falls. The speaking, addresses, and resolutions of this extraordinary meeting was almost wholly conducted by women; and although they evidently felt themselves in a novel position, it is but simple justice to say that their whole proceedings were characterized by marked ability and dignity. No one present, we think, however much he might be disposed to differ from the views advanced by the leading speakers on that occasion, will fail to give them credit for brilliant talents and excellent dispositions. In this meeting, as in other deliberative assemblies, there were frequent differences of opinion and animated discussion; but in no case was there the slightest absence of good feeling and decorum. Several interesting documents setting forth the rights as well as the grievances of women were read. Among these was a Declaration of Sentiments, to be regarded as the basis of a grand movement for attaining the civil, social, political, and religious rights of women. We should not do justice to our own convictions, or to the excellent persons connected with this infant movement, if we did not in this connection offer a few remarks on the general subject which the Convention met to consider and the objects they seek to attain. In doing so, we are not insensible that the bare mention of this truly important subject in any other than terms of contemptuous ridicule and scornful disfavor, is likely to excite against us the fury of bigotry and the folly of prejudice. A discussion of the rights of animals would be regarded with far more complacency by many of what are called the *wise* and the *good* of our land, than would a discussion of the rights of women. It is, in their estimation, to be guilty of evil thoughts, to think that woman is entitled to equal rights with man. Many who have at last made the discovery that the Negroes have some rights as well as other members of the human family, have yet to be convinced that women are entitled to any. Eight years ago a number of persons of this description actually abandoned the anti-slavery cause, lest by giving their influence in that direction they might possibly be giving countenance to the dangerous heresy that woman, in respect to rights, stands on an equal footing with man. In the judgment of such persons the American slave system, with all its concomitant horrors, is less to be deplored than this *wicked* idea. It is perhaps needless to say, that we cherish little sympathy for such sentiments or respect for such prejudices. Standing as we do upon the watch-tower of human freedom, we cannot be deterred from an expression of our approbation of any movement, however humble, to improve and elevate the character of any members of the human family. While it is impossible for us to go into this subject at length, and dispose of the various objections which are often urged against such a doctrine as that of female equality, we are free to say that in respect to political rights, we hold woman to be justly entitled to all we claim for man. We go farther, and express our conviction that all political rights which it is expedient for man to exercise, it is equally so for woman. All that distinguishes man as an intelligent and accountable being, is equally true of woman, and if that government only is just which governs by the free consent of the governed, there can be no reason in the world for denying to woman the exercise of the elective franchise, or a hand in making and administering the laws of the land. Our doctrine is that "right is of no sex." We therefore bid the women engaged in this movement our humble Godspeed.

# 2 GIVE WOMEN FAIR PLAY

*[An address delivered in Washington, D.C.,
on March 31, 1888]*

## FREDERICK DOUGLASS

Boston *Woman's Journal*, 14, 21 April 1888. Other texts in Speech File, reel 16, frames
306–09, 310–15, 320–23, reel 19, frames 765–76, FD Papers, DLC; Foner, *Life and
Writings*, 4: 448–54, misdated April 1888; Foner, *Douglass on Women's Rights*, 109–15,
misdated April 1888.

The International Council of Women met in Washington, D.C., between 25
March and 1 April 1888 with representatives attending from the United
States, France, England, Ireland, Canada, Norway, Denmark, Finland, and
India. Divided into sixteen different sessions with some eighty speakers, the
major activities of the convention occurred at Albaugh's Grand Opera House.
Douglass sat on the platform during many of the sessions and occasionally
made brief remarks to the audience. The text that follows is his principal
address, delivered on 31 March 1888, at a morning meeting designated "Pioneers' Day." Susan B. Anthony called that meeting to order. The audience
observed a moment of silence in memory of Lucretia Mott and then sang John
G. Whittier's hymn, "The Reformers." The session's first speaker was Elizabeth Cady Stanton who reminisced about the pioneers in the woman suffrage
movement. After John W. Hutchinson sang an original song, "Greeting to the
Pioneers," Anthony introduced Douglass. Lucy Stone, Henry B. Blackwell,
Antoinette Brown Blackwell, Robert Purvis, Mary Grew, Matilda Joslyn Gage,
Samuel C. Pomeroy, and May Wright Sewall followed Douglass. When Anthony asked Amy Post to stand and described her relation to Douglass, he
added his own brief words of praise for the old friend of Rochester days. The
meeting concluded with Anthony reading letters received from those unable
to attend the celebration and the singing of "Auld Lang Syne" by the audience.
The Washington *Post* commented favorably on the meeting and called the

presence of Douglass and Purvis there "poetic justice," on account of the
earlier aid of many women to the abolitionist movement. Susan B. Anthony to
Douglass, 6 February 1888, Douglass to [Caroline F.] Putnam, 16 April 1888,
General Correspondence File, reel 4, frames 712–21, 764–65, FD Papers,
DLC; Washington *Post*, 27 March, 1 April 1888; Washington *National Repub-
lican*, 1, 4 April 1888; Boston *Woman's Journal*, 7 April 1888; Stanton et al.,
*History of Woman Suffrage*, 4: 124–37; Holland, *Frederick Douglass*, 366–67.

*Mrs. President,*[1] *Ladies and Gentlemen:* I come to this platform with
unusual diffidence. Although I have long been identified with the Woman's
Suffrage movement, and have often spoken in its favor, I am somewhat at a
loss to know what to say on this really great and uncommon occasion, where
so much has been said.

When I look around on this assembly, and see the many able and eloquent
women, full of the subject, ready to speak, and who only need the opportunity to impress this audience with their views and thrill them with "thoughts
that breathe and words that burn,"[2] I do not feel like taking up more than a
very small space of your time and attention, and shall not. I would not, even
now, presume to speak, but for the circumstance of my early connection
with the cause, and of having been called upon to do so by one whose voice
in this Council we all gladly obey.[3] Men have very little business here as
speakers, anyhow; and if they come here at all they should take back benches
and wrap themselves in silence. For this is an International Council, not of
men, but of women, and woman should have all the say in it. This is her day
in court.

I do not mean to exalt the intellect of woman above man's; but I have
heard many men speak on this subject, some of them the most eloquent to
be found anywhere in the country; and I believe no man, however gifted
with thought and speech, can voice the wrongs and present the demands of
women with the skill and effect, with the power and authority of woman
herself. The man struck is the man to cry out. Woman knows and feels her
wrongs as man cannot know and feel them, and she also knows as well as he
can know, what measures are needed to redress them. I grant all the claims
at this point. She is her own best representative. We can neither speak for
her, nor vote for her, nor act for her, nor be responsible for her; and the thing
for men to do in the premises is just to get out of her way and give her the
fullest opportunity to exercise all the powers inherent in her individual
personality, and allow her to do it as she herself shall elect to exercise them.
Her right to be and to do is as full, complete and perfect as the right of any
man on earth. I say of her, as I say of the colored people, "Give her fair play,
and hands off."

There was a time when, perhaps, we men could help a little. It was when
this woman suffrage cause was in its cradle, when it was not big enough to go
alone, when it had to be taken in the arms of its mother from Seneca Falls,
N.Y., to Rochester, N.Y., for baptism. I then went along with it and offered
my services to help it, for then it needed help; but now it can afford to

dispense with me and all of my sex.[4] Then its friends were few—now its friends are many. Then it was wrapped in obscurity—now it is lifted in sight of the whole civilized world, and people of all lands and languages give it their hearty support. Truly the change is vast and wonderful.

I thought my eye of faith was tolerably clear when I attended those meetings in Seneca Falls and Rochester, but it was far too dim to see at the end of forty years a result so imposing as this International Council, and to see yourself and Miss Anthony alive and active in its proceedings. Of course, I expected to be alive myself, and am not surprised to find myself so; for such is, perhaps, the presumption and arrogance common to my sex. Nevertheless, I am very glad to see you here to-day, and to see this grand assembly of women. I am glad that you are its president. No manufactured "boom," or political contrivance, such as make presidents elsewhere, has made you president of this assembly of women in this Capital of the Nation. You hold your place by reason of eminent fitness, and I give you joy that your life and labors in the cause of woman are thus crowned with honor and glory. This I say in spite of the warning given us by Miss Anthony's friend against mutual admiration.

There may be some well-meaning people in this audience who have never attended a woman suffrage convention, never heard a woman suffrage speech, never read a woman suffrage newspaper, and they may be surprised that those who speak here do not argue the question. It may be kind to tell them that our cause has passed beyond the period of arguing. The demand of the hour is not argument, but assertion, firm and inflexible assertion, assertion which has more than the force of an argument. If there is any argument to be made, it must be made by the opponents, not by the friends of woman suffrage. Let those who want argument examine the ground upon which they base their claim to the right to vote. They will find that there is not one reason, not one consideration, which they can urge in support of man's claim to vote, which does not equally support the right of woman to vote.

There is to-day, however, a special reason for omitting argument. This is the end of the fourth decade of the woman suffrage movement, a kind of jubilee which naturally turns our minds to the past.

Ever since this Council has been in session, my thoughts have been reverting to the past. I have been thinking more or less, of the scene presented forty years ago in the little Methodist Church at Seneca Falls, the manger in which this organized suffrage movement was born. It was a very small thing then. It was not then big enough to be abused, or loud enough to make itself heard outside, and only a few of those who saw it had any notion that the little thing would live. I have been thinking, too, of the strong conviction, the noble courage, the sublime faith in God and man it required at that time to set this suffrage ball in motion. The history of the world has given to us many sublime undertakings, but none more sublime than this. It was a great thing for the friends of peace to organize in opposition to war; it

was a great thing for the friends of temperance to organize against intemperance; it was a great thing for humane people to organize in opposition to
slavery; but it was a much greater thing, in view of all the circumstances, for
woman to organize herself in opposition to her exclusion from participation
in government. The reason is obvious. War, intemperance and slavery are
open, undisguised, palpable evils. The best feelings of human nature revolt
at them. We could easily make men see the misery, the debasement, the
terrible suffering caused by intemperance; we could easily make men see
the desolation wrought by war and the hell-black horrors of chattel slavery;
but the case was different in the movement for woman suffrage. Men took
for granted all that could be said against intemperance, war and slavery. But
no such advantage was found in the beginning of the cause of suffrage for
women. On the contrary, everything in her condition was supposed to be
lovely, just as it should be. She had no rights denied, no wrongs to redress.
She herself had no suspicion but that all was going well with her. She floated
along on the tide of life as her mother and grandmother had done before her,
as in a dream of Paradise. Her wrongs, if she had any, were too occult to be
seen, and too light to be felt. It required a daring voice and a determined
hand to awake her from this delightful dream and call the nation to account
for the rights and opportunities of which it was depriving her. It was well
understood at the beginning that woman would not thank us for disturbing
her by this call to duty, and it was known that man would denounce and
scorn us for such a daring innovation upon the established order of things.
But this did not appall or delay the word and work.

At this distance of time from that convention at Rochester, and in view of
the present position of the question, it is hard to realize the moral courage it
required to launch this unwelcome movement. Any man can be brave when
the danger is over, go to the front door when there is no resistance, rejoice
when the battle is fought and the victory is won; but it is not so easy to
venture upon a field untried with one-half the whole world against you, as
these women did.

Then who were we, for I count myself in, who did this thing? We were few
in numbers, moderate in resources, and very little known in the world. The
most that we had to commend us was a firm conviction that we were in the
right, and a firm faith that the right must ultimately prevail. But the case was
well considered. Let no man imagine that the step was taken recklessly and
thoughtlessly. Mrs. Stanton had dwelt upon it at least six years before she
declared it in the Rochester convention. Walking with her from the house of
Joseph and Thankful Southwick,[5] two of the noblest people I ever knew,
Mrs. Stanton, with an earnestness that I shall never forget, unfolded her
views on this woman question precisely as she has in this Council.[6] This was
six and forty years ago, and it was not until six years after, that she ventured
to make her formal, pronounced and startling demand for the ballot. She
had, as I have said, considered well, and knew something of what would be
the cost of the reform she was inaugurating. She knew the ridicule, the

rivalry, the criticism and the bitter aspersions which she and her co-laborers would have to meet and to endure. But she saw more clearly than most of us that the vital point to be made prominent, and the one that included all others, was the ballot, and she bravely said the word. It was not only necessary to break the silence of woman and make her voice heard, but she must have a clear, palpable and comprehensive measure set before her, one worthy of her highest ambition and her best exertions, and hence the ballot was brought to the front.

There are few facts in my humble history to which I look back with more satisfaction than to the fact, recorded in the history of the Woman Suffrage Movement, that I was sufficiently enlightened at that early day, and when only a few years from slavery, to support your resolution for woman suffrage. I have done very little in this world in which to glory except this one act — and I certainly glory in that. When I ran away from slavery, it was for myself; when I advocated emancipation, it was for my people; but when I stood up for the rights of woman, self was out of the question, and I found a little nobility in the act.

In estimating the forces with which this suffrage cause has had to contend during these forty years, the fact should be remembered that relations of long standing beget a character in the parties to them in favor of their continuance. Time itself is a conservative power — a very conservative power. One shake of his hoary locks will sometimes paralyze the hand and palsy the tongue of the reformer. The relation of man to woman has the advantage of all the ages behind it. Those who oppose a readjustment of this relation tell us that what is always was and always will be, world without end. But we have heard this old argument before, and if we live very long we shall hear it again. When any aged error shall be assailed, and any old abuse is to be removed, we shall meet this same old argument. Man has been so long the king and woman the subject — man has been so long accustomed to command and woman to obey — that both parties to the relation have been hardened into their respective places, and thus has been piled up a mountain of iron against woman's enfranchisement.

The same thing confronted us in our conflicts with slavery. Long years ago Henry Clay said, on the floor of the American Senate, "I know there is a visionary dogma that man cannot hold property in man," and, with a brow of defiance, he said, "That is property which the law makes property. Two hundred years of legislation has sanctioned and sanctified negro slaves as property."[7] But neither the power of time nor the might of legislation has been able to keep life in that stupendous barbarism.

The universality of man's rule over woman is another factor in the resistance to the woman suffrage movement. We are pointed to the fact that men have not only always ruled over women, but that they do so rule everywhere, and they easily think that a thing that is done everywhere must be right. Though the fallacy of this reasoning is too transparent to need refutation, it still exerts a powerful influence. Even our good Brother Jasper yet believes, with the ancient church, that the sun "do move," notwithstanding all the astronomers of the world are against him.[8] One year ago I stood on the Pincio in Rome and witnessed the unveiling of the statue of Galileo.[9] It was an imposing sight. At no time before had Rome been free enough to permit such a statue to be placed within her walls. It is now there, not with the approval of the Vatican. No priest took part in the ceremonies. It was all the work of laymen. One or two priests passed the statue with averted eyes, but the great truths of the solar system were not angry at the sight, and the same will be true when woman shall be clothed, as she will yet be, with all the rights of American citizenship.

All good causes are mutually helpful. The benefits accruing from this movement for the equal rights of woman are not confined or limited to woman only. They will be shared by every effort to promote the progress and welfare of mankind everywhere and in all ages. It was an example and a prophecy of what can be accomplished against strongly opposing forces, against time-hallowed abuses, against deeply entrenched error, against world-wide usage, and against the settled judgment of mankind, by a few earnest women, clad only in the panoply of truth, and determined to live and die in what they considered a righteous cause.

I do not forget the thoughtful remark of our president in the opening address to this International Council, reminding us of the incompleteness of our work.[10] The remark was wise and timely. Nevertheless, no man can compare the present with the past, the obstacles that then opposed us, and the influences that now favor us, the meeting in the little Methodist chapel forty years ago, and the Council in this vast theatre to-day, without admitting that woman's cause is already a brilliant success. But, however this may be, and whatever the future may have in store for us, one thing is certain—this new revolution in human thought will never go backward.[11] When a great truth once gets abroad in the world, no power on earth can imprison it, or prescribe its limits, or suppress it. It is bound to go on till it becomes the thought of the world. Such a truth is woman's right to equal liberty with man. She was born with it. It was hers before she comprehended it. It is inscribed upon all the powers and faculties of her soul, and no custom, law nor usage can ever destroy it. Now that it has got fairly fixed in the minds of the few, it is bound to become fixed in the minds of the many, and be supported at last by a great cloud of witnesses, which no man can number and no power can withstand.

The women who have thus far carried on this agitation have already embodied and illustrated Theodore Parker's three grades of human greatness. The first is greatness in executive and administrative ability; second, greatness in the ability to organize; and thirdly, in the ability to discover truth.[12] Wherever these three elements of power are combined in any movement, there is a reasonable ground to believe in its final success; and these elements of power have been manifest in the women who have had the movement in hand from the beginning. They are seen in the order which has characterized the proceedings of this Council. They are seen in the depth and comprehensiveness of the discussions had upon them in this Council. They are seen in the fervid eloquence and downright earnestness with which women advocate their cause. They are seen in the profound attention with which woman is heard in her own behalf. They are seen in the steady growth and onward march of the movement, and they will be seen in the final triumph of woman's cause, not only in this country, but throughout the world.

[Speeches by Lucy Stone, Henry B. Blackwell, Antoinette Brown Blackwell, and Robert Purvis; song by Ormiston Chant; speeches by Mary Grew, Matilda Joslyn Gage, Samuel C. Pomeroy, May Wright Sewall, and Susan B. Anthony.]

Mr. DOUGLASS—I only want to say that all that Miss Anthony has said of Amy Post,[13] and more than all she said, and more than all that anybody can say in her praise, will not be too much. Her home, her house, her shelter, as it has been well said, has been the shelter of the poor castout. The Indian, the African, the despised of every class, have been with Isaac Post[14] and Amy Post. They have found shelter with them, and I rejoice to see her here to-day, because she was the first in whose eyes I found sympathy and from whose lips I heard a word of cheer after I escaped the chains of slavery.

### NOTES

1. The International Council of Women chose Elizabeth Cady Stanton to be the president of its Washington meeting. Susan B. Anthony however, presided over the Pioneers' Day session of the council and Douglass might be referring to either woman. Boston *Woman's Journal*, 14 April 1888.

2. Douglass quotes from the final stanza of "The Progress of Posey," by English poet Thomas Gray (1716–71). Edmund Gosse, ed., *The Works of Thomas Gray in Prose and Verse*, 4 vols. (New York, 1895), 1: 36.

3. Susan B. Anthony had written to Douglass the preceding month to invite him to speak at the Pioneers' Day ceremonies at the meeting of the International Council of Women and she called upon him at that session to speak. Susan B. Anthony to Douglass, 6 February 1888, reel 4, frames 712–21. General Correspondence File, FD Papers, DLC; Boston *Woman's Journal*, 14 April 1888.

4. Douglass attended the first women's rights convention in Seneca Falls, New York, on 19–20 July 1848 and thirteen days later attended a second one held in Rochester, New York. NS, 28 July, 11 August 1848.

5. Born in South Danvers, Massachusetts, Joseph Southwick (1791–1861) was a prominent Quaker abolitionist and merchant. He resided for a time in Maine but settled in Boston around the early 1830s and participated in numerous business enterprises. He was one of the founders of the American Anti-Slavery Society in 1833 and a longtime officer of the Massachusetts Anti-Slavery Society. In 1835, he and his wife Thankful Southwick gave refuge to British abolitionist George Thompson during the violent Boston riot. The Southwick home on Sumner Street was a frequent gathering place for Garrisonian abolitionists, including Douglass. Although Southwick was openly critical of disunionism, William Lloyd Garrison still spoke respectfully of him at his funeral. NASS, 2 February 1867; Douglass, *Life and Times*, 520; Garrison and Garrison, *Garri-*

*son Life,* 1: 396, 2: 46–48, 3: 100, 4: 412; Walter M. Merrill and Louis Ruchames, eds., *The Letters of William Lloyd Garrison,* 6 vols. (Cambridge, Mass., 1971–81), 2: 80.

6. The precise date of this meeting cannot be confirmed although both Douglass and Stanton recalled the incident in later years. In 1843 Stanton moved to Boston where her husband, Henry B. Stanton, had established a law practice the previous year. She was a frequent visitor at that time to the home of Joseph and Thankful Southwick, a Quaker couple long active in Boston Garrisonian circles. Stanton attended several antislavery meetings while in Boston and at one of them heard Douglass for the first time and soon after revealed to him in a conversation her desire to hold a women's rights convention. Douglass, *Life and Times,* 521; Elizabeth Cady Stanton, *Eighty Years and More: Reminiscences, 1815–1897* (1898; New York, 1971), 126: Alma Lutz, *Created Equal: A Biography of Elizabeth Cady Stanton, 1815–1902* (New York: 1940), 38–39; Lois W. Banner, *Elizabeth Cady Stanton: A Radical for Woman's Rights* (Boston, 1980), 126.

7. Douglass quotes Henry Clay's address on the issue of antislavery petitions delivered in the U.S. Senate on 7 February 1839. *Congressional Globe,* 25th Cong., 3d sess., 357–58; *Speech of Mr. Clay of Kentucky, on the Subject of Abolition Petitions, Delivered in the Senate of the United States, February 7, 1839* (Washington, D.C., 1839), 11.

8. An allusion to the sermon, "The Sun Do Move," by the Reverend John Jasper.

9. In his travel diary, Douglass recalls attending the dedication of a granite monument to Galileo on 21 April 1887 on the Pincian Hill in Rome. He also noted that "there was neither prayer nor priests imployed in its unveiling[,] for the monument is an honor to science and not to superstition." FD Diary, reel 1, frame 37, FD Papers, DLC.

10. Douglass alludes to the welcoming address by Elizabeth Cady Stanton to the first formal session of the International Council of Women on the morning of 26 March 1888. Boston *Woman's Journal,* 31 March 1888.

11. Douglass paraphrases a comment from William H. Seward's "Irrepressible Conflict" speech delivered in Rochester, New York, on 25 October 1858. Seward, *Irrepressible Conflict,* 7.

12. Theodore Parker suggested these classifications of human greatness in a memorial sermon for John Quincy Adams in 1848. Theodore Parker, *Historic Americans,* edited by Samuel A. Eliot (Boston, 1908), 204–12.

13. Amy Kirby Post (1802–89) was born in Jericho, New York and married Isaac Post, the husband of her deceased sister, in 1828. Originally Hicksite Quakers, the Posts left that denomination in 1845 because they felt their membership in it impeded their abolitionist activities. Three years later, Margaret Fox converted both to spiritualism. A mainstay of many Rochester reform efforts, Amy Post also served as a vice president of the Garrisonian American Anti-Slavery Society in the 1850s and 1860s. Douglass first met the Posts during a lecture tour of the West in 1843 and their friendship was one of the factors that led him to choose Rochester as the site for his newspaper. Douglass to Amy Post, 28 April 1846, 28 October 1847, 22 April 1849, 26 January 1868, 15 January 1877, 14 July 1882, Isaac and Amy Post Family Papers, NRU; Nancy A. Hewitt, *Woman's Activism and Social Change: Rochester, New York, 1822–1872* (Ithaca, N.Y., 1984), 143, 184, 188, 190, 258; Douglass, *Life and Times,* 255–56, 293, 505; *DAB,* 15: 117.

14. Isaac Post (1798–1872) was the husband of Amy Post and a fellow Garrisonian abolitionist and Underground Railroad agent. Born to a family of Hicksite Quaker farmers on Long Island, Post moved to Rochester in 1836 and became a prosperous druggist. After his conversion to spiritualism in 1848, he became a well-known medium. Douglass, *Life and Times,* 255–56, 293, 300; Merrill and Ruchames, *Letters of William Lloyd Garrison,* 5: 157; *ACAB,* 5: 84; *DAB,* 15: 117.

# 3

# I AM A RADICAL WOMAN SUFFRAGE MAN

*[An address delivered in Boston, Massachusetts, on May 28, 1888]*

FREDERICK DOUGLASS

Boston *Woman's Journal*, 2 June 1888. Other texts in Speech File, reel 19, frames 756–63, FD Papers, DLC; Foner, *Douglass on Women's Rights*, 116–24.

Continuing his campaign for women's rights, Douglass attended the annual convention of the New England Woman Suffrage Association, which met in Boston on 28–31 May 1888. Although Douglass made a few brief remarks during the business sessions of the convention, he delivered his major address at the public session at Tremont Temple on the evening of 28 May. Lucy Stone, president of the association, presided over that gathering and introduced Douglass. The Reverend Henry Blanchard of Maine, Laura Ormiston Chant of England, William Dudley Foulke of Indiana, and Thomas Wentworth Higginson spoke after Douglass. The audience expressed appreciation for Douglass's speech with "prolonged applause," the Boston *Woman's Journal* reported. The association later paid Douglass $50 to defray his expenses while attending their convention. Lucy Stone to Douglass, 31 May 1888, General Correspondence File, reel 4, frame 808, FD Papers, DLC; Boston *Globe* 27, 29, 30, 31 May 1888; Washington *Bee*, 9 June 1888; Boston *Woman's Journal*, 9 June 1888.

*Madam President, Ladies and Gentlemen:* While I esteem it an honor to stand on this New England woman suffrage platform, I do not feel that I have a right to the prominence you have been pleased to give me in your proceedings by calling upon me at this time. It is, perhaps, about time that

I should decline to be a speaker on occasions like the present. Having survived the anti-slavery conflict, and lived to rejoice in the victory over slavery, and being no longer as young as I once was, I am a little too late for efficiency and prominence in the great cause you have in hand. My special mission in the world, if I ever had any, was the emancipation and enfranchisement of the negro. Your mission is the emancipation and enfranchisement of woman. Mine was a great cause. Yours is a much greater cause, since it comprehends the liberation and elevation of one-half of the whole human family. Happily, however, I have two good reasons for coming upon this platform to-night. The first is, I live near the city of Washington; not a very strong reason, perhaps, but I come to you from an atmosphere largely pervaded with the woman suffrage sentiment, and am so much in sympathy with it, that it is more difficult to be silent than to speak in its favor. In the second place, this cause has a valid claim upon my "service and labor," outside of its merits. The New England Woman Suffrage Association is composed in part of the noble women who dared to speak for the freedom of the slave, at a time when it required far more courage to do so than is required to speak in the woman suffrage cause at this day.

I have said I reside near Washington, the capital of the nation. Let me say a word about that city in connection with this and kindred reforms. Its behavior of late has been worthy of praise. In the old times, prior to the war and the abolition of slavery, there was no room in it for woman suffrage or negro suffrage or for many other good things. It shuddered at the thought of a new idea — slavery, the slave-trade, slave auctions, horse-racing, duels, and revivals of religion were the popular excitements in the Washington of that day. But now old Washington has passed away, and a new Washington has come into existence. Under our much-abused Gov. Sheppard,[1] its physical features have been visibly improved, and under the influence of Northern ideas, its moral features have equally improved. The time is not distant, I hope, when it will symbolize all that is good, great, glorious and free, and much of the glory of that result will be due to the efforts of women.

It will next year be the theatre of a grand international exposition. Its attractive power is destined to increase with every year, and Boston itself as a reformatory centre may begin to look to its laurels.

Boston was once known as the hot-bed of abolitionism. Washington, if it keeps well on its way, will soon become the hot-bed of woman suffrage. One of the most imposing demonstrations in favor of the rights and dignity of woman was held there only a few weeks ago. You may have heard something of this before. Women from the East, women from the West, women from the North, and women from the South; women from home and women from abroad, met there in International Council,[2] and united in a solemn demand for a larger measure of liberty, and a fuller participation in the government of the world, than has ever yet been accorded to woman. No assemblage, to my knowledge, can be pointed to in the history of this republic, which ever presented a more sublime spectacle than did this

International Council. Its presence was an argument in favor of its cause. Its refinement, earnestness, ability and dignity repelled criticism and overcame opposition. In the hope and enthusiasms it inspired, some of us were made to think, or rather to feel, that the year of woman's jubilee had already dawned.

But this Council has adjourned, and although its beneficent influence will continue to be felt far and wide over the world, we are still confronted with the same old conflict, and must fight it out on the line of agitation though it shall take a century. There is still a delinquent, tardy, and reluctant Massachusetts to be converted,[3] there is still a mass of bigotry and superstition to overcome. There is still a Methodist Episcopal Conference confronting us and barring the way to woman's progress, as it once barred the way to emancipation.[4] There is still a great nation to be brought to a knowledge of the truth. We are not to be appalled by the magnitude of the work, or discouraged by this or any form of opposition.

We old abolitionists never allowed ourselves to be dismayed by repulses, however grievous. Those engaged in this cause are of the self-same material. In some respects this woman suffrage movement is but a continuance of the old anti-slavery movement. We have the same sources of opposition to contend with, and we must meet them with the same spirit and determination, and with much the same arguments which we employed against what Charles Sumner called the "seven-headed barbarism of slavery."[5]

In reform, as in war, it is always a point gained to know just where the enemy is, and just what he is about. It is not easy to deal with an enemy in the dark. It was a great thing for the abolition cause, fifty years ago, when the Methodist Episcopal Conference at Cincinnati declared itself opposed to abolitionism, and that it had no right, wish, or intention to abolish slavery.[6] It is now equally something to know that this same great organization takes its stand against the movement for the equal rights of women in its ecclesiastical assemblies. That older conference was not able, by its opposition to abolitionism, to save slavery, nor will this later conference be able to continue the degradation of woman, by denying her a voice and a vote in its councils. The Methodist Church is rich in resources, but it cannot well afford to enforce this Mahometan idea of woman upon American women —an idea in which woman has no recognized moral, social, or religious existence. In the mosques of the East, her presence among the faithful is held a defilement.[7] She is deemed incapable of self-direction—a body without a soul. No more distressing thing confronted us during our recent tour in Egypt[8] than this social and religious annihilation of woman. Religion there strikes woman dead. Her face is not to be seen; her voice is not to be heard; her moral influence is not to be exerted. She is cushioned, cabined, confined and guarded, and treated more like a criminal than like an innocent person. She sees the world only through a veil, or from behind a lattice-work. She is constantly under the surveillance of a sentinel, wearing the human form, but destitute of all manly sympathy. This Methodist attempt to exclude woman from the conference of the church, has in it a strong element of this Mahometan idea of the proper sphere and treatment of woman.

Whatever may be said of the pious Mahometan, men and women here will ask, and demand to know, what harm could possibly come to the Methodist Church and its ministers, from the presence of a few or many Christian women in its conference? The sexes meet together in prayer-meeting, in class-meeting, in "love feast," and in the great congregations of the church. Why should these gospel preachers, who mingle everywhere else in the church with women, be afraid to meet women in their conferences? What work have they to do there which women should not know? I will press this question no further, but I call upon the Methodist Church to assist us in separating woman's condition in America as far apart from her condition in Egypt as the east is from the west. We have heard a great deal of late as to what Christianity has done for woman. We have a right to call upon these Christian ministers to show that what has been done, has not been done in spite of the church, but in accordance with its teachings. One thing is certain, when the chains of woman shall be broken, when she shall become the recognized equal of man, and is put into the full enjoyment of all the rights of an American citizen, as she will be, the church and ministry will be among the first to claim the honor of the victory, and to say, "We did it!"

It is hardly necessary for me to say, after what I have already said, that I am a radical woman suffrage man. I was such a man nearly fifty years ago. I had hardly brushed the dust of slavery from my feet and stepped upon the free soil of Massachusetts, when I took the suffrage side of this question. Time, thought and experience have only increased the strength of my conviction. I believe equally in its justice, in its wisdom, and in its necessity.

But, as I understand the matter, woman does not ask man for the right of suffrage. That is something which man has no power to give. Rights do not have their source in the will or the grace of man. They are not such things as he can grant or withhold according to his sovereign will and pleasure. All that woman can properly ask man to do in this case, and all that man can do, is to get out of the way, to take his obstructive forces of fines and imprisonment and his obstructive usages out of the way, and let woman express her sentiments at the polls and in the government, equally with himself. Give her fair play and let her alone.

But we are told that suffrage is not a right, that it is neither a right for man nor for woman, but that it is simply a privilege. I do not know when or by whom this startling discovery was made, but it is evidently deemed very important and highly satisfactory by the opponents of woman suffrage.

Well, for argument's sake, let it be conceded that suffrage is not a natural right, but that it is simply a privilege, something that is created and exists only by conventional arrangement; something that can be granted or withheld at the option of those who make it a privilege. I say let all this be conceded, which I do not concede. Several important questions must be answered by those who support this pretension, before the friends of woman suffrage can be silenced or be made to accept it as final.

In the first place we have a right to know by what authority, human or divine, suffrage was made a privilege and not a right; we have a right to know when, where, how, and in the light of what doctrine of human liberty, suffrage was made a privilege and not a right. We have a right to know if such an arrangement could be properly created without the cooperation of woman herself. We have a right to know if men, acting alone, have a right to decide what is right and what is privilege where their action in the case is to determine the position of woman. We have a right to know, if suffrage is simply a privilege, by what right the exercising of that privilege is conferred only upon men. If it is a privilege, we have the right to know why woman is excluded. If it is a privilege, we have the right to know why woman is not as fully, fairly entitled to exercise that privilege as man himself.

After all, we see that nothing has been gained by the opponents of women suffrage, by sheltering themselves behind this assumption that suffrage is a privilege and not a right. The argument is an old one, and has been answered a thousand times, and will, perhaps, have to be answered a thousand times more, before woman suffrage shall be the law of the land.

I suppose we must do here, as was done in the case of the anti-slavery agitation, give line upon line and precept upon precept, as we had to do forty years ago.

Woman's claim to the right of equal participation in government with man, has its foundation in the nature and personality of woman and in the admitted doctrine of American liberty and in the authority and structure of our Republican government. When the rich man wanted some one sent from the dead to warn his brothers against coming where he was, he was told that if they heard not Moses and the prophets, neither would they be persuaded though one rose from the dead.[9] Now our Moses and our prophets, so far as the rights and privileges of American citizens are concerned, are the framers of the Declaration of American Independence. If the American people will not hear these, they will not be persuaded though one rose from the dead.

According to the Declaration of Independence and to the men who signed that great charter of human liberty, all rightful powers of government are derived from the consent of the governed.

No man has yet been able to state when, where and how woman has ever given her consent to be deprived of all participation in the government under which she lives, or why women should be excepted from the principles of the American Declaration of Independence. We are told that man derived his authority thus to disenfranchise woman from Nature; well, we should all have great respect for Nature. We cannot too often listen to her voice and learn the lessons she teaches. She is the great storehouse of knowledge, wisdom and truth. It was here that Hooker learned that beautiful

sentiment that law has her seat in the bosom of God and her voice is the
harmony of the universe.[10] I think the friends of woman suffrage have no
reason to refuse to have the question of their rights tried in this august court
we call Nature.

Let us begin then with Nature in the family. This is the starting-point of
life, the natural starting-point of organized society and of the State. Here are
a son and a daughter in the same household. They have nursed at the same
breast in their infancy; they have been supplied from the same board; they
have talked, sung, prayed, and played together on equal terms in their youth;
they have grown to manhood and womanhood together; in a word, they have
been equal members of the same family together all their young lives, with
substantially the same rights and privileges in the common family; they have
received the same moral and intellectual training, and have enjoyed the
same freedom of thought and expression around the family board—the right
to ask and to answer questions. They are equal in moral and intellectual
endowments, or if not so equal, the one is as likely to be superior as the other,
the daughter as the son, the sister as the brother. Now the question to be
answered at this point is just this: At what time and under what conditions
does nature step in to change the relations of these two people and make the
son and brother the ruler of this daughter and sister? When does Nature say
that he shall elect law-makers, and make laws, institute governments, define
for her the metes and bounds of her liberty, and that she, a rational creature
like himself, shall have no voice or vote in determining any question concerning the government under which she, equally with him, is to live? They
were equal in the cradle, equal in the family, equal in childhood, equal in
youth, equal at maturity, equal in the right to life, to liberty, and in the
pursuit of happiness. I demand to know, then, what fiat of nature, what
moral earthquake from below, or what thunder-bolt from above, has driv-
en these two people asunder—raised one to the sky and struck the other to
earth—one to freedom and the other to slavery. The only answer that Nature
is alleged to give here in opposition to woman, is one which no just and
generous man can or should accept, for it bases a moral and intellectual
conclusion—one which excludes woman from all freedom of choice in the
affairs of government—upon a purely physical fact. The logic is that man is
physically stronger than woman, and that he has the right to make her a
subject of his will; that since she cannot shoulder a musket and fight, she
shall not select a ballot and vote—that though she may have the ability to
think, she shall not have the right to express her thought and give effect to
her thought by her vote. There is no getting away from the conclusion here
other than that the essence of this anti-woman suffrage doctrine is that might
makes right. It is the right of the usurper, the slave-holder, the tyrant, the
robber and pirate—a right which better befits wild beasts than reasoning
men and women—a right which no woman ought to admit and no man
should claim. The only thing that saves it from execration is the fact that
men are too humane and too civilized to make their practice conform to the

full measure of their theory. They deny rights, but admit influence. She may not vote herself, they say, but she may influence the man who does vote, and it is precisely this which constitutes the vice of this relation, for it gives influence and excludes responsibility. A sense of responsibility is an essential element in all our exertions and relations. We need it; woman needs it, not less than man, to work out the best results of her conduct. Divest woman of power and you divest her of a sense of responsibility and duty—two of the essential attributes of all useful exertion and existence.

In tracing the moral and intellectual progress of mankind from barbarism to civilization, we see that any and every advance, however simple and reasonable, has been sternly resisted. It appears that the more simple the proposition of reform, the more stern and passionate has been the resistance. Victory has always been found, when found at all, on the other side of the battle field.

The proposition underlying the anti-slavery movement was one of the plainest that ever dropped from the lips of man. It was so simple and self-evident that argument seemed a waste of breath, and appeal an insult to the understanding, and yet this simple proposition held within itself an explosive force more powerful than dynamite—a force which divided and drove asunder the nation, rent it in twain at the centre, and filled the land with hostile armies. The fundamental proposition of anti-slavery was simply this: Every man is himself, or in other words, is *his* self, or, which is the same thing, every man is the rightful owner of himself. Nothing could be plainer than this, yet press and pulpit, church and State, saint and sinner, North and South, denounced the proposition as full of mischief and one to be put down at all hazards. Man's right to his religious faith, to believe what he could not do otherwise than believe, shared the same fate and filled Europe with nearly a century of war. With these and other and similar examples before us we are not to think it strange that the proposition to enfranchise woman, to clothe her with all the rights and dignity of American citizenship, meets with resistance.

The fundamental proposition of the woman suffrage movement is scarcely less simple than that of the anti-slavery movement. It assumes that woman is herself. That she belongs to herself, just as fully as man belongs to himself—that she is a person and has all the attributes of personality that can be claimed by man, and that her rights of person are equal in all respects to those of man. She has the same number of senses that distinguish man, and is like man a subject of human government, capable of understanding, obeying and being affected by law. That she is capable of forming an intelligent judgment as to the character of public men and public measures, and she may exercise her right of choice in respect both to the law and the lawmakers. Than all this nothing could be more simple or more reasonable.

The generation that has come on the stage since the war can hardly now realize, in view of the fundamental principles of American government, that slavery ever existed here, that the pulpit and press, that the church and the

State ever defended it. So, when this battle for woman suffrage shall have been fought and the victory won, men will marvel at the injustice and stupidity which so long deprived American women of the ballot.

Let me say in conclusion, if human nature is totally depraved, if men and women are incapable of thinking or doing anything but evil and that continually, if the character of this government will inevitably be the expression of this universal and innate depravity—then the less men and women have to do with government the better. We should abandon our Republican government, cease to elect men to office, and place ourselves squarely under the Czar of Russia, the Pope of Rome, or some other potentate who governs by divine right. But if, on the contrary, human nature is more virtuous than vicious, as I believe it is, if governments are best supported by the largest measure of virtue within their reach, if women are equally virtuous with men, if the whole is greater than a part, if the sense and sum of human goodness in man and woman combined is greater than in that of either alone and separate, then the government that excludes women from all participation in its creation, administration and perpetuation, maims itself, deprives itself of one-half of all that is wisest and best for its usefulness, success and perfection.

## NOTES

1. Alexander R. Shepherd.

2. The International Council of Women met at Albaugh's Grand Opera House in Washington, D.C., between 25 March and 1 April 1888.

3. As late as 1915, a popular referendum in the state of Massachusetts to extend the right to vote to women received only a 35.5% yes vote. Women could not vote in that state until after the ratification of the Nineteenth Amendment. Eleanor Flexner, *Century of Struggle: The Woman's Rights Movement in the United States* (Cambridge, Mass., 1959), 276–71, 292–93.

4. The position of women in the Methodist Episcopal Church had never been formally defined prior to the General Conference of 1880. At that meeting, the all-male delegates ruled that women could not become ordained ministers or local preachers but could serve in such subordinate offices as Sunday school superintendent. The question of admitting women as lay delegates to the general conference arose at the meeting of 1888 when four female delegates appeared as representatives of midwestern annual conferences. The general conference refused to seat these women and referred the issue to a referendum of church members. The results of this referendum, held in 1890 and 1891, failed to provide the necessary three-fourths majority required to amend the church constitution. The issue was finally resolved in 1906 when the church acknowledged the complete equality of women in all lay roles. *Journal of the General Conference of the Methodist Episcopal Church, Held in New York, May 1–31, 1888* (New York, 1888), 51, 83, 97–98, 103–06, 463; *AAC, 1888*, 540; Rosemary Skinner Keller, "Creating a Sphere for Women: The Methodist Episcopal Church, 1869–1906," in *Women in New Worlds: Historical Perspectives on the Wesleyan Tradition*, ed. Hilah F. Thomas and Rosemary Skinner Keller (Nashville, 1981), 246–60.

5. The precise phrase the "seven-headed barbarism of slavery" has not been located in Charles Sumner's speeches or letters. Douglass probably alludes to the arguments of

Sumner's "The Barbarism of Slavery" address delivered in the U.S. Senate on 4 June 1860 soon after the Massachusetts senator's return to the body following his slow recuperation from the attack by Preston Brooks in 1856. In this carefully reasoned speech, Sumner analyzed the barbarism of slavery under various "heads" and at one point denounced slavery as: "Barbarous in origin, barbarous in law, barbarous in all its pretensions, barbarous in the instruments it employs, barbarous in consequences, barbarous in spirit, barbarous wherever it shows itself, Slavery must breed Barbarians, while it develops everywhere, alike in the individual and the society to which he belongs, the essential elements of Barbarism." *Charles Sumner: His Complete Works*, 6: 119–237.

6. Douglass alludes to the position taken by the General Conference of the Methodist Episcopal Conference at their meeting in Cincinnati, Ohio, on 13 May 1836. John R. McKivigan, *The War Against Proslavery Religion: Abolitionism and the Northern Churches, 1830–1865* (Ithaca, N.Y., 1984), 46.

7. No prohibition against the admission of women to Islamic mosques exists in the Koran. Over the centuries, some Islamic religious leaders argued for this exclusion and in many regions women were confined to certain sections of the mosque. *The Encyclopaedia of Islam: A Dictionary of Geography, Ethnography and Biography of the Muhammadan Peoples*, 4 vols. (Leiden, The Netherlands, 1913–36), 3: 326.

8. The Douglasses toured Egypt from 15 February to 16 March 1887. FD Diary, reel 1, frames 27–35, FD Papers, DLC.

9. Douglass summarizes the biblical parable of the rich man and the beggar Lazarus. Luke 16: 19–31.

10. Douglass, substituting "universe" for "world," makes only minor errors in quoting from *Of the Laws of Ecclesiastical Polity* (1594–97) by English theologian Richard Hooker (1554–1600). *The Works of That Learned and Judicious Divine Mr. Richard Hooker, Containing Eight Books of Ecclesiastical Polity*, 2 vols. (Oxford, Eng., 1807), 1: 291.

# THE BLACK WOMAN OF THE SOUTH
## Her Neglects and Her Needs

[*Address before the "Freedman's Aid Society," (Meth. Epis. Church) Ocean Grove, N.J., August 15, 1883. From Alex Crummell,* Africa and America: Addresses and Discourses *(Springfield, Mass.: Willey and Co., 1891), 59–82.*]

ALEXANDER CRUMMELL

It is an age clamorous everywhere for the dignities, the grand prerogatives, and the glory of woman. There is not a country in Europe where she has not risen somewhat above the degradation of centuries, and pleaded successfully for a new position and a higher vocation. As the result of this new reformation we see her, in our day, seated in the lecture-rooms of ancient universities, rivaling her brothers in the fields of literature, the grand creators of ethereal art, the participants in noble civil franchises, the moving spirit in grand reformations, and the guide, agent, or assistant in all the noblest movements for the civilization and regeneration of man.

In these several lines of progress the American woman has run on in advance of her sisters in every other quarter of the globe. The advantage she has received, the rights and prerogatives she has secured for herself, are unequaled by any other class of women in the world. It will not be thought amiss, then, that I come here to-day to present to your consideration the one grand exception to this general superiority of women, viz., "THE BLACK WOMAN OF THE SOUTH."

In speaking to-day of the "black woman," I must needs make a very clear distinction. The African race in this country is divided into two classes, that is—the *colored people* and the *negro population*. In the census returns of

1860 this whole population was set down at 4,500,000. Of these, the *colored* numbered 500,000; the *black* or *negro* population at 4,000,000. But notice these other broad lines of demarkation between them. The colored people, while indeed but *one-eighth* of the number of the blacks, counted more men and women who could read and write than the whole 4,000,000 of their brethren in bondage. A like disparity showed itself in regard to their *material* condition. The 500,000 colored people were absolutely richer in lands and houses than the many millions of their degraded kinsmen.

The causes of these differences are easily discovered. The colored population received, in numerous cases, the kindness and generosity of their white kindred—white fathers and relatives. Forbidden by law to marry the negro woman, very many slave-holders took her as the wife, despite the law; and when children were begotten every possible recognition was given those children, and they were often cared for, educated, and made possessors of property. Sometimes they were sent to Northern schools, sometimes to France or England. Not unfrequently whole families, nay, at times, whole colonies, were settled in Western or Northern towns and largely endowed with property. The colored population, moreover, was, as compared with the negro, the *urban* population. They were brought in large numbers to the cities, and thus partook of the civilization and refinement of the whites. They were generally the domestic servants of their masters, and thus, brought in contact with their superiors, they gained a sort of education which never came to the field hands, living in rude huts on the plantations. All this, however casual it may seem, was a merciful providence, by which some gleams of light and knowledge came, indirectly, to the race in this land.

The rural or plantation population of the South was made up almost entirely of people of pure negro blood. And this brings out also the other disastrous fact, namely, that this large black population has been living from the time of their introduction into America, a period of more than two hundred years, in a state of unlettered rudeness. The Negro all this time has been an intellectual starvling. This has been more especially the condition of the black woman of the South. Now and then a black man has risen above the debased condition of his people. Various causes would contribute to the advantage of the *men*: the relation of servants to superior masters; attendance at courts with them; their presence at political meetings; listening to table-talk behind their chairs; traveling as valets; the privilege of books and reading in great houses, and with indulgent masters—all these served to lift up a black *man* here and there to something like superiority. But no such fortune fell to the lot of the plantation woman. The black woman of the South was left perpetually in a state of hereditary darkness and rudeness. Since the day of Phillis Wheatly no Negress in this land (that is, in the South) has been raised above the level of her sex. The lot of the black *man* on the plantation has been sad and desolate enough; but the fate of the black woman has been awful! Her entire existence from the day she first landed, a naked victim of the slave-trade, has been degradation in its extremest forms.

In her girlhood all the delicate tenderness of her sex has been rudely outraged. In the field, in the rude cabin, in the press-room, in the factory, she was thrown into the companionship of coarse and ignorant men. No chance was given her for delicate reserve or tender modesty. From her childhood [she] was the doomed victim of the grossest passions. All the virtues of her sex were utterly ignored. If the instinct of chastity asserted itself, then she had to fight like a tigress for the ownership and possession of her own person; and, ofttimes, had to suffer pains and lacerations for her virtuous self-assertion. When she reached maturity all the tender instincts of her womanhood were ruthlessly violated. At the age of marriage—always prematurely anticipated under slavery—she was mated, as the stock of the plantation were mated, *not* to be the companion of a loved and chosen husband, but to be the breeder of human cattle, for the field or the auction block. With that mate she went out, morning after morning to toil, as a common field-hand. As it was *his,* so likewise was it her lot to wield the heavy hoe, or to follow the plow, or to gather in the crops. She was a "hewer of wood and a drawer of water." She was a common fieldhand. She had to keep her place in the gang from morn till eve, under the burden of a heavy task, or under the stimulus or the fear of a cruel lash. She was a picker of cotton. She labored at the sugar mill and in the tobacco factory. When, through weariness or sickness, she has fallen behind her allotted task then came, as punishment, the fearful stripes upon her shrinking, lacerated flesh.

Her home life was of the most degrading nature. She lived in the rudest huts, and partook of the coarsest food, and dressed in the scantiest garb, and slept, in multitudinous cabins, upon the hardest boards!

Thus she continued a beast of burden down to the period of those maternal anxieties which, in ordinary civilized life, give repose, quiet, and care to expectant mothers. But, under the slave system, few such relaxations were allowed. And so it came to pass that little children were ushered into this world under conditions which many cattle raisers would not suffer for their flocks or herds. Thus she became the mother of children. But even then there was for her no suretyship of motherhood, or training, or control. Her own offspring were *not* her own. She and husband and children were all the property of others. All these sacred ties were constantly snapped and cruelly sundered. *This* year she had one husband; and next year, through some auction sale, she might be separated from him and mated to another. There was no sanctity of family, no binding tie of marriage, none of the fine felicities and the endearing affections of home. None of these things were the lot of Southern black women. Instead thereof a gross barbarism which tended to blunt the tender sensibilities, to obliterate feminine delicacy and womanly shame, came down as her heritage from generation to generation; and it seems a miracle of providence and grace that, notwithstanding these terrible circumstances, so much struggling virtue lingered amid these rude cabins, that so much womanly worth and sweetness abided in their bosoms, as slaveholders themselves have borne witness to.

But some of you will ask: "Why bring up these sad memories of the past? Why distress us with these dead and departed cruelties?" Alas, my friends, these are not dead things. Remember that

> "The evil that men do lives after them."

The evil of gross and monstrous abominations, the evil of great organic institutions crop out long after the departure of the institutions themselves. If you go to Europe you will find not only the roots, but likewise many of the deadly fruits of the old Feudal system still surviving in several of its old states and kingdoms. So, too, with slavery. The eighteen years of freedom have not obliterated all its deadly marks from either the souls or bodies of the black woman. The conditions of life, indeed, have been modified since emancipation; but it still maintains that the black woman is the Pariah woman of this land! We have, indeed, degraded women, immigrants, from foreign lands. In their own countries some of them were so low in the social scale that they were yoked with the cattle to plow the fields. They were rude, unlettered, coarse, and benighted. But when they reach *this* land there comes an end to their degraded condition.

> "They touch our country and their shackles fall."

As soon as they become grafted into the stock of American life they partake at once of all its large gifts and its noble resources.

Not so with the black woman of the South. Freed, legally she has been; but the act of emancipation had no talismanic influence to reach to and alter and transform her degrading social life.

When that proclamation was issued she might have heard the whispered words in her every hut, "Open Sesame"; but, so far as her humble domicile and her degraded person was concerned, there was no invisible but gracious Genii who, on the instant, could transmute the rudeness of her hut into instant elegance, and change the crude surroundings of her home into neatness, taste, and beauty.

The truth is, "Emancipation Day" found her a prostrate and degraded being; and, although it has brought numerous advantages to her sons, it has produced but the simplest changes in her social and domestic condition. She is still the crude, rude, ignorant mother. Remote from cities, the dweller still in the old plantation hut, neighboring to the sulky, disaffected master class, who still think her freedom was a personal robbery of themselves, none of the "fair humanities" have visited her humble home. The light of knowledge has not fallen upon her eyes. The fine domesticities which give the charm to family life, and which, by the refinement and delicacy of womanhood, preserve the civilization of nations, have not come to *her*. She has still the rude, coarse labor of men. With her rude husband she still shares the hard service of a field-hand. Her house, which shelters, perhaps, some six or eight children, embraces but two rooms. Her furniture is of the rudest kind. The clothing of the household is scant and of the coarsest material, has ofttimes the garniture of rags; and for herself and offspring is marked, not seldom, by the absence of both hats and shoes. She has rarely been taught to sew, and the field labor of slavery times has kept her ignorant of the habitudes of neatness, and the requirements of order. Indeed, coarse food, coarse clothes, coarse living, coarse manners, coarse companions, coarse surroundings, coarse neighbors, both black and white, yea, every thing coarse, down to the coarse, ignorant, senseless religion, which excites her sensibilities and starts her passions, go to make up the life of the masses of black women in the hamlets and villages of the rural South.

This is the state of black womanhood. Take the girlhood of this same region, and it presents the same aspect, save that in large districts the white man has not forgotten the olden times of slavery, and, with, indeed, the deepest sentimental abhorrence of "amalgamation," still thinks that the black girl is to be perpetually the victim of his lust! In the larger towns and in cities, our girls, in common schools and academies, are receiving superior culture. Of the fifteen thousand colored school teachers in the South, more than half are colored young women, educated since emancipation. But even these girls, as well as their more ignorant sisters in rude huts, are followed and tempted and insulted by the ruffianly element of Southern society, who think that black *men* have no rights which white men should regard, and black *women* no virtue which white men should respect!

And now look at the *vastness* of this degradation. If I had been speaking of the population of a city, or a town, or even a village, the tale would be a sad and melancholy one. But I have brought before you the condition of millions of women. According to the census of 1880 there were, in the Southern States, 3,327,678 females of all ages of the African race. Of these there were 674,365 girls between twelve and twenty, 1,522,696 between twenty and eighty. "These figures," remarks an observing friend of mine, "are startling!" And when you think that the masses of these women live in the rural districts; that they grow up in rudeness and ignorance; that their former masters are using few means to break up their hereditary degradation, you can easily take in the pitiful condition of this population, and forecast the inevitable future to multitudes of females, unless a mighty special effort is made for the improvement of the black womanhood of the South.

I know the practical nature of the American mind, I know how the question of values intrudes itself into even the domain of philanthropy; and, hence, I shall not be astonished if the query suggests itself, whether special interest in the black woman will bring any special advantage to the American nation.

Let me dwell for a few moments upon this phase of the subject. Possibly the view I am about suggesting has never before been presented to the American mind. But, Negro as I am, I shall make no apology for venturing the claim that the Negress is one of the most interesting of all the classes of women on the globe. I am speaking of her, not as a perverted and de-

graded creature, but in her natural state, with her native instincts and peculiarities.

Let me repeat just here the words of a wise, observing, tender-hearted
philanthropist, whose name and worth and words have attained celebrity. It
is fully forty years ago since the celebrated Dr. Channing said: "We are
holding in bondage one of the best races of the human family. The Negro is
among the mildest, gentlest of men. He is singularly susceptible of improvement from abroad. . . . His nature is affectionate, easily touched, and hence
he is more open to religious improvement than the white man. . . . The
African carries with him much more than *we* the genius of a meek, long-
suffering, loving virtue."[1]

I should feel ashamed to allow these words to fall from my lips if it were
not necessary to the lustration of the character of my black sisters of the
South. I do not stand here to-day to plead for the black *man*. He is a man; and
if he is weak he must go the wall. He is a man; he must fight his own way, and
if he is strong in mind and body, he can take care of himself. But for the
mothers, sisters, and daughters of my race I have a right to speak. And when
I think of their sad condition down South, think, too, that since the day of
emancipation hardly any one has lifted up a voice in their behalf, I feel it a
duty and a privilege to set forth their praises and to extol their excellencies.
For, humble and benighted as she is, the black woman of the South is one of
the queens of womanhood. If there is any other woman on this earth who in
native aboriginal qualities is her superior, I know not where she is to be
found; for, I do say, that in tenderness of feeling, in genuine native modesty,
in large disinterestedness, in sweetness of disposition and deep humility, in
unselfish devotedness, and in warm, motherly assiduities, the Negro woman
is unsurpassed by any other woman on this earth.

The testimony to this effect is almost universal—our enemies themselves
being witnesses. You know how widely and how continuously, for generations, the Negro has been traduced, ridiculed, derided. Some of you may
remember the journals and the hostile criticisms of Coleridge and Trollope
and Burton, West Indian and African travelers. Very many of you may
remember the philosophical disquisitions of the ethnological school of
1847, the contemptuous dissertations of Hunt and Gliddon. But it is worthy
of notice in all these cases that the sneer, the contempt, the bitter gibe, have
been invariably leveled against the black *man*—never against the black
woman! On the contrary, *she* has almost everywhere been extolled and
eulogized. The black man was called a stupid, thick-lipped, flat-nosed, long-
heeled, empty-headed animal; the link between the baboon and the human
being, only fit to be a slave! But everywhere, even in the domains of slavery,
how tenderly has the Negress been spoken of! She has been the nurse of
childhood. To her all the cares and heart-griefs of youth have been intrusted.
Thousands and tens of thousands in the West Indies and in our Southern
States have risen up and told the tale of her tenderness, of her gentleness,

patience, and affection. No other woman in the world has ever had such tributes to a high moral nature, sweet, gentle love, and unchanged devotedness. And by the memory of my own mother and dearest sisters I can declare it to be true!

Hear the tribute of Michelet: "The Negress, of all others, is the most loving, the most generating; and this, not only because of her youthful blood, but we must also admit, for the richness of her heart. She is loving among the loving, good among the good (ask the travelers whom she has so often saved). Goodness is creative, it is fruitfulness, it is the very benediction of a holy act. The fact that woman is so fruitful I attribute to her treasures of tenderness, to that ocean of goodness which permeates her heart. . . . Africa is a woman. Her races are feminine. . . . In many of the black tribes of Central Africa the women rule, and they are as intelligent as they are amiable and kind."[2]

The reference in Michelet to the generosity of the African woman to travelers brings to mind the incident in Mungo Park's travels, where the African women fed, nourished, and saved him. The men had driven him away. They would not even allow him to feed with the cattle; and so, faint, weary, and despairing, he went to a remote hut and lay down on the earth to die. One woman, touched with compassion, came to him, brought him food and milk, and at once he revived. Then he tells us of the solace and the assiduities of these gentle creatures for his comfort. I give you his own words: "The rites of hospitality thus performed toward a stranger in distress, my worthy benefactress, pointing to the mat, and telling me that I might sleep there without apprehension, called to the female part of her family which had stood gazing on me all the while in fixed astonishment, to resume the task of spinning cotton, in which they continued to employ themselves a great part of the night. They lightened their labors by songs, one of which was composed extempore, for I was myself the subject of it. It was sung by one of the young women, the rest joining in a sort of chime. The air was sweet and plaintive, and the words, literally translated, were these: 'The winds roared and the rains fell; the poor white man, faint and weary, came and sat under our tree. He has no mother to bring him milk, no wife to grind his corn. Let us pity the white man, no mother has he,'" etc., etc.

Perhaps I may be pardoned the intrusion, just here, on my own personal experience. During a residence of nigh twenty years in West Africa, I saw the beauty and felt the charm of the native female character. I saw the native woman in her *heathen* state, and was delighted to see, in numerous tribes, that extraordinary sweetness, gentleness, docility, modesty, and especially those maternal solicitudes which make every African boy both gallant and defender of his mother.

I saw her in her *civilized* state, in Sierra Leone; saw precisely the same characteristics, but heightened, dignified, refined, and sanctified by the training of the schools, the refinements of civilization, and the graces of Christian sentiment and feeling. Of all the memories of foreign travel there are none more delightful than those of the families and the female friends of Freetown.

A French traveler speaks with great admiration of the black ladies of Hayti. "In the towns," he says, "I met all the charms of civilized life. The graces of the ladies of Port-au-Prince will never be effaced from my recollections."[3]

It was, without doubt, the instant discernment of these fine and tender qualities which prompted the touching Sonnet of Wordsworth, written in 1802, on the occasion of the cruel exile of Negroes from France by the French Government:

> "Driven from the soil of France, a female came
>   From Calais with us, brilliant in array,
>   A Negro woman like a lady gay,
> Yet downcast as a woman fearing blame;
>   Meek, destitute, as seemed, of hope or aim
>   She sat, from notice turning not away,
> But on all proffered intercourse did lay
>   A weight of languid speech—or at the same
> Was silent, motionless in eyes and face.
>   Meanwhile those eyes retained their tropic fire,
>   Which burning independent of the mind,
>   Joined with the luster of her rich attire
> To mock the outcast—O ye heavens be kind!
> And feel thou earth for this afflicted race!"[4]

But I must remember that I am to speak not only of the neglects of the black woman, but also of her needs. And the consideration of her needs suggests the remedy which should be used for the uplifting of this woman from a state of brutality and degradation.

I have two or three plans to offer which, I feel assured, if faithfully used, will introduce widespread and ameliorating influences amid this large population.

(a) The *first* of these is specially adapted to the adult female population of the South, and is designed for more immediate effect. I ask for the equipment and the mission of "sisterhoods" to the black women of the South. I wish to see large numbers of practical Christian women, women of intelligence and piety; women well trained in domestic economy; women who combine delicate sensibility and refinement with industrial acquaintance — scores of such women to go South; to enter every Southern State; to visit "Uncle Tom's Cabin"; to sit down with "Aunt Chloe" and her daughters; to show and teach them the ways and habits of thrift, economy, neatness, and order; to gather them into "Mothers' Meetings" and sewing schools; and by both lectures and "talks" guide these women and their daughters into the modes and habits of clean and orderly housekeeping.

There is no other way, it seems to me, to bring about this domestic revolution. — We can not postpone this reformation to another generation.

Postponement is the reproduction of the same evils in numberless daughters now coming up into life, imitators of the crude and untidy habits of their neglected mothers, and the perpetuation of plantation life to another generation. No, the effect must be made immediately, in *this* generation, with the rude, rough, neglected women of the times.

And it is to be done at their own homes, in their own huts. In this work all theories are useless. This is a practical need, and personal as practical. It is emphatically a personal work. It is to be done by example. The "Sister of Mercy," putting aside all fastidiousness, is to enter the humble and, perchance, repulsive cabin of her black sister, and gaining her confidence, is to lead her out of the crude, disordered, and miserable ways of her plantation life into neatness, cleanliness, thrift, and self-respect. In every community women could be found who would gladly welcome such gracious visitations and instructors, and seize with eagerness their lessons and teachings. Soon their neighbors would seek the visitations which had lifted up friends and kinsfolk from inferiority and wretchedness. And then, erelong, whole communities would crave the benediction of these inspiring sisterhoods, and thousands and tens of thousands would hail the advent of these missionaries in their humble cabins. And then the seed of a new and orderly life planted in a few huts and localities, it would soon spread abroad, through the principle of imitation, and erelong, like the Banyan-tree, the beneficent work would spread far and wide through large populations. Doubtless they would be received, first of all, with surprise, for neither they nor their mothers, for two hundred years, have known the solicitudes of the great and cultivated for their domestic comfort. But surprise would soon give way to joy and exultation. Mrs. Fanny Kemble Butler, in her work, "Journal of a Residence on a Georgian Plantation in 1838–39," tells us of the amazement of the wretched slave woman on her husband's plantation when she went among them, and tried to improve their quarters and to raise them above squalor; and then of their immediate joy and gratitude.

There is nothing original in the suggestion I make for the "Sisters of Mercy." It is no idealistic and impractical scheme I am proposing, no new-fangled notion that I put before you. The Roman Catholic Church has, for centuries, been employing the agency of women in the propagation of her faith and as dispensers of charity. The Protestants of Germany are noted for the effective labors of holy women, not only in the Fatherland but in some of the most successful missions among the heathen in modern times. The Church of England, in that remarkable revival which has lifted her up as by a tidal wave, from the dead passivity of the last century, to an apostolic zeal and fervor never before known in her history, has shown, as one of her main characteristics, the wonderful power of "Sisterhoods," not only in the conversion of reprobates, but in the reformation of whole districts of abandoned men and women. This agency has been one of the most effective instrumentalities in the hands of that special school of devoted men called "Ritualists." Women of every class in that Church, many of humble birth, and as many more from the ranks of the noble, have left home and friends and the choicest circles of society, and given up their lives to the lowliest service of the poor and miserable. They have gone down into the very slums of her great cities, among thieves and murderers and harlots; amid filth and disease and pestilence; and for Christ's sake served and washed and nursed the most repulsive wretches; and then have willingly laid down and died, either exhausted by their labors or poisoned by infectious disease. Any one who will read the life of "Sister Dora" and of Charles Lowder, will see the glorious illustrations of my suggestion. Why can not this be done for the black women of the South?

(b) My *second* suggestion is as follows, and it reaches over to the future. I am anxious for a permanent and uplifting civilization to be engrafted on the Negro race in this land. And this can only be secured through the woman-hood of a race. If you want the civilization of a people to reach the very best elements of their being, and then, having reached them, there to abide, as an indigenous principle, you must imbue the *womanhood* of that people with all its elements and qualities. Any movement which passes by the female sex is an ephemeral thing. Without them, no true nationality, patriotism, religion, cultivation, family life, or true social status is a possibility. In *this* matter it takes *two* to make one—mankind is a duality. The *male* may bring, as an exotic, a foreign graft, say of a civilization, to a new people. But what then? Can a graft live or thrive of itself? By no manner of means. It must get vitality from the *stock* into which it is put; and it is the women who give the sap to every human organization which thrives and flourishes on earth.

I plead, therefore, for the establishment of at least one large "INDUS-TRIAL SCHOOL" in every Southern State for the black girls of the South. I ask for the establishment of schools which may serve especially the *home* life of the rising womanhood of my race. I am not soliciting for these girls scholastic institutions, seminaries for the cultivation of elegance, conservatories of music, and schools of classical and artistic training. I want such schools and seminaries for the women of my race as much as any other race; and I am glad that there are such schools and colleges, and that scores of colored women are students within their walls.

But this higher style of culture is not what I am aiming after for *this* great need. I am seeking something humbler, more homelike and practical, in which the education of the land and the use of the body shall be the specialties, and where the intellectual training will be the incident.

Let me state just here definitely what I want for the black girls of the South:

1. I want boarding-schools for the *industrial training* of one hundred and fifty or two hundred of the poorest girls, of the ages of twelve to eighteen years.

2. I wish the *intellectual* training to be limited to reading, writing, arithmetic, and geography.

3. I would have these girls taught to do accurately all domestic work, such as sweeping floors, dusting rooms, scrubbing, bed making, washing and ironing, sewing, mending, and knitting.

4. I would have the trades of dressmaking, millinery, straw-platting, tailoring for men, and such like, taught them.

5. The art of cooking should be made a specialty, and every girl should be instructed in it.

6. In connection with these schools, garden plats should be cultivated, and every girl should be required, daily, to spend at least an hour in learning the cultivation of small fruits, vegetables, and flowers.

I am satisfied that the expense of establishing such schools would be insignificant. As to their maintenance, there can be no doubt that, rightly managed, they would in a brief time be self-supporting. Each school would soon become a hive of industry, and a source of income. But the *good* they would do is the main consideration. Suppose that the time of a girl's schooling be limited to *three*, or perchance to *two* years. It is hardly possible to exaggerate either the personal family or society influence which would flow from these schools. Every class, yea, every girl in an outgoing class, would be a missionary of thrift, industry, common sense, and practicality. They would go forth, year by year, a leavening power into the houses, towns, and villages of the Southern black population; girls fit to be thrifty wives of the honest peasantry of the South, the worthy matrons of their numerous households.

I am looking after the domestic training of the MASSES; for the raising up women meet to be the helpers of *poor* men the RANK AND FILE of black society, all through the rural districts of the South. The city people and the wealthy can seek more ambitious schools, and should pay for them.

Ladies and gentlemen, since the day of emancipation millions of dollars have been given by the generous Christian people of the North for the intellectual training of the black race in this land. Colleges and universities have been built in the South, and hundreds of youth have been gathered within their walls. The work of your own Church in this regard has been magnificent and unrivaled, and the results which have been attained have been grand and elevating to the entire Negro race in America. The complement to all this generous and ennobling effort is the elevation of the black woman. Up to this day and time your noble philanthropy has touched, for the most part, the male population of the South, given them superiority, and stimulated them to higher aspirations. But a true civilization can only then be attained when the life of woman is reached, her whole being permeated by noble ideas, her fine taste enriched by culture, her tendencies to the beautiful gratified and developed, her singular and delicate nature lifted up to its full capacity; and then, when all these qualities are fully matured, cultivated and sanctified, all their sacred influences shall circle around ten thousand firesides, and the cabins of the humblest freedmen shall become the homes of Christian refinement and of domestic elegance through the influence and the charm of the uplifted and cultivated black woman of the South!

### NOTES

1. "Emancipation." By Rev. W. E. Channing, D.D. *Works of W. E. Channing, D.D. A.U.A.Ed.* p. 820.
2. "Woman." From the French of M. J. Michelet, p. 132. Rudd & Carleton, N.Y.
3. See "Jamaica in 1850." By John Bigelow.
4. Wordsworth. Sonnets dedicated to Liberty.

# 5 THE DAMNATION OF WOMEN

*[From* Darkwater: Voices from Within the Veil *(1920).]*

## W. E. B. Du Bois

I remember four women of my boyhood: my mother, cousin Inez, Emma, and Ide Fuller. They represented the problem of the widow, the wife, the maiden, and the outcast. They were, in color, brown and light-brown, yellow with brown freckles, and white. They existed not for themselves, but for men; they were named after the men to whom they were related and not after the fashion of their own souls.

They were not beings, they were relations and these relations were en-filmed with mystery and secrecy. We did not know the truth or believe it when we heard it. Motherhood! What was it? We did not know or greatly care. My mother and I were good chums. I liked her. After she was dead I loved her with a fierce sense of personal loss.

Inez was a pretty, brown cousin who married. What was marriage? We did not know, neither did she, poor thing! It came to mean for her a litter of children, poverty, a drunken, cruel companion, sickness, and death. Why?

There was no sweeter sight than Emma—slim, straight, and dainty, darkly flushed with the passion of youth; but her life was a wild, awful struggle to crush her natural, fierce joy of love. She crushed it and became a cold, calculating mockery.

Last there was that awful outcast of the town, the white woman, Ide Fuller. What she was, we did not know. She stood to us as embodied filth and wrong —but whose filth, whose wrong?

Grown up I see the problem of these women transfused; I hear all about me the unanswered call of youthful love, none the less glorious because of its clean, honest, physical passion. Why unanswered? Because the youth are too poor to marry or if they marry, too poor to have children. They turn aside, then, in three directions: to marry for support, to what men call shame, or to that which is more evil than nothing. It is an unendurable paradox; it must be changed or the bases of culture will totter and fall.

The world wants healthy babies and intelligent workers. Today we refuse to allow the combination and force thousands of intelligent workers to go childless at a horrible expenditure of moral force, or we damn them if they break our idiotic conventions. Only at the sacrifice of intelligence and the chance to do their best work can the majority of modern women bear children. This is the damnation of women.

All womanhood is hampered today because the world on which it is emerging is a world that tries to worship both virgins and mothers and in the end despises motherhood and despoils virgins.

The future woman must have a life work and economic independence. She must have knowledge. She must have the right of motherhood at her own discretion. The present mincing horror at free womanhood must pass if we are ever to be rid of the bestiality of free manhood; not by guarding the weak in weakness do we gain strength, but by making weakness free and strong.

The world must choose the free woman or the white wraith of the prostitute. Today it wavers between the prostitute and the nun. Civilization must show two things: the glory and beauty of creating life and the need and duty of power and intelligence. This and this only will make the perfect marriage of love and work.

> God is Love,
> Love is God;
> There is no God but Love
> And Work is His Prophet!

All this of woman—but what of black women?

The world that wills to worship womankind studiously forgets its darker sisters. They seem in a sense to typify that veiled Melancholy:

> Whose saintly visage is too bright
> To hit the sense of human sight,
> And, therefore, to our weaker view
> O'er-laid with black.

Yet the world must heed these daughters of sorrow, from the primal black All-Mother of men down through the ghostly throng of mighty womanhood, who walked in the mysterious dawn of Asia and Africa; from Neith, the primal mother of all, whose feet rest on hell, and whose almighty hands uphold the heavens; all religion, from beauty to beast, lies on her eager breasts; her body bears the stars, while her shoulders are necklaced by the dragon; from black Neith down to

That starr'd Ethiop queen who strove
To set her beauty's praise above
The sea-nymphs

through dusky Cleopatras, dark Candaces, and darker, fiercer Zinghas, to our own day and our own land—in gentle Phillis; Harriet, the crude Moses; the sibyl, Sojourner Truth; and the martyr, Louise De Mortie.

The father and his worship is Asia; Europe is the precocious, self-centered, forward-striving child; but the land of the mother is and was Africa. In subtle and mysterious way, despite her curious history, her slavery, polygamy, and toil, the spell of the African mother pervades her land. Isis, the mother, is still titular goddess, in thought if not in name, of the dark continent. Nor does this all seem to be solely a survival of the historic matriarchate through which all nations pass—it appears to be more than this—as if the great black race in passing up the steps of human culture gave the world, not only the Iron Age, the cultivation of the soil, and the domestication of animals, but also, in peculiar emphasis, the mother-idea.

"No mother can love more tenderly and none is more tenderly loved than the Negro mother," writes Schneider. Robin tells of the slave who bought his mother's freedom instead of his own. Mungo Park writes: "Everywhere in Africa, I have noticed that no greater affront can be offered a Negro than insulting his mother. 'Strike me,' cries a Mandingo to his enemy, 'but revile not my mother!'" And the Krus and Fantis say the same. The peoples on the Zambezi and the great lakes cry in sudden fear or joy: "O, my mother!" And the Herero swear (endless oath) "By my mother's tears!" "As the mist in the swamps," cries the Angola Negro, "so lives the love of father and mother."

A student of the present Gold Coast life describes the work of the village headman, and adds: "It is a difficult task that he is set to, but in this matter he has all-powerful helpers in the female members of the family, who will be either the aunts or the sisters or the cousins or the nieces of the headman, and as their interests are identical with his in every particular, the good women spontaneously train up their children to implicit obedience to the headman, whose rule in the family thus becomes a simple and an easy matter. 'The hand that rocks the cradle rules the world.' What a power for good in the native state system would the mothers of the Gold Coast and Ashanti become by judicious training upon native lines!"

Schweinfurth declares of one tribe: "A bond between mother and child which lasts for life is the measure of affection shown among the Dyoor" and Ratzel adds:

"Agreeable to the natural relation the mother stands first among the chief influences affecting the children. From the Zulus to the Waganda, we find the mother the most influential counsellor at the court of ferocious sovereigns, like Chaka or Mtesa; sometimes sisters take her place. Thus even with chiefs who possess wives by hundreds the bonds of blood are the strongest and that the woman, though often heavily burdened, is in herself held in no small esteem among the Negroes is clear from the numerous Negro queens, from the medicine women, from the participation in public meetings permitted to women by many Negro peoples."

As I remember through memories of others, backward among my own family, it is the mother I ever recall—the little, far-off mother of my grandmothers, who sobbed her life away in song, longing for her lost palm-trees and scented waters; the tall and bronzen grandmother, with beaked nose and shrewish eyes, who loved and scolded her black and laughing husband as he smoked lazily in his high oak chair; above all, my own mother, with all her soft brownness—the brown velvet of her skin, the sorrowful black-brown of her eyes, and the tiny brown-capped waves of her midnight hair as it lay new parted on her forehead. All the way back in these dim distances it is mothers and mothers of mothers who seem to count, while fathers are shadowy memories.

Upon this African mother-idea, the westward slave trade and American slavery struck like doom. In the cruel exigencies of the traffic in men and in the sudden, unprepared emancipation the great pendulum of social equilibrium swung from a time, in 1800—when America had but eight or less black women to every ten black men—all too swiftly to a day, in 1870—when there were nearly eleven women to ten men in our Negro population. This was but the outward numerical fact of social dislocation; within lay polygamy, polyandry, concubinage, and moral degradation. They fought against all this desperately, did these black slaves in the West Indies, especially among the half-free artisans; they set up their ancient household gods, and when Toussaint and Cristophe founded their kingdom in Haiti, it was based on old African tribal ties and beneath it was the mother-idea.

The crushing weight of slavery fell on black women. Under it there was no legal marriage, no legal family, no legal control over children. To be sure, custom and religion replaced here and there what the law denied, yet one has but to read advertisements like the following to see the hell beneath the system:

> One hundred dollars reward will be given for my two fellows, Abram and Frank. Abram has a wife at Colonel Stewart's, in Liberty County, and a mother at Thunderbolt, and a sister in Savannah.
>
> "WILLIAM ROBERTS."

> Fifty dollars reward—Ran away from the subscriber a Negro girl named Maria. She is of a copper color, between thirteen and fourteen years of age—bare-headed and barefooted. She is small for her age—very sprightly and very likely. She stated she was going to see her mother at Maysville.
>
> "SANFORD THOMSON."

> Fifty dollars reward—Ran away from the subscriber his Negro man Pauladore, commonly called Paul. I understand General R. Y. Hayne has purchased his

wife and children from H. L. Pinckney, Esq., and has them now on his plantation at Goose Creek, where, no doubt, the fellow is frequently lurking.

"T. DAVIS."

The Presbyterian synod of Kentucky said to the churches under its care in
1835: "Brothers and sisters, parents and children, husbands and wives, are
torn asunder and permitted to see each other no more. These acts are daily
occurring in the midst of us. The shrieks and agony often witnessed on such
occasions proclaim, with a trumpet tongue, the iniquity of our system. There
is not a neighborhood where these heart-rending scenes are not displayed.
There is not a village or road that does not behold the said procession of
manacled outcasts whose mournful countenances tell that they are exiled by
force from all that their hearts hold dear."

A sister of a president of the United States declared: "We Southern ladies
are complimented with the names of wives, but we are only the mistresses of
seraglios."

Out of this, what sort of black women could be born into the world of
today? There are those who hasten to answer this query in scathing terms
and who say lightly and repeatedly that out of black slavery came nothing
decent in womanhood; that adultery and uncleanness were their heritage
and are their continued portion.

Fortunately so exaggerated a charge is humanly impossible of truth. The
half-million women of Negro descent who lived at the beginning of the 19th
century had become the mothers of two and one-fourth million daughters at
the time of the Civil War and five million granddaughters in 1910. Can all
these women be vile and the hunted race continue to grow in wealth and
character? Impossible. Yet to save from the past the shreds and vestiges of
self-respect has been a terrible task. I most sincerely doubt if any other race
of women could have brought its fineness up through so devilish a fire.

Alexander Crummell once said of his sister in the blood: "In her girlhood
all the delicate tenderness of her sex has been rudely outraged. In the field,
in the rude cabin, in the press-room, in the factory she was thrown into the
companionship of coarse and ignorant men. No chance was given her for
delicate reserve or tender modesty. From her childhood she was the doomed
victim of the grossest passion. All the virtues of her sex were utterly ignored.
If the instinct of chastity asserted itself, then she had to fight like a tiger for
the ownership and possession of her own person and ofttimes had to suffer
pain and lacerations for her virtuous self-assertion. When she reached maturity, all the tender instincts of her womanhood were ruthlessly violated. At
the age of marriage—always prematurely anticipated under slavery—she
was mated as the stock of the plantation were mated, not to be the companion of a loved and chosen husband, but to be the breeder of human cattle for
the field or the auction block."

Down in such mire has the black motherhood of this race struggled—
starving its own wailing offspring to nurse to the world their swaggering

masters; welding for its children chains which affronted even the moral sense of an unmoral world. Many a man and woman in the South has lived in wedlock as holy as Adam and Eve and brought forth their brown and golden children, but because the darker woman was helpless, her chivalrous and whiter mate could cast her off at his pleasure and publicly sneer at the body he had privately blasphemed.

I shall forgive the white South much in its final judgment day: I shall forgive its slavery, for slavery is a world-old habit; I shall forgive its fighting for a well-lost cause, and for remembering that struggle with tender tears; I shall forgive its so-called "pride of race," the passion of its hot blood, and even its dear, old, laughable strutting and posing; but one thing I shall never forgive, neither in this world nor the world to come: its wanton and continued and persistent insulting of the black womanhood which it sought and seeks to prostitute to its lust. I cannot forget that it is such Southern gentlemen into whose hands smug Northern hypocrites of today are seeking to place our women's eternal destiny—men who insist upon withholding from my mother and wife and daughter those signs and appellations of courtesy and respect which elsewhere he withholds only from bawds and courtesans.

The result of this history of insult and degradation has been both fearful and glorious. It has birthed the haunting prostitute, the brawler, and the beast of burden; but it has also given the world an efficient womanhood, whose strength lies in its freedom and whose chastity was won in the teeth of temptation and not in prison and swaddling clothes.

To no modern race does its women mean so much as to the Negro nor come so near to the fulfillment of its meaning. As one of our women writes: "Only the black woman can say 'when and where I enter, in the quiet, undisputed dignity of my womanhood, without violence and without suing or special patronage, then and there the whole Negro race enters with me.'"

They came first, in earlier days, like foam flashing on dark, silent waters— bits of stern, dark womanhood here and there tossed almost carelessly aloft to the world's notice. First and naturally they assumed the panoply of the ancient African mother of men, strong and black, whose very nature beat back the wilderness of oppression and contempt. Such a one was that cousin of my grandmother, whom western Massachusetts remembers as "Mum Bett." Scarred for life by a blow received in defense of a sister, she ran away to Great Barrington and was the first slave, or one of the first, to be declared free under the Bill of Rights of 1780. The son of the judge who freed her, writes:

> Even in her humble station, she had, when occasion required it, an air of command which conferred a degree of dignity and gave her an ascendancy over those of her rank, which is very unusual in persons of any rank or color. Her determined and resolute character, which enabled her to limit the ravages of Shays' mob, was manifested in her conduct and deportment during her whole life. She claimed no distinction, but it was yielded to her from her superior experience, energy, skill, and sagacity. Having known this woman as familiarly as I knew either of my parents, I cannot believe in the moral or physical

inferiority of the race to which she belonged. The degradation of the African
must have been otherwise caused than by natural inferiority.

It was such strong women that laid the foundations of the great Negro
church of today, with its five million members and ninety millions of dollars
in property. One of the early mothers of the church, Mary Still, writes thus
quaintly, in the forties:

> When we were as castouts and spurned from the large churches, driven from
> our knees, pointed at by the proud, neglected by the careless, without a place
> of worship, Allen, faithful to the heavenly calling, came forward and laid the
> foundation of this connection. The women, like the women at the sepulcher,
> were early to aid in laying the foundation of the temple and in helping to carry
> up the noble structure and in the name of their God set up their banner; most
> of our aged mothers are gone from this to a better state of things. Yet some
> linger still on their staves, watching with intense interest the ark as it moves
> over the tempestuous waves of opposition and ignorance. . . .
>     But the labors of these women stopped not here, for they knew well that
> they were subject to affliction and death. For the purpose of mutual aid, they
> banded themselves together in society capacity, that they might be better able
> to administer to each others' sufferings and to soften their own pillows. So we
> find the females in the early history of the church abounding in good works
> and in acts of true benevolence.

From such spiritual ancestry came two striking figures of war-time—
Harriet Tubman and Sojourner Truth.

For eight or ten years previous to the breaking out of the Civil War, Harriet
Tubman was a constant attendant at anti-slavery conventions, lectures, and
other meetings; she was a black woman of medium size, smiling countenance, with her upper front teeth gone, attired in coarse but neat clothes,
and carrying always an old-fashioned reticule at her side. Usually as soon as
she sat down she would drop off in sound sleep.

She was born a slave in Maryland, in 1820, bore the marks of the lash on
her flesh; and had been made partially deaf, and perhaps to some degree
mentally unbalanced by a blow on the head in childhood. Yet she was one
of the most important agents of the Underground Railroad and a leader of
fugitive slaves. She ran away in 1849 and went to Boston in 1854, where she
was welcomed into the homes of the leading abolitionists and where every
one listened with tense interest to her strange stories. She was absolutely
illiterate, with no knowledge of geography, and yet year after year she pen-
etrated the slave states and personally led North over three hundred fugitives
without losing a single one. A standing reward of $10,000 was offered for her,
but as she said: "The whites cannot catch us, for I was born with the charm,
and the Lord has given me the power." She was one of John Brown's closest
advisers and only severe sickness prevented her presence at Harpers Ferry.

When the war cloud broke, she hastened to the front, flitting down along
her own mysterious paths, haunting the armies in the field, and serving as
guide and nurse and spy. She followed Sherman in his great march to the sea

and was with Grant at Petersburg, and always in the camps the Union officers silently saluted her.

The other woman belonged to a different type—a tall, gaunt, black, unsmiling sybil, weighted with the woe of the world. She ran away from slavery and giving up her own name took the name of Sojourner Truth. She says: "I can remember when I was a little, young girl, how my old mammy would sit out of doors in the evenings and look up at the stars and groan, and I would say, 'Mammy, what makes you groan so?' And she would say, 'I am groaning to think of my poor children; they do not know where I be and I don't know where they be. I look up at the stars and they look up at the stars!'"

Her determination was founded on unwavering faith in ultimate good. Wendell Phillips says that he was once in Faneuil Hall, when Frederick Douglass was one of the chief speakers. Douglass had been describing the wrongs of the Negro race and as he proceeded he grew more and more excited and finally ended by saying that they had no hope of justice from the whites, no possible hope except in their own right arms. It must come to blood! They must fight for themselves. Sojourner Truth was sitting, tall and dark, on the very front seat facing the platform, and in the hush of feeling when Douglass sat down she spoke out in her deep, peculiar voice, heard all over the hall:

"Frederick, is God dead?"

Such strong, primitive types of Negro womanhood in America seem to some to exhaust its capabilities. They know less of a not more worthy, but a finer type of black woman wherein trembles all of that delicate sense of beauty and striving for self-realization, which is as characteristic of the Negro soul as is its quaint strength and sweet laughter. George Washington wrote in grave and gently courtesy to a Negro woman, in 1776, that he would "be happy to see" at his headquarters at any time, a person "to whom nature has been so liberal and beneficial in her dispensations." This child, Phillis Wheatley, sang her trite and halting strain to a world that wondered and could not produce her like. Measured today her muse was slight and yet, feeling her striving spirit, we call to her still in her own words:

"Through thickest glooms look back, immortal shade."

Perhaps even higher than strength and art loom human sympathy and sacrifice as characteristic of Negro womanhood. Long years ago, before the Declaration of Independence, Kate Ferguson was born in New York. Freed, widowed, and bereaved of her children before she was twenty, she took the children of the streets of New York, white and black, to her empty arms, taught them, found them homes, and with Dr. Mason of Murray Street Church established the first modern Sunday School in Manhattan.

Sixty years later came Mary Shadd up out of Delaware. She was tall and slim, of that ravishing dream-born beauty—that twilight of the races which we call mulatto. Well-educated, vivacious, with determination shining from her sharp eyes, she threw herself singlehanded into the great Canadian

pilgrimage when thousands of hunted black men hurried northward and
crept beneath the protection of the lion's paw. She became teacher, editor,
and lecturer; tramping afoot through winter snows, pushing without blot or
blemish through crowd and turmoil to conventions and meetings, and
finally becoming recruiting agent for the United States government in
gathering Negro soldiers in the West.

After the war the sacrifice of Negro women for freedom and uplift is one
of the finest chapters in their history. Let one life typify all: Louise De
Mortie, a free-born Virginia girl, had lived most of her life in Boston. Her
high forehead, swelling lips, and dark eyes marked her for a woman of
feeling and intellect. She began a successful career as a public reader. Then
came the War and the Call. She went to the orphaned colored children of
New Orleans—out of freedom into insult and oppression and into the teeth
of the yellow fever. She toiled and dreamed. In 1887 she had raised money
and built an orphan home and that same year, in the thirty-fourth of her
young life, she died, saying simply: "I belong to God."

As I look about me today in this veiled world of mine, despite the noisier
and more spectacular advance of my brothers, I instinctively feel and know
that it is the five million women of my race who really count. Black women
(and women whose grandmothers were black) are today furnishing our
teachers; they are the main pillars of those social settlements which we call
churches; and they have with small doubt raised three-fourths of our church
property. If we have today, as seems likely, over a billion dollars of accumulated goods, who shall say how much of it has been wrung from the hearts of
servant girls and washerwomen and women toilers in the fields? As makers of
two million homes these women are today seeking in marvelous ways to
show forth our strength and beauty and our conception of the truth.

In the United States in 1910 there were 4,931,882 women of Negro
descent; over twelve hundred thousand of these were children, another
million were girls and young women under twenty, and two and a half-
million were adults. As a mass these women were unlettered—a fourth of
those from fifteen to twenty-five years of age were unable to write. These
women are passing through, not only a moral, but an economic revolution.
Their grandmothers married at twelve and fifteen, but twenty-seven per cent
of these women today who have passed fifteen are still single.

Yet these black women toil and toil hard. There were in 1910 two and a
half million Negro homes in the United States. Out of these homes walked
daily to work two million women and girls over ten years of age—over half of
the colored female population as against a fifth in the case of white women.
These, then, are a group of workers, fighting for their daily bread like men;
independent and approaching economic freedom! They furnished a million farm laborers, 80,000 farmers, 22,000 teachers, 600,000 servants and
washerwomen, and 50,000 in trades and merchandizing.

The family group, however, which is the ideal of the culture with which
these folk have been born, is not based on the idea of an economically

independent working mother. Rather its ideal harks back to the sheltered harem with the mother emerging at first as nurse and homemaker, while the man remains the sole breadwinner. What is the inevitable result of the clash of such ideals and such facts in the colored group? Broken families.

Among native white women one in ten is separated from her husband by death, divorce, or desertion. Among Negroes the ratio is one in seven. Is the cause racial? No, it is economic, because there is the same high ratio among the white foreign-born. The breaking up of the present family is the result of modern working and sex conditions and it hits the laborers with terrible force. The Negroes are put in a peculiarly difficult position, because the wage of the male breadwinner is below the standard, while the openings for colored women in certain lines of domestic work, and now in industries, are many. Thus while toil holds the father and brother in country and town at low wages, the sisters and mothers are called to the city. As a result the Negro women outnumber the men nine or ten to eight in many cities, making what Charlotte Gilman bluntly calls "cheap women."

What shall we say to this new economic equality in a great laboring class? Some people within and without the race deplore it. "Back to the homes with the women," they cry, "and higher wage for the men." But how impossible this is has been shown by war conditions. Cessation of foreign migration has raised Negro men's wages, to be sure—but it has not only raised Negro women's wages, it has opened to them a score of new avenues of earning a living. Indeed, here, in microcosm and with differences emphasizing sex equality, is the industrial history of labor in the 19th and 20th centuries. We cannot abolish the new economic freedom of women. We cannot imprison women again in a home or require them all on pain of death to be nurses and housekeepers.

What is today the message of these black women to America and to the world? The uplift of women is, next to the problem of the color line and the peace movement, our greatest modern cause. When, now, two of these movements—women and color—combine in one, the combination has deep meaning.

In other years women's way was clear: to be beautiful, to be petted, to bear children. Such has been their theoretic destiny and if perchance they have been ugly, hurt, and barren, that has been forgotten with studied silence. In partial compensation for that narrowed destiny the white world has lavished its politeness on its womankind—its chivalry and bows, its uncoverings and courtesies—all the accumulated homage disused for courts and kings and craving exercise. The revolt of white women against this preordained destiny has in these latter days reached splendid proportions, but it is the revolt of an aristocracy of brains and ability—the middle class and rank and file still plod on in the appointed path, paid by the homage, the almost mocking homage, of men.

From black women of America, however, (and from some others, too, but chiefly from black women and their daughters' daughters) this gauze has been withheld and without semblance of such apology they have been frankly trodden under the feet of men. They are and have been objected to, apparently for reasons peculiarly exasperating to reasoning human beings. When in this world a man comes forward with a thought, a deed, a vision, we ask not, how does he look—but what is his message? It is of but passing interest whether or not the messenger is beautiful or ugly—the *message* is the thing. This, which is axiomatic among men, has been in past ages but partially true if the messenger was a woman. The world still wants to ask that a woman primarily be pretty and if she is not, the mob pouts and asks querulously, "What else are women for?" Beauty "is its own excuse for being," but there are other excuses, as most men know, and when the white world objects to black women because it does not consider them beautiful, the black world of right ask two questions: "What is beauty?" and, "Suppose you think them ugly, what then? If ugliness and unconventionality and eccentricity of face and deed do not hinder men from doing the world's work and reaping the world's reward, why should it hinder women?"

Other things being equal, all of us, black and white, would prefer to be beautiful in face and form and suitably clothed; but most of us are not so, and one of the mightiest revolts of the century is against the devilish decree that no woman is a woman who is not by present standards a beautiful woman. This decree the black women of America have in large measure escaped from the first. Not being expected to be merely ornamental, they have girded themselves for work, instead of adorning their bodies only for play. Their sturdier minds have concluded that if a woman be clean, healthy, and educated, she is as pleasing as God wills and far more useful than most of her sisters. If in addition to this she is pink and white and straight-haired, and some of her fellow-men prefer this, well and good; but if she is black or brown and crowned in curled mists (and this to us is the most beautiful thing on earth), this is surely the flimsiest excuse for spiritual incarceration or banishment.

The very attempt to do this in the case of Negro Americans has strangely over-reached itself. By so much as the defective eyesight of the white world rejects black women as beauties, by so much the more it needs them as human beings—an enviable alternative, as many a white woman knows. Consequently, for black women alone, as a group, "handsome is that handsome does" and they are asked to be no more beautiful than God made them, but they are asked to be efficient, to be strong, fertile, muscled, and able to work. If they marry, they must as independent workers be able to help support their children, for their men are paid on a scale which makes sole support of the family often impossible.

On the whole, colored working women are paid as well as white working women for similar work, save in some higher grades, while colored men get from one-fourth to three-fourths less than white men. The result is curious and three-fold: the economic independence of black women is increased, the breaking up of Negro families must be more frequent, and the number of illegitimate children is decreased more slowly among them than other evidences of culture are increased, just as was once true in Scotland and Bavaria.

What does this mean? It forecasts a mighty dilemma which the whole world of civilization, despite its will, must one time frankly face: the unhusbanded mother of the childless wife. God send us a world with woman's freedom and married motherhood inextricably wed, but until He sends it, I see more of future promise in the betrayed girl-mothers of the black belt than in the childless wives of the white North, and I have more respect for the colored servant who yields to her frank longing for motherhood than for her white sister who offers up children for clothes. Out of a sex freedom that today makes us shudder will come in time a day when we will no longer pay men for work they do not do, for the sake of their harem; we will pay women what they earn and insist on their working and earning it; we will allow those persons to vote who know enough to vote, whether they be black or female, white or male; and we will ward [off] race suicide, not by further burdening the over-burdened, but by honoring motherhood, even when the sneaking father shirks his duty.

"Wait till the lady passes," said a Nashville white boy.

"She's no lady; she's a nigger," answered another.

So some few women are born free, and some amid insult and scarlet letters achieve freedom; but our women in black had freedom thrust contemptuously upon them. With that freedom they are buying an untrammeled independence and dear as is the price they pay for it, it will in the end be worth every taunt and groan. Today the dreams of the mothers are coming true. We have still our poverty and degradation, our lewdness and our cruel toil; but we have, too, a vast group of women of Negro blood who for strength of character, cleanness of soul, and unselfish devotion of purpose, is today easily the peer of any group of women in the civilized world. And more than that, in the great rank and file of our five million women we have the up-working of new revolutionary ideals, which must in time have vast influence on the thought and action of this land.

For this, their promise, and for their hard past, I honor the women of my race. Their beauty—their dark and mysterious beauty of midnight eyes, crumpled hair, and soft, full-featured faces—is perhaps more to me than to you, because I was born to its warm and subtle spell; but their worth is yours as well as mine. No other women on earth could have emerged from the hell of force and temptation which once engulfed and still surrounds black women in America with half the modesty and womanliness that they retain. I have always felt like bowing myself before them in all abasement, searching to bring some tribute to these long-suffering victims, these burdened sisters of mine, whom the world, the wise, white world, loves to affront and ridicule and wantonly to insult. I have known the women of many lands and nations—I have known and seen and lived beside them, but none have I known more sweetly feminine, more unswervingly loyal, more desperately earnest, and more instinctively pure in body and in soul than the daughters of my black mothers. This, then—a little thing—to their memory and inspiration.

# 6

# "WHEN AND WHERE [WE] ENTER"
## In Search of a Feminist Forefather—Reclaiming the *Womanist* Legacy of W. E. B. Du Bois

GARY L. LEMONS

Womanist . . . A black feminist or feminist of color[1]

> —ALICE WALKER

. . . the race question is at bottom simply a matter of the ownership of women. . . .[2]

> —W. E. B. DU BOIS, *The Crisis*

All this of woman,—but what of black women?

The uplift of women is, next to the problem of the color line and the peace movement, our greatest modern cause. When, now, two of these movements—woman and color—combine in one, the combination has deep meaning.[3]

> —W. E. B. DU BOIS, "The Damnation of Women"

We live in a society that along with being racist, classist, homophobic and capitalist, is also fundamentally sexist. Just as all whites socialized in a white society will be racists, so too will all men socialized in a sexist society be sexists. The Fact that we are black does not make us immune.

> —BLACK MEN FOR THE ERADICATION OF SEXISM

In *When and Where I Enter: The Impact of Black Women on Race and Sex in America*, Paula Giddings declares that "W. E. B. Du Bois . . . took Frederick Douglass's place as the *leading male feminist of his time*" (121; emphasis added). And in *Daughters of Sorrow: Attitudes Toward Black Women, 1880 – 1920*, a text whose title comes from his 1920 essay "The Damnation of Women," Beverly Guy-Sheftall records the germinal place of his work in her own: "This study was inspired by my reading of W. E. B. Du Bois who was, in my opinion, the most passionate defender of black women, to whom he referred as 'daughters of sorrow'" (13). Moreover, she states, "Only Du Bois, the most outspoken feminist among the group [of Black men] examined, felt compelled to devote his life's work to the emancipation of blacks *and* women" (161).

*Daughters of Sorrow* becomes a crucial piece of documentation in the recovery of the feminist legacy of Du Bois; in particular it documents his attitudes toward Black women. However, his womanist activism remains to be fully claimed by contemporary Black men, as he continues to be viewed primarily as a "race" man. His feminist/womanist writings place him in a completely new light—as a Black man advocating the rights of women. This essay moves to reclaim Du Bois as a "womanist forefather" to a new generation of profeminist Black men. We have come to own the history of his life and those of other Black men like himself and Frederick Douglass committed to the political struggle of women during the Woman Suffrage Movement. We have come not only to know our feminist past but to document its particularities. Through the power of this reclaimed knowledge, we actively participate in the creation of (re)visionary strategies to move the contemporary Black liberation struggle into the new millennium—beyond the masculinist agenda under which it currently labors. Toward establishing a genealogy of Black male womanist positionality, this essay situates W. E. B. Du Bois at its historical center as "womanist forefather" to contemporary Black men committed to contesting patriarchal and sexist power. Furthermore, it seeks to place "The Damnation of Women" at the forefront of a tradition of womanist discourse, as one of the premiere texts of the twentieth century composed by a Black man written in defense of Black women's rights.

We are sorely in need of an emancipatory vision of liberation that honors our past struggles—struggles in which Black women and men fought together against race *and gender* oppression. Recovering the history of Black men's woman suffrage activism is personally inspiring for me as a man of color, but it is politically instructive as well. As longstanding advocates of women's right to vote, *pro*feminist Black men like Du Bois and Douglass, among others, refute the notion that we are monolithically *anti*feminist. They also illustrate the value of coalitional politics within Black communities, where efforts against racial oppression can be linked to other struggles— without undermining our resistance to racism. Though this essay focuses only on the women's rights activism of Du Bois, extended studies like those of Giddings and Guy-Sheftall—as well as critical works by Angela Davis, bell hooks, and Rosalyn Terborg-Penn, among others—document Black male support for the rights of women specifically during the period of the Woman Suffrage Movement.

## *Womanist* Feminism: Du Bois and the Vindication of Black Womanhood

W. E. B. Du Bois never ceased to champion the right of women to vote. He launched a campaign for women's rights devoted to the political, social, and economic empowerment of Black women. Considering the unmitigated commitment he made to Black female liberation, not only was his conception of antiracist resistance feminist-inspired, his worldview was profoundly influenced by Black women. Nellie McKay documents the personal impact they had upon Du Bois:

> More than any other black man in our history, his three autobiographies demonstrate that black women [were] central to the development of his intellectual thought.[4]

It is precisely the fact that "[no] other black man in our history" has displayed an advocacy of feminism as intellectually and politically engaged as did Du Bois. In 1920, the year women won the right to vote, he published what surely may be taken as his womanist manifesto on the rights of women —"The Damnation of Women." In it Du Bois proclaimed, "To no modern race does its women mean so much as to the Negro nor come so near to the fulfillment of its meaning" (173). In these words, he directly echoed (as well as quoted directly in the text) the revolutionary proclamation of Black feminist activist Anna Julia Cooper who articulated over 30 years before, in 1892, the necessity of a conjoined struggle for Black liberation: "Only the black woman can say when and where I enter, in the quiet, undisputed dignity of my womanhood, without violence and without suing or special patronage, then and there the whole Negro race enters with me" (173). In the spirit of her pronouncement, Du Bois would say, "Every argument for Negro suffrage is an argument for woman's suffrage; every argument for woman's suffrage is an argument for Negro suffrage; both are great movements in democracy" (*The Crisis*, IX, April 1915, 285). At the core of this statement lies the principled foundation of Du Bois's feminist standpoint: the belief in the coterminous relationship between democratic movements for race and gender rights.

Just as Du Bois was influenced by Anna Julia Cooper, so a generation of Black men committed to the eradication of sexism have had their vision of womanhood, manhood, and masculinity changed by Black women feminist/womanist scholars, teachers, mothers, sisters, friends, and lovers. Thus, as prowomanist men, the antisexist activist work we perform is historically linked to that of Du Bois. His work as a womanist/feminist and the unyielding support of equal rights for Black women he voiced exemplifies the depth of his political commitment to them. The extraordinary manner in which Du Bois employed antiracist movement to press the case for woman suffrage had not been witnessed in the Black liberation struggle since the campaign Frederick Douglass began in the 1870s, who also surely inspired him as Jean Fagan Yellin notes in "DuBois' *Crisis* and Woman's Suffrage":

> The coupling of rights for women with rights for black people was not new. DuBois educated his readers in the history of the struggle for the franchise by both groups in September, 1912, in the first special issue of *The Crisis*. His central theme is suggested on the cover, which features a portrait of Frederick Douglass and the message, "Woman's Suffrage Number." (367)

Inspired by the radical race/gender politics Du Bois set into motion during his editorship of *The Crisis*, I am affirmed as a profeminist Black man by the history of Black male struggle forged in progressive antisexist coalition. And just as women were central to the development of Du Bois's vision of the world, so have they been to mine. Their influence on my work as a (male) feminist college professor and scholar has been profound.

As the founding editor of *The Crisis*, from 1910 to 1935, Du Bois envisioned a movement for Black liberation struggle in which gender and racial oppression were to be fought on equal fronts. Over the course of twenty years, *The Crisis* functioned as a political platform from which Du Bois launched a sustained attack against racism and sexism as they impacted the lives of both Black and white women. As stated earlier, unlike Frederick Douglass, Du Bois strategized woman suffrage and female equality from a standpoint grounded in the lived experiences of Black women. "[W]hen the triumph of woman's suffrage was imminent," Yellin observes, "DuBois repeatedly addressed himself to black women, urging them to prepare themselves to vote" (374). And it is, as I also stated from the outset, "The Damnation of Women" which articulates the foundational ideas of his womanist beliefs. Relating an affinity for African goddess mythology to the deep affection he bore for Black women, Du Bois imaginatively recoups the idea of ancestral female power to construct a vision of modern Black womanhood. The essay at once laments the condition of Black women he had known from his childhood, while celebrating the heroic achievement of Black women in U.S. history. It praises Black motherhood, while elaborating the devastating interrelated effects of race and sex discrimination on all mothers. Defying Western ideas of female beauty, it exposes their damning consequences on Black and white women, while asserting the superiority of an African feminine mystique.

I read "The Damnation of Women" as a personal narrative on the evolution of a Black man's journey toward the advocacy of women's rights through the politicization of the personal. In the childhood recollection of four women, Du Bois laid the foundation for a sustained critique of all women's oppression. And the adult views he held on womanhood have much to do with how he perceived the ways race and sex had determined the experience of his own mother as a Black woman. "There can be little doubt that Du Bois' remarkable regard for women, especially black women, had its roots in his deep regard for his mother," asserts Arnold Rampersad.[5] The vindication of Black motherhood and its liberatory relation to the idea of "woman" form a central trope in the evolution of a Du Boisian feminist nationalism. Its use as a political location from which Du Bois could call out the racial and economic subjugation of the Black mother reminds us how crucial her representation was in the formation of his African-centered ideology concerning the Black woman. For him, motherhood embodied the "essence" of Black womanhood idealized in the form of the mythological African goddess—Neith, his universal symbol of maternalism.

In fact, Du Bois's critique of women's oppression originated in a cultural nationalism rooted in African mythology popularized in the early 1900s.[6] By the early twentieth century, Black women liberationists had articulated their platform in the concept of "racial uplift"—frequently alluding to Africa as a source of inspiration. During the Harlem Renaissance, Amy Jacques Garvey, feminist writer for the *Negro World*—the official journal of the Universal Negro Improvement Association (founded by her husband Marcus Garvey)—voiced an African nationalist stance to protest what she saw was a lack of Black male political agency:

> Mr. Black Man watch your step! Ethiopia's queens will reign again, and her Amazons protect her shores and people. Strengthen your shaking knees and move forward, or we will displace you and lead on to victory and glory.[7]

Her symbolic representation of Black women (as Ethiopian queens protecting the land) placed them in a heroic position, one that Du Bois replicated in his version of feminist nationalism.

Few Black feminists of his day would have taken issue with an African-identified portrayal of themselves. They had already begun to redefine Black womanhood in nationalist terms in the late nineteenth century. Critically aware that gender-based inequity operated across racial, political, and economic divisions, he spoke both universally and in racially specific terms when necessary. But Du Bois never lost sight of the race/gender oppression Black women experienced. Never assuming the universality of the meaning of "woman," he asked: "All this of woman,—but what of black women?" (165).

## Where the Personal, Political, and Poetical Merge: Du Bois and the Idealization of the Black Mother

> Their beauty,—their dark and mysterious beauty of midnight eyes, crumpled hair, and soft, full-featured faces—is perhaps more to me than to you, *because I was born to its warm and subtle spell* [emphasis added]; but their worth is yours as well as mine.

> —"The Damnation of Women" (185–86)

> Despite the struggle for women's rights . . . the majority of black
> men, like their white male counterparts, were reluctant to
> challenge accepted notions of True womanhood. Doing so would
> free black women to develop their full potential. Instead, they
> wished that black women could climb on the pedestal and take
> their rightful place beside white women.

—*Daughters of Sorrow* (160)

In writing "The Damnation of Women" to marshal an incisive critique against the racist and sexist treatment of Black women, Du Bois brought together his critical acumen as a sociologist, journalist, litterateur, and cultural critic to challenge the damaging effects of racism and sexism in the lives of women. Stylistically, the essay may be characterized as a womanist pastiche, a composite of discursive styles that illustrate the writer's rhetorical skill in blending literary forms. Couched in autobiography, the treatise on the rights of women strategically integrates socio-political discourse with poetic prose to create a more intimate form to politicize the condition of women in Du Bois's personal life. In this manner, the autobiographical and political become one, producing a style much associated with a number of feminist writers today.

Often Du Bois lifted images of heroic Black women from his extensive body of autobiographical texts. He put to use cultural and political history to affect his own brand of literary social realism as represented in his first novel *The Quest of the Silver Fleece* (1911), perhaps the feminist-inspired source of "The Damnation of Women." Four impressionistic portraits of women open the text. Their sensuous, poetic stylization is reflected in the emphasis on their skin color ranging from dark to light. While differing in skin tone, they share in common their oppression as women. They represent the dispossessed, powerless, and *self*less women Du Bois recalled from his childhood:

> I remember four women of my boyhood: my mother, cousin Inez, Emma, and
> Ide Fuller. They represented the problem of the widow, the wife, the maiden,
> and the outcast. They were, in color, brown and light-brown, yellow with
> brown freckles and white. *They existed not for themselves, but for men; they
> were named after the men to whom they were related and not after the fashion of
> their own souls.* They were not beings, they were relations and these relations
> were enfilmed with mystery and secrecy. We did not know the truth or believe
> it when we heard it. Motherhood! What was it? We did not know or greatly
> care. (163; emphasis added)

In the passage above, he began a critique of female domination against the devaluation of womanhood and motherhood tragically resulting in the loss of female autonomy, forfeited in the *relation*ship of domestic subjugation. Questioning the foundation of patriarchal power and its relation to the family, Du Bois argued that female *self*-possession lay sacrificed to the will of the "father." In other words, a woman's worth and status in society was always already measured by her domestic and maternal service. Even as Du Bois mounted a strategic attack against the devaluation of motherhood and the racist dehumanization of the Black mother, like other Black and white feminists in the Woman Suffrage Movement, he remained wedded to the Cult of True Womanhood. "Though very few men in the history of America were as opposed to male supremacy as was Du Bois," Guy-Sheftall maintains, "even he was not totally free of conventional ideas about women's roles, especially where domesticity was concerned. Du Bois can also illustrate how one can be in favor of equal rights for women but still hold tenaciously to the ideology of motherhood" (72).

But Du Bois held to the notion that women should not have to choose between a career and motherhood. As much as he extolled the virtues of the maternal, he staunchly supported the economic independence of women. Acknowledging the limitations of conventional motherhood, he maintained that for women who chose it, it most often meant

> [the] sacrifice of intelligence and the chance to do their best work. . . . This is the damnation of women. All womanhood is hampered today because the world on which it is emerging is a world that tries to worship both virgins and mothers and in the end despises motherhood and despoils virgins. (164)

He also denounced the prevailing attitude that a woman had to choose one over the other, believing she had the right to achieve economic security through her own work and the right to become a mother if she so desired. "The future woman," he insisted, "must have a life work and economic independence. She must have the right of motherhood at her own discretion" (164). He cited poverty as the main determining factor in her victimization, boldly asserting that the path to female self-autonomy was obstructed by three things: marriage, prostitution ("to what men call shame"), and "to that which is more evil than nothing"—the refusal of men to accept women as capable of being intelligent, productive individuals as well as being mothers at the same time (164).

Yet the fact remains that the womanist politics of "The Damnation of Women" reside in a defense of Black womanhood rendered almost entirely through the idealization of motherhood—sometimes liberatory, other times not. Filtered through childhood memories of Black mothers, the representation of maternal womanhood in the text was drawn chiefly from the iconographic image of his mother: "with all her soft browness—the brown velvet of her skin, the sorrowful black-brown of her eyes, and the tiny brown-capped waves of her midnight hair as it lay parted on her forehead" (168). Repeatedly, Black womanhood and femininity are measured against the maternal in the text. Du Bois's understanding of it rested in an unwavering respect for Black women. For him, their "instinctively pure" nature originated in a familial relationship that was female-identified:

> I have known the women of many lands and nations,—I have known and seen and lived beside them but one have I known more sweetly feminine, more unswervingly loyal, more desperately earnest, *and more instinctively pure in*

*body and in soul than the daughters of my black mothers.* (186; emphasis added)

Black women, "the daughters of my black mothers," are depicted here as models of womanhood, standing comparatively above all other women. "The Damnation of Women" is a paean to Black motherhood defying its racist exploitation. Working against white supremacist notions of womanhood, Du Bois constructs a Black nationalist version of the maternal. Attesting to the courage of Black women in the face of slavery's horrific effect upon their lives, he declares, "I most sincerely doubt if any other race of women could have brought its fineness up through so devilish a fire" (171). Well aware of the fact that even after the end of slavery Black women exercised little control over their bodies, either as workers and/or child bearers, he praised their resiliency: "They [were] asked to be efficient, to be strong, fertile, muscled, and able to work" (184). In praising Black women's will to survive, Du Bois elevated Black mother to a mythic level—creating a racialized reversal of the pedestalized Southern belle. In dismantling one stereotype, however, Du Bois reified another in the myth of the "superwoman,"[8] a symbol of strength, self-sacrifice, and long-suffering.

As stated, Du Bois sets up a (race/class) double standard between Black and white women in which he views the maternal as "instinctively" Black, Southern, lower class, and innocent. Ultimately, for Du Bois the question of female liberation is one integrally connected to "married motherhood"—a preferred condition for women religiously and morally:

> God send us a world with woman's freedom and *married motherhood* [emphasis added] inextricably wed, but until He sends it, I see more of future promise in the betrayed girl-mothers of the black belt than the childless wives of the white North, and I have more respect for the colored servant *who yields to her frank longing for motherhood* than for her white sister who offers up children for clothes. (184; emphasis added)

Comparing the life of a married white woman of the North to that of an "[unwed] colored servant" from the South, Du Bois has nothing but admiration for her "yield[ing] to her frank longing for motherhood." There is only castigation for her childless "white sister" who chooses materialistic pleasure over that of motherhood. In both instances, he ironically glosses over the economic implications of child-bearing for a woman—wed or unwed, Black or white. Furthermore, the reinscription of certain racist as well as sexist notions of child-bearing onto the bodies of Black women undercuts any attempt to create a truly liberatory image of them. But rather than a further interrogation of the impact of class on motherhood across race, Du Bois privileges cultural nationalism, mythology, and symbolism over women's material condition in order to protect the image of Black womanhood from racist denigration.

Thus, in "The Damnation of Women" the affirmation of Black women comes as praise for their status as mothers, precisely because Du Bois believed that they had suffered most in this position.[9] In her critique of Du Bois and other Black men's idealization of the Black mother, Guy-Sheftall calls into question the root of its formulation. She observes that while these Black men were

> opposed to the abuse of black mothers in white households, they nonetheless embrace the ideology of motherhood, for they believe in the fundamental values associated with the mammy—home, nurturance, and maternal influence. In other words, black mothers should be removed from white homes so that they can devote themselves full time to the needs of their own homes. (84)

While Du Bois based his argument for the veneration of Black womanhood on the defense of the ideology of mother, he firmly supported the idea of women's work outside the home. Unlike other Black men who simply wanted to redress the exploitation of Black women by placing them upon a pedestal—completely powerless—Du Bois envisioned a time in which female labor outside the domestic space would be justly compensated. Looking to a future of women's equality, he affirmed the right of Black women to enter the work force and emphatically called for universal suffrage, while upholding the preeminence of motherhood as the surest means of Black people's survival:

> Out of a sex freedom that today makes us shudder will come in time a day when we will no longer pay men for work they do not do, for the sake of their harem; we will pay women what they earn and insist on their working and earning it; we will allow those persons to vote who know enough to vote, whether they be black or female, white or male; and we will ward [off] race suicide, not by further burdening the over-burdened, but by honoring motherhood. . . . (184–85)

Informed by a prophetic message of female economic independence, "The Damnation of Women" is both a defense of Black motherhood and an homage to the heroism of Black women—as women, mothers, workers, and revolutionary womanists. It stands as a testament to Du Bois's devotion to Black women and supreme admiration for their courage:

> No other women on earth could have emerged from the hell of force and temptation which once engulfed and still surrounds black women in America with half the modesty and womanliness that they retain. I have always felt like bowing myself before them in all abasement, searching to bring some tribute to these long-suffering victims, these burdened sisters of mine, whom the work, the wise, white world, loves to affront and ridicule and wantonly to insult. (186)

"If these comments seem exaggerated," Guy-Sheftall maintains, "one should be reminded of the prevailing stereotypes of black women that Du Bois and others were attempting to counteract. . . . The attempt to place black women on a pedestal should be seen against the backdrop of the elevation of the white woman. Black men wanted their women to be worshipped in the same manner" (63). Thus, Du Bois transforms Harriet Tubman and Sojourner

Truth into the daughters of Neith, whom he imagined as the African mythical mother of all civilization. Not only offering historical background of
their lives, as slaves and freedom fighters, he profiles other Black women of
heroic stature. They include poet, Phillis Wheatley; Kate Ferguson, homeless children's advocate and founder of the first Sunday school in New York;
Mary Shadd Cary, teacher, editor, lecturer, as well as a recruiting officer for
Black soldiers out West; and Louise De Mortie, who in 1877 established a
home for orphans (960–63). Black women's achievement and contribution
to racial uplift, according to Du Bois, surpassed that of Black men:

> As I look about me today in this veiled world of mine, despite the noisier and
> more spectacular advance of my brother, I instinctively feel and know that it is
> the five million women of my race who really count. . . . (179)

Describing the attainment of his "brother" as "noisier and more spectacular" (adjectives which in this case are not to be read as necessarily compli-
mentary), Du Bois is obviously more impressed with the achievements of
"five million" Black women. In foregrounding the public accomplishments
of outstanding Black women, he states: "All the way back in these dim
distances it is mothers and mothers who seem to count. . . ." Men, on the
other hand, as fathers "are shadowy memories" (168). In fact, *fathers* are
both nearly—figuratively and literally—absent in "The Damnation of Wom-
en." They function more as patriarchal specters, whose "shadowy" presence,
in the course of history, has "count[ed]" less than that of mothers. The
missing figure of the father in the text may be partly accounted for by the
absence of him in the childhood of the author. According to Du Bois
biographer David Levering Lewis, he "almost surely came to suspect years
later that his father was something more than a well-meaning, romantic
rakehell, 'indolent, kind, unreliable,' who came and soon departed from the
valley (Great Barrington, Connecticut) and his family, only to die shortly
thereafter."[10]

In the text, the "ghost" of the father is supplanted by the power of the
embodied, self-sacrificing mother—the symbolic center of the womanist
ideas Du Bois supported. Yet in the romanticization of motherhood, coupled
with an unyielding desire to celebrate a history of Black female heroism, his
critique of women's oppression reveals an unresolved ambivalence between
an uncompromising belief in the freedom of women and a devotion to the
maternal. On the one hand, his support for women's economic independence is progressive, even emancipatory. However, the womanist sensibility
exhibited in this position is repeatedly undercut by a strong allegiance to the
"cult of motherhood," couched in language affirming a woman's choice not
to bear children.

Nevertheless, we should not lose sight of the principled aims "The Damnation of Women" puts forward as a prowoman suffrage text. First and
foremost, it asserts the necessity of women's right to vote. Secondly, while it
affirms motherhood, it seeks to dismantle sexist attitudes that pitted the

maternal against the economic empowerment of women. As a womanist testament to the courage and achievement of Black women in light of the nearly insurmountable racial, sexual, and economic odds facing them—the text rejects the racist ideology of the Cult of True Womanhood that positioned the white woman as the universal representative of the feminine. But most aggressively it is the wrong against the Black mother that Du Bois determines to correct above all, writing in defiance of the historical racist and sexist devaluation of Black motherhood. Despite the limits of the (domestic) feminism Du Bois espoused, he, like other Black and white feminists during the time "The Damnation of Women" was published, convincingly argued for the self-governance of women as mothers and workers—as independent, autonomous individuals. In the end, it is the visionary belief that no woman should have to choose between motherhood and a career outside the home that stands as the hallmark of the feminist ideas he expressed. Boldly he asserted:

> We cannot abolish the new economic freedom of women. We cannot imprison women again in a home or require them all on pain of death to be nurses and housekeepers. . . . *The uplift of women is, next to the problem of the color line and the peace movement, our greatest modern cause. When, now, two of these movements—woman and color—combine in one, the combination has deep meaning.* (181; emphasis added)

### Feminism and the Difference Race (*and Gender*) Make: Embracing Womanist Space for Black Men

What promise does a womanist view of antiracism hold for Black people in the new millennium? First and foremost for Black men, womanist thinking enables us to challenge sexism on the grounds that a progressive vision of manhood and masculinity transgresses the boundaries of patriarchy. Womanist manhood rejects masculinity which identifies itself in terms that reinscribe the dehumanization, subjugation, exploitation, and sexual and physical abuse of women. Secondly, precisely because womanism speaks to the racial and culturally specific nature of Black female identity and agency linked to the empowerment of all Black people, it offers a transformative space for Black men to reclaim an antiracist struggle integrally linked to the liberation movement of Black women. Powerfully marking the emancipatory standpoint which Alice Walker includes as a part of its definition is this dialogue: "Mama, I'm walking to Canada and I'm taking you and a bunch of other slaves with me." Reply: "It wouldn't be the first time" (xi).

Reclaiming the history of feminist/womanist Black men like Du Bois (and Frederick Douglass, among others) enables us to make a strategic connection to the political activism of Black liberationist women and men who stood at the forefront of movements to end gender and race oppression. Guy-Sheftall suggests that

[t]he most enlightening aspect of the examination of [nineteenth and early twentieth century] attitudes toward woman suffrage, which was seen as another vehicle for the improvement of the race, is the revelation that some black men and many black women saw as early as a century ago no contradiction in associating themselves with struggles for women's rights (despite the opposition of many whites) at the same time that they were fighting for the emancipation of the race. They saw themselves as fighting for the liberation of all people. (162)

In documenting the longstanding commitment of W. E. B. Du Bois to the struggle for Black women's rights, I make a crucial link between his vision of Black female autonomy and the visionary possibilities womanism offers for the future of Black self-determination in the United States. A substantial body of scholarship by Black womanist/feminist scholars has made well-known the fact that racism operates insidiously to undermine the quality of Black female/male relationships at every level. The liberatory gender and sexual space Walker conceptualizes lays the groundwork for a progressive vision of struggle — where strategies of resistance to sexism, white supremacy, and homophobia are put into place simultaneously. Can we afford to exile any one Black person to the margin of struggle if s/he does not pass the litmus test of a masculinist, heterosexist, homophobic Blackness? Womanist Black men must fight for a Black woman's right to autonomous womanhood as forcefully as we demand our right to be free men. At the same time, we must champion as aggressively the liberation of our lesbian sisters and gay brothers whose experience of racism is no less insidiously felt as that of heterosexual Black folk.

In the historic document known as "The Combahee River Collective Statement," Black lesbian feminists powerfully speak at the intersection of race, gender, and sexuality to assert their alliance with a transformed vision of struggle against racial oppression:

Although we are feminists and lesbians, we feel solidarity with progressive Black men and do not advocate the fractionalization that white women who are separatists demand. *Our situation as Black people necessitates . . . solidarity around the fact of race, which white women of course do not need to have with white men, unless it is their negative solidarity as racial oppressors. We struggle together with Black men against racism, while we also struggle with Black men about sexism.* (275; emphasis added)

All Black men need to understand that antiracist strategies which uphold sexist, patriarchal dictates of Black empowerment doom themselves to fail, for they ignore the historical centrality of Black women in the movement for racial justice. Louis Farrakhan's call for Black men to "atone" for not having owned up to a patriarchal version of manhood (to be respected as men) falsely leads many of us to believe our manhood resides in the power to dominate women. Womanist Black men reject masculinist thinking rooted in ideas of male superiority. Without acknowledging the ways Black men can oppress women and be racially oppressed simultaneously, Farrakhan refuses an analysis of white supremacy that would expose the relationship of power between racial and sexual domination. Recognizing the interrelation of oppression would mean calling into question the male supremacist rhetoric he employs to win over Black men who feel racially disenfranchised. In other words, for Farrakhan the image of the Black man as the supreme victim of white racism is a much more powerful representation to persuade us (Black men) that a battle for "manhood rights" should be won before any other. For this very reason, Farrakhan's version of *male* liberation is neither visionary nor emancipatory—not even for the men who feel empowered by him. Many of them will continue to believe that women should be dominated.

In reclaiming the womanist legacy of W. E. B. Du Bois, I act to disrupt a masculinist narrative in which he is always cast as *race* spokesman. Claiming Du Bois in this essay as womanist forefather, at the beginning of a discursive tradition of Black men writing in political support of Black women, I have argued that his legacy of progressive struggle lays the groundwork for renewed dialogue on Black sexism. From the 1960s on, we have witnessed the resurgence of a Black feminist impulse in the work of a number of Black women writers dedicated to an inclusive transformative politic. Their writings have impacted the personal, social, and political lives of Black women and men. Thinking about the evolution of Black women's movement for gender and racial justice in this country, I am led to ponder the significance of Du Bois's battle for the rights of Black women at this moment when there is a move once again to make the Black liberation struggle synonymous with an affirmation of Black power rooted in patriarchal atonement. Progressive Black men, men whose vision of Blackness resists the trap of male supremacist notions of manhood and whose sense of self is linked to liberatory ideas of masculinity embrace womanist feminism as a transformative site for rethinking who we are in relation to women in and outside our communities.

Since 1983, the year *In Search of Our Mothers' Gardens* was published, a new generation of young *pro*womanist Black men have emerged, many of whom have read or studied with some of the most well-known Black feminists of the day. We speak in womanist terms, calling for Black male accountability on the issue of sexism. Today, most Black men writing in profeminist relation to Black women are university professors. They have produced a formidable body of womanist literary scholarship and criticism. But there has surfaced in this same location another, more activist, student-inspired womanist advocacy born in college classrooms of Black women, feminist professors. I am a self-declared womanist feminist precisely because of the teaching and scholarship of Black women feminists (Lemons 1996: 158–70; 259–84).

Since my first reading of bell hooks's *Feminist Theory: From Margin to Center,* over ten years ago, I have continued to draw upon her work for inspiration in my teaching and scholarship to call out the dehumanizing effects of sexism in the lives of Black people. Her vision of feminism has been central to the foundation of my belief that a movement to end sexism and women's oppression demands the committed labor of Black men as much as the struggle to eradicate racism requires the work of devoted women. Consistently, in her work, bell hooks challenges the dehumanizing power of "white supremacist capitalist patriarchal culture,"[11] not only in the lives of Black women but all people. Moreover, she speaks pointedly to the debilitating ways sexism affects the lives of men of color.[12] Never compromising the feminist critique of sexism in favor of Black nationalist solidarity, she calls out the very real ways Black men exert power over women — even as she acknowledges the manner in which racism renders many of us powerless to take control over our own lives.

As a teacher in the classroom (1996: 158–70), my efforts to oppose anti-feminist thinking in Black communities are grounded in the pedagogical imperatives hooks articulates in the idea that education should be about the practice of freedom.[13] hooks offers a feminist pedagogy that honors the tradition of Black struggle against racism while resisting a masculinist view of Black life. Invoking the radical vision of Black struggle which Malcolm X conceived, she asserts,

> If black men and women take seriously Malcolm's charge that we must work for our liberation "by any means necessary," then we must be willing to explore the way feminism as a critique of sexism, as a movement to end sexism and sexist oppression, could aid our struggle to be self-determining. (*Black Looks*, 113)

Yet as hooks herself has shown in light of the history of discriminatory practice in the U.S. feminist movement, is there any question why many women of color have not viewed feminism as liberatory for them? Many continue to believe feminism has nothing to do with them because it has failed to address their experience as women who are racially and sexually oppressed. Much of the antifeminist sentiment voiced by many Black men has emerged around the idea that feminism exists as another form of racist emasculinization, perpetrated by white women. In other words, the term "feminism" itself continues to be associated with white female, middle-class, racist privilege. However, hooks and other Black women committed to ending sexism and gender oppression, refuse to sacrifice the history of Black women's womanist agency for the sake of racial allegiance predicated upon a male-centered notion of Black liberation. Whether we employ the term "feminism" or "womanism" (or both interchangeably) to name the politics of women (and men) against the domination of females — sexism has shown itself to be a major obstacle to Black solidarity. Black men can no longer use racism as an excuse for the subjugation, exploitation, or sexual and/or physical abuse of women. Suggesting that Black sexism is a racist myth constructed by white people solely to discredit Black men leaves male supremacist attitudes and the sexist practice of Black men uninterrogated. From the rise of the Club Movement in the last decade of the nineteenth century through the groundbreaking work of Black feminists in the contemporary period, Black women have pursued an analysis of female oppression that addresses the specificity of their own experiences and ways of knowing as Black women.

The time is right for a Black male antisexist movement, if we (progressive-minded Black men) seriously desire to advance a vision of antiracist struggle that will meet the needs of Black people in this new century. "It has become necessary," as bell hooks says, "to find new avenues to transmit the messages of black liberation struggle, new ways to talk about racism and other politics of domination" (*Yearning*, 25).

## A Womanist (Men's) Postscript: Feminist Black Men and the Call for Revolutionary Change

The manifesto of Black Men for the Eradication of Sexism (BMES) proclaims:

> We believe that sexist oppression against women pervades every aspect of our communities and must be eradicated. The oppression of women is a difficult issue for our community to deal with partly because it is such a personal one. . . . Although it has often been said that black women are held in high regard by the black community, the reality is that black women are either denigrated as whores and enemies or placed on a confining pedestal as superwomen. . . . We ultimately demand a complete and fundamental revolutionary change that eradicates oppression based on sex, race, class, and sexual orientation. . . .

Just as Du Bois heard and actively engaged Anna Julia Cooper's 1892 prototypical Black womanist proclamation asserting that when Black women entered society with the full rights and privileges of citizenship then the race would follow after her, so collectively progressive Black men need to hear the radical pronouncements of BMES. When we begin to take responsibility for "demanding" a complete and fundamental revolutionary change that eradicates oppression based on a "sex, race, class, and sexual orientation," we form a historical link to our feminist/womanist past that lays the groundwork for a vision of Black liberation struggle based on coalitional politics that moves beyond one-dimensional, balkanized notions of struggle.

During the last weekend of September 1996, a historic event occurred at Morehouse College in Atlanta, Georgia. On those two days, a group of young Black men staged a conference entitled "To Be Black, Male, and Feminist/Womanist." As an invited speaker—with bell hooks, Beverly Guy-Sheftall, Rebecca Walker, and Robert Allen, among others—I witnessed the emergence of a new generation of Black men committed to the eradication of sexism. As the central tenet of their purpose statement, these men state: "We believe that although we are oppressed because of our color, we are privileged because of our sex and must, therefore, take responsibility for ending that privilege" (see chap. 16). Advocating the co-relational politics

between feminism and womanism that Alice Walker imagined, the conference organizers had created Black Men for the Eradication of Sexism at
Morehouse the year before as a result of their experience in a course they
had taken with Spelman professor Gloria Wade-Gayles. The profound nature of the interaction between these Black male students and this Black
womanist teacher/scholar bears historic implications for the future of Black
people's struggle for personal, social, and political autonomy at the dawn of
a new millennium.

In the wake of the Million Man March, Black men continue to face an
immense challenge regarding our identity as "Black" men under white
supremacist capitalism. Against a history of physical, economic, and social
disenfranchisement, we organized and came together en masse in the
nation's capital to restate our claim to humanity. Yet collectively we have not
responded to questions related to gender oppression, patriarchy, sexism, and
homophobia in our movement to end racial oppression. Black men continue to disavow the existence of sexism, ignoring its pervasiveness and
harmful effects on Black women and children in our communities. Did we
learn anything from Black women calling out sexism in the Black Power
Movement? The masculinist rhetoric of the Million Man March suggests
that once again we have failed to recognize the interlocking nature of
oppression—willfully replaying the male-identified narratives of the 1960s.
Once again with our masculinist blinders on, we have placed the evils of
racism over the insidious ways male supremacy and white supremacy function interconnectedly to devalue Black womanhood. Once again, we have
acted as if racism is the only form of domination Black women experience.
We have, once again, determined that the agenda for Black liberation rests
on our right to be (patriarchal) men (in the eyes of the white "Man").
Critiquing Black sexual politics of the sixties in "The Black Movement and
Women's Liberation," Linda La Rue argues: "Unless we realize how thoroughly the American value of male superiority and female inferiority has
permeated our relationships with one another, we can never appreciate the
role it plays in perpetuating racism and keeping black people divided"
(*Words of Fire* 169).[14]

Black people's movement for liberation can never be liberatory as long as
Black male self-interests lie at the center. If we have anything for which we
should atone, it is the fact that many of us (Black men) do not know our
legacy of shared struggle with Black women. Beverly Guy-Sheftall has said:

> At a time when there is controversy among academics and activists alike over
> whether blacks should be fighting for the liberation of women *or* the liberation
> of the race, one can look at the lives of Frederick Douglass, Sojourner Truth,
> Du Bois, and Mary Church Terrell, to name a few, and resolve this seeming
> dilemma rather easily. (162)

Contemporary Black men struggling to contest white male hegemony
only on the grounds that it keeps us from asserting patriarchal power fail to

account for the privileged status we already hold as men—in a male supremacist culture—despite racism. Progressive Black men need to put forward an analysis of racism that exposes the (inter)relation between white
supremacist thinking and ideas of male supremacy. Such an analysis resists
the uncritical tendency to privilege the effects of racism over the combined
impact of racism and sexism on Black women. A progressive movement to
end Black people's oppression in the United States must reject an ideology
of manhood that insists upon the patriarchalization of masculinity. Progressive Black men must reject a romanticized, masculinist version of struggle in
which a fantasy of royal African antiquity is invoked to serve as a model for
contemporary Black gender relations. The representation of Black women
as African queens functions as another form of patriarchal control. In this
version of utopian sexism, the power relation between Black men and wom-
en does not change: Black women remain subjugated.

Until Black men comprehend the interrelation of race and sex domination, we will continue to behave as if sexism (like homophobia) is not a
problem that Black people need to confront. Black men claim that the
injustices we suffer under white supremacist power is tantamount to racist
castration (or "high-tech lynching" as Clarence Thomas so self-servingly
protested). Thus, we cling to the ideas that antiracist resistance must be
about defending our manhood. When Black women call out masculine bias
in the struggle, we accuse them of the same crime against our manhood. Do
we remain trapped by a self-absorbed, self-defeating quest to measure up to
the litmus test of patriarchy, as if we have no identity as men outside its
limits? Or do we acknowledge ways we act out and perpetrate male supremacist beliefs and behavior? Recognizing our male privilege begins a process of
accountability in which we account for the power we possess as men (regardless of class) to oppress women. If we continue to hold to the belief that Black
people's resistance to racism must be fought out on the terrain of sexist dogma and male supremacist ideology, Black men remain trapped by a phallic
mentality that perpetually undermines political solidarity across gender. To
further ignore the ways Black sexism is counter-productive to the eradication
of racism, as well as profoundly dehumanizing to Black women, is the worst
of racial genocide. Can we afford to launch another masculinist version of
struggle to meet the challenges of the new century when a patriarchal vision
of Black liberation is already inherently flawed? To do so, we risk—in the
womanist words of Alice Walker—the "survival and wholeness of [an] entire
people, male *and* female."[15]

Profeminist-identified Black men have begun to set the stage for a womanist men's counter-movement against sexism. Reclaiming the feminist politics of Du Bois opens up the possibility for progressive dialogue between
Black men and women about the necessity of a new vision of Black liberation—one infused with the spirit of womanist feminism. In the 1920 essay
"The Damnation of Women," W. E. B. Du Bois called for revolutionary
insurgence among Black men that would lead them to take up the cause of

women's rights in support of Black women. Today, Black men reclaiming the womanist agency of Du Bois must create critical spaces where we can engage our brothers (young and old) in dialogue about ways sexism undermines our humanity, objectifies us, and perpetuates the myth of Black macho. Womanist speaking, writing, and acting against sexism honor the profeminist legacy of Du Bois. In this way, we may begin to realize our deepest desires to live free from the dehumanizing traps of male supremacy.

## NOTES

1. Alice Walker, *In Search of Our Mothers' Gardens* (Harcourt Brace Jovanovich, 1983), xi–xii.

2. W. E. B. Du Bois, *The Crisis*, 23, no. 5 (March 1922), 201–202.

3. W. E. B. Du Bois, *Darkwater: Voices from Within the Veil* (1920; reprint, New York: AMS Press, 1969), 165, 181. Subsequent references to this work appear in the text.

4. Nellie McKay, "The Souls of Black Women Folk in the Writings of W.E.B. Du Bois," in *Reading Black, Reading Feminist: A Critical Anthology*, ed. Henry Louis Gates, Jr. (New York: Meridian, 1990), 229.

5. Arnold Rampersad, *The Art and Imagination of W.E.B. Du Bois* (New York: Schocken Books, 1990), 4.

6. The fact that "The Damnation of Women" situates itself in a non-Western perspective indicated Du Bois's political interest in Ethiopianism as a transformative vehicle for Black female liberation. Its ideological framework was frequently represented in the works of many Black writers during that time (Henry Highland Garnet, Frances E. Harper, and Paul Lawrence Dunbar, to name a few). Fundamentally, it put forth the notion of Africa as "the mother of all civilization" and the primacy of all things African.

7. Amy Jacques Garvey, *Negro World*, (Oct. 24, 1925), as quoted in Mark D. Matthews, "'Our Women and What They Think,' Amy Jacques Garvey and *The Negro World*," *The Black Scholar*, 10, no. 8, 9 (May/June 1979), 12.

8. Michele Wallace offers a provocative analysis of the superwoman myth in her groundbreaking book *Black Macho and the Myth of the Superwoman* (New York: Dial, 1979).

9. In the December 1912 issue of *The Crisis*, he wrote a brief essay entitled "The Black Mother" as a commentary on the myth of the Black woman as mammy figure heard through the voice of her elite white female mistress.

Though the white female voice we hear is a fictive one, Du Bois suggested it approximated with historical accuracy the racist positionality of those white women who possessed the power to create and control such an arrangement. The essay concludes with the assertion that once Black women achieved economic self-sufficiency, the mammy as a racist stereotype would cease to exist. He sought to reclaim the dignity of Black womanhood through the validation of its maternal power. But society, Du Bois argued, would have to undergo radical reform before motherhood could assume its rightful place.

10. David Levering Lewis, *W.E.B. Du Bois: Biography of a Race* (New York: Henry Holt and Company, 1993), 21.

11. In the context of an analysis examining the interrelation of race and sex domination, bell hooks's employment of this phrase effectively works to show the interlocking relationship between racism, capitalism, and patriarchy.

12. bell hooks, *Feminist Theory: From Margin to Center* (Boston: South End Press, 1984).

13. *Teaching to Transgress: Education as the Practice of Freedom* (New York: Routledge, 1994).

14. Linda La Rue, "The Black Movement and Women's Liberation," in *Words of Fire: An Anthology of African-American Feminist Thought,* ed. Beverly Guy-Sheftall (New York: New Press, 1995), 169.

15. Alice Walker, *In Search of Our Mothers' Gardens* (Harcourt Brace Jovanovich, 1983), xi.

# PART 2

## DISLOYALTY TO PATRIARCHY
### Resisting Sexism

# 7 IN THE DAYS OF MY YOUTH

BENJAMIN E. MAYS

I remember a crowd of white men who rode up on horseback with rifles on their shoulders. I was with my father when they rode up, and I remember starting to cry. They cursed my father, drew their guns and made him salute, made him take off his hat and bow down to them several times. Then they rode away. I was not yet five years old, but I have never forgotten them.

I know now that they were one of the mobs associated with the infamous Phoenix Riot which began in Greenwood County, South Carolina, on November 8, 1898, and spread terror throughout the countryside for many days thereafter. My oldest sister, Susie, tells me, and newspaper reports of that period reveal, that several Negroes were lynched on the ninth and others on subsequent days.

That mob is my earliest memory.

Susie says I was born on August 1, 1895. The 1900 United States Census gives my birth date as August 1, 1894, and this date I accept. My birthplace is ten miles from the town of Ninety Six, South Carolina,[1] and fourteen miles from Greenwood, the county seat. The first post office I recall was named Rambo; later it was renamed "Epworth." Epworth is four miles from my birthplace, six miles from Ninety Six, and ten miles from Greenwood. The train ran through Ninety Six, which is seventy-five miles from Columbia. My birthplace is about midway between Greenwood and Saluda, not far from Edgefield.

Both my parents were born in slavery, my father, Hezekiah Mays, in 1856 and my mother, Louvenia Carter Mays, in 1862. My mother was too young to remember anything about slavery, but Father could, for he was nine years old when the Civil War came to an end in 1865.

I know virtually nothing about my ancestors. I have been told that my grandmother, Julia Mays, and her two children were sold as slaves by some-one in Virginia to a buyer in South Carolina. Her daughter died early, and her son was shot to death in the field by a white man. After coming to South Carolina, she married my grandfather, James Mays. Six children were born to them, four girls and two boys: Frances, Roenia, Janette, Polly, Hezekiah (my father), and Isaiah.

I never knew my grandfather, James Mays, but I remember my grand-mother, Julia, quite distinctly. She lived to be ninety or more years old. As I remember her features, I think she might have had a strain of Indian or white blood. However, I do not recall ever hearing her or my parents make any reference to white ancestry. I never knew my maternal grandparents. My mother had three brothers and two sisters: Abner, Harper, John, Sarah, and Susie.

My mother and father were very dark-skinned, and the color of their children ranged from black to dark brown. Color was never a problem in my family, nor did we ever feel any discrimination based on color among Negroes in my community, whose colors ranged from black to white. To protect the "purity" of the white race, South Carolina had decreed that any person with one-eighth of Negro blood in his veins belonged to the Negro race.[2] So there were a good many mulattoes and white Negroes in my area. We never felt sorry for ourselves because we were dark, and we accepted Africa as the home of our ancestors. Although I can appreciate the current emphasis on blackness, I am mighty glad I didn't have to wait seventy years for someone in the late 1960's to teach me to appreciate what I am—black! Many times my mother, unlettered and untutored though she was, said to us children, "You are as good as anybody!" This assurance was helpful to me even though the white world did not accept my mother's philosophy!

My heroes were black. Every once in a while, some Negro came along selling pictures of, or pamphlets about, a few Negro leaders. Pictures of Frederick Douglass, Booker T. Washington, and Paul Laurence Dunbar hung on our walls. In my high school days, Booker T. Washington meant more to me than George Washington; Frederick Douglass was more of a hero than William Lloyd Garrison; Dunbar inspired me more than Long-fellow. I heard about Crispus Attucks and was thrilled. The Negro preachers and teachers in my county, I worshiped. I didn't know any of the white preachers and teachers. (I doubt that I would have worshiped them if I had!) The Negroes in the South Carolina Legislature during the Reconstruction and post-Reconstruction years were the men held up to us in high school history classes as being great men, and not the Negro-hating Benjamin Ryan Tillman and his kind, who strove so long and hard to deprive the black man of his vote. I had identity.

My mother could neither read nor write. She enjoyed having me read to her, especially sections of the Bible. Until this day, I regret that I didn't teach my mother to read, write, and figure. Father could read printing fairly well but not script. I often wondered how my father—a slave for the first nine years of his life—had learned to read as well as he did. My sister Susie, ninety years old now, told me much about our parents when I visited her in the summer of 1967 as I was beginning this book. She remembers well two of my father's stories. He frequently told how the slave children on his master's plantation were fed. While the slaves were working in the fields, the master's wife would feed the slave children. She would pour milk into a trough and then call the slave children—my father among them. The children would rush to the trough, scoop up the milk in their hands and slurp it into their mouths. The other story is delightful. The slave master's son liked my father very much. Though it was unlawful to teach a slave to read, this white boy would take my father down in the woods to a secluded spot and there teach him to read.

I am the youngest of eight—three girls and five boys: Susie, Sarah, Mary, James, Isaiah, John, Hezekiah, and Benjamin—me. I never knew Isaiah, who died early. Hezekiah was the only one of my siblings to finish high school. The others went hardly beyond the fifth grade in our ungraded one-room school. The maximum school term of the Negro school was four months—November through February. The white school usually ran six months. Discrimination and farm work accounted for the shorter term for Negroes. Most of the cotton was picked in September and October; and early in March work on the farm began. It would never have occurred to the white people in charge of the schools that they should allow school to interfere with the work on the farms. I was nineteen years old before I was able to remain in school for the full term.

Education was not considered essential in those days, not even by or for whites. By law, slaves were kept illiterate. Consequently, when four million Negroes were freed in 1865 most of them were unable to read or write. It is not surprising, therefore, that, according to the Census of 1900, 57 percent of the Negro males of voting age in my county were illiterate.[3] Even the 43 percent who could read and write could not vote. In the state as a whole 52.8 percent of Negroes ten years old and above were illiterate in 1900 as against 64.1 percent in 1890. I suppose that the literacy in my family was slightly above the average of Negroes in my county.

Two of my brothers, James and John, tried farming. James stuck with it until he was killed at the age of forty-eight or fifty by a brother-in-law. Earlier, however, John had left for the city. Another brother, Hezekiah, after an altercation with Father, pulled off his sack and left the cotton field and his home, never to return except on visits to the family. My three sisters all married farmers in the community.

It could hardly have been otherwise than that most of the Negroes in my county at the turn of the century were wage hands, sharecroppers, and renters. Only a very small minority owned farms or were buying them. How could it be different? Thirty-five years earlier, Negroes had been freed without being given a dime or a foot of land by the federal government.

Emancipated from Southern slavery in 1865, the Negro was promptly deserted by the North. Had forty acres and a mule been given to each emancipated slave family, as had been proposed, the economic plight of the Negro would have been greatly ameliorated. Today the harvest might well have been of wheat and not tares.

In 1900, Greenwood County, in which I lived, had a population of 28,343, of which 18,906, or 66.7 percent, were Negroes. The fact that Negroes so far outnumbered the whites contributed to the whites' determination to exclude them from politics. The evil result of this determination was the infamous Phoenix Riot. Negroes in my county were heavily dependent upon the white people for land to till; the whites were equally dependent upon the Negroes to get their farms worked. In 1900, close to 20 percent of the Negro farmers in South Carolina owned their homes. However, in Greenwood County in 1910 only 112 Negroes owned their farms free of debt; ninety-five had farms but they were mortgaged; sixty-eight were part owners; 1,230 were cash tenants; 1,296 were share tenants; forty-three share-cash tenants; and eighty-nine were not specifically designated.[4] These figures add up to 2,933 farms run by Negroes. The free-of-debt owners, plus the owners with the mortgages, and the part-owners totaled 275, or 9.4 percent who had some ownership in their farms. Roughly speaking, only one Negro farmer in ten owned his land, and only one in twenty-six owned a farm absolutely free of debt. Ninety percent of the Negro farmers in Greenwood County were renters, sharecroppers, and wage hands. Despite poverty, however, Negro life was very stable. As a rule, men did not desert their families. There were not many illegitimate children in my community. A girl who had an illegitimate child was usually looked down on as having brought disgrace to her family.

My father was a renter. As far back as I can remember, I think we owned our mules. Any man who owned his mules or horses, buggy, wagon, or other farm equipment occupied a little higher status than the one who worked for wages or was a sharecropper. The wage hand was one who worked by the month for ten, twelve, or fifteen dollars a month. The sharecropper, or the one who worked on "halves," had his house, mules, and other farm implements provided for him. The owner of the land received half of all the sharecropper made.

As I recall, Father usually rented forty acres of land for a two-mule farm, or sixty acres if we had three mules. The rent was two bales of cotton, weighing 500 pounds each, for every twenty acres rented. So the owner of the land got his two, four, or six bales out of the first cotton picked and ginned. Many Negroes rented as many as sixty acres of land, paying as rent six bales of cotton weighing 500 pounds each. From the first bales ginned, Father got only the money that came from selling the cottonseeds. I was elated when that time came, for my father always celebrated by buying a big wheel of sharp yellow cheese out of the first cottonseed money. I still enjoy the taste of cheese. I have eaten the finest varieties in many parts of the world, but nothing has ever tasted as good to me as the cheese my father used to bring home from the sale of cottonseeds.

Although I do not recall that we were ever hungry and unable to get food, we did have very little to go on. To make sixteen bales of cotton on a two-mule farm was considered excellent farming. After four bales were used to pay rent, we would have twelve bales left. The price of cotton fluctuated. If we received ten cents a pound, we would have somewhere between five and six hundred dollars, depending upon whether the bales of cotton weighed an average of 450, 475, or 500 pounds. When all of us children were at home we, with our father and mother, were ten. We lived in a four-room house, with no indoor plumbing—no toilet facilities, no running water. When my oldest brother got his own farm, and after the death of Isaiah, there were eight of us; and things changed as my sisters got married and the oldest brothers, James and John, began to fend for themselves. If we were lucky enough to get twelve or fifteen cents a pound for cotton, things were a little better. But six or seven hundred dollars a year was not much when Father had to pay back, with interest, money borrowed to carry us from March to September, and when shoes, clothing, and food for all of us had to be bought out of this money. Then there were the mules, the buggies, wagons, and farm tools to be bought and paid for.

We were never able to clear enough from the crop to carry us from one September to the next. We could usually go on our own from September through February; but every March a lien had to be placed on the crop so that we could get money to buy food and other necessities from March through August, when we would get some relief by selling cotton. Strange as it may seem, neither we nor our neighbors ever raised enough hogs to have meat the year round, enough corn and wheat to insure having our daily bread, or cows in sufficient numbers to have enough milk. The curse was cotton. It was difficult to make farmers see that more corn, grain, hogs, and cows meant less cash but more profit in the end. Cotton sold instantly, and that was *cash* money. Negro farmers wanted to *feel* the cash—at least for that brief moment as it passed through their hands into the white man's hands!

Though never hungry, we were indeed poor. We supplemented our earnings by working at times as day hands, hoeing, chopping, and picking cotton for white farmers in the neighborhood. The price paid for this work usually was forty cents a day, sometimes only thirty-five, though when a man was desperate for help on his farm he would pay fifty cents a day. One made more money picking cotton, especially if he were a good cotton picker. The pay was forty or fifty cents per hundred pounds. All of us worked on the farm, including my sisters. Except in cases of dire necessity, Negro fathers preferred to have their daughters work on the farm rather than cook in the white man's kitchen. My sisters did not plow or cut wood, but they hoed and chopped and picked cotton. We usually got to the field about sunup and worked until sundown.

It was and still is a belief among Negroes that most white people who had

Negro tenants cheated them. This belief had no lack of confirming evidence! Many Negroes did not know how to keep their own accounts, and even when they could, all too many of them were afraid to question a white man's figures. His word was not to be disputed, and if he said a Negro owed him so much, questions were not in order and no explanations were forthcoming. If he told John, "We broke even this year; neither of us owes the other," even if John knew he had cleared a hundred dollars, he would ask no questions, register no protest.

To support my own recollections about a great deal of my past, I have either personally interviewed or had someone else interview 118 Negroes who were born about the same time I was.[5] The majority believed that Negroes who worked for white people in the South were grossly cheated by their white "bosses." Of the 118 interviewed for this study, 101 (85.6 percent) expressed the belief, from their own experiences and observations, that Negroes were cheated by white people. One was emphatic: "Whites didn't cheat Negroes — they robbed them!" Seven disagreed. Ninety-one (77.1 percent) were convinced that Negroes were also cheated in the courts. I share these majority opinions. In my county, whenever a white man was involved, the Negro was automatically guilty. As these interviews showed, it is difficult even now to get Negroes to believe otherwise. They know that Negroes were cheated in slavery, were worked and treated like animals. They know that Negroes are still cheated by whites on such things as rentals or contract buying, so they are certain that Negroes were taken advantage of on the plantations of the South after emancipation.

Despite the fact that I share this widespread belief, I feel that William Mays (no relative of mine), on whose land we lived, was fair in his transactions with my father. I did not know Dr. Childs, on whose place we lived until we moved to the "Bill" Mays place; but according to what I heard my parents say about him, he was a kindly white man. I never knew Bill Mays well. In my entire youth, for that matter, I did not know any white person well. I never had a white playmate. I saw Bill Mays when he made fairly frequent visits to the farm to see how Father was getting along, and occasionally we saw him in Greenwood. I suppose I never talked with him ten minutes at one time during our whole tenure on his place. I got the impression that he took some interest in Father's welfare. I do not believe William Mays ever cheated my father; but I was really hurt one day when I heard him tell Father, when I was trying to get away to school, that he should keep me home to work on the farm. From that moment on, I put him down as being against me. In fact, I considered anyone my enemy who was not in sympathy with my aspiration to get an education. I never forgot what Mr. Mays said to my father. A few years later when I was home from school and he visited the farm, my mother asked me to go out and speak to him and I refused. I felt that he was still against my going away to school. If Bill Mays did not cheat my father, I am sure that there must have been other white men in the South — however few — who did not cheat Negroes who worked for them.

I believe my mother had a kind of affection for the wives of Dr. Childs and Bill Mays, and for their children, who sometimes paid brief visits to our house. I recall that on more than one occasion the sons of Betty Childs came to see Mother after their family had moved to Greenville, and Mother always appeared glad to see them. As I recall, one of them gave Mother a half dollar. The way Mother spoke of Betty Childs and Nona Mays indicated affection for them—an affection which my father, I am sure, did not share. My own contact with them and their children was so slight that I never had a chance to develop any real friendship or affection. In Greenwood County, for the most part, black was black and white was white, and never the twain did meet except in an *inferior-superior* relationship; this relationship I never sought, cherished, or endured.

I did not know the meaning of it at the time, but I recall going to Greenwood with my mother when she went to see "Miss Nona," as she was called by the Negroes. Mother and I went to the back door. I do not know whether "Miss Nona" required this, or whether Mother was following the custom for Negroes to go to the back door when they went to a white man's house. I remember seeing Negroes go to the back door of a white man's house even when the white people were sitting on the front porch. Most of the 118 persons interviewed for my study reported that Negroes went to white people's back doors in their communities. When asked "Why?" forty of them, or 33 percent, said it was custom or tradition. Eighteen said white people demanded it. One person said, "It would have been accepting Negroes as equals if whites had allowed them to enter the front door." Another said that Negroes were sent to the back door because they were not considered persons. As for me, I learned the hard way, later on when I was in Orangeburg, South Carolina, that a Negro was not to go see a white man by way of the front door. But as a child, even when we had "worked out" by the day, the back-door custom had not struck me as odd, for we had no need to go to the front door, the noon meal being served on the back porch, as a rule, and not in the dining room.

I did not leave the farm because it was repulsive to me. I enjoyed work on the farm and am proud to proclaim that I was a *good* farmhand—much better than the average. At the age of twelve, I was able to take the lead row in hoeing and chopping cotton. I was an excellent "fodder puller" at the same age. I "knocked cotton stalks" in preparation for the next crop. Whenever we had three mules, I could, with sack and horn, keep ahead of three plow hands, pouring the guano in the furrows. I was not much at cutting cordwood. We were all good at plowing. When it came to picking cotton, my brother Hezekiah and I were the best in the family, and among the best cotton pickers in the county. We often competed with each other to see which could pick the most cotton. One day we carried "grab" rows all day. Each had his own row of cotton to pick and the middle row between us was the "grab" row. The fun came for the one who could pick fast enough to be getting more of the cotton on the grab row than the other. Hezekiah, "H. H."

as we called him, and I competed all day, from sunup to sundown. We picked cotton steadily and fussed just as steadily, each claiming that the other was getting all of the cotton off of the grab row. We both exaggerated, for when father weighed the cotton that evening, H. H. had picked 424 pounds and I had picked 425.

I did not mind being hired out to pick cotton at forty or fifty cents a hundred. Picking only 300 pounds earned me $1.20 or $1.50 a day, whereas I could make only forty or fifty cents a day plowing or hoeing cotton. Unfortunately, I did not always get to keep the money I made after being hired out. If Father needed it, he got it.

I loved the farm. To this day I enjoy seeing a beautiful crop of green corn blowing in the wind, or a patch of growing cotton, especially when nature has cooperated with the right amount of sunshine and rain and the cotton has been well tilled.

The few Negroes in my county who owned their land—and they were rare—were looked up to by other Negroes but had to be exceedingly careful not to be accused by white people of being "uppity," or of trying to "act like a white man." Both were serious charges. The more a Negro owned, the more humble he had to act in order to keep in the good graces of the white people. When a landowning Negro, living in a nice-looking, painted house decided to buy an automobile, he had to get permission from the leading white people in Ninety Six before he dared purchase it.

We wanted Father to buy land, but we did not succeed in persuading him to do so. I wanted him to be like Tom Waller, perhaps the wealthiest Negro in the county, despite the fact that he was illiterate. He had Negro sharecroppers and wage hands just like the landowning white farmers. His land was owned, not mortgaged; and he was a solid citizen. As I look back, I feel sure that it was just as well that Father never owned any land, because there would soon have been no one to work it. My oldest brother, James, was killed by a brother-in-law who was envious because his sister, whom James had married, had fallen heir to their father's home place. When the sister, my brother's wife, died and he married again, the brother-in-law couldn't endure having two "foreign" people in his parents' home, so he followed James into the field one day and shot him down. And since nothing in the racial situation in my county was conducive to encouraging sensitive Negroes to remain, my brother John soon left, ending up in Cleveland, and H. H. made his home in New York. I was "called" or driven to do something other than farming.

I cannot say that my home life was pleasant. Quarreling, wrangling, and sometimes fighting went on in our house. I got the impression early that Father was mean to our mother. He fussed at her; and when he drank too much he wanted to fight and sometimes did. All too many times we children had to hold him to keep him from hurting Mother. He would take out his knife and threaten to cut her. Often at night, we were kept awake by Father's loud and abusive raging. I think if Mother had said nothing, there would have been fewer arguments. But Mother had to talk back. Our sympathy was with her.

Father did his trading and buying in Greenwood, and it was there that he bought his liquor. We knew when he was "high," as he would come roaring home in the wagon, beating the mules (normally he was very careful about keeping the mules in good condition) for no other reason than that he had been drinking too much. When we heard him coming at such times we knew that there would be fussing and feuding that night.

Father's drinking embarrassed me, especially so when he did it at church. Largely under the influence of my mother, I made a vow at twelve years of age that I would never drink liquor. I have kept that pledge, not because I felt this made me better than those who drink but because I never discovered any good reason for breaking it. My decision was not based on religious or moral grounds but on what I saw drinking do to my father and our family. I claim no virtue for keeping this pledge. For the same reason, I never developed the habit of smoking. Father smoked and chewed tobacco, and was not always careful where he spat. Here again I claim no special virtue; I was repelled and disgusted by my father's indulgence in these habits and I never found any reason to follow his example. At Christmastime, we used to share a little toddy, a mixture of whiskey, sugar, and water. After I was twelve, I didn't take any more of the toddy.

As I look back over the years, I am convinced that my father was not a heavy drinker. He simply could not hold his liquor. I believe that a little whiskey "did him up." When he was under the influence of drink, his eyes sparkled and became bloodshot. At most times he was a very kindly man, but when he was otherwise one would shiver in his presence and feel like running for safety. I was afraid of my father until I was past eighteen. I was then ready to defy him when he scolded me or said harsh things to me. But he was not really an alcoholic. He lived to be eighty-two years old, and in his older years he stopped drinking altogether. When he lived with me in Washington, D.C., during the time when I was dean of the School of Religion at Howard University, he never took a drink.

My mother was very religious. Every night she called the children together for evening prayer before going to bed. She always led in prayer. Occasionally all the children said short prayers, too. Father usually prayed with us. Any one of us who got sleepy and went to bed early would say prayers alone. Often I read the Bible before evening prayer, and when Father was in good humor he would read. Frequently I would read the Bible to my mother, especially certain consoling passages in the Psalms and sections of the Sermon on the Mount. How often I read to her the Thirty-seventh Psalm after one of Father's tirades!

There was no doubt in Mother's mind that God answered prayers. She believed this to her dying day. When I made a trip around the world in the latter part of 1936 and the early months of 1937, Mother "knew" that it was her prayers that brought me safe home. Shouting in church was common in my youth, and Mother did her share. The preaching was usually other-worldly, and the minister often stirred up and exploited the emotions of the people. This fact, along with her somewhat turbulent home life, accounted for Mother's emotional outbursts in church. The depth and sincerity of her religious faith had great influence on me.

In later years, my wife was shocked when she first saw the Brickhouse School, for she had expected to see a real brick building. It was named the Brickhouse School after a large brick house nearby owned by a white man. It was a frame, one-room building with a wood stove in the center of the room, with boys seated on one side and girls on the other. The school ran for four months, from the first of November through February. When we moved from the Childs' place to the Mays' place, the round trip to school was increased from about six to approximately seven miles.

It was a happy day for me when I entered the Brickhouse School at the age of six. I discovered on that eventful day that I knew more than any of the other children who were entering school for the first time. Susie, my oldest sister, had taught me to say the alphabet, to count to a hundred, and to read a little. Since I was the only one in the beginners' class who could do these things, I was praised and highly complimented by the surprised teacher. As we put it, she "bragged on me." The next church Sunday, the second Sunday in November, my teacher sought my parents and told them, with other people standing around, "Bennie is smart." From that moment on, I was the star of that one-room school. The experience made a tremendous impression on me, so much so that I felt I had to live up to my teacher's expectations. I became Exhibit A when visitors came around and I was called upon to recite, which I was always eager and ready to do. I dearly loved the spelling class, where the best speller stood at the head of the class. If the boy or girl at the head of the class missed a word, the one who spelled the word correctly moved to the head of the class. I had been so impressed with myself that first day that I always strove thereafter to occupy the first place in class. I loved school so well that when the weather was bad and Mother kept me home I would weep. The student who was out of school a day had to go to the foot of the class, even though he had been standing at the head. When it did happen that I had to go to the foot for being absent, I took great delight in working my way up from the foot to the head.

I fell in love with my teacher, and I am sure I studied hard to please her as well as to learn. My first teacher was Ellen Waller, daughter of Tom Waller, the wealthy Negro farmer. Miss Waller was a high school graduate from Benedict College in Columbia, South Carolina. Very few Negroes went to college from my county. I can think of only four, before my time, who went to college and received degrees. A fair number went to high school and were graduated.

At the close of the school year, we had what was called an "Exhibition." Students sang, took part in dialogues, and made speeches. I was always one of the students to say a little speech of some kind, and whether or not I deserved it, the people applauded generously. I was a "great" baseball player at school in those days, and I recall two events in connection with the Exhibition which were somewhat unpleasant. Once, beautifully dressed in a white suit to give my Exhibition speech, I got pretty dirty sliding bases and had to speak in soiled clothes, much to my mother's disgust. Another time, when I was tagging a runner, he fell and his shoe hit me in the mouth, breaking off a piece of one of my front teeth, which naturally didn't improve my appearance when it came time for me to speak.

Like any normal, healthy boy I had my fights with a few of the tough guys in the community. I recall one fight when I was cut by one of the two boys with whom I was fighting. I was cut on the hand, the arm, and the head. When I got home, I was bloody. Before I could explain to my father what had happened, he kicked me off the porch and proceeded to beat me thoroughly. He never let me explain what had happened, that the two boys had "laid" for me when I passed their house returning from the store. They had jumped me. I had only two choices: run or fight. I chose to fight. I still think that I did not deserve the whipping my father gave me. I had other fights in school, but none as serious.

Father gave me another whipping which I did deserve. Although I never owned a pistol, my brothers did, and most of the boys in the county carried pistols. The young men who called on my sisters usually had their pistols. Since the firearms were a little heavy, they would put them on the table while visiting my sisters. One night one of the visitors left a loaded pistol on the table in one of our rooms. I found the pistol, assumed it was empty, and pulled the trigger. It went off with an awful noise, the bullet hitting the fireplace. I was so frightened that when Father asked me what the noise was about I told him I didn't know. H. H. showed Father the pistol. The whipping I got was indeed impressive. It has been vivid in my memory ever since.

Old Mount Zion was an important institution in my community. Negroes had nowhere to go but to church. They went there to worship, to hear the choir sing, to listen to the preacher, and to hear and see the people shout. The young people went to Mount Zion to socialize, or simply to stand around and talk. It was a place of worship and a social center as well. There was no other place to go.

This was my church, six miles from the town of Ninety Six and four miles from our house. Preaching was held every second Sunday, the pastor having other churches. If all of us were to go to church, we had to ride in a two-mule wagon, seated either on chairs or on wheat straw in the bottom of the wagon. As a rule, however, someone stayed home, and then two buggies were ample for the rest of us.

On the farm, we worked hard six days a week. Father wanted the mules to rest on the Sabbath; but he never tried to keep them rested on the first and second Sundays when there were services at Mount Olive and at Mount Zion, our own church. Mount Olive, though not our church, was closer, and we usually worshiped there on the first Sunday in each month. Fairly often on the third and fourth Sundays, however, Father would insist that the mules needed rest, so if we wished to go to Sunday school at Mount Zion on those Sundays we had to walk—round trip, eight miles.

Although the members of Mount Zion were poor and most of them were renters, they were a proud lot, and many of them owned good-looking buggies and at least a couple of fine-looking horses or mules, although it is highly probable that most of them were in debt. As a youngster, I watched them driving up in beautiful rubber-tired buggies drawn by fine horses or mules. I think some of them came late to church just so they could be seen. This was the one place where the Negroes in my community could be free and relax from the toil and oppression of the week. Among themselves they were free to show off and feel important. My brother John was the sporty one in our family. He worked and saved until he could buy a white rubber-tired buggy and a beautiful white mule which he named Kate. John and Kate created quite a sensation in the community and at Mount Zion. When the boys came to church alone, they were expected to take their girl friends home—a duty which they did not find at all burdensome.

Fighting and heavy drinking on church property were common practices in many churches, but not much of this went on at Mount Zion, thanks largely to the man who pastored Mount Zion for fifty years or more.

The Reverend James F. Marshall was hardly more than a fifth-grade scholar, but he knew the Scriptures, at least so far as knowing where certain passages were to be found. He could quote almost any passage of Scripture from memory. He accepted the Bible as it was printed and held it was "wicked" to doubt any part of it. We thought he was the best preacher in the world (our world was Greenwood County). He was eloquent. He could moan, and did. Almost invariably he made some of the people shout. If he did not moan a bit and make the people shout, his congregation felt he had not preached well. The intellectual content of his sermons was not nearly as important as the emotional appeal.

The Reverend Marshall set a good example for the people. I believe no one ever accused him of any dishonesty or immorality. Wives and daughters were safe in his presence. He did not touch liquor. The same could not be said of all the ministers who pastored in Greenwood County. The Reverend Marshall, who lived twenty-four miles away from the church, usually held Conference on the second Saturday afternoon and stayed overnight with a family of the church. It was a rare privilege to have the pastor spend the night in one's home. The house was spic and span when the preacher came, and the best food was served. He was the only hero we had around Zion to worship. So impeccable (or discreet) was the Reverend Marshall's conduct that the only story circulated about him was that once he got up in the middle of the night and left a certain woman's house because she had approached him in an immoral way. The young people heard all the gossip the old people talked, and if there had been any scandal about Marshall, the young people would have heard and no doubt circulated it. He was accused of loving money too well, but he was never accused of stealing it. Why shouldn't he have loved it? Why, indeed, should he not have lusted for it? He had ten children or more; and from his four churches he received a total of only $800 a year.

The Reverend Marshall's preaching was highly other-worldly, emphasizing the joys of heaven and the damnation of hell. He preached funerals according to the life the deceased had lived. He didn't hesitate to preach the dead "smack into heaven" or into hell, according to the life he or she had lived. The church was usually full at funerals, especially if the deceased had been well known; and when a man of bad reputation died the church was jammed. The people wanted to hear what kind of funeral sermon Marshall would preach. I am sure that a burning hell and a golden-streeted heaven were as real as their farms to a majority of the people in Mount Zion and in the community at large. They believed the trials and tribulations of the world would all be over when one got to heaven. Beaten down at every turn by the white man, as they were, Negroes could perhaps not have survived without this kind of religion.

There was no doubt in the minds of some that Marshall had special power with God. Even when he prayed for rain and it didn't come, they still believed he had influence with God. If he prayed for rain on the second Sunday in the month and it came the next day, it was obviously in answer to Marshall's prayer.

Members who had done great wrongs were brought before the Church Conference on the second Saturday in the month. Frequently they were turned out of the church if the Conference proclaimed them guilty. But a person could repent, or make a pretense of repentance, and be taken right back into the fold. I was present at a Church Conference when a young couple appeared who had been sexually intimate; the young woman was pregnant. They admitted what they had done. Marshall advised the young man to marry the girl. With his right hand lifted toward heaven, Marshall told the young man that if he didn't marry the young woman and live with her, fulfilling the duties of a husband, something unspeakably bad would happen to him. The young man married the girl on the spot, but then went on his way, never assuming any responsibility for his wife or child. Not long afterward, he was killed one midnight, so viciously beaten to death with a club that his brains were spattered all over the ground. In the summer of 1968, my sister told me Negroes believed that this young man had been killed by a certain white man because he was hanging around a Negro woman with whom the white man was having relations. Neither whites nor Negroes did anything to apprehend the murderer. The apparent fulfillment

of Marshall's prophecy in this case skyrocketed his prestige in the community. Thereafter nobody wanted Preacher Marshall to "put bad mouth" on
them.

Although Marshall taught the people to be honest and upright, the Gospel he preached was primarily an opiate to enable them to endure and
survive the oppressive conditions under which they lived at the hands of the
white people in the community. I never heard him utter one word against
lynching. If he had, he would probably have been run out of the community—or lynched. When a visiting minister attempted to condemn white
people, Pastor Marshall stopped him. I was there. I saw it and I heard it. I am
not necessarily condemning the use of religion as an opiate. Sometimes an
opiate is good in medicine. Sometimes it may be good in religion. Certainly
religious faith has helped me in my struggles.

As my pastor accepted the system and made no effort to change it, so it was
in other churches—Negro and white—in my day. Of the 118 persons interviewed who could remember what kind of sermons were being preached
around the turn of the century, fifty-nine (50 percent) said that their ministers taught them nothing about white people. Twenty (17 percent) reported
that their ministers instructed them to obey white people, be submissive and
humble, and get along with whites. Twenty-one said their ministers taught
them to be respectful to whites. Nineteen did not answer the question on the
church and race. Only four said that their ministers taught them to demand
their rights. One woman said that her pastor was bitter about the racial
situation. The vast majority of them said the church was helpful to them.

Pastor Marshall "stayed in" with the local white Methodist preacher,
although Marshall believed that all who were not Baptists were hellward
bound. When certain elements in the church wanted to get rid of Marshall,
he invited the Reverend Pierce Kinard, a white Methodist, to come to Zion
and advise the Negroes to keep Marshall, which of course effectively ended
the incipient move to have Preacher Marshall removed.

The Reverend Marshall baptized every member in my family, including
Mother and Father. Father did not join the church until after the earthquake
in 1886. My parents told me that, after the quake, the Reverend Marshall
baptized a hundred men at one session. "God moves in mysterious ways!"

Mother believed, as Marshall did, that only Baptists could get to heaven—
that is, she did until my brother, H. H., joined the Presbyterian Church!
When I teased her about this, Mother replied, "All things are possible with
God." As a small boy, I really felt sorry for the Methodists who passed our
house going to the Methodist church. Not for long, however, could I believe
that they were all bound for hell, for some of my best friends were non-
Baptists; some of the girls I began to like were not Baptists; and indeed I
ended up marrying a member of the CME Church.

Though the people of Mount Zion, for the most part, were poor and
unlettered, nevertheless they did much for me. As I sat as a boy in Sunday
school, discussing the Sunday school lessons with the adults, asking ques-

tions and making comments, they encouraged me and gave me their blessings. Each Sunday in June, we had what was called "Children's Day." I do not remember exactly how old I was—possibly nine—when I participated, having committed to memory a portion of the Sermon on the Mount. After my recitation, the house went wild: old women waved their handkerchief, old men stamped their feet, and the people generally applauded long and loud. It was a terrific ovation, let alone a tremendous experience, for a nine-year-old boy. There were predictions that I would "go places" in life. The minister said I would preach; and from that moment on the Reverend Marshall manifested a special interest in me. All of this was part of the motivation that had started with my oldest sister's teaching me how to count and read and write, thereby winning for me the encouragement and praise given me by my first teacher, Ellen Waller. The people in the church did not contribute one dime to help me with my education. But they gave me something far more valuable. They gave me encouragement, the thing I most needed. They expressed such confidence in me that I always felt that I could never betray their trust, never let them down.

After the Phoenix Riot, never a year passed in my county that there were not several brutal incidents involving Negroes and whites. In the months following the Phoenix Riot, I had seen bloodhounds on our land with a mob looking for a Negro. I saw a Negro hiding in the swamps for fear of being caught and lynched. Negroes always got the worst of it. Guilt and innocence were meaningless words: the Negro was always blamed, always punished. Among themselves, Negroes talked much about these tragedies. They were impotent to do anything about them. They dared not even mention them to whites.

I was twelve years old when I read about the Atlanta Riot in the Greenwood *Index* and the Atlanta *Journal*, the two papers to which we subscribed. As I recall, the papers played up the fact that the Atlanta Riot was the result of a series of attacks that Negro men were supposed to have made on white women. It was not until I was older that I realized that Hoke Smith, who campaigned for governor of Georgia on a white supremacy platform, and the four Atlanta newspapers which played up the accusations against the Negroes, not only struck the match but supplied the combustible material to ignite the flames that produced the Atlanta Riot.

It was in this connection that I received a stern lecture from the man who was later to marry my sister Susie. He was an unlettered but highly intelligent man. Like Susie, he would have done well in anybody's college had he been given half a chance to go. He often walked miles to see my sister, and frequently if he left before dark he would invite me to walk a distance with him. During one of our walks, the Atlanta Riot was mentioned. I was old enough at the time to hear what my parents talked about in the home. I heard the gossip about things that happened in the community. My older brothers and sisters learned all the rumors of the county and talked freely about them at home and in the cotton fields. We knew that a beautiful, light-brown-skinned Negro woman was living in the house with a white man, and that Negro men knew enough to leave her alone. It was common knowledge that "Hamp," the mulatto Negro who lived in a house a white man built for him in his backyard and whom the white man kept there to work in his house and to drive his daughters around, was really the white man's son, born to a Negro woman, and therefore half brother to the white daughters. It was an accepted fact that "Polly," a beautiful Negro woman, was the paramour of "Lowden," a white man. Once Polly was caught in a buggy with a Negro man, and rumor had it that Lowden made her get out of the buggy and threatened to shoot the Negro man. This story was so deeply believed that fifty years later Negroes living in that community were still talking about Polly and Lowden, who both lingered ill and suffered for years before they died. Negroes say even now that God punished them for their sins. It no doubt was a comfort to believe that God would mete out the punishment that Negroes were powerless to inflict. Occasionally, too, a white baby turned up in a black home.

In the Atlanta Riot, which began on Saturday night, September 22, 1906, and extended through Tuesday, September 25, many Negroes were killed and many more wounded. One or two whites were killed and several wounded. The riot was allegedly caused by black men attacking white women. It was in this context that I asked my brother-in-law-to-be why it was that white men could do anything they wanted to Negro women but Negro men were lynched and killed if they did the same to white women or even if they were merely accused and innocent. My prospective brother-in-law stopped by the side of the road and gave me a stern lecture. He told me in positive language never to discuss that matter again. It was dangerous talk, and if I said such a thing in the presence of a white person it would not be good for me.

Years later, when I thought it necessary to do some research on both the Phoenix and the Atlanta riots for this autobiography, I discovered that the four Atlanta papers—the Atlanta *Constitution*, the Atlanta *Journal*, the *Georgian*, and the *Evening News*—played up the reported attacks on white women out of all proportion to the facts; and that John Temple Graves, editor of the *Georgian*, really whooped it up. I learned as recently as the summer of 1968 that an analysis of the twelve alleged attacks on white women, *committed six months before the riot*, showed that two were cases of rape, three were cases of attempted rape, three were cases producing no definite proof of attempted rape, three were purely cases of fright on the part of white women, and a final one said at first that a Negro had assaulted her but finally confessed that she had attempted suicide.[6] Attacks were made on Negroes indiscriminately in the Atlanta Riot with as many as five thousand white men participating. Charles Crowe, associate professor of history at the University of Georgia, writing of the Atlanta Riot in the April, 1969, issue of the *Journal of Negro History*, says:

As a result of the riot, one white person died and several dozen were hurt. Twenty-five black men perished, about one hundred and fifty suffered serious wounds, hundreds had less critical injuries, and more than a thousand black men, women and children fled the city. For several months to come white leaders busied themselves with public apologetics as black people concentrated on the restoration of "normal" patterns of work and life. The Atlanta race riot was not soon forgotten by black people who remembered with particular vividness the evening of September 22 as the terror-ridden night of the white assassins.[7]

Another incident happened in my county two years after the Atlanta Riot of 1906, which I remember vividly—I was fourteen at the time. Jack Johnson, a Negro, defeated Jim Jeffries, a white man, in Reno, Nevada, and became the first black heavyweight champion of the world. White men in my county could not take it. A few Negroes were beaten up because a Negro had beaten a white man in far-away Nevada. Negroes dared not discuss the outcome of this boxing match in the presence of whites. In fact, Johnson's victory was hard on the white man's world. Race riots broke out in a number of places and many Negroes were killed. Jack Johnson committed two grave blunders as far as whites were concerned: He beat up a white man and he was socializing with a white woman—both deadly sins in 1908.

This was the pattern during slavery and long after the post-Reconstruction years. In this relationship, white men and Negro women were free. Perhaps the best portrayal of the relationship between white men and Negro women, and, in the colonial days, between the Negro male and the white female servant, is to be found in E. Franklin Frazier's *The Negro Family in the United States.*[8] Writing of the relationship that existed between white men and Negro women, Frazier says: "cohabitation of the men of the master race with the women of the slave race occurred on every level, and became so extensive that it nullified to some extent the monogamous mores."

I cannot close this chapter without words of commendation for my parents. My father was bitterly opposed to my efforts to get an education; and yet I owe much to my parents. I shall mention only two things:

My parents were industrious. There wasn't a lazy bone in their bodies. They didn't sit back and make the children do it. They did their part on the farm. In addition to cooking, seeing that our clothes were washed and ironed, and keeping the house clean, Mother hoed and picked cotton, and Father worked equally hard. I must have caught their spirit of work. To this day, I am impatient with lazy people. Father believed that a man should earn his living by the sweat of his brow, and that, to him, meant working on the farm in the blazing hot sun. And my parents were honest. I never heard them scheming how they might get something for nothing. I never suspected them of stealing anything from anybody. They taught their children honesty. I believe that not a single child in our family expected to get anything except through honest channels and by his own efforts. I am reminded of what John Hope, president of Morehouse College in Atlanta, once said. He admitted that Morehouse was poor, but added, "We live in respectable poverty!" The Mays family was poor and lived on the ragged edge of poverty, but we lived in "respectable poverty."

The rugged honesty of my parents has stuck with me through all these years. I am intolerant of dishonesty, particularly intellectual dishonesty, wherein men ignore or distort the truth and plot to take advantage of others for their own indulgence. My parents did little or no ethical philosophizing, but they *lived* their ideals of industry and honesty. I am indebted to them for their living example, and I am grateful.

There were only a few books in the Mays' house and no magazines. We had the Bible, a dictionary, picture books about Booker T. Washington, Frederick Douglass, and Paul Laurence Dunbar, and Sunday school books. We read the Atlanta *Journal* and the Greenwood *Index*. And we had the school textbooks from which we learned to read, spell, and figure to a certain level. This was about it. Nobody in the family had gone beyond the fourth or fifth grade. I didn't seem to have much to go on. But I had learned industry and honesty from my parents. I had been inspired by my county teachers, encouraged by the Reverend Marshall, and motivated by the people in the church who made me believe that I could become something worthwhile in the world. These are the things that drove me on and, when they are summed up, I guess they amount to quite a lot.

## NOTES

1. According to local legend, the town of Ninety Six, South Carolina, got its name from an event during the Revolutionary War when a Cherokee Indian maiden rode from the Cherokee reservation to Old Star Fort, then occupied by the British, to warn the British that the Americans were approaching. The distance was ninety-six miles; the warning was not successful; the Americans overcame the British; but the name Ninety Six was born.

2. South Carolina Constitution, 1895. *States' Laws on Race and Color*, compiled and edited by Pauli Murray (Cincinnati, Ohio, 1951), p. 407.

3. Negroes in the United States, U.S. Bureau of the Census, 1900.

4. Negro Population in the United States: 1780–1915, U.S. Bureau of the Census, p. 746.

5. A team of interviewers composed of teachers, senior and graduate college students, using a carefully prepared schedule of questions, conducted in-depth personal interviews of 118 selected persons living in the Atlanta area and born in the South just before and after the turn of the century.

6. Glenn Weddington Rainey, *Race Riots in Atlanta in 1906* (Master of Arts thesis, Emory University, Atlanta, 1929), p. 8.

7. Charles Crowe, "Racial Massacre in Atlanta, September 22, 1906" (*Journal of Negro History*, LIV, No. 2, April, 1969), p. 168.

8. E. Franklin Frazier, *The Negro Family in the United States* (The University of Chicago Sociological Series, Chicago, 1939), p. 482.

# 8 FEMINISM AND EQUALITY

*[From the* New York Amsterdam News, *August 27, 1970.]*

BAYARD RUSTIN

The women's liberation movement, which has created much controversy in recent months, is not a new phenomenon but part of a long struggle for women's equality. The fact that a major feminist demonstration was held on August 26, 1970, indicates the historical character of this movement, since the date was the fiftieth anniversary of the passage of the Nineteenth Amendment, granting female suffrage.

The modern feminist movement differs from the suffragette movement of a half-century ago in that its demands have to do more with economic equality than with political rights. To a considerable degree, this is a reflection of technological changes that have taken place in the society—changes which have freed the more affluent women from household chores and enabled them to gain a high degree of education. These women are now demanding that jobs and other opportunities be opened to them on a nondiscriminatory basis. The force of their argument is reflected in economic statistics showing that the income differential between men and women is greater than it is between whites and blacks.

If the women's liberation movement should be criticized, it is not because its demands are unjust but because they do not go far enough. The three demands put forth at the August 26 demonstrations were for free abortions, twenty-four-hour day-care centers for children of working mothers, and equal educational and employment opportunities.

I would personally take issue with none of these demands, but they are inadequate in that they are proposed in isolation from the broad social and economic context of American life. The feminists are making the same mistake that many other social protesters have made: they do not relate their demands to the larger issues which ultimately will determine whether the demands are met.

For example, I am entirely for free abortions on demand, since I think women should be able to choose whether they want to have children. But I think that the feminists would be wiser to make this specific demand part of a larger demand for socialized medicine. Our current health system does not permit all women, or all Americans, to obtain adequate medical care, and good health is a prerequisite for "liberation," however one cares to define that word. Similarly, it is not enough to have day-care centers that will free mothers from constant supervision of their children. There should also be a demand for the expansion of preschool education and for high-quality integrated schools that will liberate the minds of the children and enable them to develop their potential to the fullest. Finally, the demand for equal employment opportunities cannot be met in the absence of full employ-ment. As long as a sizable portion of the population is unemployed, workers, regardless of their sex or race, will have to compete for jobs and employers will be able to hire those willing to work for the least pay. Here it should be added that the demand for female equality is too often stated in terms of giving women the same rights as men. What happens then is that women consider their own special rights—such as the legal protection of women workers—to be expendable. Rather than give up these rights, they should be demanding that such provisions be extended to all workers.

Thus far the women's liberation movement has failed to make its de-mands within this larger social context. That failure is not accidental; it is, in fact, a commentary on the affluent background of many of the feminists. They are, for the most part, women who already have access to adequate health care, whose children (if they have them) probably attend excellent schools, and who don't need jobs, just *better* jobs. This is one reason why so few black women have participated in the feminist movement. If the femi-nists do not make the larger demands I have suggested, their movement will become just another middle-class foray into limited social reform, the main result of which will be to divert valuable social energies away from the prob-lem of fundamentally transforming our society's institutions. Without such a transformation, leading to full social equality for all Americans—female and male, black and white, poor and rich—our people will not be free.

# 9
# WOMEN'S RIGHTS ARE HUMAN RIGHTS

Kalamu Ya Salaam

My position, succinctly stated, is simply this: any discussion of the issue of human rights should include a discussion of women's rights.

The reason for my statement, while complex in its subtleties, is simple in its substance. Simply said, women are human beings.

Our struggle for human rights must be grounded in a rejection of the oppression of any identifiable segment or stratum of human societies, regardless of the criterion of differentiation or discrimination, e.g. race, class or sex.

Based on my study and analysis of my own experiences and environment, as well as study and analysis of the experiences and environments of other peoples, in other places and other periods of time, I draw the conclusion that the issue of women's rights has and continues to be a central concern of every progressive force in the world, as well as a critical concern of millions of women who daily suffer the degradations and deprivations of sexual chauvinism in its institutionalized and individual forms. The suffering of women in general, third world women in particular, and especially the suffering of the Afrikan-american woman, hurts me in ways too numerous to delineate. Yet beyond the personal pain, there is a social reality which must be recognized, namely, that sexism is a means, used by our enemies, to help maintain our subjugation as a people.

Perhaps some are wondering why should an Afrikan-american man be concerned with an issue like women's rights, an issue which is often erroneously identified with "bored, middle class white women" who are tired of staying home. My response to that question is a query of my own: is there any reason why I shouldn't be concerned with women's rights, after all am I not born of woman, aren't we all born of woman?

I am concerned about the issue of women's rights because I understand that women's rights is a political issue and I am a political person. I understand that the oppression and exploitation of women is an integral aspect of every reactionary social system which ever existed and I am struggling to be a progressive. I understand that women, like land, are primary to life, and I am a living being.

I am concerned about the issue of women's rights because I am striving to be a revolutionary, and without the eradication of sexism there will be no true and thorough going revolution.

At this moment in history, asserting a position which I feel is my revolutionary responsibility to put forward, I hear the echoes of our heritage urging me to be firm. I hear Frederick Douglass, who also spoke out strongly in support of women's rights. Douglass was villified and shunned by former friends who could not understand his concern for the rights of women. I hear Douglass being called an "hermaphrodite" and other terms which questioned his sexuality because of his stand on sexism. But in the spirit of Frederick Douglass, I do declare that I too should rather be called "hermaphrodite" and other names because of my support for women's rights, than have women continually referred to as "bitch," and "broad" in everyday American speech.

There are those who argue that raising the issue of women's liberation is devisive of Black unity. They argue that, in reality, the women's movement drives a "wedge" between Black women and Black men in our social relationships. They argue that the promotion of women in the work force cuts down on the employment opportunities for men and effectively throws Black men out of work. They argue that Black women don't want to be lesbians and live with other women but rather that they want to be united with Black men and live together with Black men in peace and harmony. Some even argue that women should not work outside of the home because the work that they do of raising the children in the home is one of the most important tasks of nationbuilding or socialization. These are some of the arguements sincerely and seriously raised against our full and active involvement in the struggle for women's rights.

But the profound truth of the matter is that all of these arguments deny women the option to excercise their rights, to control their lives in whatever manner they see fit. Full rights for women does not ipso facto mean that women will all have to conform to some mythical "liberated norm." It means, instead, that women will decide for themselves their social lifestyles and social relationships.

Women's liberation has not driven a wedge betwen women and men. Firstly, women do not control this society. This society is controlled by a ruthless, racist, sexist, and capitalist patriarchy. If we would look past the propaganda pushed in the establishment press, we would clearly recognize whose hand is on the hammer attempting to beat us into submission, we would see who actually wields the wedge of division. To divide and conquer has always been a tactic of a minority who are opposing and exploiting a majority.

Secondly, issues such as "women's lib is denying or stopping Black men from getting jobs" is not true. We must understand that women do not do most of the hiring and firing in America. Women do not run the major or minor corporations. With very few exceptions, it is a man or some group of men, and usually white, who make those kinds of decisions.

We are all for the unity of our women with our men, but not if that unity is to be male superior/female inferior. The emotional crux of most of the arguments against women's liberation is, when mouthed by men, actually a fear of independent women, a hatred of independent women, an ideological opposition to any women being independent of a man's control. When espoused by women, most of those arguments simply amount to the attempts by an insecure woman, whose sense of self is that of an inferior entity, to maintain the certainties of a slavery she "thinks" she understands and to one degree or another has learned to cope with, rather than face a challenging liberation which she finds difficult to envision.

Cabral has noted that within the context of liberation struggle, the emancipation of women is a difficult issue; " . . . during the fight the important thing is the political role of women . . . It is all a part of the process of transformation, of change in the material conditions of the existence of our people, but also in the minds of the women, because sometimes the greatest difficulty is not only in the men but in the women too."[1]

In all of the contemporary national liberation movements in the Third World, whether in Africa, Asia, Latin America, Oceania or the Caribbean, great attention is always paid to the eradication of sexism and the development of women. Why is this the case?

Is sexism a universal constant? Is it true, as we have been taught, that beginning with Adam and Eve there has been a battle of the sexes going on, that one sex has, is and, in all probability, will continue to try to dominate the other sex? Do we really believe these fairy tales, these rationalizations? Do we really believe that men and women are "naturally" antagonistic to each other?

Sexism is not a biological necessity, it is rather the reflection of reactionary ideas, particularly "bourgeois individualism." In a bourgeois society, private ownership is the basic goal of most endeavors, whether it is to own land and material wealth, hence private property; or to own labor and industry, hence private enterprise in the form of capitalism; or to ultimately own other human beings, hence slavery and sexism. Couple this type of thinking with the belief that the individual is supreme, and what will result will be a society peopled by selfish and self-centered human beings who have no true concern for those around them or those who will follow them.

The roots of modern day sexism are to be found in "prehistoric" Europe and the trunk of sexism is a patriarchy watered by capitalism and imperialism. Understand that sexism is the systematic oppression and/or exploitation of a group of people based on the criterion of sex. In America today, and everywhere else where capitalism and imperialism have gone unchecked, unchallenged and unchanged, sexism is deeply entrenched into the social fabric. Indeed, in self proclaimed socialist societies also, remnants of sexism remain to be rooted out.

We do not have the time to analyze in detail my assertion that the roots of modern day sexism are found in prehistoric Europe. However, the statement, I am sure, is too provocative to most of us to be accepted simply at face value. So for purposes of brevity I sight a reference. The reference is *The Cultural Unity of Black Africa*, by Cheikh Anta Diop, published in America by Third World Press.[2]

Diop's book traces and analyzes the development of patriarchy and matriarchy, the class characteristics and clashes of the two social systems, the merging of the two, and the domination of patriarchy over matriarchy. At the risk of oversimplifying a complex topic, we summarize Diop's findings to include the positing of a two cradle concept. These two cradles are Aryan and African, northern and southern, patriarchal and matriarchal. According to Diop's analysis, which contests that of most social scientists, including Marx and Engles, matriarchy is not universal. The history of human development in its progressive movement did not go from matriarchy to patriarchy, for in fact, there never was a matriarchy in Europe. "As far as we can go back into the Indo-European past, even so far back as the Eurasian steppes, there is only to be found the patrilineal genos with the system of consanguinity which at the present day still characterized their descendents."

What is matriarchy? Is matriarchy the domination of women over men? Is matriarchy amazonism? Is matriarchy lesbianism? Is matriarchy strong women and weak men? No. Matriarchy is a social system within which blood relationships are traced through the maternal line and within which women enjoy equal political and economic rights.

Why should a wife and child assume the husband/father's name? Traditionally this was done for the purposes of the protection of property rights, namely the identification of property and the succession of property.

Today, we continue using this patriarchal form of naming alledgedly in order to identify the parents of children and vice versa. How unscientific to trace parentage via the father, when there is no known conclusive proof of male parentage. How much more scientific and simple it is to trace parentage via the mother, because regardless of whether the actual father of the child is known or unknown, the mother of the child is identified conclusively by the act of giving birth to that child.

In a patriarchal society, the concern is not with identifying parents but rather with identifying property, hence children born socalled "out of wedlock" are rarely given the same rights and protection as children born "in wedlock."

This is just one small example of the pervasivness and perverseness of the patriarchal social system. However, let us return to our central concern. Regardless of the roots of sexism, it should be clear that sexism is a real and reactionary way of life that must be eradicated.

Today, women continue to get less pay for equal work, and lack equal access to both educational and employment opportunities. Today, women continue to be regarded as the sexual toys of powerful men, men whose social relationships with women are controlled more by the heads of their penises than the heads on their shoulders, men whose main mode of reasoning conditions them to think that they can either buy or take a woman's body. Today, rape continues to be one of the most common and underreported crimes in America. Today, childcare continues to be virtually nonexistent and/or exorbitantly priced.

I view with dismay the return of sexually suggestive and nearly nude bodies of women used to sell commercial items, particularly consumable items such as cigarettes, liquor and automobiles, and leisure items such as films and records. Surely you have noticed that pornography is increasing at an alarming rate.

One sure sign of sexism is the objectification of women's bodies, the turning of women into commodities to be bought, sold, bartered for or stolen. The gains in women's rights, just as the gains in civil rights for Afrikan-americans, are seemingly becoming little more than paper formalities and highly touted token adjustments.

Afrikan-american women are still the most exploited stratum of american society. In fact, throughout the world, the lower class woman of color is on the bottom of nearly every society within which she is found.

Virtually every indicator of social inequality proves this to be the case, whether we are discussing employment or illness, educational development or access to leadership and decision making positions.

In conclusion, I urge that we open our eyes to the reality of sexism and fight it. I urge everyone, particularly men, to speak out against sexism and support the struggles of women to defend and develop themselves. I urge greater attention to be paid to the social and material conditions which lead to and reinforce sexism; a deeper and more accurate analysis needs to be done, and resolute and uncompromising action needs to be taken.

The denial of any human right is always based in the political repression of one group by another group. Sexism does not exist because women are "unclean during their monthly periods," nor because women are weaker than men, nor because "god" was unhappy with the behavior of women. Sexism exists because men have organized themselves to oppress and exploit women.

Sexism will be eradicated only through organized resistance and struggle. Women's rights will be won only when we consciously overturn all vestiges of patriarchy and "bourgosie" right. No person has the right to either own, oppress, enslave or exploit another person. Sexism is not a right, it is a wrong.

We must stand for what is right and fight against what is wrong.

My attempt has not been to analyze in detail the denial of human rights for women, rather I had a more modest goal in mind. I seek to place on the agenda of human rights the question of women's rights as a top priority item.

I hope that this topic has shown "pandora's box" to be a myth created by men who want to keep "women, coloreds, and other inferiors" hidden in the dank caves of injustice and reaction.

I hope that I have broadened the view on what human rights is, and indeed, on who human beings are. It is so easy in america to forget that women are human beings, to forget that women have rights. Hopefully, this presentation will stir up opposition to sexism, will bring women and men out of their shells of self-denial and isolation, and into the light of truth and justice.

It will not be easy to win rights for women, just as it will not be easy to defeat South Africa, just as it will not be easy to stop nuclear power, to clean up the environment, to end economic exploitation, to plan and control the economy, or to win national liberation for Afrikan-americans. But it can be done. Sexism can be smashed.

My hope is that from this day forward we will not hesitate to stand for women's rights, to place it on any and every agenda of progressive social development. Know that when you stand for women's rights you stand beside the most courageous and progressive people who have ever lived. You stand next to men and women who are not afraid of the future because they are willing to struggle in the present to correct historical wrongs.

A great woman by the name of Sojourner Truth once gave a brilliant speech which included the famous phrase "ain't I a woman!" This is continuance of that woman's work. In the spirit of Sojourner Truth, I urge you to join in the struggle for women's rights, whether you are woman or man. If Sojourner were here today she would challenge you in the same way. Sojourner is not here, but her spirit is. Although I ain't a woman, I say without hesitation that women's rights are human rights. I am committed to and call for the smashing of sexism and the securing of women's rights. I believe that we will win women's rights.

**NOTES**

1. Amilcar Cabral, "Return to the Source," *Monthly Review*, 1973, p. 85.
2. Cheikh A. Diop, *The Cultural Unity Of Black Africa*, Third World Press, 1959, p. 45.

# 10 GROUNDINGS WITH MY SISTERS
## Patriarchy and the Exploitation of Black Women

MANNING MARABLE

> ain't I a woman? Look at me! Look at my arm! . . . I have plowed,
> and planted, and gathered into barns, and no man could head
> me—and ain't I a woman? I could work as much as any man
> (when I could get it), and bear de lash as well—and ain't I a
> woman? I have borne five children and seen 'em mos all sold off
> into slavery, and when I cried out with a mother's grief, none but
> Jesus hear—and ain't I a woman?
>
> —SOJOURNER TRUTH, 1852

> We are the slaves of slaves; we are exploited more ruthlessly than
> men.
>
> —LUCY PARSONS, 1905

## I

Black women comprise a significant minority within the Black laboring
population, and have for many years experienced higher rates of unemployment than their male counterparts. Over one-third of all Black women are
officially classified as "poor" by the Federal government. This economic
profile graphically illustrates the effects of patriarchy, racism and capitalist
exploitation. But it does not begin to present the unique dimensions of the
Black woman's historical experience.

Black social history, as it has been written to date, has been profoundly patriarchal. The sexist critical framework of American white history has been accepted by Black male scholars; the reconstruction of our past, the reclamation of our history from the ruins, has been an enterprise wherein women have been too long segregated. Obligatory references are generally made to those "outstanding sisters" who gave some special contribution to the liberation of the "Black man." Even these token footnotes probably do more harm than good, because they reinforce the false belief that the most oppressed victim of white racial tyranny has been *the Black man*. It is true that the numerical majority of those Blacks who have been lynched, executed and forced to work in penal institutions have been males. But these numbers ignore a critical reality of racism and capitalist development. From the dawn of the slave trade until today, U.S. capitalism was both racist and deeply sexist. The superexploitation of Black women became a permanent feature in American social and economic life, because sisters were assaulted simultaneously as workers, as Blacks, and as women. This triple oppression escaped Black males entirely. To understand the history of all Blacks within the Black majority, the "domestic Black periphery," special emphasis is required in documenting the particular struggles, ideals and attitudes of Black women. To do less would be to reinforce capitalist patriarchy's ideological hegemony over the future struggles of all Black working people. Black male liberationists must relearn their own history, by grounding themselves in the wisdom of their sisters.

## II

During the entire slave period in the U.S. a brutal kind of equality was thrust upon both sexes. This process was dictated by the conditions of slave production within the overall process of capital accumulation in the South. Black women working in the fields on rice, sugar and cotton plantations were expected to labor at least twelve hours a day without complaint, breaking their backs just like their sons, husbands and fathers. Angela Davis has recognized that "the slave system could not confer upon the Black man the appearance of a privileged position vis-a-vis the Black woman." Since slavery itself was authoritarianism in the extreme, with the white slaveowner exercising physical violence to maintain political hegemony, no "family provider" or Black patriarch could be allowed. "The attainment of slavery's intrinsic goals was contingent upon the fullest and most brutal utilization of the productive capacities of every man, woman and child. The Black woman was therefore wholly integrated into the productive force."[1]

It must be remembered that the Afro-American slave was chattel: a thing, a privately owned commodity. Some slave masters tolerated the marriages of Blacks on their own farms or on their white neighbors' property to marry each other. But even the most "humane" master, when confronted with the inevitable economic declines that are a permanent feature of capitalism, would disrupt Black families by selling off a spouse or several children. "Here and there one can find sufficient respect for basic human rights or ample sentimentality to prevent the separation of families," John Hope Franklin indicates, "but it was not always good business to keep families together." Black women were sold separately to bring a more competitive price on the open market. Children over the age of fourteen were viewed as prime field hands, and were routinely taken from their mothers and fathers. Historians disagree on the precise number of families that were divided during slavery. One fair estimate is provided by Herbert Gutman, who describes the intersectional sale of slaves as "one of the great forced migrations in world history." 835,000 Afro-Americans were moved from the Upper South to Lower South between 1790 and 1860. Most of these persons were transported in the decades immediately before the Civil War, 575,000 slaves between 1830 and 1860. No fewer than one million Blacks were sold from 1820 to 1860, roughly one percent of the total slave population every year. Estimates of the number of Black women who were sold and thereby separated from their children, parents or husbands are, of course, difficult to assess. Gutman's work indicates that anywhere from 35 to 71 percent of marriage-age Black women who were sold in the interregional slave trade were involuntarily separated from their husbands. The public sale of young Black girls above the age of 12 who were bought to satisfy the sexual needs of white racist males was notorious. A few slavers even specialized in selling Black children between the ages of 8 to 12.[2]

One decisive form of oppression which befell the Black woman was slave breeding. Here again, the overwhelming majority of white male historians insist that either slave breeding did not exist or that it was rarely attempted by white planters. Usually this volatile term is employed narrowly to describe owner-coerced matings, where little actual documentation exists. However, the concept of slave breeding should be extended to mean all and any forms of slavery which, in Kenneth Stampp's definition, "indicate that slaves were reared with an eye to their marketability." Massive evidence exists illustrating that "many masters counted the fecundity of Negro women as an economic asset and encouraged them to bear children as rapidly as possible. Masters who prized prolific Negro women not only tolerated but sometimes came close to promoting sexual promiscuity among them."[3] Some white owners voided Blacks' marriages if they suspected that the men or women were sterile. In their own literature, Southern whites were absolutely candid about the centrality of slave breeding to the accumulation of profits. One Mississippian declared that fecund slave women "are the most profitable to their owners of any others . . . It is remarkable the number of slaves which may be raised from one woman in the course of forty or fifty years with the proper kind of attention."[4] Nearly every Black woman interviewed by Fannie Kemble in her 1838–1839 journal on slavery had a number of children. One woman under thirty had borne ten children and had subsequently developed a "nervous disorder, brought on by frequent childbearing." Venus, a mulatto slave "terribly crippled with rhematism," had "eleven children, five of whom had died, and two miscarriages."[5] U. B. Phillips observed that "one phenomenal slave mother bore forty-one children, mostly of course as twins; and the records of many others ran well above a dozen each."[6] One ingenious master, James Hammond of South Carolina, gave each of his Black slave mothers "a muslin or calico frock—but only when her newborn infant was thirteen months old." Another ordered that any Black "women with six children alive at any one time are allowed all Saturday to themselves."[7]

Many masters did not wait for the slaves themselves to reproduce in sufficient numbers, and took matters into their own hands. As property, Black women were expected to produce wealth for their owners. But as females, Black women were also constantly subjected to the physical and sexual assault of white males. As Angela Davis observed, "the integration of rape (into slavery) harks back to the feudal 'right of the first night,' the *jus primae noctis*. The feudal lord manifested and reinforced his authority to have sexual intercourse with all the females." In the context of American slavery, in the United States and elsewhere, the white man sought to reduce Black women to the lowest level of biological being. "The act of copulation, reduced by the white man to an animal-like act, would be symbolic of the effort to conquer the resistance the Black woman could unloose."[8] White American historians have usually been extremely reluctant to discuss this "normal" and universal aspect of any slave order. Brazilian sociologist Gilbert Freyre discussed the issue frankly with the initial observation that "there is no slavery without sexual depravity. Depravity is the essence of such a regime." Freyre noted that "one favorite saying of the planters was: 'The most productive feature of slave property is the generative belly.'"[9] Brazilian whites had a casual attitude toward syphilis and gonorrhea and had no reservations about spreading their affliction into Black households. From the age of thirteen, the white boy "was subject to ridicule for not having had carnal knowledge of a woman and would be the butt of jests if he could not show the scars of syphilis on his body." Many older white men believed that the only method to cure themselves of gonorrhea was to have intercourse with a young Black virgin—"the surest means of extinguishing it in oneself." Black women who wet-nursed white infants who were already infected by their parents "thus convey(ed) from the Big House to the slave hut the blight of syphilis. It killed, blinded, deformed at will."[10] Sadism and masochism were also an organic aspect of race relations, sometimes involving even small Black boys as well as females. Freyre noted that "the white lad was often initiated into the mysteries of 'physical love' through sexual games of submission wherein Black youths were forced to 'take a drubbing.'"[11]

White males who settled the United States lacked the cultural and historic relations which characterize the evolution of Portuguese and Spanish slave societies vis-a-vis Africans. Their racism was more aggressive; their neurotic fantasies were more repressively checked by the religious heritage of Calvinism and Puritanism; their knowledge of Black culture was more limited; their desire for profits, greater. For the white male American, the Black women's vagina was his private property. Like his cotton fields, the fruit of its issue belonged to him alone. His half-white child by the Black woman was usually treated just like any other slave. Raping the Black woman was not unlike plowing up fertile ground; the realities of plantation labor descended into the beds of the slaves' quarters, where the violent ritual of rape paralleled the harsh political realities of slave agricultural production. As Davis noted:

> In its political contours, the rape of the Black woman was not exclusively an attack upon her. Indirectly, its target was also the slave community as a whole.
>
> In launching the sexual war on the woman, the master could not only assert his sovereignty over a critically important figure of the slave community, he would also be aiming a blow against the Black man. . . . Clearly the master hoped that once the Black man was struck by his manifest inability to rescue his women from sexual assaults of the master, he would begin to experience deep-seated doubts about his ability to resist at all.[12]

Many Black women fought these repeated sexual assaults, and an untold number sacrificed their lives to retain their humanity. Many more carried the scars of their rapes, both physical and psychological, with them for the rest of their lives. The children of such coerced owner-slave unions, and the omnipresence of white rape, is indicated in part by the swelling number of mulattoes in the South before the Civil War. By 1850 there were 245,000 mulatto slaves; by 1860, 411,000 mulattoes out of an enslaved Black population of 3,900,000.[13]

For Black women, and their men, the only means to maintain their inner strength and integrity was through resistance. Black resistance assumed, first, the form of conscious, voluntary day-to-day protest: the destruction of agricultural implements, burning crops, stealing whites' personal food and property, deliberate slow-downs in the fields, and so forth. A number of Black women, far more than most Black historians have appreciated, ran away from their plantations or farms in search of freedom. Between 1736 and 1801 in Virginia alone, there were 141 documented instances of runaway African women. There was Hannah, a young woman of 19, "who when angered flashed a 'very passionate temper'"; Sarah, a "small and courageous girl of 14" who insisted in calling herself Mindingo; Milly, described by her owner as having grey eyes, "very large Breasts," and noted for being "a sly, subtle Wench, and a great Lyar." Cicley's master warned, "Beware to secure her Well, for she is very wicked and full of flattery." Only fifteen of the 141 women ran off in the company of slave men—a piece of evidence that indicates remarkable self-reliance in a patriarchal society. Yet many white owners, blinded by their entrenched sexism, could not contemplate that

Black women by themselves would thirst for liberation. In 1772, a typical master lamented about one African woman who departed with her husband, "I imagine she is entirely governed by him."[14]

The greatest indictment against slavery and white Southern patriarchy came from the voices of Black women. Jane Blake's *Memoirs*, written in 1897, provides all the evidence one needs to illustrate that slave breeding existed. Many slave women refused to have sex with men they did not love, and fought the sexual advances of their white owners. Blake wrote, if "all the bond women had been of the same mind, how soon the institution could have vanished from the earth, and all the misery belonging to it."[15] Jane Brown's *Narrative* of 1856 asserted that virtually every slave longed for freedom, and that both freed and enslaved Blacks covertly discussed rebellion.[16] Louisa Picquet was forced to become a concubine for white men. In her 1861 narrative, *Inside Views of Southern Domestic Life*, she argued that sexual exploitation of Black women constituted the core of white Southern hypocrisy. She observed that U.S. whites oppose the "heathenism of a Turkish harem. (But) is all this whit worse than what is constantly practiced, with scarce a word of unfavorable comment, in our Christian land? Our chivalrous 'southern gentlemen' beget thousands of slaves; and hundreds of children of our free white citizens are sold in the southern slave markets every year."[17] When the moment of freedom arrived, Black women understood better than anyone else the *ancien regime* of rape and labor exploitation was at an end. The story of one young Black woman named Caroline Gordon, or "Caddy," bears witness:

> Caddy had been sold to a man in Goodman, Mississippi. It was terrible to be sold in Mississippi. In fact, it was terrible to be sold anywhere. She had been put to work in the fields for running away again. She was hoeing a crop when she heard that General Lee surrendered . . . that meant that all the colored people were free! Caddy threw down that hoe, she marched herself up to the big house, then, she looked around and found the mistress. She went over to the mistress, she flipped up her dress and told the white woman to do something. She said it mean and ugly: *Kiss my ass!*[18]

## III

From the very beginning of Black political activism in the United States, Afro-American men had real difficulty in considering the "triple oppression" (race/class/sex) of Black women with any degree of seriousness. Part of the problem stemmed from the evolution of patriarchal institutions within Black civil society. Black churches in the free states were involved in a variety of reform activities, from the creation of economic enterprises to the building of a network of Black schools. But these churches were invariably dominated by Black men, who served as pastors, evangelists and deacons. Black mutual benefit societies, first started in Newport, Rhode Island and Philadelphia, gave members recreational facilities, provided families with modest economic protection in case of sickness or death, and created the foundations for Black business development. Yet the major societies were funded, directed and controlled by Black males. The Black newspapers established in the nineteenth century, including John Russwurm's *Freedom's Journal* (1827), Martin Delany's *Mystery* (1843), Frederick Douglass' *North Star* (1848) and the *Anglo-African* of New York City (1859), tended to print the antislavery speeches, manifestos and essays of articulate Black men. The Negro Convention Movement, a series of Black political conferences beginning in 1830 in Philadelphia, almost always involved only Black men.

Many Black male activists identified the cause of Black liberation with the ultimate attainment of "Black manhood." This definition of freedom was a conditioned response evoked by white patriarchy, whether the Black men of the period recognized this or not. Henry Highland Garnet's famous "Address to the Slaves of the United States," delivered at the 1843 Negro Convention specifically called upon every Black "man" to "resist aggression." "In every man's mind the good seeds of liberty are planted, and he who brings his fellow down so long, as to make him contented with a condition of slavery, commits the highest crime against God and man." Garnet's audience was reminded of the racists' transgressions upon its manhood:

> See your sons murdered, and your wives, mothers and sisters doomed to prostitution . . . And worse than all, you tamely submit while your lords tear your wives from your embraces and defile them before your eyes. In the name of God, we ask, are you men? Where is the blood of your fathers? Has it all run out of your veins?[19]

Radical newspaper editor T. Thomas Fortune condemned whites as "the most consummate masters of hypocrisy, of roguery, of insolence, and of cowardice" in an 1887 polemic. Fortune was quick to add, however, that "many imagine that we are compelled to submit and have not the manhood necessary to resent such conduct. We shall labor as one man to wage relentless opposition to all men who would degrade our manhood."[20] Pan-African scholar and clergyman Alexander Crummell reminded Blacks that the chief aim of civilization was the creation "of a true and lofty race of men. For manhood is the most majestic thing in God's creation."[21] Even Frederick Douglass, the leading male proponent of women's rights in the nineteenth century, asserted in 1855 that the struggle for racial liberation meant that Blacks "must develop their manhood, and not be too modest to attempt such development."[22]

Douglass was exceptional among all Black male activists in his open commitment to equality for women. Soon after his flight to freedom in the North, he identified himself with militant white and Black women in their struggle for suffrage and legal rights. In the initial issue of the *North Star*, he drew the obvious political parallels between the battles against racism and sexism, declaring that "Right is of no sex." He attended the first national women's rights convention held at Seneca Falls, New York, in July, 1848, and seconded the motion of Elizabeth Cady Stanton calling for women's voting rights. Douglass was the only male of thirty-seven men in attendance who supported women's suffrage. Douglass' advocacy for feminist causes was so well-known that both Stanton and Lucretia Mott urged women to elect him as a leader of their movement only two weeks after Seneca Falls. Susan B. Anthony notified friends to purchase the *North Star* "for announcements of women's rights gatherings." Douglass' partial break with white feminists occurred after the Civil War, when Anthony, Stanton and others opposed the ratification of the Fifteenth Amendment unless it also mandated universal suffrage. Politically pragmatic, Douglass urged his followers to support the winning of Black male voting rights first. By 1869, the Equal Rights Association split, and many white feminists began to gravitate toward racist slogans to support their own cause.[23]

The struggle to destroy slavery, and the economic and political battles of Reconstruction, coincided with the entrenchment of patriarchal relations within the Black community. The rough equality of labor imposed by the brutalities of the slave regime did not extend into the slaves' quarters. Black men universally "regarded tasks like cooking, sewing, nursing, and even minor farm labor as woman's work," according to bell hooks. Black women after slavery seldom demanded social equality between themselves and their men. "Instead, they bitterly resented that they were not considered 'women' by the dominant culture. . . . "[24] With the establishment of sharecropping, the majority of Black women farm laborers and farmers ceased work in the fields, and retreated into the kitchens and homes of their families. They expected, as a point of honor and as an element of freedom, that they would be supported by their husbands, fathers and brothers. "White plantation owners were shocked when large numbers of Black female workers refused to work in the fields."[25] Statistically this is illustrated by Census figures from 1890. Slightly less than half of all Black women between the ages of 15 to 24 years were employed in 1890; about half were domestic workers, and the remainder were field hands or farmers. Less than 40 percent of all Black women between the ages of 25 to 64 were workers, compared to 97–98 percent of all Black males. Of course, fewer white women were gainfully employed than Black women. Only 14 percent of all white women 10 years old and over were in the 1890 workforce, and the percentage dropped to 10 percent and below after age 35. Denied the right to work outside the home, the majority of Black women were expected to fulfill the "traditional" role of "mother" by giving birth to as many children as physically possible. For Black married women born between 1861 and 1865, the average number of children born to them by 1910 was 6.2.

Although the Victorian era was inhospitable to intelligent and politically active females, a number of Black women succeeded in overcoming the institutional barriers of white and Black patriarchy. Frances Ellen Watkins Harper established herself as the nineteenth century's most popular Black poet/activist. Born in Baltimore of free parents in 1824, she became involved in the Underground Railroad, the illegal network by which slaves were channelled North. In September, 1854, the Maine Anti-Slavery Society recognized her talents as an orator and hired her to speak across New England. In 1857–1858 she worked for the Pennsylvania Anti-Slavery Society, speaking two or three times each day for the cause of Black freedom, attracting "large, enthusiastic audiences." In 1860 she married a Black Ohio farmer, Fenton Harper, and retired for several years to have a child. Within five months of her husband's death in 1864, Harper was again on the lecture circuit, speaking in support of the war effort. From 1865 until 1871 Harper travelled throughout the Southern United States at her own expense, living on meager donations, speaking endlessly "at Sunday schools, day schools, churches, town meetings, in homes and village squares," usually talking twice daily. During these years she also authored several popularly acclaimed books of poetry and wrote articles for the press. In the 1870s she became Assistant Superintendent of the YMCA school in Philadelphia, and was elected national officer in the National Council of Women and the National Association of Colored Women. Until her death in 1911, Harper was a noted advocate of women's suffrage, equal rights and Black freedom.[26]

Sojourner Truth was, probably only second to Douglass, the outstanding orator of Black liberation during the mid-century. Born as "Isabella" in Ulster County, New York in 1797, she was one of twelve slave children who were sold away from their parents. Married at an early age, she gave birth to five children before she was freed; one of her sons was sold by her owner to an Alabama slavemaster. In 1843, she began to speak out on her personal ordeal as a slave at abolitionist gatherings, and assumed the name Sojourner Truth. During the Civil War Sojourner lived and worked in the "contraband" camps of Washington, D.C., teaching former slaves. She aided Black women "to protect their children against white Maryland raiders who sought to kidnap them and sell them into slavery."[27] Appointed to work with the Freedman's hospital in Washington, she led the struggle to bar Jim Crow public transportation in the capital. In the late 1860s, Sojourner returned to the lecture circuit, speaking out in favor of a massive relocation of Black families from the South into the Great Plains states. In her view, no Black political solution was possible without a general reallocation of land. In 1879, Sojourner joined the wave of "Exodusters" who fled the post-Reconstruction era South and settled in Kansas City. Unlike most Black male leaders, she urged her people to buy land and to develop a sufficient economic base from which to wage their various struggles for social and political justice. One of the central tragedies of this period is that so few Black politicians listened seriously to Sojourner's ideas on Black economic development. Their ingrained sexism made it impossible, perhaps, for Black men to internalize the agenda of an eighty-two year old Black woman.

Two of the most progressive Black activists during the post-Reconstruction period of political accommodation were Ida B. Wells and Mary Church

Terrell. Wells was born in 1862, in Holly Springs, Mississippi and was educated at Rust College and Fisk University. Arriving in Memphis in the early
1880s, she soon acquired the reputation as the Black South's most militant
journalist. Purchasing partial ownership in the Memphis *Free Speech and
Headlight,* she used the press in a campaign against Southern lynchings. In
a controversial editorial, she observed that "Nobody in this section of the
country believes the old threadbare lies that Negro men rape white women.
If Southern white men are not careful they will over-reach themselves and
public sentiment will have a reaction, or a conclusion will be reached which
will be very damaging to the moral reputation of their women." Wells' documentary on the near genocidal violence against Blacks, *United States Atroci-
ties* (1893), is a valuable precursor to the works of William Patterson and
Sidney Willhelm six decades later.[28] Mary Church Terrell was the daughter
of Robert R. Church of Memphis, a Southern Black real estate millionaire
and political leader. Educated at Oberlin College, she taught at Wilberforce
before settling in Washington, D.C. and, in 1891, marrying Robert H. Terrell, a lawyer and the principal of the District's M. Street High School. Mary
Terrell was appointed a member of the Washington, D.C. Board of Education, and quickly became a leading critic of Booker T. Washington—the
Black politician whom her husband closely supported. In fact, she created
such a furor that one of the Tuskegeean's hacks penned a *New York Age*
editorial declaring bitterly that "some one ought to muzzle Mary Church
Terrell. What we now want as a race, is less agitators and more constructors."
Terrell joined the NAACP and was promptly elected vice president of the
Washington branch. In later years, Terrell became politically quite conservative, serving as director of the Republican National Committee's campaign to reach Black women voters on the East coast in 1920 and 1932.
However, despite her support for Hoover and the Republican Party, Terrell
continued to fight racial discrimination and Jim Crow laws until her death.[29]

The first half of the twentieth century produced a new generation of
creative and intellectually prolific Black women in education and the arts.
Jessie Redmond Fauset, born in 1886, became famous both as the translator
of Black poetry from the French West Indies, and for her novels *There is
Confusion* (1924), *Plum Bun* (1929), and *The Chinaberry Tree* (1931). Georgia Douglass Johnson was perhaps the most popular Black poet between
Paul Laurence Dunbar and the rise of the Harlem Renaissance bards of the
1920s. Novelist Nella Larsen's *Quicksand* (1928) and *Passing* (1929) exam-
ined the "innumerable social problems of young Negro women in their
efforts to struggle upward both in America and in Europe."[30] Meta War-
rick Fuller became renowned as a brilliant and innovative sculptor; Laura
Wheeler Waring gained fame as a painter. Actresses Ida Anderson, Edna
Thomas and Laura Bowman performed to rave reviews in Harlem's all-
Black Lafayette Players' group during the 1920s. Among the most creative
Black minds in aesthetics during the Great Depression was unquestionably
Zora Neale Hurston—cultural anthropologist, novelist, essayist and folk-

lorist. In a brief period of twelve years she authored seven important novels. In education and politics, Black women were ably represented by Mary McLeod Bethune. Founder of Cookman College in 1905, she became a master fund raiser and proponent of higher education for young Black women. During the 1930s Bethune was named Director of the Division of Negro Affairs for the National Youth Administration. In 1945 she was one of several Blacks named as members of the United States delegation at the creation of the United Nations in April, 1945, in San Francisco.[31]

The decades after 1900 until the 1940s also produced gradual changes within both the employment patterns of Black women and in the size of Black families. More Black women were in the labor force than there were immediately after slavery: about 47 percent during the prime working ages of 20 to 54. Roughly twice the percentage of Black women were gainfully employed in 1930 as were white women (39 percent vs. 20 percent). By 1940, Black married women averaged only 2.3 children, the lowest number ever recorded for Blacks by the U.S. Census. Most married women were waiting longer to have their children, and between 22 to 29 percent of middle aged Black women were not bearing any children at all. The number of children ever born per married Black woman was reduced during this time by 53 percent. Black families during World War II were still slightly larger than those of whites, but as the Black woman acquired greater opportunities for post-secondary education, the number of her children dropped sharply. In 1940, married nonwhite women with one to three years of college training averaged only 1.7 children. With four or more years of college, nonwhite women had only 1.2 children — both figures that were below those for white college trained women. More frequently than ever before, Black women were leaving the kitchens and earning their own wages in the labor force. Black women appeared no longer as "auxilliaries" or marginal participants in Black educational, social and political life. The leading figures of Bethune, Terrell, Hurston and others provided abundant role models for young Black girls to abandon the yoke of subordination and sexual subservience.

During these years, among Black men, W. E. B. Du Bois largely filled the role of Douglass as the chief proponent of women's equality. Du Bois' commitment to women's rights began as early as 1887, when as editor of the *Fisk Herald* he predicted that "the Age of Woman is surely dawning."[32] In his essays in the *Crisis* and other periodicals, Du Bois emphasized that the struggle for Black freedom must inevitably include the demand for "the emancipation of women."[33] Constantly he chided Blacks for exhibiting any form of favoritism toward males over females. When one reader of the *Crisis* reported the birth of a girl, Du Bois suggested "the ancient idea that boys are intrinsically and naturally better than girls is a relic of barbarism that dies a hard death ... Be glad it's a girl and make life wider and safer and more equal in burden for all girls because of this one."[34] The patriarchal attitudes of politicians was a particularly favorite topic for this Black scholar. "Every statesman who yells about Children, Church and Kitchen," he declared in January, 1934, "ought to be made to bear twins, to listen to as many sermons as we have, and to wash dishes and diapers for at least ten years."[35] In 1912 Du Bois drafted a pamphlet entitled *Disfranchisement*, published by the National American Woman Suffrage Association, which advanced women's right to vote as a necessary precondition to the realization of democracy.[36] In states where universal enfranchisement was on the ballot, Du Bois encouraged Black men to cast their support behind the women's rights movement. "Is there a single argument for the right of men to vote, that does not apply to the votes for women, and particularly for black women?"[37] Although he was friendly toward feminist causes, Du Bois would not hesitate to criticize the racism found within the white women's political movement. In several *Crisis* articles, he condemned some leaders of the "Suffering Suffragettes" who advocated that white women, and not Blacks, should be allowed to vote.[38] Despite these differences, Du Bois enthusiastically supported the moves of women from the kitchens into the factory and business world. In March, 1941, he pointed with pride that many more Black women were in the labor force than white women. In January, 1947, he urged Black husbands to "share housework" and to shoulder the burdens of child-rearing equally.[39] For half a century, he reminded Black men that "the hope of the Negro rests on its intelligent and incorruptible womanhood."[40]

In contrast with Du Bois, however, many Black men were disturbed with the evolutionary transformation in sex roles and the creation of political, educational and economic opportunities for Black women. Marcus Garvey's political approach toward Black women's issues was a curious mixture of romanticism, sexism and race nationalism. In the 1923 edition of the *Philosophy and Opinions of Marcus Garvey*, the Jamaican militant suggested that women were necessary yet contradictory beings: "She makes one happy, then miserable. You are to her kind, then unkind. Constant yet inconstant. Thus we have WOMAN. No real man can do without her."[41] Like the Black activists of the nineteenth century, Garvey identified Black struggle with the attainment of manhood, the realization of a kind of masses' macho. He warned his followers, "There is always a turning point in the destiny of every race, every nation, of all peoples and we have come now to the turning point of the Negro, where we have changed from the old cringing weakling, and transformed into full-grown men, demanding our portion as MEN."[42] In his *Blackman* journal, he cautioned affluent Black women not to marry white men, and urged Black men not to "insult our womanhood" by having sexual relations with whites.[43] Garvey was profoundly concerned with statistics that showed a declining number of children in Black households. "By a decreasing birth rate and an increasing death rate," he warned in October, 1925, "it means the death of your race—the suicide of your race."[44] In 1934, Garvey's Universal Negro Improvement Association issued a resolution condemning birth control for Blacks. "Any attempt to interfere with the natural function of life is a rebellion against the conceived purpose of divinity in making man a part of his spiritual self," the sexist manifesto declared. "The theory of birth control . . . interfered with the course of nature and with the purpose of the God in whom we believe."[45] Simultaneously, Du Bois authored a stirring statement endorsing planned parenthood in *Birth Control Review*, and invited Margaret Sanger, a "birth-control pioneer," to contribute to the pages of the *Crisis.*[46]

From the 1930s to the 1950s, a number of Black men raised serious questions pertaining to the declining birth rate among Black women. University of Chicago pathologist Julian Lewis argued in 1945 that "the survival of the black race in the United States was dependent upon a high birth rate." In subsequent articles, Lewis attacked the Planned Parenthood Federation for attempting to "improve the quality of the human race at the cost of numbers." Blacks who condoned birth control were sponsoring "race suicide."[47] Some Blacks noted with apprehension that some states had sanctioned castrations and vasectomies on prison inmates and patients in mental hospitals in the 1890s, and suggested that racists now might be using birth control as a legal means to reduce the Black population. These fears were reinforced when a Mississippi state legislator introduced a bill in 1958 which would "provide for mandatory sterilization after a woman on welfare (had) given birth to a certain number of illegitimate children." By 1964 the Mississippi house ratified a law that "stipulated that any person who became the parent of a second out-of-wedlock child would be guilty of a felony punishable by a sentence of one to three years in the state penitentiary. A subsequent conviction would be punishable by three to five years in prison. However, a convicted parent had the option of submitting to sterilization in lieu of imprisonment."[48] White Republicans and Democrats alike, particularly in the South, proposed punitive sterilization for Black welfare mothers. These same male politicians had no reservations, however, in denying legal abortions or contraceptive information to Black (or white) teenage girls and women.

Conservative Black nationalist formations often surpassed white reactionaries in their opposition to birth control. An extreme case is provided by the Nation of Islam. Patriarch Elijah Muhammad informed Black followers that their women were unprepared for the "tricks the devils are using to instill the idea of a false birth control in their clinics and hospitals." Black women were created by God to serve their husbands and sons. "The woman is man's field to produce his nation," Elijah Muhammad observed. The Nation of Islam's ministers frequently attacked Black women and men who supported freedom of choice regarding birth control. Minister Louis Farrakhan wrote in a Black woman's publication, *Essence*, that "when the black woman kills her unborn child, she is murdering the advancement of her nation." One *Muhammad Speaks* article declared that population control was a covert tactic in the general "war against the nonwhite people." Muslim woman

Shirley Hazziez wrote in *Muhammad Speaks* that every Black woman should reject the pill as a "deadly poison," and that "Allah was able to feed and care for black infants." Birth control was, for the Black woman, "death for my babies and race."[49]

Well before the Civil Rights Movement, a not-so-subtle reaction began to form within Black civil society which reinforced patriarchal relations between men and women. The Depression and war years produced within the popular culture the figure of Sapphire: a Black woman who was "evil, treacherous, bitchy, stubborn, and hateful." The Sapphire stereotype was utilized by white males, who "could justify their dehumanization and sexual exploitation of black women," and by Black males, who could reasonably "claim that they could not get along with black women because they were so evil." Black patriarchal society employed Sapphire to explain away any Black woman who exhibited tendencies of strength that were designated for males only.[50] Furthermore, as greater numbers of Black women left agricultural work for domestic service employment, many Black men leaped to the illogical conclusion that white males "favored black women over black men" in all levels of the job market. As hooks observed, "white people did not perceive black women engaging in service jobs as performing significant work that deserved adequate economic reward. They saw domestic service jobs performed by black women as being merely an extension of the 'natural' female role and considered such jobs valueless." Unemployed Black men, desperate for work, perceived their wives' ability to gain employment an assault on their own manhood. At another level, Black women who adopted patriarchal perspectives "saw the black male who did not eagerly assume the breadwinner role as selfish, lazy, and irresponsible, or in white male sociological terms, 'emasculated'."[51] These cultural, social and economic forces combined after 1945 to produce the conditions for a fundamental reaction.

Within the U.S. economy, this reaction was apparent in civilian labor force participation rates between 1945 and 1960. During the early 1940s, tens of thousands of Black women went into jobs previously held by men. By the end of World War II, almost half of all Black women (46 percent) were employed full-time, compared to only 31 percent of all white women. Fifty-one to 53 percent of Black women between the ages of 25 and 54 were wage earners. Sixty percent of the Black women were employed as private household workers, 7 percent were blue-collar laborers, and 16 percent were farmers or farm laborers. Fifteen years later, the percentage of Black women workers outside the home had increased by only 2 percent, while white women workers increased by 6 percent. Only 22 percent of all nonwhite teenage women who were actively in the job market could find work in 1960, compared to 30 percent for white female teenagers. By 1965, Black females with an eighth-grade education or less had a labor force participation rate of only 38 percent.[52] Black men encouraged their wives and daughters to settle back, to return to the kitchen: the role of the husband was that of provider, and the task of wives was to produce offspring. After 1945, the birth rates for Black women climbed sharply. The percentage of all Black married women between the ages of 20 and 24 years who had two to four children increased from 34 percent in 1940 to 51 percent in 1960; in that same age group, those women with five or more children grew from 2 percent to 7 percent. The percentage of all Black married women between the ages of 25 and 29 who had five or more children doubled in two decades, from 11 percent in 1940 to 22 percent in 1960. Overall the number of children born per married Black woman increased from 2.3 percent in 1940 to 2.8 percent in 1960. Even outside of marriage, the number of Black children born during this period increased dramatically. The rate of child-births for nonmarried nonwhite women per thousand, for women between ages 25 and 29, increased from 32.5 in 1940 to 171.8 in 1960. Black fertility rates, which declined from 3.56 in 1920 to 2.62 in 1940, rebounded to 3.58 in 1950 and reached 4.54 by 1960.[53] No Black female could become a real woman, in short, unless she had a child. Work outside the home should be a secondary goal. Black unmarried teenage girls could become women by bearing children "for the race."

## IV

Sudden changes in the consciousness of oppressed people are often reflected in their poetry: the sexual and racial conflicts of the 1960s provided new directions for Black Americans in the arts. Occasionally, both Black liberation and patriarchal themes were woven together by the new Black women poets. Nikki Giovanni asked all Black men and women alike to develop their "manhood":

> Can you kill
> Can you piss on a blond head
> Can you cut [it] off
> Can you kill . . .
> Can you splatter their brains in the street
> Can you lure them to bed to kill them . . .
> Can we learn to kill WHITE for BLACK
> Learn to kill niggers
> Learn to be Black men.[54]

In "Beautiful Black Men," written in 1968, Giovanni praised "those beautiful beautiful outasight black men with their afros . . . " Her "brand new pleasure" was observing her men "running numbers, watching for their whores, preaching in churches," and "winking at me" in their "tight tight pants that hug what I like to hug."[55] Other Black women embraced the image of the Black man as the urban guerilla, and created love poetry that expressed simultaneously their fertility and sensuality for their men:

> My old man
> tells me i'm

> so full of sweet
> pussy he can
> smell me coming.
> maybe i shd
> bottle it and
> sell it
> when he goes.[56]

Along more traditional romantic lines, poet Alice Lovelace's "Wedding Song" informs her husband-to-be: "You are my man/The part I've sought that makes me whole . . . we'll raise bubbling black babies/swathed in black culture."[57] Carolyn Rogers' "For Some Black Men" counsels her brothers to recognize the inherent dependency and submissiveness of sisters: "Woman is softness, warm of warmth, need from need."[58]

Among some Black women intellectuals, there was at one point a curious inversion of the "pedestal phenomenon," the cultural dynamic wherein white males had symbolically elevated white women to the heights of aesthetic and social predominance. These sisters not only acknowledged the innate or biological leadership of Black men, but literally placed their faith, their ontological existence, within the hegemonic corpus of the Black male. Romanticists were usually the worst offenders. Poet Ann DuCille's "Lady in Waiting" combined the African mythology of the cultural nationalists with the sexist acceptance of the woman-as-womb:

> In dreams without sleep
> I lie inside myself
> waiting to be born . . .
> I am a princess
> goddess of the Nile
> Nubian daughter of Nefertiti . . .
> unsung
> yet tuned in time
> to take the milk of man
> between my thighs.[59]

Other Black women poets who reflected critically about their own "integrationist contradictions" sang high hosannas to the Black militant men who had delivered them from their former political beliefs. Lucille Clifton's "apology (to the panthers)" is reminiscent of a Catholic chant, evoking one's spiritual weaknesses before the holy altar, requesting absolution for the remission of sins:

> I was obedient
> but brothers i thank you
> for these mannish days.
> . . . brothers
> i thank you
> i praise you
> i grieve my whiteful ways.[60]

Most Black men accepted these *mea culpas* in stride. "The role of the black woman in the black liberation is an important one and cannot be forgotten," Black sociologist Robert Staples wrote in 1970. "From her womb have come the revolutionary warriors of our time."[61] Thus, the Black woman's most significant factor to contribute to the Movement, in short, was her uterus.

But behind these glowing exhaltations of the Black man there remained the bitter embers of sexual oppression and subordination. Half-hidden even during Black Power's hey-day, but becoming ever more dominant into the 1970s, were the contradictory stirrings of a Black feminist criticism. Often these expressions began in the form of an attack on all "brothers" who chose to have sexual relations with white females. Sonia Sanchez's "to all brothers" is a clear warning:

> yeah.
> they hang you up
> those grey chicks
> parading their tight asses
> in front of you.
> Some will say out right
> baby I want
> to ball you
> while smoother ones
> will integrate your
> blackness
> yeah.
> brother
> this sister knows
> and waits.[62]

And in her finest work, "Woman Poem," Giovanni illustrates the basic exploitation of Black women within a patriarchal and racist social order:

> a sex object if you're pretty
> and no love
> or love and no sex if you're fat
> get back fat black woman be a mother
> grandmother strong thing but not woman
> manseeker dick eater sweat getter
> fuck needing love seeking woman.[63]

Poet/playwright Ntozake Shange, author of *For Colored Girls Who Have Considered Suicide When the Rainbow is Enuf,* was one of the first major writers to examine the problems of abortion, alienation between Black women and men, and the hostilities between Black women over males.

> she been there for years wid this dude
> but he needed a change and well, she wd manage
> nothin gonna last forever/
> but i hesitated cuz she seemed so fragile

i wax fulla vitality and gall
'get ridda that bitch or leave me alone'
he did.
i ignored all that talk bout the woman who tried to
burn herself alive/waznt none of my business
what some weak bitch did to herself.[64]

The obvious contradictions relating the issues of race and gender within these and other poems were, of course, a product of the turbulent politics of the period. The Civil Rights Movement had begun coming unglued by 1964, with the successful desegregation of Southern civil society. Young Black women and men, the vanguard of freedom fighters in the Student Nonviolent Coordinating Committee (SNCC), rejected integration as "subterfuge for the maintenance of white supremacy."[65] Black nationalism as a cultural and political expression was seized by substantial elements of the Black petty bourgeoisie and working class. Across the country, hundreds of new political and educational institutions were created that were developed within the specious theoretical framework of Black Power. Yet remarkably few Black activists elevated the question of sexism to the level of primacy, within their practical political activities or in their intellectual work. Patriarchy had been historically more compatible with most Black nationalist groupings than among cultural pluralists or even integrationists. As a result, it is not surprising that the actual practice of Black militants did precious little to overturn the rampant sexism within Black life.

The fountainhead of contemporary Black nationalism, Malcolm X, was likewise not immune from this dynamic. For many young Black militants, both in the streets and the universities, Malcolm symbolized the best that Black humanity had produced. Black actor Ossie Davis eulogized Malcolm at his funeral, declaring that he "was our manhood . . . our own black shining Prince—who didn't hesitate to die, because he loved us so."[66] Though Malcolm's views on Black women changed considerably for the better throughout his life, like so many other male leaders, he usually thought of politics as a preserve for men only; sisters were an invaluable but secondary factor in the race war. Even today, any serious criticism of Malcolm's views is akin to traitorous behavior in most Black activist circles. But it serves Malcolm's memory poorly if we simply reify the entire body of his ideas and actions without a detailed and serious analysis of his own contradictions. As bell hooks observes, "it is impossible to read his autobiography without becoming aware of the hatred and contempt he felt toward women for much of his life."[67] At one point in his discussions with Alex Haley, the Black novelist/ journalist, Malcolm admitted that "you never can fully trust any woman":

> I've got the only one I ever met whom I would trust seventy-five percent. I've told her that. . . .Too many men (have been) destroyed by their wives, or their women. Whatever else a woman is, I don't care who the woman is, it starts with her being vain. I'll prove it . . . You think of the hardest-looking, meanest-acting woman you know, one of those women who never smiles. Well, every

day you see that woman you look her right in the eyes and tell her 'I think
you're beautiful,' and you watch what happens. The first day she may curse
you out, the second day, too—but you watch, you keep on, after a while one
day she's going to start smiling just as soon as you come in sight.[68]

Malcolm X was not the only, and certainly not the worst of the Black
Power leaders with respect to the issue of gender. For Stokely Carmichael,
leader of SNCC in 1966, young Black men had to assert themselves as
males—politically, and sexually. "Every Negro is a potential black man,"
Carmichael taught nascent activists.[69] Black militants cultivated a righteous
contempt for white women as a *sine qua non* of activist practice. When
whites asked Carmichael if integration meant interracial marriage, he replied that "the white woman is not the queen of the world, she is not the
Virgin Mary, she can be made like any other woman."[70] The revolutionary
responsibilities of sisters in the cause of Black liberation were somewhat
different. In a speech given at Morgan State on January 28, 1967, Carmichael outlined his thoughts on Black women:

> Girls, are you ready? Obviously it is your responsibility to begin to define the
> criteria for black people concerning their beauty. You are running around with
> your Nadinola cream. The black campuses of this country are becoming in-
> fested with wigs and Mustangs and you are to blame for it. You are to blame for
> it. What is your responsibility to your fellow black brothers? So that you can
> become a social worker or so that you can kick down a door in the middle of
> the night to look for a pair of shoes? Is that what you come to college for? . . .
> Is it so that you can just get over? Do you not know that your black mothers
> scrubbed floors so you can get here—and the minute you get out, you turn
> your back on them?[71]

Like the Garveyites, many later-day nationalists vigorously opposed contraceptives, abortions and planned parenthood measures. In 1970, Brenda
Hyson, a female leader of the Black Panthers, attacked a New York state law
which made legal abortions available to Black and poor women. The "oppressive ruling class will use this law to kill off Blacks and other opposed people before they are born," Hyson warned. Voluntary abortions would lead to
forced sterilization. Black women had a political responsibility to oppose
"legalized murder" and forced "family planning in the guise of pills and
coils." The *Black News*, a nationalist publication based in Brooklyn, described birth control for sisters as "deceptive genocide" in one 1971 essay.
Black women were too frequently "duped into having unnecessary hysterectomies and surgical sterilization." For the survival of "the Black man," Black
women would have to put away all forms of contraceptives—even the traditional and most unreliable device, the condom. "The hidden meaning of
the Trojan," *Black News* declared, "was to emasculate the Black man by convincing him that he should throw away his living sperm into the white man's
rubber contraption rather than to put it into his woman's fertile womb."[72]
Haki Madhubuti, director of Chicago's Black Nationalist Institute of Positive Studies, argued that "the entire white system is geared toward the total

destruction of the *Black man first*—mentally, physically and spiritually. If the Black man is not allowed to take care of and build his family, where is the Black woman?" Zero population growth campaigns and liberal abortion laws would destroy the Black race.[73]

No single Black activist was more profoundly sexist than the celebrated ex-convict/writer of the Black Panther Party, Eldridge Cleaver. His infamous and bizarre expositions against Black women, gays, and others need no re-counting here.[74] What is most important about Cleaver's writing is that it falls squarely into the century-old tradition of viewing Black liberation first and last as the effort to assert one's manhood, in the sense of patriarchal hegemony exhibited by the old planter class. In a pathetic passage, Cleaver contemplates the impact of white racism upon the Black male:

> Across the naked abyss of negated masculinity, of four hundred years minus my Balls, we face each other today, my Queen. I feel a deep, terrifying hurt, the pain of humiliation of the vanquished warrior. For four hundred years I have been unable to look squarely into your eyes . . . Instead of inciting the slaves to rebellion with eloquent oratory, I soothed their hurt and eloquently sang the Blues! Instead of hurling my life with contempt into the face of my Tormentor, I shed your precious blood! My spirit was unwilling and my flesh was weak. . . . Divested of my Balls, (I) walked the earth with my mind locked in Cold Storage. I would kill a black man or woman quicker than I'd smash a fly, while for the white man I would pick a thousand pounds of cotton a day.[75]

From this standpoint, the white master had succeeded in erecting a barrier between all Black men and women. Cleaver's conclusion was to mimic the worst features of white patriarchy. "We shall have our manhood," he vowed. "We shall have it or the earth will be leveled by our attempts to gain it." This struggle for freedom did not involve Black women, since by their gender, they already possessed what Cleaver dubbed "pussy power."[76]

Robert Staples merits special commentary at this juncture, for few Black sociologists writing about the Black woman have been more consistently wrong than he has. Writing on the "Mystique of Black Sexuality" in 1967, Staples gave his views on the "guilt-free attitude towards the sex act" among sisters. In a totally bankrupt interpretation of slavery historiography, Staples insisted first that "the women of Africa were brought to this country to service the lust of the white master class." Black men were unable to shield their women from "the carnal desires" of white males. Because virtually every Black woman experienced rape, "the worth of virginity" lost all its value. "What good was it to value something one was not allowed to have?" Staples reasoned. "As a consequence the deeply rooted feelings of guilt about sex never became entrenched in the psyche of Black women as they did in her white counterpart . . . Black women receive more satisfaction in marriage and are more aggressive partners during coitus than white women." Ergo, the collective rapes of Black women were, in retrospect, a liberating force which allowed sisters to "at least salvage the spirit of eros for their own."[77] Black women were judged to have become slightly too aggressive, by Staples, as a result.

Further reflecting on the Black woman in a later publication, Staples writes: "Many black females assume that a male with an athletic build possesses large sex organs, which will guarantee them sexual pleasure." The term Staples employed to describe this process is surely a classic in the history of Black sociology: "the masculinization of female mate selection standards." "For those of us who are not built like athletes," he admitted, "this is a most disheartening trend." Describing the social phenomenon of "tipping out," or Black extramarital sex, the Black sociologist's fear of cuckoldry is plainly visible:

> The independence of the black female leads her to sexual dalliance whenever things do not go right or she feels the desire to 'make it' with another male. This practice has become quasi-institutionalized . . . Sexual dalliance must, however, be discreet so as not to damage the male ego. It is most common among black females attending college some miles away from their boyfriends and in the lower class.[78]

Regrettably, the historical legacy of racial and sexual oppression has also led some Black women to defend patriarchal definitions of manhood. In her 1968 essay in the *Liberator*, Black writer Gail Stokes denounced all Black men who were unable or unwilling to assume the role of provider and family patriarch. Stokes equated manhood with the economic function of "bringing home the bacon":

> Of course you will say, "How can I love you and want to be with you when I come home and you're looking like a slob? Why, white women never open the door for their husbands the way you black bitches do." I should guess not, you ignorant man. Why should they be in such a state when they've got maids like me to do everything for them? There is no screaming at the kids for her, no standing over the hot stove; everything is done for her, and whether her man loves her or not, he provides . . . provides . . . do you hear that, nigger? PROVIDES![79]

The material base that provided the impetus for such statements was the unprecedented proliferation of Black female one-parent households and growing Black unemployment. The percentage of Black families with no husband present increased from 21.7 percent in 1960 to 34.6 percent in 1973. The percentage of Black children who lived with both of their parents declined from 75 percent in 1960 to 54 percent by 1975. Single female-parent households within the Black community tended to become younger, with 42 percent of such homes having Black female householders between the ages of 14 and 34 years in 1975. Less than half of all Black women were married in 1975. As unemployment rates for nonwhite married men increased by 332 percent between 1969 and 1975, even Black households with two parents found it more difficult to provide the basic necessities of life. Black women who viewed themselves and their children through the prism

of patriarchy could draw the conclusion that their male counterparts—
unemployed, underemployed, or sometimes absent from home for indefi-
nite periods of time—were somehow less than real men. The vicious cycle of
sexism, fostered by white exploiters of the Black community, would be
perpetuated in the actual social practices and relations between Black
women and men.[80]

As the contemporary women's movement gained impetus during the early
1970s, Black intellectuals and activists were forced to confront the rampant
sexist traditions within their own community and underlying their own
theoretical practice. At the outset, the majority of Blacks who wrote on
feminism were decidedly hostile. In one widely read 1971 essay published in
*Ebony* magazine, Helen King denounced "women's lib" as a white petty
bourgeois fad that had little or nothing to do with the interests of Black
women.[81] In the *Black Scholar*, Elizabeth Hood charged that white feminists
had opportunistically usurped issues such as affirmative action from Blacks.
"It can be argued that women's liberation not only attached itself to the
black movement," Hood explained, "but did so with only marginal concern
for black women and black liberation, and functional concern for the rights
of white women." Any coalition between Black and white women was
unlikely because both groups had been socialized to perceive each other as
the "enemy."[82] Staples' view on the women's movement was decidedly
antagonistic and betrayed a pathetic inability to grasp the essential character
of the economic reforms feminists proposed that would have benefited poor
and working class Black women. First, he suggested that "female liberation"
was tantamount to a "hatred of men." Second, any discussion of the "sex-role
antagonisms extant in the black community will only sow the seed of dis-
unity and hinder the liberation struggle." Black women must tolerate, for the
time being, any sexist behavior of their brothers and the patriarchal institutions developed by nationalists. "One must be cognizant of the need to avoid
a diffusion of energy devoted to the liberation struggle lest it dilute the overall effectiveness of the movement," Staples warned. "Black women cannot
be free *qua* women until all blacks attain their liberation."[83]

Perhaps the most "eloquent" assault against "white feminism" was written
by Linda LaRue in 1970. Unlike other critics of the women's movement,
LaRue attempted to put forward a clear theoretical argument against feminism. In her view, the basic dynamics of sexual exploitation were concretely
different and secondary in nature to those of white racism. "Blacks are *oppressed*, and that means unreasonably, cruelly and harshly fettered by white
authority. White women . . . are only *suppressed*," contrasted LaRue, "and
that means checked, restrained, excluded from conscious and overt activity."
For LaRue, it was a farce for Black women to align themselves with white
women—a social group who benefited materially from white supremacy:

> With few exceptions, the American white woman has had a better opportunity
> to live a free and fulfilling life . . . than any other group in the United States,
> with the exception of her white husband. Thus, any attempt to analogize black

oppression with the plight of the American white woman has the validity of
comparing the neck of a hanging man with the hands of an amateur mountain
climber with rope burns . . . Is there any logical comparison between the
oppression of the black woman on welfare who has difficulty feeding her children and the discontent of the suburban mother who has the luxury to protest
the washing of the dishes on which her family's full meal was consumed.

LaRue's analysis rested solely on two other basic points. White women
were, after all, white, and there was no reason to assume that they would be
less racist or "more open-minded than their male counterparts." With millions of white housewives moving into the labor force, Black women and
men would be forced inevitably to compete with them. "The black labor
force, never fully employed and always representing a substantial percentage of the unemployed . . . will now be driven into greater unemployment as
white women converge at every level on an already dwindling job market."[84]
What is interesting about LaRue and other Black critics of feminism was
their perception that all white women were inside the "middle class." Statistically, the majority of women who depended on food stamps were, and are,
white; the majority of women living in Federally-subsidized public housing
were, and are, white. The poverty and educational backwardness of white
female householders in the Appalachian hills of Kentucky is often worse
than that of the South Bronx. There exists, in short, a unity of political and
economic interests between women across the color line that LaRue and
others failed to recognize. Furthermore, LaRue's economic analysis was
premised on the incorrect belief that all white women benefited materially
from the continuation of racism—a view which is not substantially supported by economic data.

At the founding convention of the Congress of African People, held in
Atlanta in September, 1970, over 2,700 delegates gathered to chart the
development of new Black social, political and economic institutions. One
major feature at the convention included a series of workshops relating to
Black women. Coordinator Bibi Amina Baraka set the tone for the sisters'
dialogue, by first quoting West Coast cultural nationalist Maulana Ron
Karenga: "What makes a woman appealing is femininity and she can't be
feminine without being submissive." Baraka stated that Black females had to
internalize "submitting to (their) natural roles" by studying their attitudes
toward their "man, house, and children." Sisters needed to take cooking
classes, learn to create tasty recipes, and improve their personal hygiene.[85] In
her paper on the Black family, Akiba ya Elimu suggested that Black males
were the natural leaders of the Black community in all social, cultural and
political relations. "He is the leader of the house/nation because his knowledge of the world is broader, his awareness is greater, his understanding is
fuller and his application of this information is wiser" than that of Black
women.[86] Kasisi Washao summarized the proceedings with a few appropriately sexist remarks. The Black family was "like an organ and the woman's
function must be to inspire her man, to educate the children, and participate

in social development. The man must provide security . . . " Black women fortunate enough to have a man in their lives should "be humble and loving, appreciative, and resourceful, faithful, respectful and understanding . . . to provide continuous inspiration" for their husbands.[87]

Nationalists were aware of the climbing rate of Black single parent households and the economic pressures that fractured many of the relations between Black females and males. Madhubuti's *Enemies: The Clash of Races*, started from the assumption that "the destruction of the Black family was a crucial move in laying the ground for the destruction and total enslavement of Black people in America." If this destruction was a *fait accompli*, what evolved in the manner of social relations and male/female institutions among Blacks?

Madhubuti claimed that the most serious immediate effect of contemporary racism for Black women "depends upon and revolves around how they are able to effectively solve the problem of no men in their lives." The options available for Black women were unpleasant. Going "without Black men," sexual abstinence, was "unnatural and against life." Lesbianism, according to Madhubuti, "has only recently become popular among some Black women as a compensating move toward fulfilling their sexual desires, possible as a result of not having comfortable and non-frustrating relationships with a Black man." Homosexual activity among women was abnormal, "for it does not generate reproduction . . . with the opposite sex." The most dangerous option, of course, was the prospect of Black women/white men's sexual relationships. When "white men are pushed on Black women or if white men become the accepted option for Black women . . . there is a very serious consequence in terms of Black genocide." Miscegenation was a white supremacist/integrationist plot because the white man would eventually "control the reproductive process of Black women, which goes hand in hand with the physical destruction of Black men and Black families." The fourth option, prostitution, meant that the Black single woman would obtain some security by "(becoming) the property of her pimp." Within the Black community prostitution "is rampant not only for financial means but as (an acceptable) social norm" for Black females. The Black pimp was a kind of "semi-hero" for some, although the entire process "continues to degrade Black women . . . (who) end up as dead property . . . " The final option was in keeping with the African heritage of polygyny—the "quality of sharing" Black males by groups of Black females. Where a brother could economically support more than one household, and satisfy the sexual, emotional and social needs of more than one Black woman at once, such sharing agreements could be achieved for the mutual benefit of all. Sharing would "create a climate and conditions" wherein Black women would willingly permit "their men" to engage in extramarital sex and Black family-building, "while at the same time not damaging existing relationships."[88]

Even outside the boundaries of cultural nationalism, Black political activities did little to challenge institutional sexism. The continuing patterns of Black patriarchy were evident within electoral politics in the 1960s and

1970s. A few Black women politicians gained national prominence after the Civil Rights Movement, including Yvonne Burke of California, Barbara Jordan of Houston, Shirley Chisholm of New York City, and Cardiss Collins of Chicago. The percentage of Black women holding elective office increased 522 percent between 1969 and 1976. Of 508 Black delegates and alternates who participated in the 1976 Democratic National Convention, 310 were women. This "success" in challenging patriarchy was more apparent than real, however. Only 22.2 percent of all Black Federal elected officials and 13.5 percent of all Black state representatives were Black women. Black women comprised only 9.5 percent of all Afro-American judges, and 11 percent of all county officials. 80.5 percent of all Black women who were elected officials in 1976 served either at the municipal level or on boards of education. Despite the formation of the National Association of Black Women Legislators by Tennessee politician Hannah Atkins, and the activities of Nellis Saunders' National Black Women's Leadership Caucus, the effective participation of Black women in electoral politics still grossly underrepresented the potential weight of Black women nationally and regionally.[89] Both integrationist and nationalist-oriented Black men had little to say concretely about the exploitation of Black women by their own institutions. In theory and practice, the Black protest movemement was compromised and gutted by its inability to confront squarely the reality of patriarchy. Black leadership—in the workplace, in street demonstrations, in electoral politics and in the bedroom—was the province of Black men.

By the mid-1970s, a number of women emerged within the Black Movement who advocated key political and economic reforms suggested first by the feminist movement. Many, although by no means all, were also identified as socialists. Angela Davis' essays in the *Black Scholar*, her deep commitment to an antisexist and antiracist politics, were profoundly influential for many Black women. Cathy Sedgewick and Reba Williams, young Black women who were also members of the Trotskyist Socialist Workers Party, advocated Black support for the Equal Rights Amendment as a necessary and progressive reform which aided women of all races. Advocacy of feminism, they argued, aided and enriched the struggle for Black liberation. For Black women who were pessimistic about the viability of joint political work with white feminists, they pointed out that the real political and economic advances acquired by women of color involved in the women's movement more than made up for the very real problems and personal contradictions evident among certain petty bourgeois white women's "leaders."[90]

Many of the theoretical gains achieved by Black feminists within the Black Movement and community were briefly compromised with the publication of Michele Wallace's controversial diatribe, *Black Macho and the Myth of the Superwoman*. Wallace emerged as a female version of Eldridge Cleaver, praised by *Ms.* magazine, the central publication of white liberal feminists, and exalted by pseudofeminist/racists such as Susan Brownmiller. Her vulgar polemic combined historical truth with crude fiction, racial mythology with a neo-Freudian, psycho-sexual analysis of Black politics.

"Come 1966, the Black man had two pressing tasks before him: a white woman in every bed and a Black woman under every foot," she pronounced. Wallace viewed the entire history of Black Power as "nothing more nor less than the Black man's struggle to attain his presumably lost 'manhood'":

> To most of us Black Power meant wooly heads, big Black fists and stern Black faces, gargantuan omnipotent Black male organs, big Black rifles and foot-long combat boots, tight pants over young muscular asses, dashikis, and broad brown chests; Black men looting and rioting in the streets . . . [Stokely Carmichael] was a Black spokesman unlike any other that had come before him. He was a Black man with an erect phallus, and he was pushing it up in America's face.[91]

Wallace contended that virtually every Black male leader of the 1960s accepted and perpetuated the idea of Black Macho, the notion that all political and social power was somehow sexual, and that the possession of a penis was the symbol of revolution. "Black Macho allowed for only the most primitive notion of women—women as possessions, women as the spoils of war, leaving Black women with no resale value," Wallace charged. "The Black woman was a symbol of defeat, and therefore of little use to the revolution except as the performer of drudgery (not unlike her role in slavery)." The Black man was a pathetic failure, and "when [he] went as far as the adoration of his own genitals could carry him, his revolution stopped."[92] The obvious criticism of Wallace's work begins with her crude acceptance of Cleaver and the most blatantly sexist spokespersons of Black liberation as representative of all Black males. But the dilemma for genuine progressives was that her book served absolutely no purpose in facilitating an urgent dialogue between Black women and men on the very real and pressing questions of patriarchy within their community. *Black Macho* raised at its core several historically valid issues, but due to its distorted and acrid context, it actually reinforced sexism and a hostility towards feminism among many Blacks.

## V

The emergence of a militant Black feminism since the mid-1970s, which has since continued and deepened in organizational character, is the product of the convergence of several specific social and economic factors. As illustrated previously, the actual practice of the Black Power Movement was the perpetuation of the structures of patriarchy, under the guise of "Blackness." With the passage of affirmative action legislation, many Black males drew the conclusion that Black women were now taking away newly-won middle income jobs from them. The vulgarly sexist thesis was based on the belief that Black women were indeed submissive, or less threatening to the white, male power apparatus than Black males. Their lack of a penis, in short, was an automatic ticket to employment and job advancement during economically austere times.

Black women knew better than men that the dynamics of sexist exploitation were not altered by bourgeois legislation: Black women remained at the very bottom of the income ladder within the U.S. social order. According to the 1979 Census statistics, for example, 68,000 Black males and only 8,000 Black females earned salaries between $30,000 to $35,000. 46,000 Black men and 6,000 Black women collected annual wages between $35,000 to $50,000 in 1979. 14,000 Black men and 2,000 Black women received wages between $50,000–$75,000. Within the highest income levels, in excess of $75,000, there were 548,000 white men and 4,000 Black men. Less than 500 Black women were in this category. The illusion that Black women, even within the so-called middle class, had achieved parity or had exceded Black men's earnings was not simply false, but a gross reversal of economic reality. Black female unemployment rates were generally higher than those of Black men, especially for all blue collar workers, clerical workers and sales personnel.[93]

Responding to this chasm between Black liberation rhetoric and the harsh realities of Black women's existence, progressive Black female activists fought back. They helped to provide the political base for the fight to acquit Joanne Little, a North Carolina Black woman who was accused of murdering her jailer when he sexually assaulted her.[94] They helped to rally a majority of the national Black community in favor of the Equal Rights Amendment.[95] Progressive Black women in Boston formed the Combahee River Collective in 1974, to begin bringing together Black women who were "actively committed to struggling against racial, sexual, heterosexual, and class oppression" and who viewed as their "particular task the development of integrated analysis and practice based upon the fact that the major systems of oppression are interlocking."[96]

They criticized white feminists who tended to ignore Black women's fears about forced sterilizations and who emphasized only abortion rights. Black female activist veterans of SNCC recalled with some bitterness that a few of the white women who now championed feminism and gave lip-service to antiracist politics had eagerly slept with Black male leaders and saddled Black women with the Movement's "shit work" a decade before. Lorraine Bethel's "What Chou Mean We, White Girl? Or, The Cullud Lesbian Feminist Declaration of Independence," spoke for thousands of Black women who view themselves as the historic victims of suppression by males (white and Black) and white females:

> I bought a sweater at a yard sale from a white-skinned (as opposed to Anglo-Saxon) woman. When wearing it I am struck by the smell — it reeks of a soft, privileged life without stress, sweat, or struggle. When wearing it I often think to myself, this sweater smells of a comfort, a way of being in the world I have never known in my life, and never will. . . . It is moments/infinities of conscious pain like these that make me want to cry/kill/roll my eyes suck my teeth hand on my hip scream at so-called radical white lesbians/feminists "WHAT CHOU MEAN WE, WHITE GIRL?"[97]

The final history of the systematic exploitation of Black women in capitalist America will not be written by whites, or by Black men, no matter how sympathetic they might be to the struggle against racism and patriarchy. Historically, Black women have carried the greatest burden in the battle for democracy in this country.

Women have been the foundation of Black culture and society, yet their contributions have been generally ignored, or relegated to second class status by most Black male activists, historians and social scientists. They felt the sting of the lash upon their backs in Georgia's cotton fields; they knew the pain of losing children from lack of decent medical care; they felt the hot sun beating down upon their foreheads as they walked to work as maids in whites' homes; they fought to preserve their humanity from white and/or Black men's sexual abuse. The underdevelopment of Black America will end only when Black men begin to seriously challenge and uproot the patriarchal assumptions and institutions which still dominate Black civil and political society. In the words of Michele Barrett, the oppression of all women "is entrenched in the structure of capitalism. Just as we cannot conceive of women's liberation under the oppression of capitalism so we cannot conceive of a socialism whose principles of equality, freedom and dignity are vitiated by the familiar iniquities of gender."[98] Similarly, no road toward the ultimate emancipation of the U.S. Black working class exists outside of a concomitant struggle, in theory and in practice, to destroy every vestige of sexual oppression within the Black community.

## NOTES

1. Angela Davis, "Reflections on the Black Woman's Role in the Community of Slaves," Black Scholar, Vol. 3 (December, 1971), p. 7.

2. John Hope Franklin, From Slavery to Freedom: A History of Negro Americans (New York: Vintage, 1969), p. 179; Herbert Gutman, Slavery and the Numbers Game (Urbana: University of Illinois Press, 1975) pp. 102-103, 112, 126, 128.

3. Kenneth M. Stampp, The Peculiar Institution, pp. 245–247.

4. Ibid., p. 249.

5. Frances Anne Kemble, Journal of a Residence on a Georgian Plantation in 1838–1839 (New York: New American library, 1975), pp. 76, 245.

6. Ulrich B. Philips, Life and Labor in the Old South, (Boston: Little, Brown and Company, 1963), p. 204.

7. Gutman, Slavery and the Numbers Game, p. 98.

8. Davis, "Reflections on the Black Woman," p. 13.

9. Gilberto Freyre, The Masters and the Slaves (New York: Alfred A. Knopf, 1971), p. 324.

10. Ibid., pp. 325–326.

11. Ibid., pp. 74–75.

12. Davis, "Reflections on the Black Woman," p. 13.

13. Franklin, From Slavery to Freedom, p. 205.

14. Gerald W. Mullin, Flight and Rebellion: Slave Resistance in Eighteenth Century Virginia (New York: Oxford University Press, 1972), pp. 103–105.

15. Jane Blake, Memoirs of Margaret Jane Blake (Philadelphia: Innes and Son, 1897), p. 13.

16. Jane Brown, *Narrative of the Life of Jane Brown and Her Two Children* (Hartford: G.W. Offley, 1860), pp. 47–49.

17. Louisa Picquet, *Louisa Picquet, the Octoroon; or, Inside Views of Southern Domestic Life* (New York: the author, 1860), pp. 50–52. Other slave narratives written by Black women include Annie L. Burton, *Memories of Childhood's Slavery Days* (Boston: Ross Publishing Company, 1919); Elizabeth Keckley, *Behind the Scenes* (New York: G.W. Carlton, 1868); Sylvia Dubois, *A Biography of the Slave Who Whipt Her Mistress and Gained Her Freedom* (New Jersey: C. W. Larison, 1883).

18. Lawrence W. Levine, *Black Culture and Black Consciousness: Afro-American Folk Thought From Slavery To Freedom* (New York: Oxford University Press, 1977), pp. 392–393.

19. Quoted in John Bracey, August Meier, and Elliott Rudwick, eds., *Black Nationalism in America* (Indianapolis and New York: Bobbs-Merrill, 1970), pp. 70–71, 75–76.

20. *Ibid.*, pp. 215–216.

21. *Ibid.*, pp. 140–141.

22. *Ibid.*, p. 62.

23. Benjamin Quarles, *Frederick Douglass* (New York, Atheneum, 1969), pp. 131–136, 244–247.

bell hooks' treatment of Douglass in *Ain't I A Woman* seems somewhat monolithic. She argues that Douglass "saw the entire racial dilemma as a struggle between white man and black men. . . . By emphasizing that the right to vote was more important to men than [to] women, Douglass and other Black male activists allied themselves with white male patriarchs on the basis of shared sexism." hooks does not discuss Douglass' significant role in the early evolution of the suffragist cause, and does not mention Du Bois even once in her study.

The record of white feminists and early supporters of women's suffrage on racism is more contradictory than hooks suggests. In 1851, white suffragists protested the appearance of Sojourner Truth at an Ohio women's convention because they opposed both "abolition and niggers." In her debate with Douglass, Elizabeth Cady Stanton asserted that she would not trust "the colored man with my rights; degraded, oppressed himself, he would be more despotic with the governing power than even our Saxon rulers are. If women are still to be represented by men, then I say let only the highest type of manhood stand at the helm of State." Robert L. Allen, *Reluctant Reformers: Racism and Social Reform Movements in the United States* (Garden City, New York: Anchor Books, 1975), pp. 141, 153–154; hooks, *Ain't I A Woman* (Boston: South End Press, 1981), pp. 89–90.

24. hooks, *Ain't I A Woman*, pp. 44–45.

25. [No text in original]

26. Joan R. Sherman, *Invisible Poets: Afro-Americans of the Nineteenth Century* (Urbana: University of Illinois Press, 1974), pp. 62–74.

27. John E. Fleming, "Slavery, Civil War and Reconstruction: A Study of Black Women in Microcosm," *Negro History* Bulletin, Vol. 38 (August–September, 1975), pp. 430–433; Hertha Ernestine Pauli, Her Name Was Sojourner Truth (New York: Appleton-Century Crofts, 1962); Sojourner Truth, *Narrative of Sojourner Truth* (Battle Creek, Michigan: the author, 1878); Marie Harlowe, "Sojourner Truth, the First Sit-In," *Negro History Bulletin*, Vol. 29 (Fall, 1966), pp. 173–174; E. Jay Ritter, "Sojourner Truth," *Negro History Bulletin*, Vol. 26 (May, 1963), p. 254; Arthur H. Fausett, *Sojourner Truth: God's Faithful Pilgrim* (New York: Russell and Russell, 1971).

28. David M. Tucker, "Miss Ida B. Wells and the Memphis Lynching," *Phylon*, Vol. 32 (Summer, 1971), pp. 111–122; Alfreda M. Duster, ed., *Crusade for Justice: The Autobiography of Ida B. Wells* (Chicago: University of Chicago Press, 1969).

29. Elizabeth Chittenden, "As We Climb: Mary Church Terrell," *Negro History Bulletin*, Vol. 38 (February–March, 1975), pp. 351–354; August Meier, *Negro Thought in America, 1880–1915* (Ann Arbor: University of Michigan Press, 1963), pp. 239–241; Gladys B. Shepperd, *Mary Church Terrell* (Baltimore: Human Relations Press, 1959);

Mary Church Terrell, *A Colored Woman in a White World* (Washington, D.C.: Ransdell Publishing Company, 1940); Terrell, "Lynching From a Negro's Point of View," *North American Review*, Vol. 178 (July, 1904), pp. 853–898.

30. Franklin, *From Slavery to Freedom*, pp. 505–506, 511.

A *caveat* must be registered concerning Hurston's views on politics. At the end of her career, Hurston drafted a letter attacking the 1954 *Brown* decision of the Supreme Court as an "insult" to all Blacks. "Since the days of the never-to-be-sufficiently-deplored Reconstruction, there has been currently the belief that there is no greater delight to Negroes than physical association with whites . . . It is to be recalled that Moscow made it the main plank in their campaign to win the American Negro from 1920s on. It was the come-on stuff. Join the party and get yourself a white wife or husband." Not surprisingly, the viciously racist Mississippi State Sovereignty Commission reprinted and widely distributed her remarks. James Graham Cook, *The Segregationists* (New York: Appleton-Century Crofts, 1962), p. 311.

31. *Ibid.*, pp. 511, 532, 601–602; Rackham Holt, *Mary McLeod Bethune: A Biography* (New York: Doubleday, 1964); C. O. Pearce, *Mary McLeod Bethune* (New York: Vanguard Press, 1951); "Life of Mary McLeod Bethune," *Our World*, Vol. 5 (December, 1950), pp. 32–35; Bethune, "Clarifying Our Vision With the Facts," *Journal of Negro History*, Vol. 23 (January, 1938), pp. 12–15.

32. W. E. B. Du Bois, editorial, *Fisk Herald*, Vol. 5 (December, 1887), p. 9.

33. Du Bois, "Fifty Years Among the Black Folk," *New York Times* (December 12, 1909).

34. Du Bois, "Postscript," *Crisis*, Vol. 40 (February, 1933), p. 45.

35. Du Bois, "As the Crow Flies," *Crisis*, Vol. 41 (January, 1934), p. 5.

36. Du Bois, *Disfranchisement* (New York: National American Woman Suffrage Association, 1912).

37. Du Bois, "Suffering Suffragettes," *Crisis*, Vol. 4 (June, 1912).

38. Du Bois, "As the Crow Flies," *Amsterdam News* (March 22, 1941); Du Bois, "The Winds of Time," *Chicago Defender* (January 25, 1947).

39. Du Bois, "Ohio," *Crisis*, Vol. 4 (August, 1912), p. 182.

40. Du Bois, "Opinion," *Crisis*, Vol. 19 (March, 1920), p. 234.

Du Bois' writings on women's rights and Black women include: *An Attack* (Atlanta: Published by author, 1906); "The Work of Negro Women in Society," *Spelman Messenger*, Vol. 18 (February, 1902), pp. 1–3; "Suffrage Workers," *Crisis*, Vol. 4 (September, 1912); "The Burden of Black Women," *Crisis*, Vol. 9 (November, 1914), p. 31; "A Question of Facts," *Crisis*, Vol. 21 (February, 1921), p. 151; *The Gift of Black Folk: Negroes in the Making of America* (Boston: Stratford Company, 1924); "Greetings to Women," *Women of the Whole World* (1959), p. 24.

41. Amy Jacques-Garvey, ed., *The Philosophy and Opinions of Marcus Garvey* (New York: Reprinted, Atheneum, 1977), p. 7.

42. *Ibid.*, p. 9.

43. John Henrik Clarke, ed., *Marcus Garvey and the Vision of Africa* (New York: Vintage, 1974), pp. 309-310.

44. Garvey, ed., *The Philosophy and Opinions of Marcus Garvey*, p. 348.

45. Robert G. Weisbord, *Genocide? Birth Control and the Black American* (Westport, Connecticut: Greenwood Press, 1975), p. 43.

This criticism of the sexist character of the Universal Negro Improvement Association's program should not be construed as a condemnation of the legitimate achievements of Garveyism. C.L.R. James is correct in his characterization of this Black nationalist leader: "Garvey is the only Negro who has succeeded in building a mass movement among American Negroes. Garvey never set foot in Africa. He spoke no African language . . . but Garvey managed to convey to Negroes everywhere (and to the rest of the world) his passionate belief that Africa was the home of a civilisation which had once been great and would be great again. When you bear in mind the slenderness of his resources, the vast material forces and the pervading social conceptions which automatically sought to destroy him, his achievement remains one of the propagandistic miracles of this century." James, *The Black Jacobins*, p. 396.

46. W. E. B. Du Bois, "Black Folk and Birth Control," *Birth Control Review* (June, 1932), pp. 166–167; Margaret Sanger, "The Case for Birth Control," *Crisis*, Vol. 41 (June, 1934).

47. Weisbord, *Genocide?*, pp. 52–53.

48. *Ibid.*, pp. 141–142.

In some Southern counties, doctors refused to deliver a third or even a second child of a welfare mother unless she agreed to be sterilized. In a number of U.S. hospitals, particularly those with large numbers of Black and Latino patients, white doctors still perform sterilizations "without bothering to get permission." Linda Jenness, "Black Women Fight Sterilization," in Willie Mae Reid, ed., *Black Women's Struggle For Equality* (New York: Pathfinder Press, 1980), pp. 9–10.

49. *Ibid.*, pp. 96–104.

A note on the intimate relationship between religion and patriarchy is appropriate here. The ancient Jews stoned young brides to death "if the village elders agreed" with their husbands' charges that they were not virgins. The Orthodox Jewish prayer— "Blessed art Thou O Lord our God, King of the Universe who has not made me a woman"—speaks for itself. Muhammad taught his disciples, "When Eve was created, Satan rejoiced." The Hindu Code of Manu states: "In childhood a woman must be subject to her father; in youth to her husband; when her husband is dead, to her sons. A woman must never be free of subjugation." From its origins, Christianity promulgated misogyny. The Holy Bible taught that "all wickedness is but little to the wickedness of a woman." The woman was "an unescapable punishment" and "a necessary evil." In his correspondence to the Corinthians, St. Paul declared that "the head of every man is Christ, and the head of the woman is the man."

St. Augustine commented that women were as a temple built over a sewer. Later-day Christian leaders were generally worse than their forefathers. John Calvin, the Protestant patriarch, argued that the sole function of women was to bear as many offspring as possible. Political responsibilities for females were a "deviation from the original and proper order of nature." Martin Luther "thought that sexual relations carried on Original Sin." In colonial America, evangelical ministers delivered solemn prayers while burning "witches" and "adulteresses" at the stake. At the level of popular ideology and cultural tradition, therefore, the various rituals of faith have often dictated an overtly hostile policy of suppressing women. The "good Christian" could beat his wife in "the name of the Father." The crude and often vicious practices of many Black male Christians and Muslims toward Afro-American women historically is to a degree an expression of a much older cultural heritage. See Lucy Komisar, *The New Feminism* (New York: Warner, 1972), pp. 69–72, 111–112.

50. hooks, *Ain't I A Woman*, pp. 85–86.

51. *Ibid.*, pp. 91, 93.

52. Bureau of the Census, *The Social and Economic Status of the Black Population*, pp. 67, 74.

53. *Ibid.*, pp. 124, 131.

Considerable sociological evidence exists indicating that Black women wanted to bear fewer children than white women. This was particularly true for low- to lower-middle-income Black women, even in the 1950s and 1960s. Researchers Adelaide Cromwell Hill and Frederick S. Jaffe point to a 1960 national survey demonstrating that "the average number [of children] wanted by nonwhite [women] was 2.9, compared to 3.3 by the white wives . . . Furthermore, 46 percent of nonwhites said they wanted no more than 2 children, compared to 29 percent of whites." They also noted a Chicago study in which "twice as many nonwhites as whites said they wanted only two children, and 90 percent of a group of A. F. D.C. mothers of out-of-wedlock children said they did not want to have the child." See Hill and Jaffe, "Negro Fertility and Family Size Preferences—Implications for Programming of Health and Social Services," in Talcott Parsons and Kenneth Clark, eds., *The Negro American* (Boston: Beacon Press, 1967), pp. 160–204.

54. Nikki Giovanni, "The True Import of Present Dialogue: Black vs. Negro," in Dudley Randall, ed., *The Black Poets* (New York: Bantam, 1972), pp. 318–319.

55. Giovanni, "Beautiful Black Men," in *Ibid.*, pp. 320–321.

56. Sonia Sanchez, "Homecoming," in Don L. Lee, ed., *Dynamite Voices* (Detroit: Broadside Press, 1971), p. 48.

57. Alice Lovelace, "Wedding Song," *Gumbo Literary Anthology, Vol. I* (Winter, 1978–1979), p. 46.

58. Carolyn Rodgers, "For Some Black Men," In Lee, ed., *Dynamite Voices*, p. 57.

59. Ann DuCille, "Lady in Waiting," in Pat Crutchfield Exum, ed., *Keeping the Faith: Writings by Contemporary Black American Women* (Greenwood, Connecticut: Fawcett, 1974), pp. 70–71.

60. Lucille Clifton, "Apology (to the panthers)," in *Ibid.*, pp. 67–68.

61. Robert Staples, "The Myth of the Black Matriarchy," *Black Scholar*, Vol. I January–February, 1970), p. 16.

62. Sonia Sanchez, "to all brothers," in Randall, ed., *The Black Poets*, p. 231.

63. Nikki Giovanni, "Woman Poem," in Lee, ed., *Dynamite Voices*, pp. 70–71.

64. Ntozake Sbange, poem in *Black Scholar*, Vol. 12 (November-December, 1981), p. 61.

65. Stokely Carmichael, *Stokely Speaks: Black Power Back to Pan-Africanism* (New York: Vintage, 1971), p. 23.

66. Malcolm X, *The Autobiography of Malcolm X* (New York: Grove Press, 1965), p. 454.

67. hooks, *Ain't I A Woman*, p. 109.

68. Malcolm X, *The Autobiography of Malcolm X*, pp. 389–390.
Following his second journey to Africa in 1964, Malcolm X began to question his profoundly sexist education via the Nation of Islam, and was gradually embracing more progressive thoughts on the role of women in political struggle. In a Paris interview in November, 1964, he contended: "The degree of progress (in the Third World) can never be separated from the woman. If you're in a country that's progressive . . . the woman is progressive . . . One of the things I became thoroughly convinced of in my recent travels is the importance of giving freedom to the woman, giving her education, and giving her the incentive to get out there and put that same spirit and understanding in her children." Despite the political advance, the discourse on women is still framed in a primarily patriarchal caste. Malcolm X, *By Any Means Necessary*, p. 179.

69. Carmichael, *Stokely Speaks*, p. 114.

70. *Ibid.*, pp, 64–65.

71. *Ibid.*, p. 73.

72. Weisbord, *Genocide?*, pp. 94–95.

73. Haki R. Madhubuti, *Enemies: The Clash of Races* (Chicago: Third World Press, 1978), p. 188.

74. In *Soul on Ice* (New York: Delta, 1968), Cleaver described homosexuality as "a sickness, just as are baby-rape or wanting to become the head of General Motors . . . Many Negro homosexuals are outraged and frustrated because in their sickness they are unable to have a baby by a white man. . . . The fruit of their miscegenation is not the little half-white offspring of their dreams, though they redouble their efforts and intake of the white man's sperm" (pp. 102,110).

75. Eldridge Cleaver, *Soul on Ice*, pp. 206–209.

76. *Ibid.*, p. 61.

77. Robert Staples, "Mystique of Black Sexuality," *Liberator*, Vol. 7 (March, 1967), pp. 8–10.

78. Staples, ed., *The Black Family: Essays and Studies* (Behnont, California: Wadsworth Publishing Company, 1971), p. 74.
Not surprisingly, Staples also justified the sexual relations between Black males and white females. "Since the interracial sex taboo is mostly centered around Negro men/white women, it is not strange that these two groups may have a certain curiosity about the sex ability of each other. Inflaming their curiosity" is the "common stereotype" that the Black man "possesses an overly large penis and has an abnormal sex drive." Many Black men "are preoccupied with the sexual conquest of women . . . Sexual conquest of women is generally seen as a sign of masculinity in American culture . . . being mascu-

line, in a sexual sense, is very important to Negro males because the ordinary symbols of masculinity have often been denied them in the past." Staples, "Negro-White Sex: Fact and Fiction," *Sexology Magazine*, Vol. 35 (August, 1968), pp, 46–51.

79. Quoted in hooks, *Ain't I A Woman*, pp. 92–93.

80. Bureau of the Census, *The Social and Economic Status of the Black Population*, pp. 70, 103, 106, 107, 109.

81. Helen King, "The Black Woman and Women's Lib," *Ebony* (Much, 1971), pp. 68–76.

82. Elizabeth Hood, "Black Women, White Women: Separate Paths to Liberation," *Black Scholar*, Vol. 9 (April, 1978), pp. 45–46.

83. Staples, "The Myth of the Black Matriarchy," pp. 15–16.

84. Linda LaRue, "The Black Movement and Women's Liberation," *Black Scholar* Vol. I (May, 1970), pp. 36–42.

One root cause for dissention between elements of the Black activist intelligentsia and feminists was competition for white-collar jobs. Throughout the 1970s, many Black women and men argued that white women were seizing many of the avenues for upward mobility within the corporate and political hierarchies that had been offered originally as concessions to the Black Movement. Between 1966 and 1979, the percentage of total professional jobs that various groups held were: white women, 13 percent in 1966 to 31.6 percent in 1979; white men, 83.5 percent to 58.9 percent; Black women, 0.6 percent to 2.2 percent; Black men, 0.7 percent to 1.9 percent; and others (including Latinos, Asians, and Native Americans), 2.2 percent to 5.4 percent. White corporate executives and employment experts interviewed by the *New York Times* suggested several factors for the apparent preference for white women over Black women/men in executive hiring practices. "The white men who control advancement are more at ease with white women than with Blacks of either sex," some pointed out. Others noted that Blacks had a disturbing "lack of faith in the fairness" of capitalism whereas the majority of white middle-class females did not. See Sheila Rule, "Blacks Believe White Women Lead in Job Gains," *New York Times* (March 25,1982).

85. Bibi Amina Baraka, "Coordinator's Statement," in Imamu Amid Baraka, ed., *African Congress: A Documentary of the First Modem Pan-African Congress* (New York: William Morrow, 1972), pp. 177–178.

86. Akiba ya Elimu, "The Black Family," in *Ibid.*, pp. 179–180.

87. Kasisi Washao, "Marriage Ceremony," in *Ibid.*, pp. 181–186.

88. Madhubuti, *Enemies: The Clash of Races*, pp. 139–158.

The academic interest in polygyny transcended the Black Movement in the 1970s. Other works on the subject as it relates to Blacks include Jacquelyne Jackson, "But Where Are the Men?" *Black Scholar*, Vol. 2 (December, 1971), pp. 30–41; Melvin Ember, "Warfare, Sex Ratio, and Polygyny," *Ethnology*, Vol. 8 (1974), pp. 197–206; Joseph W. Scott, "Polygamy: A Futuristic Family Arrangement for African Americans," *Black Books Bulletin* (Summer, 1976), pp, 13–19; Leachim T. Semaj, "Male/Female Relationships: Polygamy Reconsidered," in Semaj, *Working Papers in Cultural Science* (Ithaca, New York: the author, 1980).

89. Joint Center for Political Studies, *National Roster of Black Elected Officials* (Washington, D.C.: Joint Center, 1976), pp. xliii-li.

Works by or about Black women politicians include Shirley Chisholm, *Unbought and Unbossed* (Boston: Houghton and Mifflin, 1970); Chisholm, *The Good Fight* (New York: Harper and Row, 1973); Herrington J. Bryce and Allan E. Warrick, "Black Women in Elective Offices," *Black Scholar*, Vol. 6 (October, 1974), pp. 17–20; Jewel L. Prestage, "Political Behavior of American Black Women: An Overview," in La Frances Rodgers-Rose, ed., *The Black Woman* (Beverly Hills and London: Sage Publications, 1980), pp. 233–245.

90. Cathy Sedgewick and Reba Williams, "Black Women and the Equal Rights Amendment," *Black Scholar*, Vol. 7 (July–August, 1976), pp. 24–29.

91. Michele Wallace, *Black Macho and the Myth of the Superwoman* (New York: Warner Books, 1980), pp. 52–53.

92. *Ibid.*, pp. 103–104, 118.

Predictably, the reviews of *Black Macho* were mixed. The bourgeois press embraced Wallace's analysis with gusto. "With this rude, witty polemic—part political broadside, part personal memoir—a 26-year-old Black writer makes a striking debut," declared *Newsweek* (February 5, 1979). The *Library Journal* (March 1, 1979, p. 616) was impressed with Wallace's "simple yet brilliant thesis . . . laser-like in its probing of Black sexual politics. Wallace ranges easily over a vast array of contemporary thought and culture." *Kirkus Reviews* judged *Black Macho* as "thoughtful and temperate." Former SNCC activist Julius Lester wrote in the *Nation* (February 17, 1979, pp. 181–182) that he liked "the book and agree with its thrust and energy when she calls for a Black feminism that is not imitative of what white feminists have done before." Most Black intellectuals' responses to Wallace were divided along feminist lines. Black males who were explicitly sexist provided the most caustic commentary. Harvard psychiatrist Alvin F. Poussaint bristled that "the Black macho response during the Black Liberation Movement was primarily and appropriately a response to white macho and was only secondarily directed at women." In Poussaint's view, Wallace and other Black women had now joined "with whites to destroy the number one object of racism—the Black male." (Poussaint, "White Manipulation and Black Oppression," *Black Scholar* (May/June, 1979), p. 54.) Robert Staples' response was loaded with sexist stereotypes. "The attack on Black men is occurring when Black women threaten to overtake them, in terms of education, occupation, and income," he wrote. "True, lower-class Black women are not faring well. But lower-class Black men are in even worse condition." (Staples, "The Myth of Black Macho," *Black Scholar* (May/June, 1979), pp. 24–33.) Antisexist Black males such as Kalamu ya Salaam recognized the problems with Wallace's polemic, but also insisted that a feminist perspective was imperative for progressive struggle. Salaam stated that "regardless of our [Black men's] power, the fact remains that we routinely act our sexist behavior and the controllers of society at large condone, seldom punish, and even sometimes reward such sexist behavior." (Salaam, "Revolutionary Struggle/Revolutionary Love," *Black Scholar* (May/June, 1979), p. 21.) Black women intellectuals Sherely A. Williams, Pauline Terrelonge Stone, Sarah Webster Fabio, and Julianne Malveaux critiqued both *Black Macho* and the obvious sexism inherent in Staples' and Poussaint's analysis of the Black community.

93. In 1977, for example, Black women workers in sales jobs suffered more than twice the unemployment rate of Black men, 19.6 percent v. 9.2 percent. Black women in blue-collar jobs had an overall unemployment rate of 16.9 percent v. 11.8 percent for men. Bureau of the Census, *The Social and Economic Status of the Black Population*, p. 214.

94. Cindy Jaquith, "Joanne Little's Victory," in Reid, ed., *Black Women's Struggle For Equality*, pp. 10–13.

95. Sedgewick and Williams, "Black Women and the Equal Rights Amendment."

96. hooks, *Ain't I A Woman*, p. 151.

97. *Ibid.*, pp, 152.

98. Michele Barrett, *Women's Oppression Today: Problem in Marxist Feminist Analysis* (London: Verso Editions, 1980), pp. 258–259.

Sheila Rowbotham also provides some insights on the continuing contradictions between socialism and feminist politics: "Marxists have in general assumed that the overthrow of capitalist society will necessitate the fundamental transformation in the organization and control of production and the social relations which came from the capitalist mode of production. Women's liberation implies that, if the revolutionary movement is to involve women . . . as equals, then the scope of production must be seen in a wider sense and cover also the production undertaken by women in the family and the production of self through sexuality . . . The connection between the oppression of women and the central discovery of Marxism, the class exploitation of the worker in capitalism, is still forced. I believe the only way in which their combination will become living and evident is through a movement of working-class women, in conscious resistance to both, alongside black, yellow and brown women struggling against racialism and imperialism." Rowbotham, *Women, Resistance and Revolution: A History of Women and Revolution in the Modern World* (New York: Vintage, 1972), pp. 246–247.

# 11 BREAKING SILENCES

Calvin Hernton

The sex war and the race war in the United States have always been ruled by the politics of a common ideology—the Ideology of Race First and Sex Second.

The machinations of this ideology have been indelibly manifested in three historical moments of truth. First, the long struggle for freedom bore fruit between 1865 and 1870. For both women and men, the 13th Amendment abolished slavery. But the 14th and 15th Amendments, which granted citizenship, equal protection, and the ballot to black men, deliberately excluded women, rendering them without any civil rights whatsoever. A half century later, in 1920, women won the vote with the passage of the 19th Amendment, marking the second moment of truth in which, again, black women were effectively excluded, since "women" meant white women only. The third time around, the Civil Rights *cum* Black Power Movement of the 1960s and early 1970s was thoroughly dominated by men whose values and practices relegated women to the "prone position." Women were objectified as being either "queens" or "bitches," which meant anything from a house-serving, baby-producing, "glorified slave," to a subservient, stamp-licking "piece of ass." Indeed, from slavery until now, at the close of every cycle of racial upheaval in America, the nefarious machinations of the ideology of race first and sex second have resulted in black women getting "screwed" every time.

The ideology of race first and sex second fosters both white supremacy and male supremacy, and it underpins the racial oppression of black women and men. At the same time it underpins the sexual oppression of both black and white women. Specifically, in terms of race this Hydra-headed ideology empowers white over black and, in terms of sex, it empowers male over female. Race is sexualized and sex is racialized, but race is ranked higher than sex, which means that racial equality between white and black men is more important than the "lesser question" of sex equality. Thus, race and sex are abstracted and "polarized," then they are manipulated and played off against one another. But the politics of sex and the politics of race are one and the same politics. The most recent enactment of the vulgarity of this politics was the televised gang rape of Anita Hill before the gaze of the world.

Because it is impossible to separate their sex from their race, and since they are at once sexually and racially oppressed, the primary target of the ideology of race first and sex second is black women. Their sex and race are split in two, which requires them to choose and be loyal to *either* their race *or* their sex. In this fashion the ideology of race first and sex second verifies and denies that sexual oppression exists, and it prohibits and penalizes anyone who says that sexism and racism are intertwined and that they should be fought as one. Vitiating and deforming their sex and race, the ideology of race first and sex second seeks to smear the integrity of being a woman.

The mandate that authorizes the sexual abuse of women is implicitly coded and explicitly sanctioned in the ideology of race first and sex second. Sexually, this ideology empowers men over women; it teaches that the penis is first and the vagina is last; that the "dick" is supposed to be all-powerful and the "pussy" is supposed to be powerless. In its most barbaric form, male power is the penis seeking to subdue, conquer and ravish women as objectified "pieces of ass." Male power over women is "dick over pussy," where ideas such as "Long Dong Silver" and a battery of men's "dirty" jokes and references are designed to degrade women sexually and pornographize the act of coitus.

Sexual harassment then is merely the tip of the iceberg. For the power that men wield over women consists of more than sexual insults and insinuations by individual men. All male power is located in and backed up by the institutional orders and cultural *norms* of society; male domination over women is realized in and through these institutions, particularly in the economic and political structures of the Corporation and State.

Men first, women second, moreover, is individually and collectively vested in the concept of Manhood, which is significantly based on and actualizes itself in the sexual degradation of the female sex. Altogether, male power is *patri-power*, where the ideas, feelings, beliefs and practices of violence against femaleness are embodied in and authorized by hierarchal structures of patriarchy throughout society and culture. In a patriarchy, men are the officers of power, and women are viewed as spoils of the powerful. Accordingly, women are supposed to be attracted to power and to the men who claim this power as theirs alone. Especially in political jobs women are regarded as sexual game. This is particularly true in bureaucratic places like the nation's capital where women—secretaries, typists, stamp-lickers, filers, and so forth—exist as a colony of sex for men in command of the most powerful patri-structures in the world. But, in all work places where men predominate—from the halls of academe to the fire department, from the corporate board room to the sweat shop, and from the auto plant to the halls of Congress—women employees are constant victims of sexual intimidation, vulgarity and profanity. This is the key, the power to exploit and degrade women in all places of work. For the work place is the traditional bulwark of penis power. No matter what the job or the status, sexual exploitation of women is taken for granted as a built-in benefit, a "perk" and a privilege for men.

Women and men are never treated as equals, only people with penises can be equals; never mind how much money a woman might earn, no vagina can ever be equal to a penis. When the signs read: "Men at Work," it means, "Penises at Work." Whoever heard of "Vaginas at Work?" Such a sign would be taken that prostitutes were in the area. These are the living sexways of the ideology of race (men) first and sex (women) last. Thus, we witnessed on television the sexual and racial *smearing* of Anita Hill by members of an all-white-male Senate Judiciary Committee, along with a black man and his supporters, including a majority of the public, as reported by the polls.

Race first and sex second is a misogynist ideology that mandates male appropriation of women's bodies as objects of pornography and abuse. Sexual harassment, politically considered, is a power variant and is a manifestation of the macho politics concocted, practiced and exemplified by the Reagan-Bush regime. The Reagan-Bush men make up a typical locker room gang; football is their metaphor and paradigm. Every man is a jock with a killer instinct. Bush and his jocks have "kicked ass" from Grenada to Libya to Panama and back to Iraq. The locker room attitude and behavior in the political world are matched by the locker room attitude and behavior in the world of men and women—for, like football, sex and women are regarded as "sport" for men. In the locker room, profanity, vulgarity and pornography. In the locker room, men "joke" with themselves about "sex" that is always degrading to women. Derisive palaver about "faggots," "freaks," "nymphomaniacs," "sucking dick" and "eating cunt" are standard pastime activities among men. Just to say "fucking bitch," to feel these obscenities on the tongue and in the mouth, and to hear oneself say them, socializes in men a hateful, violent, and righteous feeling of *power* over women.

This is the ethos that characterizes all places where women and men work. This is the world in which Anita Hill works and lives. Lawyers, doctors, professors, preachers, judges, politicians, business men, as well as construction workers and garbage men, black and white, yellow and brown, share the attitude and the behavior that men are primary and righteous, and women are secondary and profane.

Three boys come upon a cabin in the woods. They go in and overpower a black woman writer and rape her for nearly four hours. Fearing to report it to the authorities, the writer shared it with some of her close peers who gossiped among themselves that perhaps the writer had "made up" the story, or had "embellished" it—after all, the writer was known to have a "vivid imagination." On October 12, 1991, women sympathetic to Anita Hill held a demonstration in front of the U.S. Supreme Court. A man yelled to them that they were interfering with him watching football. "Fuck you, bitches!" he yelled to them.

Let's face it. Very few if any black folk, let alone white folk, doubt that Clarence Thomas did what Anita says he did. What turned people away from Hill was their perception of her as "uppity" by class position, education, job, presumed equality in a world of men. The public got mad at Hill for jeopardizing a black man getting his piece of the American pie. Anita Hill was supposed to devote her energies to fighting white racism, and do nothing about black or white sexism. But by breaking the silence, inadvertently or not, Anita Hill put her sex and humanity and the sex and humanity of all women on par with men and race. Hill's translation of silence into words and action was perceived as insubordination and a challenge to male power.

The ideology of race first and sex second means that no act that a man commits against a woman can warrant the woman telling on the man. When a woman does tell, as Anita Hill told, the whole race reacts as if the woman told on the entire race. The ideology of race first and sex second decrees that women belong to a race, which is to say that they belong to men, and not vice versa, the first identification then, is with men and the only loyalty is to the race. Not only would Anita Hill be punished. Women feared that all women who took her side would be punished, they feared that men would backlash them. So they turned away from Anita and sex, and supported Clarence and race.

Punishment consists of re-victimization where the victim, the one who tells, is made to be the criminal. When a Cleveland woman kills her batterer of fifteen years, she is labelled a traitor to the race for aiding white men in destroying black males. Women are *blackmaled* into silence for fear of being attacked as "sluts," "whores" and "nymphos." Classic examples are slave women who often broke the silence on their white masters at the risk of their lives. Branded as not merely a traitor to her race, but as being a mentally unstable, love-starved sex-teaser and fantasizing liar, the punishment dealt to Anita Hill was a message to other women not to follow in Hill's footsteps. Every woman testifying for Thomas told of having been harassed by every employer they ever had, *except Thomas!* Thomas was supported by not just the spectre of the entire black and white male population, but there was Senator Danforth in person. During slavery a free Negro was behooved to have some influential white man as his protector-guardian. Because every-body knew he was Ole Massa John's nigger, you did not mess with such a Negro. There is little need to argue that Hill herself is a cut off of the same block as Thomas. The only difference is that Thomas is a black man and Hill is a black woman, which is all the difference in the world. The primacy of race before sex demands that black women split themselves in two, and that they deny their sex and behave as if race is everything and their sex is worth absolutely nothing. Nearly every black man in America, and a majority of women too, would have us believe that black women are oppressed solely because of their race and not because of their sex. Historically, the ideology of race first and sex second has been utilized to divide and conquer. Black women are stigmatized by two "negatives" — femaleness and blackness, and are required to split themselves and become "schizophrenic." Race *vs.* sex as an *either/or* proposition has always rendered black women on the bottom of the power structure in America.

On the other hand, women identifying with Hill are organizing. One such organization is African American Women in Defense of Ourselves. They recognize that sexual harassment is part and parcel of the mores and practices of male violence and women's oppression the world over. For feminist or womanist/feminist women, Hill's breaking of silence has greatly raised and illuminated their awareness and strengthened their commitment. In *Sister Outsider,* Audre Lorde has written, "Your silence will not protect you. I am not only a casualty, I am also a warrior. And of course I am afraid, because the transformation of silence into language and action is an act of self-revelation. . . . For it is not difference which immobilizes us, but silence. And there are so many silences to be broken."

# 12 ON BECOMING ANTI-RAPIST

Haki R. Madhubuti

> If we men, of all races, cultures, and continents would just
> examine the inequalities of power in our own families, businesses,
> and political and spiritual institutions, and decide today to reassess
> and reconfigure them in consultation with the women in our
> lives, we would all be doing the most fundamental corrective act
> of a counter-rapist.

> There are mobs & strangers
> in us
> who scream of the women
> we wanted and
> will get
> as if the women are ours for the
> taking.

In 1991 the crime of rape in the United States entered our consciousness with the power of the dissolution of the U.S.S.R. The trials of William Kennedy Smith (of the Camelot family) and Iron Mike Tyson, former heavyweight boxing champion of the entire world, shared front pages and provided talk-show hosts with subject matter on a topic that is usually confined to women's groups and the butt jokes of many men. Since women are over fifty percent of the world's population and a clear majority in this country, one would think that the question of rape would not still be hidden in the minor concerns files of men.

However, what is not hidden is that Mr. Kennedy Smith and Mr. Tyson both tried defenses that blamed the women in question. For Smith that tactic was successful; for Tyson, it failed. Pages of analysis have been written in both cases, and I do not wish to add to them. But one can safely state that no woman wants to be raped, and that if men were raped at the frequency of women, rape would be a federal crime rivaling those of murder and bank robbery. If car-jacking can command federal attention, why are we still treating rape as if it's a "boys will be boys" sport or a woman's problem as in "blame the victim"? In the great majority of sex crimes against women in the United States, the women are put on trial as if they planned and executed their own rapes.

Male acculturation (or a better description would be males' "seasoning") is antifemale, antiwomanist/feminist, and antireason when it comes to women's equal measure and place in society. This flawed socialization of men is not confined to the West but permeates most, if not all, cultures in the modern world. Most men have been taught to treat, respond, listen, and react to women from a male's point of view. Black men are not an exception here; we, too, are imprisoned with an intellectual/spiritual/sexual understanding of women based upon antiquated male culture and sexist orientation—or should I say miseducation. For example, sex or sexuality is hardly ever discussed, debated, or taught to black men in a nonthreatening or nonembarrassing family or community setting.

Men's view of women, specifically black women outside of the immediate family, is often one of "bitch," "my woman," "ho," or any number of designations that demean and characterize black women as less than whole and productive persons. Our missteps toward an understanding of women are compounded by the cultural environments where much of the talk of women takes place: street corners, locker rooms, male clubs, sporting events, bars, military service, business trips, playgrounds, workplaces, basketball courts, etc. Generally, women are not discussed on street corners or in bars as intellectual or culturally compatible partners. Rather the discussion focuses on what is the best way to "screw" or control them.

These are, indeed, learning environments that traditionally are not kind to women. The point of view that is affirmed all too often is the ownership of women. We are taught to see women as commodities and/or objects for men's sexual releases and sexual fantasies; also, most women are considered "inferiors" to men and thus are not to be respected or trusted. Such thinking is encouraged and legitimized by our culture and transmitted via institutional structures (churches, workplaces), mass media (*Playboy* and *Penthouse*), misogynist music (rap and mainstream), and R-rated and horror films that use exploitative images of women. And of course there are the ever-present, tall, trim, "Barbie-doll" women featured in advertising for everything from condoms to the latest diet "cures." Few men have been taught, really taught, from birth—to the heart, to the gut—to respect, value, or even, on occasion, to honor women. Only until very recently has it been confirmed in Western culture that rape (unwelcomed/uninvited sex) is criminal, evil and antihuman.

our mothers, sisters, wives and
daughters ceased to be the
women men want we think of them as
loving family music & soul bright wonderments.
they are not locker room talk
not the hunted lust or dirty
cunt burnin hos.
bright wonderments are excluded by association as
blood & heart bone & memory
& we will destroy a rapist's knee caps,
& write early grave on his thoughts
to protect them.

Human proximity defines relationships. Exceptions should be noted, but in most cultures and most certainly within the black/African worldview, family and extended family ties are honored and respected. One's sexual personhood in a healthy culture is nurtured, respected, and protected. In trying to get a personal fix here, that is, an understanding of the natural prohibitions against rape, think of one's own personhood being violated. Think of one's own family subjected to this act. Think of the enslavement of African people; it was common to have breeding houses on most plantations where one's great-great-grandmothers were forced to open their insides for the sick satisfaction of white slave owners, overseers, and enslaved black men. This forced sexual penetration of African women led to the creation of mixed-race people here and around the world. There is a saying in South Africa that the colored race did not exist until nine months after white men arrived. This demeaning of black women and other women is amplified in today's culture, where it is not uncommon for young men to proclaim that "pussy is a penny a pound." However, we are told that such a statement is not meant for one's own mother, grandmother, sister, daughter, aunt, niece, close relative, or extended family. Yet the point must be made rather emphatically that incest (family rape) is on the rise in this country. Incest between adults and children is often not revealed until the children are adults. At that point their lives are so confused and damaged that many continue incestuous acts.

it will do us large to recall
when the animal in us rises
that all women are someone's
mother, sister, wife, or daughter
and are not fruit to be stolen when hungry.

Part of the answer is found in the question: Is it possible or realistic to view all women as precious persons? Selective memory plays an important role here. Most men who rape are seriously ill and improperly educated. They do not view women outside of their "protected zone" as precious blood, do not see them as extended family, and do not see them as individuals or independent persons to be respected as most men respect other men. Mental illness or brain mismanagement blocks out reality, shattering and negating respect for self and others, especially the others of which one wishes to take advantage. Power always lurks behind rape. Rape is an act of aggression that asserts power by defaming and defiling. Most men have been taught—either directly or indirectly—to solve problems with force. Such force may be verbal or physical. Violence is the answer that is promoted in media everywhere, from Saturday morning cartoons to everyday television to R-rated films. Popular culture has a way of trivializing reality and confusing human expectations, especially with regards to relationships between men and women. For too many black people, the popular has been internalized. In many instances, the media define us, including our relationships to each other.

Women have been in the forefront of the anti-rape struggle. Much of this work has taken place in nontraditional employment, such as serving in police and fire departments, as top professors and administrators in higher education, as elected and appointed public servants in politics, and in the fields of medicine and law. However, the most pronounced presence and "advancement" of women has been seen in the military. We are told that the military, in terms of social development, remains at the cutting edge of changes, especially in the progress of blacks and female soldiers. However, according to Gary A. Warner in the *San Francisco Examiner* (December 30, 1992), the occurrence of rape against women in the military is far greater than in civilian life:

> A woman serving in the Army is 50 percent more likely to be raped than a civilian, newly released military records obtained by the Orange County Register show.
>
> From 1981 to 1987, 484 female soldiers were raped while on active duty, according to Department of the Army records released after a Freedom of Information Act request.
>
> The Army rate of 129 rape cases per 100,000 population in 1990 exceeds nationwide statistics for the same year compiled by the FBI of 80 confirmed rape cases per 100,000 women. The 1990 statistics are the latest comparable ones available.

The brutality of everyday life continues to confirm the necessity for caring men and women to confront inhuman acts that cloud and prevent wholesome development. Much of what is defined as sexual "pleasure" today comes at the terrible expense of girls and often boys. To walk Times Square or any number of big city playgrounds after dark is to view how loudly the popular, throwaway culture has trapped, corrupted, and sexually abused too many of our children. In the United States the sexual abuse of runaway children, and children sentenced to foster care and poorly supervised orphanages, is nothing less than scandalous. The proliferation of battered women's shelters and the most recent revelation of the sexual abuse of women incarcerated in the nation's prisons only underscores the prevailing view of women by a substantial number of men, as sex objects for whatever sick acts that enter their minds.

Such abuse of children is not confined to the United States. Ron O'Grady, coordinator of the International Campaign to End Child Prostitution in Asiatic Tourism, fights an uphill battle to highlight the physical and economic maltreatment of children. Murray Kempton reminds us in his essay "A New Colonialism" (The *New York Review of Books*, November 19, 1992) of Thailand's "supermarkets for the purchases of small and disposable bodies." He goes on to state that:

> Tourism is central to Thailand's developmental efforts; and the attractions of its ancient culture compare but meagerly to the compelling pull its brothels exercise upon foreign visitors. The government does its duty to the economy by encouraging houses of prostitution and pays its debt to propriety with its insistence that no more than 10,000 children work there. Private observers concerned with larger matters than the good name of public officials estimate the real total of child prostitutes in Thailand at 200,000.
>
> The hunters and others of children find no border closed. They have ranged into South China carrying television sets to swap one per child. The peasants who cursed the day a useless girl was born know better now: they can sell her for consumers overseas and be consumers themselves. Traffickers less adventurous stay at home and contrive travel agencies that offer cheap trips to Kuala Lumpur that end up with sexual enslavement in Japan or Malaysia.

That this state of affairs is not better known speaks loudly and clearly to the devaluation of female children. The war in Sarajevo, Bosnia, and Herzegovina again highlights the status of women internationally. In the rush toward ethnic cleansing and narrow and exclusive nationalism, Serbian soldiers have been indicted for murder and other war crimes. The story of one such soldier, Borislav Herak, is instructive. According to an article by John F. Burnes in the *New York Times* (November 27, 1992) entitled "A Serbian Fighter's Trial of Brutality," Mr. Herak and other soldiers were given the go-ahead to rape and kill Muslim women:

> The indictment lists 29 individual murders between June and October, including eight rape-murders of Muslim women held prisoner in an abandoned motel and cafe outside Vogosca, seven miles north of Sarajevo, where, Mr. Herak said, he and other Serbian fighters were encouraged to rape women and then take them away to kill them in hilltops and other deserted places.
>
> The indictment also covers the killings of at least 220 other Muslim civilians in which Mr. Herak has confessed to being a witness or taking part, many of them women and children. (Also see the January 4, 1993 issue of *Newsweek*.)

Much in the lives of women is not music or melody but is their dancing to the beat of the unhealthy and often killing drums of men and male teenagers. Rape is not the fault of women; however, in a male-dominated world, the victims are often put on the defensive and forced to rationalize their gender and their personhood.

Rape is not a reward for warriors
it is war itself

a deep, deep tearing, a dislocating of
the core of the womanself.
rape rips heartlessly
soul from spirit,
obliterating colors from beauty and body
replacing melody and music with
rat venom noise and uninterrupted intrusion and beatings.

The brutality of rape is universal. Most modern cultures—European, American, African, Asian, religious, and secular—grapple with this crime. Rarely is there discussion, and, more often than not, women are discouraged from being a part of the debates and edicts. Rape is cross-cultural. I have not visited, heard of, or read about any rape-free societies. The war against women is international. Daily, around the world, women fight for a little dignity and their earned place in the world. And men in power respond accordingly. For example, Barbara Crossette reported in the *New York Times* (April 7, 1991) about an incident in Batamaloo, Kashmir:

> In this conservative Muslim Society, women have moved to the forefront of demonstrations and also into guerrilla conclaves. No single event has contributed more to this rapidly rising militancy among women than reports of a gang rape a month ago by Indian troops in Kunan, a remote village in northwestern Kashmir.
>
> According to a report filed by S. M. Yasin, district magistrate in Kupwara, the regional center, the armed forces "behaved like violent beasts." He identified them as members of the Fourth Rajputana Rifles and said that they rampaged through the village from 11 P.M. on Feb. 23 until 9 the next morning.
>
> "A large number of armed personnel entered into the houses of villagers and at gunpoint they gang-raped 23 ladies, without any consideration of their age, married, unmarried, pregnancy etc.," he wrote. "There was a hue and cry in the whole village." Local people say that as many as 100 women were molested in some way.

As a man of Afrikan descent, I would like to think that Afrikans have some special insight, enlightened hearts, or love in us that calms us in such times of madness. But my romanticism is shattered every day as I observe black communities across this land. The number of rapes reported and unreported in our communities is only the latest and most painful example of how far we have drifted from beauty. However, it is seldom that I have hurt more than when I learned about the "night of terror" that occurred in Meru, Kenya, on July 13, 1991, at the St. Kizito boarding school. A high school protest initiated by the boys, in which the girls refused to join, resulted in a night of death, rapes, and beatings unparalleled in modern Kenya, in Africa or in the world. As Timothy Dwyer reported in the *Chicago Tribune* (April 18, 1991):

> The night of terror a month ago at the boarding school near Mount Kenya has torn the soul of the Kenyan people. What had the girls done to invoke the wrath of their male schoolmates? They dared say no to the boys, who wanted them to join a protest against the school's headmaster, according to police and to those girls who lived through the night.

In Kenya, one-party rule has resulted in a tyranny of the majority. Dissent, even in politics, is not welcome. "Here, the minority must always go along with the majority's wishes," said a businessman who has done a lot of work with the government in the last 15 years and asked not to be named. "And it is said that a woman cannot say no to a man."

Woman's groups have said the rapes and deaths were an extreme metaphor for what goes on in the Kenyan society. The girls of St. Kizito dared to say no to the boys, and 19 paid with their lives while 71 others were beaten and raped. . . .

There have been many school protests in Kenya this year. This summer alone, some 20 protests have turned into riots resulting in the destruction of school property. There have been rapes at other schools when girls have refused to join boys in their protests.

A growing part of the answer is that we men, as difficult as it may seem, must view all women (no matter who they are—race, culture, religion, or nationality aside) as extended family. The question is, and I know that I am stretching: Would we rape our mothers, grandmothers, sisters, or other female relatives, or even give such acts a thought? Can we extend this attitude to all women? Therefore we must:

1. Teach our sons that it is their responsibility to be anti-rapist; that is, they must be counter-rapist in thought, conversations, raps, organizations, and actions.

2. Teach our daughters how to defend themselves and maintain an uncompromising stance toward men and boys.

3. Understand that being a counter-rapist is honorable, manly, and necessary for a just society.

4. Understand that anti-rapist actions are part of the black tradition; being an anti-rapist is in keeping with the best Afrikan culture and with Afrikan family and extended family configurations. Even in times of war we were known to honor and respect the personhood of children and women.

5. Be glowing examples of men who are fighting to treat women as equals and to be fair and just in associations with women. This means at the core that families as now defined and constructed must continually be reassessed. In today's economy most women, married and unmarried, must work. We men must encourage them in their work and must be intimately involved in rearing children and doing housework.

6. Understand that just as men are different from one another, women also differ; therefore we must try not to stereotype women into the limiting and often debilitating expectations of men. We must encourage and support them in their searching and development.

7. Be unafraid of independent, intelligent, and self-reliant women. And by extension, understand that intelligent women think for themselves and may not want to have sex with a particular man. This is a woman's prerogative and is not a comment on anything else other than the fact that she does not want to have sex.

8. Be bold and strong enough to stop other men (friends or strangers) from raping and to intervene in a rape in process with the fury and destruction of a hurricane against the rapist.

9. Listen to women. Listen to women, especially to womanist/feminist/Pan-Africanist philosophies of life. Also, study the writings of women, especially black women.

10. Act responsibly in response to the listening and studying. Be a part of and support anti-rape groups for boys and men. Introduce anti-rape discussion into men's groups and organizations.

11. Never stop growing, and understand that growth is limited and limiting without the input of intelligent women.

12. Learn to love. Study love. Even if one is at war, love and respect, respect and love must conquer, if there is to be a sane and livable world. Rape is anti-love, anti-respect. Love is not easy. One does not fall in love but *grows* into love.

We can put to rest the rape problem in one generation if its eradication is as important to us as our cars, jobs, careers, sport-games, beer, and quest for power. However, the women who put rape on the front burners must continue to challenge us and their own cultural training, and position themselves so that they and their messages are not compromised or ignored.

> A significant few of their
> fathers, brothers, husbands, sons
> and growing strangers
> are willing to unleash harm onto the earth
> and spill blood in the eyes
> of
> maggots in running shoes
> who do not know the sounds of birth
> or respect the privacy of the human form

If we are to be just in our internal rebuilding we must challenge tradition and cultural ways of life that relegate women to inferior status in the home, church/mosque/temple, workplace, political life, and education. Men are not born rapists; we are taught very subtly, often in unspoken ways, that women are ours for the taking. Generally, such teachings begin with the family. Enlightenment demands fairness, impartiality, and vision; it demands confrontation of outdated definitions and acceptance of fair and just resolutions. One's sex, race, social class, or wealth should not determine entitlements or justice. If we are honest, men must be in the forefront of eradicating sex stereotypes in all facets of private and public life. I think that being honest, as difficult and as self-incriminating as it may be, is the only way that we can truly liberate ourselves. If men can liberate themselves (with the help of women) from the negative aspects of the culture that produced them, maybe a just, fair, good, and liberated society is possible in our lifetime.

The liberation of the male psyche from preoccupation with domination, power hunger, control, and absolute rightness requires an honest and fair assessment of patriarchal culture. This requires commitment to deep study, combined with a willingness for painful, uncomfortable, and often shocking change. We are not where we should be. That is why rape exists; why families are so easily formed and just as easily dissolved; why children are confused and abused; why our elderly are discarded, abused, and exploited; and why teenage boys create substitute families (gangs) that terrorize their own communities.

I remain an optimistic realist, primarily because I love life and most of what it has to offer. I often look at my children and tears come to my eyes because I realize how blessed I am to be their father. My wife and the other women in my life are special because they know that they are special and have taken it upon themselves, at great cost, to actualize their dreams, making what was considered for many of them unthinkable a few years ago a reality today. If we men, of all races, cultures, and continents would just examine the inequalities of power in our own families, businesses, and political and spiritual institutions, and decide today to reassess and reconfigure them in consultation with the women in our lives, we would all be doing the most fundamental corrective act of a counter-rapist.

It is indeed significant, and not an arbitrary aside, that males and females are created biologically different. These profound differences are partially why we are attracted to each other and are also what is beautiful about life. But too often due to hierarchical and patriarchal definitions one's sex also relegates one to a position in life that is not necessarily respected. Sex should not determine moral or economic worth, as it now does in too many cultures. In a just society, one's knowledge and capabilities, that is, what one is actually able to contribute to the world, is more valuable than if the person is male or female.

Respect for the woman closest to us can give us the strength and knowledge to confront the animal in us with regards to the women we consider "others." Also, keep in mind that the "others" often are the women closest to us. If we honestly confront the traditions and histories that have shaped us, we may come to the realize that women should be encouraged to go as far as their intellect and talents will take them—burdened only by the obstacles that affect all of us. Most certainly the sexual energies of men must be checked before our misguided maleness manifests itself in the most horrible of crimes—rape.

> No!
> Means No!
> even when men think
> that they are "god's gift to women"
> even after dropping a week's check & more
> on dinner by the ocean,
> the four tops, temptations and intruders memory tour,

imported wine & rose that captured her smile,
suggested to you private music & low lights
drowning out her inarticulated doubts.

Question the thousand years teachings
crawling through your lower depths and
don't let your little head
out think your big head.
No! means No!
even when her signals suggest yes.

# 13 THE SEXUAL DIVERSION
## The Black Man / Black Woman Debate in Context

DERRICK BELL

Rayford Logan, the great black historian, called the period at the turn of the last century the nadir for black people. Hundreds of blacks were lynched, thousands were victims of racist violence and intimidation, and literally millions were exploited on farms and at mostly menial labor where their pay failed to cover the food and other necessities they were often required to purchase from their employers.

For Dr. Logan, the nadir meant the bottom, a status that arguably was only a small step up from slavery itself. It is a measure of the fragility of our current condition that a great many thoughtful black people now worry that we are heading toward another nadir, this one marked by far more self-destruction than anyone living a century ago could easily imagine. The statistics supporting these concerns are all too familiar.[1] Maya Angelou transforms them into words that highlight the pain of our plight:

> In these bloody days and frightful nights when an urban warrior can find no face more despicable than his own, no ammunition more deadly than self-hate and no target more deserving of his true aim than his brother, we must wonder how we came so late and lonely to this place.[2]

If African Americans are to survive the storms we are now experiencing—and those storms now brewing on the horizon—we must reconnect ourselves, eschewing in the process divisive behaviors that distract us from the dangers lurking outside our community, dangers we know all too well and prefer to deny.

It is sad but hardly remarkable that oppressed black people vent far more of their rage on other blacks than on their oppressors. The very power that defines the status of those on the top and those on the bottom serves to deflect frustrated rage from the perpetrators of oppression to fellow sufferers. Diversion is now, and likely has always been, an important tactic in preventing the oppressed from recognizing the true sources of their oppression. Those in power recognize the value of diversion to redirect victim rage away from themselves and seldom miss the chance to promote its paranoid permutations.

Once sown, the seeds of distrust and enmity seem to flourish on their own. Those in power need do no more than appear to favor one subordinate group over another to quell even a possibility that the feuding groups will either recognize the similar character of their lowly state or identify the source of their condition. The lowly ones engage in spirited expressions of hostility against each other, exhausting time, energy, and resources that might otherwise be employed against their oppressors. In the process, their squabbling provides their real enemies with a seemingly impenetrable insulation from intergroup strife among those who, while fearing their differences, are quite similar in their subordination. Subordination, by its very nature, generates beliefs and behaviors that lead to antagonism among subordinate groups. Victims often look for the less powerful and attempt to victimize them in turn. Those harmed seek to retaliate, and soon there is a vicious cycle of hostility that creates disorder and chaos among victims of the status quo while serving to ensure the position of those in power.

The stability and even the survival of the economic system in this country depends on maintaining divisions between people based on race, gender, and class. The success of this strategy can be measured in the fact that (for example) there is little outcry about the gap in income and wealth between the rich and the rest of us, even though this gap is larger than at any time in this century. The reason is not hard to find. Those at the short end of the income and wealth gap are easily convinced that they should vent their otherwise unfocused upset on those on welfare, newly arrived immigrants, those who commit street crimes, and the society's traditional scapegoat—black people. A great many whites across the socioeconomic spectrum are vocal in their opposition to affirmative action policies that they view as aiding less qualified members of minorities at their expense; there is no similar opposition to all manner of priorities and preferences aimed at privileging those who are already well-off.

It would be a most welcome but quite unlikely miracle if black people, we who from our earliest days in this country have occupied the very bottom of society's well, were able to avoid the victim's predisposition to battle others within our group rather than those responsible for our lowly status. Alas, it is likely that because of our long history of subordinate status in this country we are more rather than less prone to this affliction. Because sexism and patriarchy are deeply rooted in this society, all too many black men have fallen into patterns of physical and emotional abuse of women, behavior that black women understandably fear and resent.

For a generation now, a host of writers—many of them black women—have been telling the world about the inadequacies of black men. This often emotional testimony ranges from mournful frustration to flat-out rage. These revelations contain both deeply felt disappointment about what often is and a yearning hope about what might be. And while there are many, many black males who do not fit the woeful patterns, we know from statistics and personal experience that these criticisms are based in reality as well as myth. Rather than either condone or condemn, I want to examine this phenomenon in the context of a society where the deflection of oppression is the norm.

Who can deny it? Life for black men in racist America is devilishly difficult. Surely, a factor in our failings is the hostility we encounter at every level. While slavery is over, a racist society continues to exert dominion over black men and their maleness in ways more subtle but hardly less castrating than during slavery, when male-female relationships between black people generally were not formalized, and even when a marriage was recognized, the black man's sexual access to his wife was controlled by the master or his sons or his overseer.

Black women also suffered the pains of slavery. Black women were exploited, abused, and demeaned, and that harm was serious. Forced to submit to the sexual desires of their masters or to slaves selected by their masters, they then suffered the agony of watching helplessly as their children were sold off. Black men were also dealt a double blow. They were forced to stand by powerless and unable to protect black women from sexual access by white men, and they were denied access to white women as a further symbol of their subordinate status. The harm done black men by this dual assault has never been fully assessed. Moreover, the assault continues in less blatant but still potent forms.

James Baldwin asserts that "the action of the White Republic, in the lives of Black men, has been, and remains, emasculation. Hence, the Republic has absolutely no image, or standard, of masculinity to which any man, Black or White, can honorably aspire."[3] The vain effort to protect black males against this ever-present danger, Baldwin explains, results in what Andy Young calls "sorriness," a disease that attacks black males. Baldwin writes:

> It is transmitted by Mama, whose instinct—and it is not hard to see why—is to protect the Black male from the devastation that threatens him the moment he declares himself a man. All of our mothers, and all of our women, live with this small, doom-laden bell in the skull, silent, waiting, or resounding, every hour of every day. Mama lays this burden on Sister, from whom she expects (or indicates she expects) far more than she expects from Brother; but one of the results of this all too comprehensible dynamic is that Brother may never grow up—in which case, the community has become an accomplice to the Republic.[4]

Women may well respond that here is one more effort, albeit a well-written one, to blame male failure on female love. There is a chicken and egg aspect to this position. This society has not much loved either black men or black women, and debate as to whether society's hostility or parental efforts to shield males from this hostility is more damaging does not move us much closer toward the relief that both need. Even so, in Baldwin's view, "this dilemma has everything to do with the situation of the Black man in the American inferno."[5]

Black women do not accept racism as the reason for sorry behavior—they have experienced it firsthand, and for them it is an excuse, not a justification. Alice Walker's character Grange Copeland speaks her mind on this subject:

> I'm bound to believe that that's the way white folks can corrupt you even when you done held up before. 'Cause when they got you thinking that they're to blame for everything they have you thinking they's some kind of gods! You can't do nothing wrong without them being behind it. You gits just as weak as water, no feeling of doing nothing yourself. Then you begins to think up evil and begins to destroy everybody around you, and you blames it on the crackers. Shit! Nobody's as powerful as we make them out to be. We got our own souls, don't we?[6]

In addition to rejecting the traditional, patriarchal notion that women must be protected by men, black women cannot see why black men must try to emulate the macho sexism of their white counterparts rather than work toward a more natural and healthy equality between the sexes. As a woman student wrote in an essay, quoting Fran Sanders's "Dear Black Man,"

> Talk to me like the woman that I am and not to me as that woman who is the inanimate creation of someone's overactive imagination. Look at me with no preconceived notions of how I must act or feel and I will try to do the same with you. No presumption, no assumptions, no banal rhetoric substituted for real person-to-person giving and receiving. Look at my face when you speak to me; look into my eyes and see what they have to say. Think about the answers that you give to my questions. . . . I am a woman and you are a man and I have always known it. If you love me, tell me so. Don't approach me as you would an enemy. I am on your side and have always been. We have survived, and we may just be able to teach the world a lesson.[7]

That, of course, is a wonderful homily of how life should be for sexual partners, regardless of race. It is an ideal, and as is obvious from the charges and countercharges, a far from fulfilled ideal for many black men and women.[8] It can hardly be denied that black women bear much of the brunt of black male frustration and suppressed rage.

During my twenty-five years of law school teaching, I have listened to dozens of black women—and more than a few white ones—voice their disappointments with many black men. Much of the problem is due to the paucity of black men at the professional level rather than to their behavior. The statistics regarding the number of black men who fall by the wayside long before professional school are harsh. Most law school classes contain many more black women than men. This disparity heightens black women's sense of betrayal when potentially available black men choose white women. As one of my students put it, "We black women are always being reminded of how marginal and unworthy we are. We're never smart enough or beautiful enough or supportive, sexy, understanding, and resourceful enough to deserve a good black man."[9]

Another former student, Kirsten Levingston, makes clear that she would not encourage a black woman to stay with a black man if he made her unhappy, nor would she discourage a black man from marrying a white woman who makes him happy. Even so, she believes black Americans must do all they can to unite and develop. This unity begins at home with our children, and, she contends, "the key to producing strong and proud black children is to raise them in an environment with strong and proud black parents."[10] Ms. Levingston's call for unity may be unrealistic in a society where one-half of all marriages end in divorce, but hers is a view shared by many, perhaps most, black women.

Recently, while discussing this issue in a civil rights class, two black women prepared a fictional dialogue among friends regarding interracial relationships. As reported by the black woman commentator, the black and white law students discussed the tendency of handsome and promising black men to prefer or at least look with admiration on white women, while disliking ethnic hair styles and other Afrocentric "looks" on black women. They raised the often unspoken question regarding black women's suspicion that any expression of interest in them by white men is based on the stereotype of black women as super-sensual, and discussed the refusal of some black women to date white men for that reason. The narrator shares this concern, but feels trapped by it because the "bottom line is that there just aren't enough brothers to go around." She recognizes that many black men are not very sensitive to this dilemma, resent black women who date white men, and sometimes ask, "How come a garbage collector isn't good enough for you?" The fictional group discusses several variations on this theme and then the narrator closes with this observation:

> As I took a sip from my wine glass, I realized that there were no definitive answers. I could say I am black, female, and bright in a white mediocre world, but that hardly explains why I sit on the beaches of St. Croix feeling so abandoned.

In the same class, a young Indian woman, after conceding the burdening nature of male hegemony in Indian culture, posed the question,

> Why is it that struggle and racial adversity create strong black women and "weak and disempowered" black men? The African-American female has fewer job opportunities and just as many stereotypes heaped upon her as does the African-American male. Why does the most oppressed class, women of color, derive strength from oppression, whereas black men may scapegoat oppression to justify unjustifiable behavior (often against women of color).

Both my student's question and the issue deserve to be more firmly grounded in the societal environment out of which they come. I shared my student's observations with a black social worker friend, Gwen Jordan, who felt that the Indian woman posed an ultimate dilemma for all people of color. When we attempt to work through the difficulties in relationships that are fundamental to the preservation of our culture and well-being in public, within the view of others who do not share our cultural issues, we unconsciously place that struggle in the context of an alien culture whose values and mores do not support—and are often hostile to—the core of our definition and being. And then it is from this perspective that we evaluate and judge the quality of these relationships and the sincerity of our mates.

In Ms. Jordan's view, African-Americans in their relationships must struggle to achieve a level of unconditional love in a systemic context—racism—which places conditions upon our being. Within that context, we trivialize ourselves when we attempt to define African-American male/ female relationships in terms of the prevailing culture: we attribute to black females mystical powers and strengths that become burdensome in their superficiality, and we attribute weakness and defeat to black males. These, according to Jordan, are really just more sophisticated versions of the stereotypes that we have carried since slavery. The result is that we disempower ourselves and imperil our capacity to love unconditionally and, through that love, to grow and create together.

The threat of disempowerment is certainly real, but the effort to define differences can be both revealing and strengthening in our understanding of how we function as male and female human beings. James Baldwin, for example, provides an enlightening statement about the psychological make-up of men and their weakness, too often masked by a show of muscle and—it must be said—all too often manifested in the physical abuse of those very women who would, if given a chance, love and care for them. Baldwin writes:

> One is confronted, first of all, with the universal mystery of men—as we are, of a man, as he is; with the legend and the reality of the masculine force and the masculine role—though these last two realities are not always the same. Men would seem to dream more than women do—always have, it would seem, and very probably, always will. They must, since they assume that their role is to alter and conquer reality. If women dream less than men—for men know very little about a woman's dreams—it is certainly because they are so swiftly confronted with the reality of men. They must accommodate this indispensable creature, who is, in so many ways, more fragile than a woman. Women know much more about men than men will ever know about women—which may, at bottom, be the only reason that the race has managed to survive so long.
>
> In any case, the male cannot bear very much humiliation; and he really cannot bear it, it obliterates him. All men know this about each other, which is one of the reasons that men can treat each other with such a vile, relentless, and endlessly inventive cruelty. Also, however, it must be added, with such depthless respect and love, conveyed mainly by grunts and blows. It has often

seemed to me that men need each other in order to deal with women, and women, God knows, must need each other in order to deal with men.

Women manage, quite brilliantly, on the whole, and to stunning and unforeseeable effect, to survive and surmount being defined by others. They dismiss the definition, however dangerous or wounding it may be—or even, sometimes, find a way to utilize it—perhaps because they are not dreaming. But men are neither so supple nor so subtle. A man fights for his manhood: that's the bottom line. A man does not have, simply, the weapons of a woman. Mama must feed her children—that's another bottom line; and there is a level on which it can be said that she cannot afford to care how she does it.

But when a man cannot feed his women or his children, he finds it, literally, impossible to face them. The song says, Now, when a woman gets the blues, Lord/She hangs her head and cries/But when a man gets the blues, Lord/He grabs a train and rides.[11]

Even we black men fortunate enough to provide for our families must defend against the myriad forms of emasculation that the society has placed in our path. Success as the society measures it exacts a very real and often terrible price. None of us escapes, really, and those of us who feel we have established some limits to what we will put up with spend far more time than we should criticizing those who, by our measures, have been too willing to comfort whites in order to either get ahead or (usually) stay even.

Baldwin, I think, would urge more understanding—if not compassion— as he reminds us:

It is a very grave matter to be forced to imitate a people for whom you know— which is the price of your performance and survival—you do not exist. It is hard to imitate a people whose existence appears, mainly, to be made tolerable by their bottomless gratitude that they are not, thank heaven, you.[12]

Writer Jill Nelson speaks for many of us, men as well as women, when she describes how difficult it is to maintain one's ethical bearings in the job market. Following a series of interviews at a major, white newspaper that was considering her as a reporter, she wrote:

I've been doing the standard Negro balancing act when it comes to dealing with white folks, which involves sufficiently blurring the edges of my being so that white folks don't feel intimidated and simultaneously holding on to my integrity. There is a thin line between Uncle Tomming and Mau-Mauing. To step over that line can mean disaster. On one side lies employment and self-hatred, on the other, the equally dubious honor of unemployment with integrity. In the middle lies something like employment with honor, although I'm not sure exactly how that works.[13]

Jill Nelson got the job. Even so, it was a constant hassle, which she writes about with pain-filled humor. Increasingly, blacks—men and women—are not getting these jobs, or much of any work. The optimist might hope that frustrated employment hopes might bring humility and compassion to the Donnells of this world and their less talented brethren. Alas, for all the reasons Baldwin asserts, it usually does not. And it is unlikely that the relations between some black men and black women will improve until societal conditions improve. Even so, we must not ignore the fact that despite all the barriers, a great many—dare we say most?—black men marry and stay with their wives and families through thick and thin. Here, again, Baldwin says it well:

> A stranger to this planet might find the fact that there are any Black people at all still alive in America something to write home about. I myself find it remarkable not that so many Black men were forced (and in so many ways!) to leave their families, but that so many remained and aided their issue to grow and flourish.[14]

This positive observation provides an important foundation on which to plan the coming struggle for our survival in a society in transition, one that appears more than ready to sacrifice our interests, our well-being, even our lives, in a desperate effort to avoid the dangers inherent in change. The black man/black woman debate should continue, but participants must be aware of the ever-present temptation of diversion and its potential to twist that debate in a way that comforts our enemies and betrays ourselves.

### NOTES

1. Typical are the figures issued by the U.S. Justice Department, reporting that young black men were almost 14 times more likely to be murdered during 1992 than the nation's general population. In that year, black males ages twelve to twenty-four were victims of homicide at a rate of 114.9 per 100,000, compared with 8.5 murder victims per 100,000 of the general population. They constituted 17.7 percent of all homicide victims, even though they were only 1.3 percent of the U.S. population. Black males age sixteen to twenty-four, were 1.5 times more likely to be victims of all types of violent crime (source: "Around the Nation," *Washington Post*, 9 December 1994, A = 10).

2. Maya Angelou, "I Dare to Hope," *New York Times*, 25 August 1991, 15.

3. James Baldwin, *The Evidence of Things Not Seen* (1985), 21.

4. Ibid., 19.

5. Ibid., 20.

6. Alice Walker, *The Third Life of Grange Copeland* (1970), 207.

7. F. Sanders, "Dear Black Man," in *The Black Woman: An Anthology*, ed. T. Cade (1970), 73, 78–79.

8. Compare Wallace, "A Black Feminist's Search for Sisterhood," in *All the Blacks Are Men, All the Women Are White, but Some of Us Are Brave*, ed. G. T. Hull et al. (1982), 5–8 ("Whenever I raised the question of a Black woman's humanity in conversation with a Black man, I got a similar reaction. Black men, at least the ones I knew, seemed totally confounded when it came to treating Black women like people"), with Staples, "The Myth of Black Macho: A Response to Angry Black Feminists," *Black Scholar*, March/April 1979, 24–32 (While black males are not free of sexism, most black men lack the institutionalized power to oppress black men, and it is their lowly societal position that most disturbs black males).

9. I used this quote in the story "The Last Black Hero," in Derrick Bell, *Faces at the Bottom of the Well: The Permanence of Racism* (1992), 75.

10. See "Racial Reflections: Dialogues in the Direction of Liberation," ed. Derrick Bell, Tracy Higgins, Sung-Hee Suh, *UCLA Law Review* 37 (1990): 1037, 1083.

11. Baldwin, *Evidence of Things Not Seen,* 20–21.

12. Ibid., 44.

13. Jill Nelson, *Volunteer Slavery* (1993), 10.

14. Baldwin, *Evidence of Things Not Seen,* 21.

# 14
## A BLACK MAN'S PLACE IN
## BLACK FEMINIST CRITICISM

Michael Awkward

Many essays by male and female scholars devoted to exploring the subject of male critics' place in feminism generally agree about the uses and usefulness of the autobiographical male "I." Such essays suggest that citing the male critical self reflects a response to (apparent) self-difference, an exploration of the disparities between the masculine's antagonistic position in feminist discourse on the one hand and, on the other, the desire of the individual male critic to represent his difference with and from the traditional andro-centric perspectives of his gender and culture. Put another way, in male feminist acts, to identify the writing self as biologically male is to emphasize the desire not to be ideologically male; it is to explore the process of rejecting the phallocentric perspectives by which men traditionally have justified the subjugation of women.[1]

In what strikes me as a particularly suggestive theoretical formulation, Joseph Boone articulates his sense of the goals of such male feminist auto-biographical acts:

> In exposing the latent multiplicity and difference in the word "me(n)," we can perhaps open up a space within the discourse of feminism where a male feminist voice *can* have something to say beyond impossibilities and apologies and unresolved ire. Indeed, if the male feminist can discover a position *from which* to speak that neither elides the importance of feminism to his work nor ignores the specificity of his gender, his voice may also find that it no longer exists as an abstraction . . . but that it in fact inhabits a body: its own sexual/ textual body.[2]

Because of an awareness that androcentric perspectives are learned, are transmitted by means of specific sociocultural practices in such effective ways that they come to appear natural, male feminists such as Boone believe that, through an informed investigation of androcentric and feminist ideologies, individual men can work to resist the lure of the normatively masculine. That resistance for the aspiring male feminist requires, he says, exposing "the latent multiplicity and difference in the word 'men,'" in other words, disrupting both ideologies' unproblematized perceptions of monolithic and/or normative maleness (as villainous, antagonistic "other" for feminism, and, for androcentricism, powerful, domineering patriarch). At this early stage of male feminism's development, to speak self-consciously— autobiographically—is to explore, implicity or explicitly, why and how the individual male experience (the "me" in men) has diverged from, has created possibilities for a rejection of, the androcentric norm.

And while there is not yet agreement as to what constitutes an identifiably male feminist act of criticism or about the usefulness of such acts for the general advancement of the feminist project, at least one possible explanation for a male critic's self-referential discourse is that it is a response to palpable mistrust—emanating from some female participants in feminism and perhaps from the writing male subject himself—about his motives. A skeptical strand of opinion with regard to male feminism is represented by Alice Jardine's "Men in Feminism: Odor di Uomo or Compagnons de Route?" Having determined that the most useful measure of an adequately feminist text is its *"inscription of struggle*—even of *pain"*—an inscription of a struggle against patriarchy which Jardine finds absent from most male feminist acts, perhaps because "the historical fact that is the oppression of women [is] . . . one of their favorite blind spots"—she admits to some confusion as to the motivations for males' willing participation: "Why . . . would men want to be in feminism if it's about struggle? What do men want to be in—in pain?"[3]

In addition to seeking to cure its blindness where the history of female oppression is concerned, a male feminism must explore the motivations for its participation in what we might call, in keeping with Jardine's formulations, a discourse of (en)gendered pain. If one of the goals of male feminist self-referentiality is to demonstrate to females that individual males can indeed serve as allies in efforts to undermine androcentric power—and it seems that this is invariably the case—the necessary trust cannot be gained by insisting that motivation as such does not represent a crucial area that must be carefully negotiated. For example, I accept as accurate and, indeed, reflective of my own situation Andrew Ross's assertion that "there are those [men] for whom the *facticity* of feminism, for the most part, goes without saying . . . , who are young enough for feminism to have been a primary component of their intellectual formation."[4] However, in discussions whose apparent function is a foregrounding of both obstacles to and possibilities of a male feminism, men's relation(s) to the discourse can never go "without saying"; for the foreseeable future at least, this relation needs necessarily to be rigorously and judiciously theorized, and grounded explicitly in the experiential realm of the writing male subject.

But no matter how illuminating and exemplary one finds self-referential inscriptions of a male feminist critical self, if current views of the impossibility of a consistently truthful autobiographical act are correct, there are difficulties implicit in any such attempt to situate or inscribe that male self. Because, as recent theorizing on the subject of autobiography has demonstrated, acts of discursive self-rendering unavoidably involve the creation of an idealized version of a unified or unifiable self, we can be certain only of the fact that the autobiographical impulse yields but some of the truths of the male feminist critic's experiences.[5] As is also the case for female participants, a male can never possess or be able to tell the whole truth and nothing but the truth about his relationship to feminist discourse and praxis.

But while autobiographical criticism, like the genre of autobiography itself, is poised tenuously between the poles of closure and disclosure, between representation and re-presentation, between a lived life and an invented one, I believe that even in the recoverable half-truths of my life are some of the materials that have shaped my perceptions, my beliefs, the self or selves that I bring to the interpretive act. In these half-truths is the source of my desire both to inscribe a black male feminism and to inscribe myself as a self-consciously racialized version of what Jardine considers a potentially oxymoronic entity—"male feminist"—whose literal, if not ideological or performative "blackness" is indisputable, and whose adequacy vis-à-vis feminism others must determine. By examining discussions of the phenomenon of the male feminist—that is to say, by reading male and female explorations of men's places in feminist criticism—and exploring responses of others to my own professional and personal relationships to feminism, I will identify autobiographically and textually grounded sources for my belief that while gendered difference might be said to complicate the prospect of a non-phallocentric black male feminism, it does not render such a project impossible.

At the outset, I acknowledge that mine is a necessary participation with regard to black feminist criticism in the half-invention, half-perception which, in Houston Baker's compelling formulation, represents every scholar's relationship to cultural criticism.[6] Such an acknowledgment is not intended to indicate that my male relationship to feminism is that of an illegitimate child, as it were. Rather, it is meant to suggest, like Elizabeth Weed's insistence on "the impossibility" of both men's and women's "relationship to feminism," my belief that while feminism represents a complex, sometimes self-contradictory "utopian vision" which no one can fully possess, a biological male can "develop political, theoretical [and, more generally, interpretive] strategies" which, though at most perhaps half-true to all that feminist ideologies are, nevertheless can assist in a movement toward actualizing the goals of feminism.[7]

I have been forced to think in especially serious ways about my own relationship to feminist criticism since I completed the first drafts of *Inspiring
Influences*, my study of Afro-American women novelists.[8] I have questioned
neither the explanatory power of feminism nor the essential importance
of developing models adequate to the analysis of black female-authored
texts, as my book—in harmony, I believe, with the black feminist project
concerned with recovering and uncovering an Afro-American female literary tradition—attempts to provide on a limited scale. Instead, I have been
confronted with suspicion about my gendered suitability for the task of
explicating Afro-American women's texts, suspicion which has been manifested in the form of both specific responses to my project and general
inquiries within literary studies into the phenomenon of the male feminist.

For example, a white female reader of the manuscript asserted—with
undisguised surprise—that my work was "so feminist" and asked how I'd
managed to offer such ideologically informed readings. Another scholar, a
black feminist literary critic, recorded with no discernible hesitation her
unease with my "male readings" of the texts of Zora Neale Hurston, Toni
Morrison, Gloria Naylor, and Alice Walker. I wondered about the possibility
of my being simultaneously "so feminist" and not so feminist (i.e., so "male"),
about the meanings of these terms both for these scholars and for the larger
interpretive communities in which they participate. Consequently, in what
was perhaps initially an act of psychic self-protection, I began to formulate
questions for which I still have found no consistently satisfactory answers.
Were the differences in the readers' perceptions of the ideological adequacy
of my study a function of their own views of feminist criticism, a product, in
other words, of the differences not simply *within me* but *within feminism
itself*? And if the differences within feminism are so significant, could I
possibly satisfy everybody with "legitimate" interests in the texts of Hurston
et al. by means of my own appropriated versions of black feminist discourse,
my unavoidably half-true myth of what that discourse is, means, and does?
Should my myth of feminism and its mobilization in critical texts be considered naturally less analytically compelling than that of a female scholar
simply as a function of my biological maleness? And how could what I took
to be a useful self-reflexivity avoid becoming a debilitating inquiry into a
process that has come to seem for me, if not "natural," as Cary Nelson views
his relationship to feminism, at least *necessary*?[9]

Compelled, and, to be frank, disturbed by such questions, I searched for
answers in others' words, others' work. I purchased a copy of *Men in Feminism*, a collection which examines the possibility of men's participation as
"comrades" (to use Toni Morrison's term) in feminist criticism and theory.
Gratified by the appearance of such a volume, I became dismayed upon
reading the editors' introductory remarks, which noted their difficulty in
"locating intellectuals, who, having shown interest in the question, would
offer, for instance, a gay or a black perspective on the problem"[10] While a

self-consciously "gay . . . perspective" does find its way into the collection, the insights of nonwhite males and females are conspicuously absent.[11]

Even more troubling for me than the absence of black voices or, for that matter, of general inquiries into the effects of racial, cultural, and class differences on males' relationship to feminism, was the sense shared by many contributors of insurmountable obstacles to male feminism. In fact, the first essay, Stephen Heath's "Male Feminism," begins by insisting that "men's relation to feminism is an impossible one."[12] For me, Heath's formulations are insightful and provocative, if not always persuasive, as when he claims: "This is, I believe, the most any man can do today: to learn and so to try to write and talk or act in response to feminism, and so to try not in any way to be anti-feminist, supportive of the old oppressive structures. Any more, any notion of writing a feminist book or being a feminist, is a myth, a male imaginary with the reality of appropriation and domination right behind.[13] Is male participation in feminism restricted to being either appropriative and domineering or not antifeminist? Must we necessarily agree with Heath and others who claim that men cannot be feminists? To put the matter differently, is gender really an adequate determinant of "class" position?

Despite the poststructuralist tenor of Heath's work generally and of many of his perspectives here, his is an easily problematized essentialist claim — that, in effect, biology determines destiny and, therefore, one's relationship to feminist ideology, that womanhood allows one to become feminist at the same time that manhood necessarily denies that status to men. And while Heath embraces its notions of history as a narrative of male "appropriation and domination" of gendered others, he appears resistant at this point in his discourse to evidence of a powerful feminist institutional *present* and *presence*. I believe that we must acknowledge that feminism represents, at least in areas of the American academy, an incomparably productive, influential, and resilient ideology and institution that men, no matter how cunning, duplicitous, or culturally powerful, will neither control nor overthrow in the foreseeable future, one whose perspectives have proved and might continue to prove convincing even to biological males. In surveying the potential implications of the participation of biological men in feminism, we must therefore be honest about feminism's current persuasiveness and indomitability, about its clarifying, transformative potential, and about the fact that the corruptive possibility of both the purposefully treacherous and the only half-convinced male is, for today at least, slight indeed. Surely it is neither naive, presumptuous, nor premature to suggest that feminism as ideology and reading strategy has assumed a position of exegetical and institutional strength capable of withstanding even the most energetically masculinist acts of subversion.

Below I want to focus specifically on the question of a black male feminism. Rather than seeing it as an impossibility or as a subtle new manifestation of and attempt at androcentric domination, I want to show that certain instances of afrocentric feminism provide Afro-American men with an invaluable means of rewriting — of re-vis(ion)ing — our selves, our history and literary tradition, and our future.

Few would deny that black feminist literary criticism is an oppositional discourse constituted in large part as a response against black male participation in the subjugation of Afro-American women. From Barbara Smith's castigation of black male critics for their "virulently sexist . . . treatment" of black women writers and her insistence that they are "hampered by an inability to comprehend Black women's experience in sexual as well as racial terms" to Michele Wallace's characterization of the "black male Afro-Americanists who make pivotal use of Hurston's work" as "a gang," Afro-American men are generally perceived as non-allied others of black feminist discourse.[14] And, as is evident in Wallace's figuration of male Hurston scholars as intraracial street warriors, they are viewed at times as always already damned and unredeemable, even when they appear to take black women's writing seriously. We — I — must accept the fact that black male investigations informed by feminist principles, including this one, may never be good enough or ideologically correct enough for some black women who are feminists.

This sense of an unredeemable black male critic/reader is in stark contrast to perspectives offered in such texts as Sherley Anne Williams's "Some Implications of Womanist Theory." In her essay, she embraces Alice Walker's term "womanist" — which, according to Williams, connotes a commitment "to the survival and wholeness of an entire people, female and male, as well as a valorization of women's works in all their varieties and multitudes" — because she considers the black feminist project to be separatist in "its tendency to see not only a distinct black female culture but to see that culture as a separate cultural form" from "the facticity of Afro-American life."[15]

I believe that a black male feminism, whatever its connections to critical theory or its specific areas of concern, can profit immensely from what female feminists have to say about male participation. For example, Valerie Smith's suggestion in "Gender and Afro-Americanist Literary Theory and Criticism" that "Black male critics and theorists might explore the nature of the contradictions that arise when they undertake black feminist projects"[16] seems to me quite useful, as does Alice Jardine's advice to male feminists. Speaking for white female feminists, Jardine addresses white males who consider themselves to be feminists: "We do not want you to *mimic* us, to become the same as us; we don't want your pathos or your guilt: and we don't even want your admiration (even if it's nice to get it once in a while). What we want, I would even say what we need, is your *work*. We need you to get down to serious work. And like all serious work, that involves struggle and pain."[17] The womanist theoretical project that has been adopted by Williams, Smith, and others provides aspiring Afro-American male feminists with a useful model for the type of self-exploration that Smith and Jardine advocate. What Williams terms "womanist theory" is especially suggestive for Afro-American men because, while it calls for feminist discussions of black women's texts and for critiques of black androcentricism, womanism foregrounds a general black psychic health as a primary objective. Williams argues that "what is needed is a thoroughgoing examination of male images in the works of black male writers"; her womanism, then, aims at "ending the separatist tendency in Afro-American criticism," at leading black feminism away from "the same hole The Brother has dug for himself—narcissism, isolation, inarticulation, obscurity," at the creation and/or continuation of black "community and dialogue."[18]

If a black man is to become a useful contributor to black feminism, he must, as Boone argues, "discover a position *from which* to speak that neither elides the importance of feminism to his work nor ignores the specificity of his gender." However multiply split we perceive the subject to be, however deeply felt our sense of "maleness" and "femaleness" as social constructions, however heightened our sense of the historical consequences and current dangers of black androcentricism, a black male feminism cannot contribute to the continuation and expansion of the black feminist project by being so identified against or out of touch with itself as to fail to be both self-reflective and at least minimally self-interested. A black male feminist self-reflectivity of the type I have in mind necessarily would include examination of both the benefits and the dangers of a situatedness in feminist discourse. The self-interestedness of a black male feminist would be manifested in part by his concern with exploring a man's place. Clearly if convincing mimicry of female-authored concerns and interpretive strategies—speaking *like* a female feminist—is not in and of itself an appropriate goal for aspiring male participants, then a male feminism necessarily must explore males' various situations in the contexts and texts of history and the present.

Perhaps the most difficult task for a black male feminist is striking a workable balance between male self-inquiry/interest and an adequately feminist critique of patriarchy. To this point, especially in response to the commercial and critical success of contemporary Afro-American women's literature, scores of black men have proved unsuccessful in this regard. As black feminist critics such as Valerie Smith and Deborah McDowell have argued, the contemporary moment of black feminist literature has been greeted by many Afro-American males with hostility, self-interested misrepresentation, and a lack of honest intellectual introspection. In "Reading Family Matters," a useful discussion for black male feminism primarily as an exploration of what such a discourse ought not do and be, McDowell speaks of widely circulated androcentric male analyses of Afro-American feminist texts by writers such as Toni Morrison and Alice Walker:

> Critics leading the debate [about the representation of black men in black women's texts] have lumped all black women writers together and have fo-

cused on one tiny aspect of their immensely complex and diverse project—the image of black men—despite the fact that, if we can claim a center for these texts, it is located in the complexities of black female subjectivity and experience. In other words, though black women writers have made black women the subjects of their own family stories, these male readers/critics are attempting to usurp that place for themselves and place it at the center of critical inquiry.[19]

Although I do not believe that "the image of black men" is as microscopic an element in Afro-American women's texts as McDowell claims, I agree with her about the reprehensible nature of unabashed androcentricism found in formulations she cites by such writers as Robert Staples, Mel Watkins, and Darryl Pinckney. Nevertheless, in relation to the potential development of a black male feminism, I am troubled by what appears to be a surprisingly explicit determination to protect turf. In their unwillingness to grant that exploration of how Afro-American males are delineated by contemporary black female novelists is a legitimate concern that might produce illuminating analyses, McDowell's formulations echo in unfortunate ways those of antifeminist male critics, white and black, who consider feminism to be an unredeemably myopic and unyielding interpretive strategy incapable of offering subtle readings of canonical, largely male-authored texts. Despite the circulation of reprehensibly masculinist responses to Afro-American women's literature, black feminist literary critics do not best serve the discourses that concern them by setting into motion homeostatic maneuvers intended to devalue all forms of inquiry except for those they hold to be most valuable (in this particular case, a female-authored scholarship that emphasizes Afro-American women's writings of black female subjectivity). If the Afro-American women's literary project is indeed "immensely complex and diverse," as McDowell claims, bringing to bear other angles of vision, including antipatriarchal male ones, can assist in analyzing aspects of that complexity.

While the views of Staples and others are clearly problematic, those problems do not arise specifically from their efforts to place males "at the center of critical inquiry" any more than feminism is implicitly flawed because it insists, in some of its manifestations, on a gynocritical foregrounding of representations of women. Rather, these problems appear to result from the fact that the particular readers who produce these perspectives do not seem sufficiently to be, in Toril Moi's titular phrase, "men against patriarchy."[20] Certainly, in an age when both gender studies and Afro-American women's literature have achieved a degree of legitimacy within the academy and outside of it, it is unreasonable for black women either to demand that black men not be concerned with the ways in which they are depicted by Afro-American women writers, or to see that concern as intrinsically troubling in feminist terms. If female feminist calls for a non-mimicking male feminism are indeed persuasive, then black men will have very little of substance to say about contemporary Afro-American women's literature, especially if we are also to consider as transgressive any attention to figurations of black manhood. It seems to me that the most black females in feminism can insist upon in this regard is that examinations which focus on male characters treat the complexity of contemporary Afro-American women novelists' delineations of black manhood with an antipatriarchal seriousness which the essays McDowell cites clearly lack.

From my perspective, what is potentially most valuable about the development of black male feminism is not its capacity to reproduce black feminism as practiced by black females who focus primarily on "the complexities of black female subjectivity and experience."[21] Rather, its potential value lies in the possibility that, in being antipatriarchal and as self-inquiring about their relationship(s) to feminism as Afro-American women have been, black men can expand the range and utilization of feminist inquiry and explore other fruitful applications for feminist perspectives, including such topics as obstacles to a black male feminist project itself and new figurations of "family matters" and black male sexuality.

For the purpose of theorizing about a black male feminism, perhaps the most provocative, enlightening, and inviting moment in feminist or in "womanist" scholarship occurs in Hortense Spillers's "Mama's Baby, Papa's Maybe: An American Grammar Book." Indeed, Spillers's essay represents a fruitful starting point for new, potentially nonpatriarchal figurations of family and of black males' relationship to the female. Toward the end of this illuminating theoretical text, which concerns itself with slavery's debilitating effects on the Afro-American family's constitution, Spillers envisions black male identity formation as a process whose movement toward successful resolution seems to require a serious engagement of black feminist principles and perspectives. Spillers asserts that as a result of those specific familial patterns which functioned during American slavery and beyond and "removed the African-American male not so much from sight as from *mimetic* view as a partner in the prevailing social fiction of the Father's name, the Father's law," the African-American male "has been touched . . . by the *mother, handed* by her in ways that he cannot escape." Because of separation from traditional American paternal name and law, "the black American male embodies the *only* American community of males which has had the specific occasion to learn *who* the female is within itself . . . It is the heritage of the *mother* that the African-American male must regain as an aspect of his own personhood—the power of 'yes' to the 'female' within."[22]

Rather than seeing the "female" strictly as other for the Afro-American male, Spillers's afrocentric revisioning of psychoanalytic theory insists that we consider it an important aspect of the repressed in the black male self.[23] Employing Spillers's analyses as a starting point, we might regard Afro-American males' potential "in-ness" vis-à-vis feminism not, as Paul Smith insists in *Men in Feminism*, as a representation of male heterosexual desires to penetrate and violate female spaces[24] but rather as an acknowledgment of what Spillers considers the distinctive nature of the Afro-American male's

connection to the "female." If Afro-American males are ever to have anything to say about or to black feminism beyond the types of reflex-action
devaluations and diatribes about divisiveness that critics such as McDowell
and Valerie Smith rightly decry, the investigative process of which womanist
acts by Spillers and Williams speak is indispensable. Such a process, if
pursued in an intellectually rigorous manner, offers a means by which black
men can participate usefully in and contribute productively to the black
feminist project.

   Black womanism demands neither the erasure of the black gendered
other's subjectivity, as have male movements to regain a putatively lost Afro-
American manhood, nor the relegation of males to prone, domestic, or other
limiting positions. What it does require, if it is indeed to become an ideology
with widespread cultural impact, is a recognition on the part of both black
females and males of the nature of the gendered inequities that have marked
our past and present, and a resolute commitment to work for change. In that
sense, black feminist criticism has not only created a space for an informed
Afro-American male participation, but it heartily welcomes—in fact, insists
upon—the joint participation of black males and females as *comrades*, to
invoke, with a difference, this paper's epigraphic reference to *Sula*.

Reading "Mama's Baby, Papa's Maybe" was of special importance to me in
part because it helped me to clarify and articulate my belief that my relationship to feminism need not mark me necessarily as a debilitatingly split
subject. The source of that relationship can only be traced autobiographically, if at all. Having been raised by a mother who, like too many women of
too many generations, was the victim of male physical and psychological
brutality—a brutality which, according to my mother, resulted in large part
from my father's frustrations about his inability to partake in what Spillers
calls masculinity's "prevailing social fiction"—my earliest stories, my familial narratives, as it were, figured "maleness" in quite troubling terms. My
mother told me horrific stories, one of which I was, in a sense, immediately
involved in: my father—who left us before I was one year old and whom I
never knew—kicked her in the stomach when my fetal presence swelled her
body, because he believed she'd been unfaithful to him and that I was only
"maybe" his baby.

   As a youth, I pondered this and other such stories often and deeply, in part
because of the pain I knew these incidents caused my mother, in part
because, as someone without a consistent male familial role model, I actively sought a way to achieve a gendered self-definition. As one for whom
maleness as manifested in the surrounding inner city culture seemed to be
represented only by violence, familial abandonment, and the certainty of
imprisonment, I found that I was able to define myself with regard to my
gender primarily in oppositional ways. I had internalized the cautionary
intent of my mother's narratives, which also served as her dearest wish for
me: that I not grow up to be like my father, that I not adopt the definitions of

"maleness" represented by his example and in the culture generally. Because the scars of male brutality were visibly etched—literally marked, as it were—on my mother's flesh and on her psyche, "maleness," as figured both in her stories and in my environment, seemed to me not to be a viable mimetic option. I grew up, then, not always sure of what or who I was with respect to prevailing social definitions of gender but generally quite painfully aware of what I could not become.

In order to begin to understand who my mother was, perhaps also who my father was, what "maleness" was and what extra-biological relationship I could hope to have to it, I needed answers that my mother was unable to provide. I found little of value in the black masculinist discourse of the time, which spoke endlessly of the dehumanization and castration of the Afro-American male by white men and black women—our central social narrative for too long—for this rhetoric seemed simplistic and unself-consciously concerned with justifying domestic violence and other forms of black male brutality.

Afro-American women's literature, to which I was introduced along with black feminism in 1977 as a sophomore at Brandeis University, helped me move toward a comprehension of the world, of aspects of my mother's life, and of what a man against patriarchy could be and do. These discourses provided me with answers, nowhere else available, to what had been largely unresolvable mysteries. I work within the paradigm of black feminist literary criticism because it explains elements of the world about which I care most deeply. I write and read what and as I do because I am incapable of escaping the meanings of my mother's narratives for my own life, because the pain and, in the fact of their enunciation to the next generation, the sense of hope for better days that characterizes these familial texts are illuminatingly explored in many narratives by black women. Afro-American women's literature has given me parts of myself that—incapable of a (biological) "fatherly reprieve"—I would not otherwise have had.

I have decided that it is ultimately irrelevant whether these autobiographical facts, which, of course, are not, and can never be, the whole story, are deemed by others sufficient to permit me to call myself "feminist." Like Toril Moi, I have come to believe that "the important thing for men is not to spend their time worrying about definitions and essences ('am I *really* a feminist?'), but to take up a recognizable anti-patriarchal position."[25] What is most important to me is that my work contribute, in however small a way, to the project whose goal is the dismantling of the phallocentric rule by which black females and, I am sure, countless other Afro-American sons have been injuriously "touched."

My indebtedness to Spillers's and other womanist perspectives is, then, great indeed, as is my sense of their potential as illuminating moments for a newborn—or not-yet-born—black male feminist discourse. But to utilize these perspectives requires that we be more inquiring than Spillers is in her formulations, not in envisioning liberating possibilities of an acknowledgment of the "female" within the black community and the male subject, but in noting potential dangers inherent in such an attempted adoption by historically brutalized Afro-American men whose relationship to a repressed "female" is not painstakingly (re)defined.

Clearly, more thinking is necessary not only about what the female within is but about what it can be said to represent for black males, as well as serious analysis of useful means and methods of interacting with a repressed female interiority and subject. Spillers's theorizing does not perform this task, in part because it has other, more compelling interests and emphases—among which is the righting/(re)writing of definitions of "woman" so that they will reflect Afro-American women's particular, historically conditioned "female social subject" status—but a black male feminism must be especially focused on exploring such issues if it is to mobilize Spillers's suggestive remarks as a means of developing a fuller understanding of the complex formulations of black manhood found in many texts and contexts, including Afro-American women's narratives.

I want to build briefly on Spillers's provocative theorizing about the Afro-American male's maturational process and situation on American shores. To this end, I will look at an illuminating moment in Toni Morrison's *Sula*, a text that is, to my mind, not only an unparalleled Afro-American woman's writing of the complexities of black female subjectivity and experience but also of black males' relationship to the female within as a consequence of their limited access to "the prevailing social fiction" of masculinity. In this novel, the difficulty of negotiating the spaces between black male lack and black female presence is plainly manifested in such figures as the undifferentiatable deweys; BoyBoy, whose name, in contrast to most of the authorial designations in *Sula*, speaks unambiguously for him; and Jude, whose difficulty in assuming the mantle of male provider leads him to view his union with Nel as that which "would make one Jude."[26]

The response of Plum, the most tragic of *Sula*'s unsuccessful negotiators of the so-called white man's world, vividly represents for me some of the contemporary dangers of black male "in-ness" vis-à-vis the "female." Despite a childhood which included "float[ing] in a constant swaddle of love and affection" and his mother's intention to follow the Father's law by bequeathing "everything" to him (38), Plum appears incapable of embracing hegemonic notions of masculinity. Instead, he returns from World War I spiritually fractured but, unlike a similarly devastated Shadrack, lacking the imaginative wherewithal to begin to theorize or ritualize a new relationship to his world. He turns to drugs as a method of anesthetizing himself from the horrors of his devastation and, in his mother's view, seeks to compel her resumption of familiar/familial patterns of caretaking. In the following passage, Eva explains to Hannah her perception of Plum's desires, as well as the motivation for her participation in what amounts to an act of infanticide:

When he came back from that war he wanted to git back in. After all that
carryin' on, just gettin' him out and keepin' him alive, he wanted to crawl back
in my womb and well . . . I ain't got the room no more even if he could do it.
There wasn't space for him in my womb. And he was crawlin' back. Being
helpless and thinking baby thoughts and dreaming baby dreams and messing
up his pants again and smiling all the time. I had room enough in my heart,
but not in my womb, got no more. I birthed him once. I couldn't do it again.
He was growed, a big old thing. Godhavemercy, I couldn't birth him twice.
. . . A big man can't be a baby all wrapped up inside his mamma no more; he
suffocate. I done everything I could to make him leave me and go on and live
and be a man but he wouldn't and I had to keep him out so I just thought of a
way he could die like a man not all scrunched up inside my womb, but like a
man. (62)[27]

What is significant about this passage for an analysis of the possibilities of
a non-oppressive black male relationship to feminism—to female experience characterized by a refusal to be subjugated to androcentric desires—is
its suggestiveness for our understanding of the obstacles to a revised male
view of the repressed "female," obstacles which result in large part from
black males' relative social powerlessness. If black feminism is persuasive in
its analysis of the limitations of Afro-American masculinist ideology, emphasizing as it does achievement of black manhood at the expense of black
female subjectivity, and if we can best describe an overwhelming number of
Africa's American male descendants as males-in-crisis, the question a black
male feminism must ask itself is, On what basis, according to what ideological perspective, can an Afro-American heterosexual male ground his notions
of the female? Beyond its heterosexual dimension, can the "female" truly
come to represent for a traditional black male-in-crisis more than a protective maternal womb from which he seeks to be "birthed" again? Can it serve
as more than a site on which to find relief from or locate frustrations caused
by an inability to achieve putatively normative American male socioeconomic status? If embracing normative masculinity requires an escape from
the protection and life-sustaining aspects symbolized by maternal umbilical
cords and apron strings and an achievement of an economic situation
wherein the male provides domestic space and material sustenance for his
dependents (including "his woman"), black manhood generally is, like
Plum, in desperate trouble. And if, as has often been the case, a black female
can be seen by an Afro-American male-in-crisis only if she has been emptied
of subjectivity and selfhood, if she becomes visible for the male only when
she is subsumed by male desire(s), then the types of refiguration and redefi-
nition of black male subjectivity and engagement with the "female" central
to Spillers's formulations are highly unlikely.

This question of seeing and not seeing, of the male gaze's erasure and
recreation of the female, is crucial to *Sula's* general thematics. It seems to
me that in all of her novels Morrison's figuration of black female subjectivity is largely incomprehensible without some serious attention both to her

representation of black manhood and to her exploration of the relationships between socially constructed gendered (and racial) positions. To return explicitly to the case of Eva: What Eva fears, what appears to be a self-interested motivation for her killing of her intended male heir, is that Plum's pitiful, infantile state has the potential to reduce *her* to a static female function of self-sacrificing mother, which, according to Bottom legend, had already provoked her decision to lose a leg in order to collect insurance money with which to provide for her children. Having personally lost so much already, Eva chooses, instead of sacrificing other essential parts of her self, to take the life of her self-described male heir. And if Plum dies "like a man" in Eva's estimation, his achievement of manhood has nothing to do with an assumption of traditional masculine traits, nothing to do with strength, courage, and a refusal to cry in the face of death. Instead, that achievement results from Eva's creation of conditions that have become essential components of her definition of manhood: death forces him to "leave" her and to "keep . . . out" of her womb. It would appear that manhood is defined here not as presence as typically represented in Western thought, but—by and for Eva at least—as liberating (domestic and uterine) absence.

One of the intentions of this chapter is to suggest that feminism represents a fruitful and potentially not oppressive means of reconceptualizing, of figuratively birthing twice, the black male subject. But, as a close reading of the aforementioned passage from *Sula* suggests, interactions between men and women motivated by male self-interest such as necessarily characterizes an aspect of male participation in feminism are fraught with possible dangers for the biological/ideological female body of an enactment of or a capitulation to hegemonic male power. Indeed, if it is the case that, as Spillers has argued in another context, "the woman who stays in man's company keeps alive the possibility of having, one day, an unwanted guest, or the guest, deciding to 'hump the hostess,' whose intentions turn homicidal," then male proximity to feminism generally creates the threat of a specifically masculinist violation.[28] If, as I noted earlier, the dangers of a hegemonic, heterosexual Euro-American male's "in-ness" vis-à-vis feminism include (sexualized) penetration and domination, then those associated with a heterosexual black male's interactions with the ideological female body are at least doubled, and potentially involve an envisioning of the black female body as self-sacrificingly maternal or self-sacrificingly sexual. Because of a general lack of access to the full force of hegemonic male power, Afro-American men could see in increasingly influential black female texts not only serious challenges to black male fictions of the self but also an appropriate location for masculine desires for control of the types of valuable resources that the discourses of black womanhood currently represent.

But a rigorous, conscientious black male feminism need not give in to traditional patriarchal desires for control and erasure of the female. To be of any sustained value to the feminist project, a discourse must provide illuminating and persuasive readings of gender as it is constituted for blacks in America and sophisticated, informed, contentious critiques of phallocentric practices in an effort to redefine our notions of black male and female textuality and subjectivity. And in its differences from black feminist texts that are produced by individual Afro-American women, a black male feminism must be both rigorous in engaging these texts and self-reflective enough to avoid, at all costs, the types of patronizing, marginalizing gestures that have traditionally characterized Afro-American male intellectuals' response to black womanhood. What a black male feminism must strive for, above all else, is to envision and enact the possibilities signaled by the differences feminism has exposed and created. In black feminist criticism, being an Afro-American male does not mean attempting to invade an /other political body like a lascivious soul snatcher or striving to erase its essence in order to replace it with one's own myth of what the discourse should be. Such a position for black men means, above all else, an acknowledgment and celebration of the incontrovertible fact that "the Father's law" is no longer the only law of the land.

## NOTES

1. Joseph Boone's and Gerald MacLean's essays in *Gender and Theory* assume that the foregrounding of gendered subjectivity is essential to the production of a male feminist critical practice. Consequently, in an effort to articulate his perspectives on the possibilities of a male feminist discourse, Boone shares with us professional secrets— he writes of his disagreement with the male-authored essays in Alice Jardine and Paul Smith's *Men and Feminism*, and of being excluded, because of his gender, from a Harvard feminist group discussion of Elaine Showalter's "Critical Cross-Dressing." And MacLean's essay discloses painfully personal information about his difficult relationship with his mother, his unsatisfying experience with psychoanalysis, and an incident of marital violence.

2. Joseph Boone, "Of Me(n) and Feminism: Who(se) is the Sex That Writes?" in *Gender and Theory*, 158–80. Here and below, I quote from p. 159. For my purposes, Boone's remarks are suggestive despite their use of language that might seem to mark them as a heterosexualization of men's participation in feminism ("open up a space," "discover a position"). I believe that Boone's passage implies less about any desire for domination on his part than it does about the pervasiveness in our language of terms which have acquired sexual connotations and, consequently, demonstrates the virtual unavoidability of using a discourse of penetration to describe interactions between males and females. But it also appears to reflect a sense of frustration motivated by Boone's knowledge that while feminism has had a tremendous impact on his thinking about the world he inhabits, many feminists do not see a place in their discourse for him or other like-minded males. In order to make such a place for himself, violation and transgression seem to Boone to be unavoidable.

3. Alice Jardine, "Men in Feminism: Odor di Uomo or Compagnons de Route?" in *Men in Feminism*, 58.

4. Andrew Ross, "No Question of Silence," in *Men in Feminism*, 86.

5. See Georges Poulet, "Criticism and the Experience of Interiority," in *Reader-Response Criticism: From Formalism to Post-Structuralism*, ed. Jane P. Tompkins (Baltimore: Johns Hopkins University Press, 1980), 41–49.

6. Houston A. Baker, Jr., *Afro-American Poetics*, 8.

7. Elizabeth Weed, "A Man's Place," in *Men in Feminism*, 75.

8. Michael Awkward, *Inspiriting Influences: Tradition, Revision, and Afro-American Women's Novels* (New York: Columbia University Press, 1989).

9. About his relationship to feminism, Nelson writes: "Feminism is part of my social and intellectual life, has been so for many years, and so, to the extent that writing is ever 'natural,' it is natural that I write about feminism" (153). Nelson's "Men, Feminism: The Materiality of Discourse" (*Men in Feminism*, 153–72) is, in my estimation, a model for self-referential male feminist inquiries that assume—or, at the very least, seek to demonstrate—a useful place for males in the discourse of feminism.

10. Jardine and Smith, *Men in Feminism*, vii–viii.

11. See Craig Owens, "Outlaws: Gay Men in Feminism," in *Men in Feminism*, 219–32. It is hard to believe that Jardine and Smith's difficulty reflected a lack of interest among Afro-Americans in exploring the relationship of men to black feminism. A number of texts give evidence of interest in "the problem": the 1979 *Black Scholar* special issue devoted to investigating black feminism as manifested primarily in Ntozake Shange's *for colored girls* and Michele Wallace's *Black Macho and the Myth of the Superwoman*; Mel Watkins, "Sexism, Racism, and Black Women Writers," *New York Times Book Review*, June 15, 1986, p. 1; Darryl Pinckney, "Black Victims, Black Villains," *New York Review of Books* 34 (January 29, 1987: 17–20); and essays by Valerie Smith and Deborah McDowell from which I draw below.

Jardine and Smith's difficulties might have stemmed from the facts that most of the men who had spoken publicly on the subject were open about their hostility to black feminism, and most of them did not speak the language of contemporary theory, a high academic idiom which demonstrates that the contributors to *Men in Feminism* are, despite significant differences among them, members of the same speech community.

12. Stephen Heath, "Male Feminism," *Men in Feminism*, 1.

13. Ibid., 9.

14. Barbara Smith, "Toward a Black Feminist Criticism," 173, 172; Michele Wallace, "Who Dat Say Dat When I Say Dat? Zora Neale Hurston Then and Now," *Village Voice Literary Supplement*, April 1988, p. 18.

15. Sherley Anne Williams, "Some Implications of Womanist Theory," *Callaloo* 9 (1986): 304.

16. Valerie Smith, "Gender and Afro-Americanist Literary Theory and Criticism," in *Speaking of Gender*, 68.

17. Jardine, "Men in Feminism," *Men in Feminism*, 60.

18. Williams, "Some Implications," 307.

19. Deborah McDowell, "Reading Family Matters," in *Changing Our Own Words: Essays on Criticism, Theory, and Writing by Black Women*, ed. Cheryl Wall (New Brunswick: Rutgers University Press, 1989), 84.

20. Toril Moi, "Men against Patriarchy," in *Gender and Theory*, 181–88.

21. McDowell's views notwithstanding, constructions of black male and black female subjectivity are too obviously interrelated in black women's narratives for feminist criticism to profit in the long run from ignoring—or urging that others ignore—the important function that delineations of black male subjectivity play in these narratives' thematics. Certainly the threat of antifeminist male critical bias is not cause to erase or minimize the significance of black male characters in these writers' work.

22. Spillers, "Mamas Baby, Papa's Maybe: An American Grammar Book," 80.

23. In this sense, Spillers's perspectives complement those of Sherley Anne Williams, for the latter demands, in effect, that we consider the extent to which black male repression of the "female" results from an attempt to follow the letter of the white Father's law.

24. Paul Smith, "Men in Feminism: Men and Feminist Theory," *Men in Feminism*, 3.

25. Moi, "Men against Patriarchy," 184.

26. Toni Morrison, *Sula* (New York: Plume, 1973), 71. Subsequent references to this novel appear in the text in parentheses.

27. At least one other reading of Eva's murder of her son is possible: as protection against the threat of incest. In a section of her explanation to Hannah—very little of which is contained in my textual citation of *Sula*—Eva discusses a dream she has had concerning Plum:

> I'd be laying here at night and he be downstairs in that room, but when I closed my eyes I'd see him . . . six feet tall smilin' and crawlin' up the stairs quietlike so I wouldn't hear and opening the door soft so I wouldn't hear and he'd be creepin' to the bed trying to spread my legs trying to get back up in my womb. He was a man, girl, a big old growed-up man. I didn't have that much room, I kept on dreaming it. Dreaming it and I knowed it was true. One night it wouldn't be no dream. It'd be true and I would have done it, would have let him if I'd've had the room but a big man can't be a baby all wrapped up inside his mamma no more; he suffocate. (72–73)

Morrison reverses to some extent the traditional dynamics of the most prevalent form of intergenerational incest. Instead of the male parent creeping to the bed and spreading the legs of his defenseless female child, in Eva's dream her man-child Plum is the active agent of violation. Eva's emphasis on Plum's immensity and her own uterus's size makes connections to incestuous creeping and spreading possible. It is not difficult to imagine, given Plum's constantly drugged state, that frustrations caused by an inability to re-insert his whole body into his mother's womb during what Eva views as an inevitable encounter might lead to a forced insertion of a part that "naturally" fits, his penis. At any rate, a reading of this scene that notes its use of language consistent with parent-child incest serves to ground what appear to be otherwise senseless fears on Eva's part concerning both the possible effects of Plum's desire for reentry into her uterine space and her own inability to deny her son access to that space ("I would have done it, would have let him").

28. Spillers, "Black, White, and in Color, or Learning How to Paint: Toward an Intramural Protocol of Reading."

# 15 MEN
## We Just Don't Get It

NATHAN McCALL

At about the tender age of sixteen, I carried around in my wallet a wrinkled piece of paper that contained a notorious list. I'm ashamed to admit it now, but back then I proudly showed off the contents of that list, often during wine-bingeing bragging sessions with the boys on the block.

The list contained the names of some twenty or so teenage girls—in our vernacular, babes, broads, bitches—who held the unlucky distinction of having been laid by me.

In most cases, I had "talked the drawers off" the girls, meaning they'd willingly yielded to empty promises designed to persuade them to prove their devotion by hopping into bed. But a few girls named on that list had been strong-armed—sexually assaulted—by me.

It never occurred to me during that time to distinguish between those girls on the list who'd willingly consented to sex and those who had not. The names of actual rape victims were jotted down on that smudgy piece of paper tucked between my driver's license and my Social Security card. There was enough written evidence of confessed sex crimes, scribbled in my distinctive handwriting, to put me away in prison for a long, long time.

But that didn't matter to me then. I wasn't afraid of exposure because I honestly didn't grasp the tragic implications of the thing. I just didn't get it.

That might seem unbelievable, but what's more stunning is this: I was far from alone in such cruel stupidity. Of course, there were many exceptions. There were lots of decent, self-respecting teenage boys who wouldn't dare take advantage of a girl even if the opportunity presented itself. Still, in addition to my hoodlum partners and me, a sizable number of other, "regular" dudes—bookworms, jocks, and other everyday, play-by-the-rules kinds of guys—also held cloudy notions about the distinction between consensual sex and rape.

I've heard all the macho men's-room talk, and I'd say the number of boys and men who harbor blurry notions about the liberties they can rightfully take with a female is nothing less than mind-boggling. If the truth be told, on some level of awareness or another, most men don't get it.

That massive male blindness accounts for the boatload of sexual-harassment cases filed by women in government and civilian workplaces every year. That obtuseness explains why some of the highest-ranking men in the nation—including the President of the United States and a U.S. Supreme Court justice—have been accused of taking indecent liberties with women.

William Kennedy Smith, Mike Tyson, the late Tupac Shakur—theirs are among the high-profile sexual-assault cases that have made headlines in recent years, but they represent only a small fraction of the incidents that do untold psychic damage to girls and women every day.

From this male's perspective, the pervasiveness of men's problem with sexual aggression suggests one of two things: Either God developed a defective sensibility gene when he assembled males, or there's a major flaw in our cultural conditioning, and that flaw feeds this madness that's corrupted us.

After much soul-searching, I'm inclined to believe the latter is true: that even in these so-called modern times, we still uphold a supermacho cultural climate that helps men feel comfortable—even justified—in forcing their attentions on the opposite sex. Certainly, the role of individual responsibility can't be dismissed, but in a sense our whole society is an accessory in this thing called rape. In America, where sex seems to sell everything, from new cars to good beer, it's not hard at all to become a sexist pig. All that's needed are eyes, ears, and a hearty store of testosterone.

As I look back on my own warped past, it's impossible to say just when the boorishness toward females first kicked in. I suspect that for me and for most other boys who mistakenly embraced sex as a rite of passage into manhood, the foundation for our brutish ways was laid early and deep.

Long before Tonka trucks and G.I. Joes assigned us our sex roles, we boys were sent clear messages about who we were to become. The sex-typed toys that we were cheerfully given at Christmastime simply reinforced the negative stereotypes that we were already being force-fed every day.

It's very likely that adolescence was the time when the crass sexism seeped in deeper for my buddies and me. Maybe it was somewhere around middle school—when zealous cheerleaders leaped in the air and did phenomenal splits in support of the boys' more celebrated exploits on the football field—that we were thoughtlessly handed the double standards that would govern us.

Somewhere amid all the TV ads showing half-naked buxom women selling products that had absolutely nothing to do with the female body, the notion of male dominance crystallized: While the girls learned to view males as the objects of their love, we boys learned to regard females as mere objects.

For many guys, that notion creates a major emotional disconnect. That disconnect makes it easier to regard females as something less on the human scale. Once that disconnect occurs, it's entirely possible to discount a female's humanity; it's entirely possible to subject a woman to sexual harassment or, worse, to rape.

For my buddies and me, our inclination to strong-arm girls related directly to our definition of masculinity. Men, who are schooled by other men, are taught to see themselves, first and foremost, as conquerors. Our movie heroes attest to that. Heros such as John Wayne were almost always big, strong, domineering men who often boasted a sharp, sexist wit. In their movies, the settings, story lines, and subplots were secondary to the underlying quest. The bottom line was obvious. It was about pussy: The conqueror got the pretty girl.

That's how the fellas and I thought of it, too. We didn't think of what we did as rape as much as we saw it as the ultimate macho conquest sport. Our competitive language reinforced that. In the male idiom, where men were called "hounds" and women were dubbed "foxes," it required no great leap of logic to extend the realm of conquest to sex. Life's purpose was made clear: The hunt was on, and females were the game.

As teenagers, operating with that kind of twisted vision as a frame of reference, we singled out as potential prey every little cute thing who even *thought* she had a crush on one of us. (Strangely enough, females in our families—mothers, sisters, cousins, and so on—were afforded respect.) With few exceptions, everybody's "phat" daughter who crossed our path was an unwitting candidate for our respective lists.

And why not keep a list? Almost from day one, we boys had been primed to score.

What is clearer now than it was back then is that the social scientists' take on rape is absolutely true: It's more about power than about sexual enjoyment. Think about it; nobody in his right mind can truly enjoy forcing someone to share something so intimate as sex.

Sometimes, the fellas and I engaged in the conquest sport alone, but we occasionally formed teams that carried out a male rite called "running trains." Often with the help of guys secretly stationed in closets in the appointed room, we simply intimidated our victims with fear or might or both, then took turns having our way.

It was a perverse exercise in male bonding; it was a bizarre camaraderie that boys and men shared as a way of showing off; it was a reenactment of the primitive caveman's rite of dividing the spoils of the hunt.

Really, we didn't get it.

Probably the clearest indication of our utter confusion about the seriousness of sexual aggression was the conflicting attitudes we held about rape.

If you'd walked into the very room at the very moment one of our sexual escapades was going down, we would've been highly offended—pissed off even—at any suggestion that we were committing a serious crime.

It's true. We frowned on rapists. We regarded rapists as deranged men, social misfits, outcasts, freaks who were so hard up they couldn't get sex on their own. Reports by the American Medical Association show that 80 percent of rape victims know their assailants. But in our limited vision, rapists were people who attacked perfect strangers to get their jollies off. Rapists were weirdos who went alone to darkened theaters, slouched low in their seats, and masturbated while gazing at the movie screen.

Looking back, I find it hard to know exactly where the moral breakdown occurred. I suspect that it erupted somewhere amid all those puzzling instructions that were handed down to us boys from men who were no more than grown-up boys themselves. Where females were concerned, we boys were given general training about right and wrong, but we also were granted broad latitude to interpret what a woman's rights *really* are.

I now know this: A woman has the right to say no whenever she wants. A woman has the right to change her mind anytime she chooses. But I remember being told, straight up, from men I respected, that it's OK for a man to take sexual liberties with a woman if she "leads him on." I recall hearing, over and over, that a woman is required to "give it up" if a man spends a fair amount of money on her during a date.

Indications are that the notions my buddies and I were taught back then are still being passed along today. In an AMA survey of high school students, 56 percent of the girls and 76 percent of the boys believed forced sex was acceptable "under some circumstances." Among eleven- to fourteen-year-olds, 51 percent of the boys and 41 percent of the girls said forced sex was acceptable if the boy "spent a lot of money" on the girl.

And so much of what we were told was male ego driven. We were assured that, regardless of what they say to the contrary, most girls and women really *want* to have sex: "They just need to be coaxed along."

If all this strikes you as appalling, then try this next thought on for size: Where the general oppression of females is concerned, there are also a good number of women unwittingly playing supporting roles. There is some subtle and blatant voodoo being worked on them that even a whole lot of young girls and grown-up women *just don't get.*

That includes the vast number of women who squeal in excited glee at men flaunting the same macho behaviors that victimize them; that includes the Miss America wanna-bes who strut across lighted stages in high heels and swimsuits so men can judge their considerable "talents"; that certainly includes the pseudodivas who shake their rounded rumps for those gold-chained misogynists in some rap-music videos.

It's no mystery why so many females are so gullible. While the boys were conditioned to be sexist oafs, the girls were socialized to seek happiness by providing the services men value most. Almost from birth, they are well primed by the likes of Barbie dolls and Suzy Homemakers to cooperate in this sex-oppression thing.

"Our parents gave us girls tea sets for Christmas," Debra Dennis, a friend, told me recently. "And we didn't even drink tea in our *fucking* house!"

The females were hit with it nonstop. Still are. And you *have* to know that for young girls there's a cumulative effect of seeing so many women everywhere serving so many men's interests—all the time. At some point, the message sinks in: Gals exist for the sole purpose of pleasing guys.

All that bull, piled high as the heavens, made it easier for my buddies and me to get our way. And the confusion that those messages created in young girls' heads is what enabled us to get away undetected with the things we did.

It's no wonder, then, that the AMA survey found that among college-age women who have been the victim of rape or attempted rape, 42 percent never even reported what happened to them.

Like so many others, my partners and I usually got away scot-free, usually without being punished for sexual assaults. But in the years since then, I've often wondered whether any of us *really* got away.

Life has a way of avenging folks who've been terribly wronged, even if the victims never get a chance to witness poetic justice firsthand. Life has a way of revisiting you with acts of meanness that you may have committed against someone in some long-forgotten time. Among the guys in my bunch, some got their wickedness shipped right back to them, almost exactly the same way they'd dished it out.

When I consider this idea, I'm reminded of something that happened during one of our street-corner bragging sessions years ago. A number of dudes were standing around in a tight circle, listening to a guy called Foots gloat over some girl he'd strong-armed the night before. A dude I'll call Alfred Towns, who'd also been known to do such things, happened to walk up and join the circle. Foots was so wrapped up in his boasting that he didn't even see Alfred approach. He went on jabbering.

And Alfred went on listening—only to get what must've been the shock of his life: Alfred heard Foots call out his sister's name.

When Foots spotted Alfred in the crowd, he smiled sheepishly and apologized. As everyone turned and looked his way, Alfred stared straight ahead. His eyes glazed over, and he stood in stunned silence. Alfred was deeply affected; he was shocked to learn that his own sister had been raped.

In the years since those crazy days, I've changed my thinking about women and sex, but still, life's revenge has come back to haunt me, too. The first time revenge paid a visit, I was involved with a woman I *really* felt strongly about. In one of our intimate conversations, she disclosed that some guys had run a train on her years ago, when she was a teen. Another time, a former girlfriend confessed that she had once been "taken advantage of" by her boyfriend in a violent episode that left her permanently scarred.

These stories hurt me. But more than anything, they forced me to face my own past cruelty and helped me understand the truth about what I'd done:

I had committed one of the worst offenses one person can commit against another and somehow had failed to see the brutality inherent in it. I just didn't get it.

Those stories told by my women friends also underscored just how widespread assaults on females are. They revealed that sexual violence is no respecter of color, race, or social standing, that it happens in all quarters, from church pews, where preachers take liberties with female members of their unsuspecting flocks, to college campuses, where frat brothers often carry on such manhood rites at the expense of hapless coeds.

Of all the life experiences that have taught me about the common threat to females' humanity, none has provided greater enlightenment than fatherhood. I think the Creator devised the best way to help me fully get the point when he gave me a daughter. She's twelve now and fast approaching that stage when boys and men will start eyeing her with that certain hungry look.

I look at her with a father's love—and also with a father's dread. As a man, I know what young predators might see when they look at her. They might see a vivacious, trusting little girl who is a stranger to no one. Or they might see a babe, a broad, a bitch, an object whose good nature makes her easy prey—a candidate for somebody's sordid list.

And I fear that my daughter may just fall for some boy who she thinks cares the world for her. He could be a nice guy. Or he could turn out to be another messed-up young man who, like me, was improperly schooled in matters of respect and sex. He might be another male who *just doesn't get it.*

# 16

## MISSION STATEMENT OF
# BLACK MEN FOR THE ERADICATION OF SEXISM
### MOREHOUSE COLLEGE (1994)

We believe that although we are oppressed because of our color, we are privileged because of our sex and must therefore take responsibility for ending that privilege. We live in a society that along with being racist, classist, homophobic and capitalist, is also fundamentally sexist. Just as all whites socialized in a white society will be racists, so too will all men socialized in a sexist society be sexists. The fact that we are black does not make us immune. We are dealing with a disease that once within us remains for the rest of our lives. As long as the society remains sexist all of our brothers to come will suffer the same fate. Because we struggle to move forward as a people we accept our responsibility of helping to dismantle this form of oppression that we help to perpetuate.

We believe that our relationships with women must be based on the principle of equality. Our notions of sexuality are based on domination. We are taught as boys to be sexual conquerors of women whose bodies are objectified and declared to be the property of men to be bought, sold and traded. We reject relationships based on domination and the violence against women and prostitution they create. We seek to establish relationships with our sisters based on equality. Men and women are complementary. We need each other in order to survive and to thrive. However two people must be held in equal standing in order to be complementary.

> "There is a profound distrust, if not hatred, between black men and women that has been nursed along largely by racism but also by an almost deliberate ignorance on the part of blacks about the sexual politics of their experience in this country." —Wallace, *Black Macho & the Myth of the Superwoman*

We recognize that present eurocentric notions of manhood and masculinity are damaging to the psyche of black men and must be replaced with a wholistic interpretation of manhood that acknowledges the oneness of men and women. Patriarchal notions of manhod, which we have internalized from our oppressors, demand that our existence as men be defined by our sexual ability and our ability to produce economically and dominate others. Following this path in a society that denies economic equality and perverts sexuality is like committing suicide. Masculinity is a one-dimensional, social creation that has nothing to do with biological reality. Notions of "masculine" and "feminine" only serve to further sexism and to suppress the abilities of both men and women. It is sexism, not biology, that confines men to being aggressive and women to being nurturers.

We believe that sexism is a global form of oppression of no less importance than any other form of oppression. All forms of oppression including, sexism, racism, and classism are interconnected and support each other. For too long the struggle for the liberation of African people in the United States has been centered around the liberation of black men. This male centered analysis inhibits us from fully confronting the oppression we constantly face and perpetuate within and without the black community. The struggle against sexism must become an issue of primary importance if we are to advance as a people.

We believe that sexist oppression against women pervades every aspect of our communities and must be eradicated. The oppression of women is a difficult issue for our community to deal with partly because it is such a personal one. It is passed onto us through media, schools, religous institutions, friends, and families. Although it has often been said that black women are held in high regard by the black community, the reality is that black women are either denigrated as whores and enemies or are placed on a confining pedestal as superwomen. The humanity of our sisters is lost in these classifications which only succeed in further dividing our people and preventing us from collectively dealing with other forms of oppression. Sexism is a radical problem that requires a radical solution. It will not be solved by simple reform. We support feminism/womanism and all efforts to eradicate sexist oppression. We ultimately demand a complete and fundamental change that eradicates oppression based on sex, race, class, and sexual orientation, both within and without.

We are not perfect. We do not claim to be. As we fight alongside our sisters we struggle to become whole; to deprogram ourselves. We have organized into one body because we know in our hearts and minds that as we hold our sisters back so will we hold ourselves back.

*be critical of sexism
in your hiphop, young men

| MARRIED COUPLE FAMILY $39,016 | MALE, living alone $17,652 |
|---|---|
| MALE householder, no spouse $26,375 | FEMALE, living alone $12,227 |
| FEMALE householder, no spouse $18,222 | |

—1990 median income for metro Atlanta, US Census Bur. Pop. Stats

## BLACK MEN: VERY MUCH ALIVE

As of late it's become very popular to refer to black men as an endangered species. As one of these men I think that's a pretty insulting phrase. It has very little to do with the actual numbers of brothers alive and more to do with income and education. When our sisters speak about a lack of "good black men" the definition usually centers around having "a decent job." Now if there's one thing we should never do, it's to allow our jobs to define us. When we do that it becomes very easy to jump out of a Wall Street office window when the stock market crashes. Unfortunately that's exactly what we do when we talk about manhood. This western idea of manhod as being connected to how much income you generate has well intentioned brothers being rejected by many of our sisters for drug dealers and corporate pimps. In this culture women are supposed to be dependent on men. Our people are no exception. This is why many of our sisters flock to the brother who can provide most. So understand that when manufacturing plants move to areas of the world where they can exploit our sisters and brothers even more, the brothers who still have jobs here and can pay the rent become the endangered few.

Believe it or not my brothers, this is about sexism. We've accepted a definition of ourselves that's killing us in a way no bullet ever could. That's why we're here, to set the record straight. We're here to redefine ourselves so one day we can all realize what it really means to be a man and to be human. So forget what "Martin" told you about man-hating feminists that really want to be men. It's all about a love thang. Dig.

## CROSSROADS

It hurts when those who got your back
suddenly grow fangs
The posse gets to the crossroads
and friendships die
　　　Memories of good times are overcome
　　　by present letdowns
　　　You talked too much and the words stung
　　　You criticized their heroes
　　　for calling your mama a bitch
　　　you exposed their weakness when

you showed you cared about the women
they claimed to
You irritated the one the rest looked to for leadership
All because you cared about your sister-
-and wanted to be whole
And now,
you're all at the crossroads
And he gives you the stare
words never exchanged
you know what it means

---

"NATIONAL LIBERATION DOES NOT COME BEARING THE
STAMP 'FOR MEN ONLY'. AND IF IT DOES, AS HAS BECOME
APPARENT IN ALGERIA, THEN THAT STANDS AS ONE INDI-
CATOR OF AN INCOMPLETE REVOLUTION, A REVOLUTION
WHICH HAS NOT FULFILLED ITS PROMISE."
                                                    —ROBERT L. ALLEN

---

"You're not wanted here anymore"
the rest look down at the ground
spineless
            You turn and walk straight,
            towards the rising sun
            on the path born of tears and blood
            shed by those who loved before you
            With more crossroads, snakes, pitfalls
            and broken glass
            to cut your feet and feed the path, you move on
            The path seems to go on and on to no end
            Sometimes you wanna just fall into the ground
            and hope the loneliness goes away
You'll meet others along the way
Many won't seem to be making the pilgrimage
But I think you'll be glad to know
"Everybody's gotta live a life under the sun"
            As long as the sun is destined to rise
            You will never be alone
lookers and hookers
    reflecting to a time in my life when the "politics of sex" or "misogyny"
were terms undefined to me. "female subjugation" and "status quo gender
roles" were inapplicable to me, a young boy who was simply trying to find
ALL of my parent's dirty magazines and satisfy some pre-pubescent curiousity about sex. the goal was to see that which i was not supposed to see,
secret things. and there was a definite reason why these things were secret,

especially to a young child. these things (pornography and its evil offsprings) reflected the adult world's most carnal thoughts, thoughts of broken up people. broken up mentals from living a life of the non-freedoms of "skirts below the knees," and "unattainable beautiful blonde blue-eyed flirtesses" and sex as a commodity and freudian misconceptions on sexuality. many confusing premises about sex. "teach it in school, don't teach it in school," and including your bible that states flesh is sin and eve was a "trick." and it all leads to obscene and mostly negative thoughts. flip through any pornographic magazine on the newsstand (or don't) and everyone's curiousities and frustrations are there.

> **north american society has a vested interest in reinforcing an individual's failure to achieve sexual maturity. by exploiting unconscious fears, forcing them to repress sexual taboos, the media guarantees blind repressed seeking for value substitutes through commercial products and consumption. sexual repression, as reinforced by media, is a most viable marketing technology.**
>
> —quote from *media sexploitation* by wilson bryan key. 1976.

## SUPPORT NBWHP
## NATIONAL BLACK WOMEN'S HEALTH PROJECT

sell the frustrations of the citizens masked in hot sex on a platter. "i don't make enough money," give him a playboy and a beer. "niggers always acting stupid," a hustler and domino's. always an escape, never a solution, or the solution is to transfer one's hopelessness onto the pages of more hopelessness. so what are the ramifications of this process on a thirteen year old boy who has no "problems" except his own curiousity? the effect of subliminal pedophilia, master/slave porno, free sex phone lines, etc. on a child? maybe one more broken up individual alienated from his/her sexuality who will grown up to be a looker or a hooker searching eternally for his/her real self and not the conditioned self created for us. freaknik showed us in one way all the break ups. the videocameras and exhibitionism satisfied a lot of people who can now go back and experience the "fun" during their times of hopelessness. nonetheless i see the revolution in all of this. the revolution-when we can overcome the drive to escapism, the "i don't give a fuck" indulges, the hundredth smoked blunt cause "shit is real, god" and being the looker upon hookers in sleaze mags. come clean in spirit.

## P E A C E

# PART 3

## MEDITATIONS FROM THE HEART
### Making Meaning Out of Masculinity

# 17 HERE BE DRAGONS

*[Originally published as "Freaks and the American Ideal of Manhood" in* Playboy, *January 1985.]*

JAMES BALDWIN

To be androgynous, *Webster's* informs us, is to have both male and female characteristics. This means that there is a man in every woman and a woman in every man. Sometimes this is recognized only when the chips are, brutally, down—when there is no longer any way to avoid this recognition. But love between a man and a woman, or love between any two human beings, would not be possible did we not have available to us the spiritual resources of both sexes.

To be androgynous does not imply both male and female sexual equipment, which is the state, uncommon, of the hermaphrodite. However, the existence of the hermaphrodite reveals, in intimidating exaggeration, the truth concerning every human being—which is why the hermaphrodite is called a freak. The human being does not, in general, enjoy being intimidated by what he/she finds in the mirror.

The hermaphrodite, therefore, may make his/her living in side shows or brothels, whereas the merely androgynous are running banks or filling stations or maternity wards, churches, armies or countries.

The last time you had a drink, whether you were alone or with another, you were having a drink with an androgynous human being; and this is true for the last time you broke bread or, as I have tried to suggest, the last time you made love.

There seems to be a vast amount of confusion in the western world concerning these matters, but love and sexual activity are not synonymous:

Only by becoming inhuman can the human being pretend that they are. The mare is not obliged to love the stallion, nor is the bull required to love the cow. They are doing what comes naturally.

But this by no means sums up the state or the possibilities of the human being in whom the awakening of desire fuels imagination and in whom imagination fuels desire. In other words, it is not possible for the human being to be as simple as a stallion or a mare, because the human imagination is perpetually required to examine, control, and redefine reality, of which we must assume ourselves to be the center and the key. Nature and revelation are perpetually challenging each other; this relentless tension is one of the keys to human history and to what is known as the human condition.

Now, I can speak only of the western world and must rely on my own experience, but the simple truth of this universal duality, this perpetual possibility of communion and completion, seems so alarming that I have watched it lead to addiction, despair, death, and madness. Nowhere have I seen this panic more vividly than in my country and in my generation.

The American idea of sexuality appears to be rooted in the American idea of masculinity. Idea may not be the precise word, for the idea of one's sexuality can only with great violence be divorced or distanced from the idea of the self. Yet something resembling this rupture has certainly occurred (and is occurring) in American life, and violence has been the American daily bread since we have heard of America. This violence, furthermore, is not merely literal and actual but appears to be admired and lusted after, and the key to the American imagination.

All countries or groups make of their trials a legend or, as in the case of Europe, a dubious romance called "history." But no other country has ever made so successful and glamorous a romance out of genocide and slavery; therefore, perhaps the word I am searching for is not idea but ideal.

The American *ideal*, then, of sexuality appears to be rooted in the American ideal of masculinity. This ideal has created cowboys and Indians, good guys and bad guys, punks and studs, tough guys and softies, butch and faggot, black and white. It is an ideal so paralytically infantile that it is virtually forbidden—as an unpatriotic act—that the American boy evolve into the complexity of manhood.

The exigencies created by the triumph of the Industrial Revolution—or, in other terms, the rise of Europe to global dominance—had, among many mighty effects, that of commercializing the roles of men and women. Men became the propagators, or perpetrators, of property, and women became the means by which that property was protected and handed down. One may say that this was nothing more than the ancient and universal division of labor—women nurtured the tribe, men battled for it—but the concept of property had undergone a change. This change was vast and deep and sinister.

For the first time in human history, a man was reduced not merely to a thing but to a thing the value of which was determined, absolutely, by that

thing's commercial value. That this pragmatic principle dictated the slaughter of the native American, the enslavement of the black and the monumental rape of Africa—to say nothing of creating the wealth of the Western
world—no one, I suppose, will now attempt to deny.

But this principle also raped and starved Ireland, for example, as well as
Latin America, and it controlled the pens of the men who signed the
Declaration of Independence—a document more clearly commercial than
moral. This is how, and why, the American Constitution was able to define
the slave as three-fifths of a man, from which legal and commercial definition it legally followed that a black man "had no rights a white man was
bound to respect."

Ancient maps of the world—when the world was flat—inform us, concerning that void where America was waiting to be discovered, HERE BE
DRAGONS. Dragons may not have been here then, but they are certainly
here now, breathing fire, belching smoke; or, to be less literary and biblical
about it, attempting to intimidate the mores, morals, and morality of this
particular and peculiar time and place. Nor, since this country is the issue of
the entire globe and is also the most powerful nation currently to be found
on it, are we speaking only of this time and place. And it can be said that the
monumental struggles being waged in our time and not only in this place
resemble, in awesome ways, the ancient struggle between those who insisted
that the world was flat and those who apprehended that it was round.

Of course, I cannot possibly imagine what it can be like to have both male
and female sexual equipment. That's a load of family jewels to be hauling
about, and it seems to me that it must make choice incessant or impossible
—or, in terms unavailable to me, unnecessary. Yet, not to be frivolous concerning what I know I cannot—or, more probably, dare not—imagine, I
hazard that the physically androgynous state must create an all-but-intoler-
able loneliness, since we all exist, after all, and crucially, in the eye of the
beholder. We all react to and, to whatever extent, become what that eye sees.
This judgment begins in the eyes of one's parents (the crucial, the definitive,
the all-but-everlasting judgment), and so we move, in the vast and claustro-
phobic gallery of Others, on up or down the line, to the eye of one's enemy
or one's friend or one's lover.

It is virtually impossible to trust one's human value without the collaboration or corroboration of that eye—which is to say that no one can live
without it. One can, of course, instruct that eye as to what to see, but this
effort, which is nothing less than ruthless intimidation, is wounding and
exhausting: While it can keep humiliation at bay, it confirms the fact that
humiliation is the central danger of one's life. And since one cannot risk love
without risking humiliation, love becomes impossible.

I hit the streets when I was about six or seven, like most black kids of my
generation, running errands, doing odd jobs. This was in the black world—
my turf—which means that I felt protected. I think that I really was, though
poverty is poverty and we were, if I may say so, among the truly needy, in

spite of the tins of corned beef we got from home relief every week, along with prunes. (Catsup had not yet become a vegetable; indeed, I don't think we had ever heard of it.) My mother fried corned beef, she boiled it, she baked it, she put potatoes in it, she put rice in it, she disguised it in corn bread, she boiled it in soup(!), she wrapped it in cloth, she beat it with a hammer, she banged it against the wall, she threw it onto the ceiling. Finally, she gave up, for nothing could make us eat it anymore, and the tins reproachfully piled up on the shelf above the bathtub—along with the prunes, which we also couldn't eat anymore. While I won't speak for my brothers and sisters, I can't bear corned-beef hash or prunes even today.

Poverty. I remember one afternoon when someone dropped a dime in front of the subway station at 125th Street and Lenox Avenue and I and a man of about forty both scrambled for it. The man won, giving me a cheerful goodbye as he sauntered down the subway steps. I was bitterly disappointed, a dime being a dime, but I laughed, too.

The truly needy. Once, my father gave me a dime—the last dime in the house, though I didn't know that—to go to the store for kerosene for the stove, and I fell on the icy streets and dropped the dime and lost it. My father beat me with an iron cord from the kitchen to the back room and back again, until I lay, half-conscious, on my belly on the floor.

Yet—strange though it is to realize this, looking back—I never felt threatened in those years, when I was growing up in Harlem, my home town. I think this may be because it was familiar; the white people who lived there then were as poor as we, and there was no TV setting our teeth on edge with exhortations to buy what we could never hope to afford.

On the other hand, I was certainly unbelievably unhappy and pathologically shy, but that, I felt, was nobody's fault but mine. My father kept me in short pants longer than he should have, and I had been told, and I believed, that I was ugly. This meant that the idea of myself as a sexual possibility, or target, as a creature capable of desire, had never entered my mind. And it entered my mind, finally, by means of the rent made in my short boy-scout pants by a man who had lured me into a hallway, saying that he wanted to send me to the store. That was the very last time I agreed to run an errand for any stranger.

Yet I was, in peculiar truth, a very lucky boy. Shortly after I turned sixteen, a Harlem racketeer, a man of about thirty-eight, fell in love with me, and I will be grateful to that man until the day I die. I showed him all my poetry, because I had no one else in Harlem to show it to, and even now, I sometimes wonder what on earth his friends could have been thinking, confronted with stingy-brimmed, mustachioed, razor-toting Poppa and skinny, popeyed Me when he walked me (rarely) into various shady joints, I drinking ginger ale, he drinking brandy. I think I was supposed to be his nephew, some nonsense like that, though he was Spanish and Irish, with curly black hair. But I knew that he was showing me off and wanted his friends to be happy for him—which, indeed, if the way they treated me can be taken as a barometer, they were. They seemed to feel that this was his business — that he would be in trouble if it became *their* business.

And though I loved him, too — in my way, a boy's way — I was mightily tormented, for I was still a child evangelist, which everybody knew, Lord. My soul looks back and wonders.

For what this really means is that all of the American categories of male and female, straight or not, black or white, were shattered, thank heaven, very early in my life. Not without anguish, certainly; but once you have discerned the meaning of a label, it may seem to define you for others, but it does not have the power to define you to yourself.

This prepared me for my life downtown, where I quickly discovered that my existence was the punch line of a dirty joke.

The condition that is now called gay was then called queer. The operative word was *faggot* and, later, pussy, but those epithets really had nothing to do with the question of sexual preference: You were being told simply that you had no balls.

I certainly had no desire to harm anyone, nor did I understand how anyone could look at me and suppose me physically capable of *causing* any harm. But boys and men chased me, saying I was a danger to their sisters. I was thrown out of cafeterias and rooming houses because I was "bad" for the neighborhood.

The cops watched all this with a smile, never making the faintest motion to protect me or to disperse my attackers; in fact, I was even more afraid of the cops than I was of the populace.

By the time I was nineteen, I was working in the Garment Center. I was getting on very badly at home and delayed going home after work as long as possible. At the end of the workday, I would wander east, to the Forty-second Street Library. Sometimes, I would sit in Bryant Park — but I discovered that I could not sit there long. I fled, to the movies, and so discovered Forty-second Street. Today that street is exactly what it was when I was an adolescent: It has simply become more blatant.

There were no X-rated movies then, but there were, so to speak, X-rated audiences. For example, I went in complete innocence to the Apollo, on Forty-second Street, because foreign films were shown there — *The Lower Depths, Childhood of Maxim Gorky, La Bête Humaine* — and I walked out as untouched (by human hands) as I had been when I walked in. There were the stores, mainly on Sixth Avenue, that sold "girlie" magazines. These magazines were usually to be found at the back of the store, and I don't so much remember them as I remember the silent men who stood there. They stood, it seemed, for hours, with the magazines in their hands and a kind of maisma in their eyes. There were all kinds of men, mostly young and, in those days, almost exclusively white. Also, for what it's worth, they were heterosexual, since the images they studied, at crotch level, were those of women.

Actually, I guess I hit Forty-second Street twice and have very nearly blotted the first time out. I was not at the mercy of the street the first time, for, though I may have dreaded *going* home, I hadn't *left* home yet. Then, I spent a lot of time in the library, and I stole odds and ends out of Woolworth's — with no compunction at all, due to the way they treated us in Harlem. When I went to the movies, I imagine that a combination of innocence and terror prevented me from too clearly apprehending the action taking place in the darkness of the Apollo — though I understood it well enough to remain standing a great deal of the time. This cunning stratagem failed when, one afternoon, the young boy I was standing behind put his hand behind him and grabbed my cock at the very same moment that a young boy came up behind me and put his cock against my hand: Ignobly enough, I fled, though I doubt that I was missed. The men in the men's room frightened me, so I moved in and out as quickly as possible, and I also dimly felt, I remember, that I didn't want to "fool around" and so risk hurting the feelings of my uptown friend.

But if I was paralyzed by guilt and terror, I cannot be judged or judge myself too harshly, for I remember the faces of the men. These men, so far from being or resembling faggots, looked and sounded like the vigilantes who banded together on weekends to beat faggots up. (And I was around long enough, suffered enough, and learned enough to be forced to realize that this was very often true. I might not have learned this if I had been a white boy; but sometimes a white man will tell a black boy anything, everything, weeping briny tears. He knows that the black boy can never betray him, for no one will believe his testimony.)

These men looked like cops, football players, soldiers, sailors, Marines or bank presidents, admen, boxers, construction workers; they had wives, mistresses, and children. I sometimes saw them in other settings — in, as it were, the daytime. Sometimes they spoke to me, sometimes not, for anguish has many days and styles. But I had first seen them in the men's room, sometimes on their knees, peering up into the stalls, or standing at the urinal stroking themselves, staring at another man, stroking, and with this miasma in their eyes. Sometimes, eventually, inevitably, I would find myself in bed with one of these men, a despairing and dreadful conjunction, since their need was as relentless as quicksand and as impersonal, and sexual rumor concerning blacks had preceded me. As for sexual roles, these were created by the imagination and limited only by one's stamina.

At bottom, what I had learned was that the male desire for a male roams everywhere, avid, desperate, unimaginably lonely, culminating often in drugs, piety, madness or death. It was also dreadfully like watching myself at the end of a long, slow-moving line: Soon I would be next. All of this was very frightening. It was lonely and impersonal and demeaning. I could not believe — after all, I was only nineteen — that I could have been driven to the lonesome place where these men and I met each other so soon, to stay.

The American idea of masculinity: There are few things under heaven more difficult to understand or, when I was younger, to forgive.

During the Second World War (the first one having failed to make the world safe for democracy) and some time after the Civil War (which had failed, unaccountably, to liberate the slave), life for niggers was fairly rough in Greenwich Village. There were only about three of us, if I remember correctly, when I first hit those streets, and I was the youngest, the most visible, and the most vulnerable.

On every street corner, I was called a faggot. This meant that I was despised, and, however horrible this is, it is clear. What was *not* clear at that time of my life was what motivated the men and boys who mocked and chased me; for, if they found me when they were alone, they spoke to me very differently—frightening me, I must say, into a stunned and speechless paralysis. For when they were alone, they spoke very gently and wanted me to take them home and make love. (They could not take *me* home; they lived with their families.) The bafflement and the pain this caused in me remain beyond description. I was far too terrified to be able to accept their propositions, which could only result, it seemed to me, in making myself a candidate for gang rape. At the same time, I was moved by their loneliness, their halting, nearly speechless need. But I did not understand it.

One evening, for example, I was standing at the bottom of the steps to the Waverly Place subway station, saying goodbye to some friends who were about to take the subway. A gang of boys stood at the top of the steps and cried, in high, feminine voices, "Is this where the fags meet?"

Well. This meant that I certainly could not go back upstairs but would have to take the subway with my friends and get off at another station and maneuver my way home. But one of the gang saw me and, without missing a beat or saying a word to his friends, called my name and came down the steps, throwing one arm around me and asking where I'd been. He had let me know, some time before, that he wanted me to take him home—but I was surprised that he could be so open before his friends, who for their part seemed to find nothing astonishing in this encounter and disappeared, probably in search of other faggots.

The boys who are left of that time and place are all my age or older. But many of them are dead, and I remember how some of them died—some in the streets, some in the Army, some on the needle, some in jail. Many years later, we managed, without ever becoming friends—it was too late for that—to be friendly with one another. One of these men and I had a very brief, intense affair shortly before he died. He was on drugs and knew that he could not live long. "What a waste," he said, and he was right.

One of them said, "My God, Jimmy, you were moving so fast in those years, you never stopped to talk to me."

I said, "That's right, baby; I didn't stop because I didn't want you to think that I was trying to seduce you."

"Man," he said, indescribably, "why didn't you?"

But the queer—not yet gay—world was an even more intimidating area of this hall of mirrors. I knew that I was in the hall and present at this company—but the mirrors threw back only brief and distorted fragments of myself.

In the first place, as I have said, there were very few black people in the Village in those years, and of that handful, I was decidedly the most improbable. Perhaps, as they say in the theater, I was a hard type to cast; yet I was eager, vulnerable, and lonely. I was terribly shy, but boys *are* shy. I am saying that I don't think I felt absolutely, irredeemably grotesque—nothing that a friendly wave of the wand couldn't alter—but I was miserable. I moved through that world very quickly; I have described it as "my season in hell," for I was never able to make my peace with it.

It wasn't only that I didn't wish to seem or sound like a woman, for it was this detail that most harshly first struck my eye and ear. I am sure that I was afraid that I already seemed and sounded too much like a woman. In my childhood, at least until my adolescence, my playmates had called me a sissy. It seemed to me that many of the people I met were making fun of women, and I didn't see why. I certainly needed all the friends I could get, male *or* female, and women had nothing to do with whatever my trouble might prove to be.

At the same time, I had already been sexually involved with a couple of white women in the Village. There were virtually no black women there when I hit those streets, and none who needed or could have afforded to risk herself with an odd, raggedy-assed black boy who clearly had no future. The first black girl I met who dug me I fell in love with, lived with and almost married. But I met her, though I was only twenty-two, many light-years too late.

The white girls I had known or been involved with—different categories—had paralyzed me, because I simply did not know what, apart from my sex, they wanted. Sometimes it was great, sometimes it was just moaning and groaning, but, ultimately, I found myself at the mercy of a double fear. The fear of the world was bearable until it entered the bedroom. But it sometimes entered the bedroom by means of the motives of the girl, who intended to civilize you into becoming an appendage or who had found a black boy to sleep with because she wanted to humiliate her parents. Not an easy scene to play, in any case, since it can bring out the worst in both parties, and more than one white girl had already made me know that her color was more powerful than my dick.

Which had nothing to do with how I found myself in the gay world. I would have found myself there anyway, but perhaps the very last thing this black boy needed were clouds of imitation white women and speculations concerning the size of his organ: speculations sometimes accompanied by an attempt at the laying on of hands. "*Ooo!* Look at him! He's cute—he doesn't like you to touch him there!"

In short, I was black in that world, and I was used that way, and by people who truly meant me no harm.

And they could *not* have meant me any harm, because they did not see me. There were exceptions, of course, for I also met some beautiful people. Yet even today, it seems to me (possibly because I am black) very dangerous to model one's opposition to the arbitrary definition, the imposed ordeal, merely on the example supplied by one's oppressor.

The object of one's hatred is never, alas, conveniently outside but is seated in one's lap, stirring in one's bowels and dictating the beat of one's heart. And if one does not know this, one risks becoming an imitation—and, therefore, a continuation—of principles one imagines oneself to despise.

I, in any case, had endured far too much debasement willingly to debase myself. I had absolutely no fantasies about making love to the last cop or hoodlum who had beaten the shit out of me. I did not find it amusing, in any way whatever, to act out the role of the darky.

So I moved on out of there.

In fact, I found a friend—more accurately, a friend found *me*—an Italian, about five years older than I, who helped my morale greatly in those years. I was told that he had threatened to kill anyone who touched me. I don't know about that, but people stopped beating me up. Our relationship never seemed to worry him or his friends or his women.

My situation in the Village stabilized itself to the extent that I began working as a waiter in a black West Indian restaurant, The Calypso, on MacDougal Street. This led, by no means incidentally, to the desegregation of the San Remo, an Italian bar and restaurant on the corner of MacDougal and Bleecker. Every time I entered the San Remo, they threw me out. I had to pass it all the time on my way to and from work, which is, no doubt, why the insult rankled.

I had won the Saxton Fellowship, which was administered by Harper & Brothers, and I knew Frank S. MacGregor, the president of Harper's. One night, when he asked me where we should have dinner, I suggested, spontaneously, the San Remo.

We entered, and they seated us and we were served. I went back to MacGregor's house for a drink and then went straight back to the San Remo, sitting on a bar stool in the window. The San Remo thus began to attract a varied clientele, indeed—so much so that Allen Ginsberg and company arrived there the year I left New York for Paris.

As for the people who ran and worked at the San Remo, they never bothered me again. Indeed, the Italian community never bothered me again— or rarely and, as it were, by accident. But the Village was full of white tourists, and one night, when a mob gathered before the San Remo, demanding that I come out, the owners closed the joint and turned the lights out and we sat in the back room, in the dark, for a couple of hours, until they judged it safe to drive me home.

This was a strange, great and bewildering time in my life. Once I was in the San Remo, for example, I was *in*, and anybody who messed with me was *out*—that was all there was to it, and it happened more than once. And no one seemed to remember a time when I had not been there.

I could not quite get it together, but it seemed to me that I was no longer black for them and they had ceased to be white for me, for they sometimes introduced me to their families with every appearance of affection and pride and exhibited not the remotest interest in whatever my sexual proclivities chanced to be.

They had fought me very hard to prevent this moment, but perhaps we were all much relieved to have got beyond the obscenity of color.

Matters were equally bewildering, though in a different way, at The Calypso. All kinds of people came into our joint—I am now referring to white people—and one of their most vivid aspects, for me, was the cruelty of their alienation. They appeared to have no antecedents nor any real connections.

"Do you really *like* your mother?" someone asked me, seeming to be astounded, totally disbelieving the possibility.

I was astounded by the question. Certainly, my mother and I did not agree about everything, and I knew that she was very worried about the dangers of the life I lived, but that was normal, since I was a boy and she was a woman. Of course she was worried about me: She was my *mother*. But she knew I wasn't crazy and that I would certainly never do anything, deliberately, to hurt her. Or my tribe, my brothers and sisters, who were probably worried about me, too.

My family was a part of my life. I could not imagine life without them, might never have been able to reconcile myself to life without them. And certainly one of the reasons I was breaking my ass in the Village had to do with my need to try to move us out of our dangerous situation. I was perfectly aware of the odds—my father had made that very clear—but he had also given me my assignment. "Do you really *like* your mother?" did not cause me to wonder about my mother or myself but about the person asking the question.

And perhaps because of such questions, I was not even remotely tempted by the possibilities of psychiatry or psychoanalysis. For one thing, there were too many schools—Freud, Horney, Jung, Reich (to suggest merely the tip of that iceberg)—and, for another, it seemed to me that anyone who thought seriously that I had any desire to be "adjusted" to this society had to be ill; too ill, certainly, as time was to prove, to be trusted.

I sensed, then—without being able to articulate it—that this dependence on a formula for safety, for that is what it was, signaled a desperate moral addiction. People went to the shrink in order to find justification for the empty lives they led and the meaningless work they did. Many turned, helplessly, hopefully, to Wilhelm Reich and perished in orgone boxes.

I seem to have strayed a long way from our subject, but our subject is social and historical—and continuous. The people who leaped into orgone boxes in search of the perfect orgasm were later to turn to acid. The people so dependent on psychiatric formulas were unable to give their children any sense of right or wrong—indeed, this sense was in themselves so fragile that during the McCarthy era, more than one shrink made a lot of money by convincing his patients, or clients, that their psychic health demanded that they inform on their friends. (Some of these people, after their surrender, attempted to absolve themselves in the civil rights movement.)

What happened to the children, therefore, is not even remotely astonishing. The flower children—who became the Weather Underground, the Symbionese Liberation Army, the Manson Family—are creatures from this howling inner space.

I am not certain, therefore, that the present sexual revolution is either sexual or a revolution. It strikes me as a reaction to the spiritual famine of American life. The present androgynous "craze"—to underestimate it— strikes me as an attempt to be honest concerning one's nature, and it is instructive, I think, to note that there is virtually no emphasis on overt sexual activity. There is nothing more boring, anyway, than sexual activity as an end in itself, and a great many people who came out of the closet should reconsider.

Such figures as Boy George do not disturb me nearly so much as do those relentlessly hetero (sexual?) keepers of the keys and seals, those who know what the world needs in the way of order and who are ready and willing to supply that order.

This rage for order can result in chaos, and in this country, chaos connects with color. During the height of my involvement in the civil rights movement, for example, I was subjected to hate mail of a terrifying precision. Volumes concerning what my sisters, to say nothing of my mother, were capable of doing; to say nothing of my brothers; to say nothing of the monumental size of *my* organ and what I did with it. Someone described, in utterly riveting detail, a scene he swore he had witnessed (I *think* it was a *he*—such mail is rarely signed) on the steps of houses in Baltimore of niggers fucking their dogs.

At the same time, I was also on the mailing list of one of the more elegant of the KKK societies, and I still have some of that mail in my files. Someone, of course, eventually realized that the organization should not be sending that mail to this particular citizen, and it stopped coming—but not before I had had time to be struck by the similarity of tone between the hate mail and the mail of the society, and not before the society had informed me, by means of a parody of an Audubon Society postcard, what it felt and expected me to feel concerning a certain "Red-breasted" Martin Luther King, Jr.

The Michael Jackson cacophony is fascinating in that it is not about Jackson at all. I hope he has the good sense to know it and the good fortune to snatch his life out of the jaws of a carnivorous success. He will not swiftly be forgiven for having turned so many tables, for he damn sure grabbed the brass ring, and the man who broke the bank at Monte Carlo has nothing on Michael. All that noise is about America, as the dishonest custodian of black life and wealth; the blacks, especially males, in America; and the burning, buried American guilt; and sex and sexual roles and sexual panic; money, success and despair—to all of which may now be added the bitter need to find a head on which to place the crown of Miss America.

Freaks are called freaks and are treated as they are treated—in the main, abominably—because they are human beings who cause to echo, deep within us, our most profound terrors and desires.

Most of us, however, do not appear to be freaks—though we are rarely what we appear to be. We are, for the most part, visibly male or female, our social roles defined by our sexual equipment.

But we are all androgynous, not only because we are all born of a woman impregnated by the seed of a man but because each of us, helplessly and forever, contains the other—male in female, female in male, white in black and black in white. We are a part of each other. Many of my countrymen appear to find this fact exceedingly inconvenient and even unfair, and so, very often, do I. But none of us can do anything about it.

# 18 IN THE LIMELIGHT

Arthur J. Robinson, Jr.

I know how it feels to be in a relationship with a dynamic, highly visible, on-the-move woman. My wife and I are 50-plus-year-old professionals in a second marriage, with five sons—and more than 1,700 daughters. My wife is the president of Spelman College in Atlanta. I am a health professional, and I am Spelman's first "First Man."

Recently, when I was asked to serve as Spelman's tennis coach, I went shopping for tennis videos. The brother who was waiting on me said, "I love that sister, Johnnetta Cole, but how do you handle a woman like that?"

"You don't *handle* a woman," I responded. Still, I could almost hear that young man thinking, *Well, what do you do when people call you Mr. Cole?*

On Dr. Martin Luther King, Jr.'s birthday, hundreds gathered to hear my wife and others speak at Ebenezer Baptist Church. As I waited to be seated, the usher approached me and said, "Mr. Cole?"

"No, Mr. Robinson." A few minutes later she returned. "Mr. Cole?"

"No, Mr. Robinson," I replied, watching the pews fill. The third time she queried, "Mr. Cole?" I responded "Yes." She immediately took me to my seat.

It finally became clear that I had to become comfortable with this. I'm married to a famous woman, and I am inevitably put in a secondary role. Because I'm at ease with myself, well grounded in who I am, there is a joy in watching someone I love being recognized. Of course, being at ease with myself was not easily come by. It isn't a birthright, but the reward of a long and difficult process.

I try to be genuinely supportive of my partner, and when I am, I know I have played an important role in whatever accolades she receives. When she is in the spotlight and reaches for my hand, as she often does, and when she includes me in the conversation or interview, the public knows what I already know: There is a partnership here.

Early in our marriage I was not happy with sharing my new bride with the world. But it is a two-way street. I now realize that because she shares her friends and acquaintances with me I'm a wealthier man, with a new and wonderful network of brother and sister friends.

My wife is constantly working, travels a lot and has far less private time than most people. Recently, for example, she made a ten-day business trip to Japan. Neither of us wanted to be apart that long, as evidenced by long distance transpacific phone calls. But between her work-related travel and mine, separations are a constant in our lives. I deal with them by fine tuning my tennis game with extra time on the court.

When we do share private moments, they are really special: a long early-morning walk, a game of tennis at midnight, window-shopping for African-American art, a hard-fought game of checkers.

Johnnetta is at the top of her profession, and her income is higher than mine. We have stopped letting money be a source of control. I now see that her high income means that for the security of our family, and for our pleasure, we have more together than either of us would have individually.

A good deal of my wife's time is spent "in a man's world." I had to accept that my on-the-move sister would lunch with rich and powerful men. Through many honest and painful talks, we have established trust, affirmed our commitment to nurture our "something special" and learned to believe in the integrity of our marriage. I believe that my partner can be trusted because I know that I can be.

Of course, being married to a highly visible woman is not as easy as an I'm-in-charge-she's-in-her-place arrangement. But my marriage is beautiful. Every day I discover that conurturing beats one partner doing it alone, that supporting a high-profile woman beats competing with her. And having confidence in our relationship is more satisfying than jealousy. The main reason my marriage works is because I have a deep sense of confidence in myself and am comfortable with who I am. So, to the young brother in the video store, I say, "I don't handle women. I've learned to handle myself."

# 19
## THE SEXIST IN ME

KEVIN POWELL

My girlfriend and I had been arguing most of the day. As we were returning from the laundromat, she ran ahead of me to our apartment building. I caught up with her at the front door, dropped the clothes at her feet, went inside and slammed the door behind me. She carried the bundle in, set it down and started back outside. Enraged, I grabbed her by the seat of her shorts and pulled her back into the apartment. We struggled in the kitchen, the dining area and the bathroom. As we were moving toward the living room, I shoved her into the bathroom door. Her face bruised, she began to cry uncontrollably, and I tried to calm her down as we wrestled on the living-room floor. When she let out a high pitched yell for help, I jumped to my feet, suddenly aware of what I was doing. Shaking with fear and exhaustion, I watched my girlfriend run barefoot out of our apartment into the street.

I still shudder when I think of that scene one year later. It was my first serious relationship and, notwithstanding my proclamations of "I'm one Black man who's gonna do the right thing," I managed to join the swelling ranks of abusive men with relative ease. Soon after "the incident," accusations of sexism flooded my guilty conscience. Like a lot of men, I tried to pin much of the blame on my now ex-girlfriend. *She must have done something to provoke my outburst*, I rationalized to myself.

But I couldn't delude myself for too long. I kept thinking of all the women I had ill-treated in some way. Without fully realizing it, I had always taken women for granted, but it wasn't until I committed a violent act that it hit me how deeply I believed women to be inferior to men.

Ashamed of what I had done, I knew that if I didn't deal with my deeply rooted sexism—that desire of man to dominate women—I could not seriously enter into another emotionally intimate relationship with a woman. Psychologically drained, I consulted young women friends my own age, older Black women and men, and any book that dealt with the issue at hand. Everywhere I turned, I found someone who was pointing out the dangers of exhibiting sexism.

For example, one woman friend drew an analogy to racism. If a child is taught from an early age to dislike another child because of his or her race, she said, the former is likely to become a hardened racist by adulthood. The same logic, she offered, applies to sexism.

Keeping in mind my friend's analogy, I recalled my childhood. I evolved as many boys do in this society: Machismo gripped my psyche, and by the time I reached my teen years we "boys" did whatever we felt like doing—which ran the gamut from squeezing girls' buttocks in gym class to "gang-banging" girls in abandoned buildings.

My chauvinistic demeanor merely ripened with age, and even after my political consciousness blossomed in college, I self-righteously continued to rationalize that the real battle was against racism, and if the "sistas" on campus couldn't fall into line, well, then, those women weren't really down with the program anyway.

In retrospect, what happened in my relationship was inevitable. Left unchecked my entire life, my sexist inclinations were building up to a breaking point. Unable to handle the pressures of a serious relationship, I first sought to "control" my girlfriend through verbal tirades and then finally through violence—the highest form of sexism.

The entire experience has been incredibly stressful—including writing about it now. I will never be able to remove the pain I inflicted on my ex-girlfriend, but at least I've taken measures to ensure that it will not happen again.

Acknowledging my inherent sexism was the first step. I then had to recognize that women are not footstools or servants or punching bags, but my equals on every level. And as I've struggled against my own sexism, I've also had to struggle against it when it manifests in my male friends. I can no longer tolerate the use of words like *bitch* or *skeezer* to describe women. Silence is acquiescence and acceptance. Moreover, true manhood does not rest on the subjugation of women—verbal or physical—and meaningful relationships between men and women won't exist until we men understand that.

# 20 A PHENOMENOLOGY OF THE BLACK BODY

CHARLES JOHNSON

A bawdy old black folktale celebrates the physical superiority of black men:

> Two white farmers sat before the stove in a general store in Alabama, arguing over who had the longest tool as an old Negro named Willis swept the front porch. They agreed to compare lengths. The man with the longest would get $25 for each additional inch. The first unzipped his fly. Six inches. The second did the same. Seven. The first turned to Willis, and said, "Let's see yours, Willis." The janitor trembled and shook his head. "Nassuh, Ah doan think Ah'd better do that, sar." The white man became angry. "I said for you to get in on this heah bet, Willis!" Afraid to say no, the janitor uncoiled his tool on the table—it took a while, friend: Willis just kept throwing it out like a fishing line. Twelve inches. Someone said, "God damn!" The two men gave Willis $125, and he raced home to show the money to his wife Maybelle. Staring skeptically at her husband, Maybelle asked. "You got alla that just for being big?" Willis whooped and went into hysterics. "Honey, that was the easiest money Ah ever made! Them white folks just better thank the Lord Ah wasn't on hard."

Laughing at the good fortune of Willis, we may lose sight of the fact that his triumph is based on cultural assumptions that lock him into the body and, to echo W. E. B. Du Bois, create in his life a "double-consciousness" in need of resolution. This essay seeks to define the ambiguity of his situation and describe the harrowing constraints upon both Willis and his white competitors.

Our past experience as a people can often be understood through its expression in language, myths, stereotypes, symbols, and folktales like this one.

As multi-layered complexes, they present collectively shared and communicated meanings. But before we can talk intelligently about the "black experience" of the body, in this or any other narrative, we must first get clear on what is essential to all experience—the correlate of consciousness and its content, *noesis-noema*, or subject and object. A rule for phenomenology is that there is never an object without a corresponding subject, and that "Consciousness is always consciousness *of* something," to quote Edmund Husserl. Given the universality of these structures for consciousness, it is reasonable to say that there is neither an impenetrable "white" or "black" experience, which are mutually exclusive, but rather that there are diverse human variations upon experience, which can always be communicated imaginatively or vicariously across racial, political, and cultural lines through language in its two analytic forms: philosophy and literature. Perhaps this point is disagreeable to proponents of cultural pluralism, but it is a presupposition of the philosophy of experience—phenomenology—that is here assumed as a working methodology. The symbol of the black body, for example, if interrogated, should disclose a racial experience wrought mythically. Our folk literature simultaneously conceals and reveals our primordial racial situation, and must be carefully unpacked if we wish to wrench self-understanding from it.

Black writers, particularly novelists and poets in search of fresh ways of seeing things familiar, frequently feel the power of folk myths and stereotypes and, so moved, wrestle with uncovering their meaning. Weaving in and out of Frantz Fanon's works are thematizations of black consciousness from the vantage point of existential phenomenology, but without a turn to the body as the radix for interpreting racial experience. In his controversial essay, "The Primevil Mitosis," Eldridge Cleaver brooks the stereotype of Black American physicality by now checking his own feelings (as an experiencing subject) against the myth, now rendering its terms rigidly abstract, now pursuing its more painful political implications. His conclusion: "The gulf between the Mind and Body will be seen to coincide with the gulf between the two races."[1] But *is* there such a gulf between the Mind and Body?

Cleaver assumes a basic division between the bodily and mental experiences of blacks and whites. Racism is the given, historically constituted and lying in wait for black consciousness, concealing the ethical dualism which has—over long centuries of Western cultural development—made white "good" and black "evil." Cleaver, focusing on one aspect of the phenomenon, the psycho-physical, finds that blacks are stripped of a mental life, which leaves them only a bodily existence (albeit a superior one like that of our janitor Willis), and he assigns them the name, "The Supermasculine Menial." He writes: "The body is tropical, warm, hot; Fire! It is soft, pleasing to the touch, luscious to the kiss. The blood is hot. Muscles are strength."[2] Alienated from this sensuous profile of the body, whites are characterized by Cleaver as "The Omnipotent Administrator." Weakness, frailty, cowardice, effeminacy, decay, and impotence are profiles associated with the white man's situation of abstraction from the body. Here, Cleaver's concerns in *Soul on Ice* are basically political, sexual, and polemical, not philosophical. But his attempt to explain our experience of embodiment may yield more philosophically than the author knows. His division recalls Paul Ricoeur's belief that, "It is possible for man to take two divergent and non-reconcilable perspectives upon himself because within man there is a non-coincidence which is that of the *finite* and the *infinite*,"[3] or of the physical and mental, consciousness and the body. It is even more illuminating when compared to Fanon's statement that, "There are times when the black man is locked into his body."[4]

Sexuality is not truly at issue in *Soul on Ice*. That is merely the manifestation of a larger problem of consciousness and the body in the black experience. The issue at stake is how blacks experience their own bodies within a world of racial restriction. By speaking descriptively, by casting the problem in absolute and often simple terms, Cleaver offers us the occasion for a broader consideration of experience, the body, and black consciousness.

Modern philosophy in the West since Descartes has entertained the idea that man is not identical with his physical being. In a crude formulation, man is presented mythologically and often philosophically as a mixture of mind and matter, spirit and flesh, consciousness and body, carnal shell and *Ka*, and remains to himself something of a mystery. The dialectic of matter and mind, subject and object, is a thread running the length of Western intellectual history, beginning with Plato's world of flux and world of forms. The later sundering of man and the world into mental and physical substances by Descartes in The *Meditations* throws light on the issue Cleaver is trying to bring to clarity—consciousness is experienced as being identical with, yet curiously distinct from, the body. One could almost categorize Western philosophy along the lines of whether a particular approach is primarily concerned with the subject of experience, consciousness, idealism, or the soul; if it emphasizes the object, matter, materialism, the body; or if it seeks a reconciliation between the two. Maurice Merleau-Ponty offers a simple but concise formulation to correct this false dualism that underlies the division between "The Omnipotent Administrator" and "The Supermasculine Menial": "I am my body."[5] It is that which reeves the subject to a world, anchors him in history, thus individualizing him, and makes possible perception and "meaning." It is my point of reference on the universe. I, as subject, am often at "one" with it, yet my relation as a human self to my body is also that of *radical otherness*. I *am* my body while I am also *not* my body (or I experience myself as not simply reducible to my body as the empirical object of physics, chemistry, neurology). Experience without "embodied consciousness" is as unthinkable as experience with the *noesis-noema* correlate: it is the irreducible way we are in the world. I am conscious of the world through the medium of my body.

To say that the body is our anchorage in the world is to bring this discussion to a consideration of "intentionality," the structure which gives meaning to experience. Intentions are at the heart of consciousness, or the *noesis-*pole, to the extent that they determine the manner in which we perceive the world. At this instant, let us say that I am a white administrator on campus. A strapping black student with a full natural, dashiki, coal-black complexion, and dark sunglasses comes into my office with a "dip-down," rolling gait. If my hobby is painting, perhaps I look toward the colorfulness of his clothing, and see him as a future subject for my canvas. Suppose I have just read Claude McKay's *Home to Harlem,* a novel which emphasizes the natural spontaneity of blacks; in this case I see the rhythms of his walk, the musicality of his movements in contrast to my own. Or, finally, suppose I am concerned that my daughter is being bused across town to a black school—Will she encounter people like this? In each instance the same student presents these multiple profiles of himself; they *are* his appearances, and each discloses a different "meaning." We have yet to speak of *his* experience upon entering the room and what my intentionality causes to arise in his consciousness. To "intend" an object or content of consciousness is to be "informed" by it as well as to *give form* to it. The mind is in no way passive; it is a participant in each act of knowing—self and object being inseparable poles of experience. It is also possible *not* to see other "meanings" or profiles presented by the object if the perceiver is locked with the "Natural Attitude," as Husserl calls it, and has been conditioned culturally or racially to fix himself upon certain "meanings." Rollo May, for example, reports of a patient who could not see an object placed before him on a table—it remained invisible on the basis of his inability to bring it forth intentionally as a content of consciousness.[6]

But consciousness is "embodied." Our desires, too, are "embodied," and it is clearly the case that every act of intending involves, to some extent, "interest." By this I mean that acting, willing, and intending are closely related. I see the student in a certain way because I fear for my daughter while she is across town. To *per*ceive a content is to *con*ceive that content. "The theory of the body image is, implicitly, a theory of perception."[7]

My body for me is not an assemblage of organs juxtaposed in space; my possession of it is undivided, and I know where my limbs are through a *body image,* know, when I sit at my desk, how my crossed feet appear, though I cannot see them. In all perception within a figure-ground relationship, where I either bring an object forth for attention or let it remain undifferentiated in the "ground," my body is the third term: it points me to the left or right, determines up and down, allows me to know space because as "embodied consciousness" I am in space, and know time because embodiment has temporality as one of its structures.

Right and left, established by the body, are sources of the lawful and forbidden; the body is emblematic; if I am "downcast," the body gestures accordingly with a drooping posture. "The body is our general medium for having a world."[8] The blind man's stick is no longer alien to him, not a mere object, but his bodily extension; the woman with a feather in her hat keeps a safe distance between it and things that might snap it off, but without looking: she *feels* these distances. All this is understood by the term *body image,* or in the work of Fanon, *body schema.* We see that motility is basic to intentionality.

Our first phenomenological act in a thematization of the black body involves a suspension or bracketing of all sociological and scientific theories concerning race. We wish to purify a field in which the body becomes the primary focus of racial consciousness. Whether black or white, the body is still experienced as having an ambiguity, a non-coincidence of mind and matter. I *am* my body, but clearly there is magic in the fact that when I say "Spread your fingers" the digits on my hand do so. I see my hand on my desk and sometimes it is alien; perhaps I do not even recognize it as *mine* when I see it in a photograph. Stranger still, I know that I cannot see myself as others see me, white and black, as if the secret of my body and the objectivity of its "outside" belongs, not to me, but to everyone else. Furthermore, I am black. I do not see what the white other sees in my skin, but I am aware of his intentionality, and—yes—aware that I often disclose something discomfiting to him. My body gives me the world, but, as that world is given, it is one in which I can be unseen. I walk down the hallway at the university and pass a professor I know well. He glances up quickly, yet does not acknowledge that he knows me. He has seen a black, a body, that remains for him always in the background, seldom figured forth save as maid, taxi driver, or janitor. Passing, he sees me as he sees the fire extinguisher to my left, that chair outside the door. I have been seen, yet not seen, acknowledged as present to him, but in a peculiar way. I call down the hallway, "Professor Peterson!" Recognizing me, he says, "Ah, Charles," and figures me forth. He offers me his hand and, shaking it, I see perhaps what he has seen: the darkness of the black body suggests "stain" primordially. For him, and at odd moments for me, this stain of my skin gives in a sudden stroke of intentionality "darkness," "guilt," "evil," an entire galaxy of meanings. Yet, it is *I* who perceive myself as "stained," as though I were an object for myself and no longer a subject. In fact, the stain of the black body seems figuratively to darken consciousness itself, to overshadow my existence as a subject. Is it this way for him? Cleaver writes:

> The chip on the Supermasculine Menial's shoulders is the fact that he had been robbed of his mind. In an uncannily effective manner, the society in which he lives assumed in its very structure that he, minus a mind, is the embodiment of Brute Power. The bias and reflexes of the society are against the cultivation of even the functioning of his mind, and it is borne in upon him from all sides that the society is deaf, dumb, and blind to his mind.[9]

That is, incapable of the intentionality that would allow the Supermasculine Menial to disclose an interiority. We shall call this situation the "black-as-body." Quoting Fanon: "In the white world the man of color encounters difficulties in the development of his bodily schema. Consciousness of the body is solely a negating activity . . . the body is surrounded by an atmosphere of uncertainty."[10] I am aware of each of my limbs through my *body image*; similarly, I am aware of my skin surface, my epidermal encasement through my *body image*, and particularly when I am "seen." "Saying that I have a body is thus a way of saying that I can be seen as an object and that I try to be seen as a subject, that another can be my master, so that shame and shame-lessness express the dialectic of the plurality of consciousness, and have a metaphysical significance."[11] Fanon warns that "though Sartre's specula-tions on the existence of the Other may be correct . . . their application to a black consciousness proves fallacious. That is because the white man is not only the Other, but also the master, whether real or imaginary." And again: "Jean-Paul Sartre has forgotten that the Negro suffers in his body quite differently from the white man."[12]

The experience of the black-as-body becomes, not merely a Self-Other conflict, nor simply Hegel's torturous Master-Slave dialectic, but a variation on both these conditions, intensified by the particularity of the body's ap-pearance as black, as "stained," lacking interiority and, as Fanon writes, as being "overdetermined from without." The body as opaque and conscious-ness as invisible is developed in Cleaver's brief essay. And if that conscious-ness is not experienced by the Other as invisible, it is the repository for the offscum of racial relations—to black subjectivity is attributed the contents that white consciousness itself fears to contain or confront: bestial sexuality, uncleanliness, criminality, all the purported "dark things." In R. W. Shu-feldt's *The Negro, A Menace to Civilization* (1907) and Thomas Dixon Jr.'s. *The Leopard's Spots*, the idea is extended to include black blood, which carries the germ of the underworld and the traits of lower orders of animals; one drop of black blood, for example, will cause a white family to revert to Negroid characteristics even after a full century; the mulatto, though pos-sessing white blood, is depicted as dangerous because his surface "outside," not being stained, betrays the criminality and animality of his interior.[13]

The stereotype with which we began discloses the black-as-body but, as a pure literary presentation, it conceals the original situation of "embodied consciousness" made a problem for itself by "stain." Consider the concern our grandparents had with body complexion, "brightening the race" through careful marriage, the terrible importance of fair skin, curly hair, and "yellah women." They were not fools, these old folks; they knew what they experi-enced. And understood skin-bleaching creams and straightening combs as important because these changed their stained "outsides" upon which, in this social system, the depth of their "insides" would be gauged by others. (Indeed, critic Robert Bone has called Christianity in James Baldwin's *Go Tell it on the Mountain* a "spiritual bleaching cream.") Stain recalls de-filement, guilt, sin, corpses that contaminate, menstruating women; and with them come the theological meanings of punishment, ostracism, and the need to be "cleansed." It was never so much that, "If you're light, you're alright," meant that whiteness was rightness on the basis of the lack of pigmentation alone; rather, it meant that, "Washing a Moor white over three generations," degree by painful degree, led to his social recognition by the Other as human subject, as—in some cases—his possessing a soul, as "inside."

I am walking down Broadway in Manhattan, platform shoes clicking on the hot pavement, thinking as I stroll of, say, Boolean expansions. I turn, thirsty, into a bar. The dimly-lit room, obscured by shadows, is occupied by whites. Goodbye, Boolean expansions. I am *seen*. But, as a black, seen as stained body, as physicality, basically opaque to others—a possibility that, of course, whites themselves have in a room of blacks. Their look, an intending beam focusing my way, suddenly realizes something larval in me. My world is epidermalized, "collapsed like a house of cards into the stained casement of my skin."[14] My subjectivity is turned inside out like a shirtcuff. "And so it is not I who make a meaning for myself, but it is the meaning that was already there, pre-existing, waiting for me,"[15] much like a mugger at a boardwalk's end. All I am, can be to them, is as nakedly presented as the genitals of a plant since they cannot see my other profiles. Epidermalization spreads throughout the body like an odor, like an echoing sound. This feeling differs little from that of sexuality: a sudden dizziness and disorientation, an acute awareness of my outside, of its being for others, a tight swell at my temples. But it is not the pathological feeling of "inferiority" alone that Fanon speaks of when my being is stolen—it is Cleaver's perception of the black-as-body. Yet, Fanon is correct. "For not only must the black man be black; he must be black in relation to the white man."[16] Because it is from whites that the intention, the "meaning" of the black body comes. I sit at the bar, ignoring the Others; but the body is acutely aware of them, knows immediately when someone outside my peripheral vision has stood up. It is intense, as though consciousness has shifted to the skin's seen surfaces.

Our body responds totally to this abrupt epidermalization; consciousness for the subject is violently emptied of content: one, in fact, draws a "blank," though clearly for the white Other my interiority is, if not invisible, a space filled with sensuality, crime, or childlike simplicity. There are physiological reactions: the pulse and adrenalin increase, the seen skin becomes moist, as if the body is in open conspiracy with the white Other to confirm the sudden eclipse of my consciousness entirely by corporeality. I feel its sleepy awkwardness, and know myself not as subject but as slumberous, torpid matter. The Other awaits my slurring my words; my mouth, dry as ash, seems ready to realize his expectation. He awaits a signal of my "Negroness"—perhaps my brutalizing the language when I order a beer: some signal that we in our bodies are not the same. If I am the sort of "Negro" brought up to be a "credit to the race," I must forever be on guard against my body betraying me in public; I must suppress the profile that their frozen intentionality brings forth—I police my actions, and take precautions against myself so the myth of stain, evil, and physicality, like a Platonic form, does not appear in me.

Or, let us say, I sit sipping espresso with a white friend in the Village, discussing Borges, Barthelme, Baraka, basketball, the incredible Pele. I've smoked myself into a sore throat; I sip the scum-surfaced coffee merely to wet my lips, to ease my throat. Our conversation turns circuitously and comes to Walt Frazier. The Other slaps my knee soundly. He says, "Man, that cat is the most beautiful animal I've ever seen on a basketball court. I mean, he moves like — like a cheetah, or a big jungle cat." Make no mistake: this comes from him as the highest compliment. He is "hip," you see, liberal, a Left Bank intellectual — it is merely a *faux pas*. He has not reduced us to a "nothingness." The reduction is to "muscles are strength." Paradoxically, we are reduced to the body as the subject of physics — Brute Power. Yet, as with the rush of sexuality, a torpor glazes over my consciousness, a languor arises like a sleepiness in my limbs. The thickness of the world's texture is thinned. The body commonly extends itself in vehicles, buildings, machines, clothing. "Consciousness is being toward the thing through the intermediary of the body — to move one's body is to aim at things through it; it is to allow oneself to respond to their call."[17] But the black-as-body must see such a call as dubious, even though the "White Only" signs have been torn down, because there remain strict territorial boundaries, real or imagined, when we experience the searing Sartrean "look" of the hate-stare, when the world is epidermalized. Our body in these cases comes awake, translates itself as total physicality — it, oddly enough, feels as if it is listening with its limbs to the Other as my interiority shrivels like something burned, falls into confusion, feels threatened and, if it does not make me constitute myself as hatred (unable to change the world, I emotionally change myself), it momentarily, like a misty field, hazes over.

But we have not completely answered the question raised by Cleaver. There are black modes of flight from the black-as-body situation to consider. So far we have said that in a situation structured by a color-caste system, a black's consciousness and his lived-world (*Lebenswelt*) are frequently epidermalized and thrown into confusion when others intend him as the black-as-body. Once I am so one-sidely seen, I have several options open to me on the level of consciousness. These are also stages in recent black history:

(A) I accept this being seen only from the outside, accept my human possibility of being matter *sans* mind for the Others. I craftily use this invisibility of my interior to deceive, and thus to win survival, as the folk-hero Trickster John frequently does in the "Old Marster and John" cycle. My stain is like the heavy make-up of a clown; it conceals me completely. The motto of this useful opacity is the rhyme: "Got one mind for whitefolks to see / Got another one that's really me." That is, not being acknowledged as a subject is my strength, my chance for cunning and masquerade, for guerrilla warfare: I am a spy in the Big House. I cynically play with their frozen intentions, presuppositions, and stereotypes; I shuffle and appear lazy to avoid work, or — if I am a modern — I manipulate their basic fear of me as Darkness and Brute Power to win concessions. It is what Ralph Ellison calls

"Rinehartism" in his novel *Invisible Man*. In Richard Wright's "novel-of-ideas," *The Outsider*, the protagonist is Cross Damon, a black existential hero with an extensive background in Heidegger, Husserl, and French phenomenology, who is freed from his former life by a freak subway wreck in Chicago. He assumes a new identity, but needs a false birth certificate. He thinks: "He would have to present to the officials a Negro so scared and ignorant that no white man would ever dream that he was up to anything deceptive." By shuffling, head-scratching, eye-blinking, and butchering the language, Cross pulls off the grotesque deception, and the author explains:

> And as he stood there manipulating their responses, Cross knew exactly what kind of man he would pretend to be to kill suspicion if he ever got into trouble. In his role as an ignorant, frightened Negro, each white man—except those few who were free from the race bias of their group—would leap to supply him with a background and an identity; each white man would project out on him his own conception of the Negro and he could safely hide behind it. . . . He knew that deep in their hearts those two white clerks knew that no human being on earth was as dense as he made himself out to be, but they wanted, needed to believe it of Negroes and it helped them to feel racially superior. They were pretending, just as he had been pretending.[18]

(B) Perhaps I vindicate my eloquence, culture, and my charm to demonstrate to the Other that I, despite my stained skin, do indeed have an inside. "Y'know, I was just thinking about Boolean expansions," I tell the barkeeper. I self-consciously sprinkle my speech with French (my interiority is Continental, you see). Perhaps I pretend that I am not Afro-American at all, but part Indian, Jamaican, or an African—a flight from the historical experience of American antebellum slavery in which epidermalization reaches its acme.

(C) Or I am radical, and seize the situation at its root by reversing the negative meaning of the body and, therefore, the black-as-body: "It is beautiful," I say, "I am a child of the Sun." The situation of the black-as-body possessing non-cognitive traits is not rejected in this most recent variation of cultural nationalism, but rather stood upon its head: the meaning still issues from the white Other. I applaud my athletic, amorous, and dancing ability, my street-wisdom and savior-faire, my "soul," the food my body eats ("Yeah," I scream at my white friend in the Village, "we're naturally superior to you at sports. Uh huhn, and we satisfy our women better *too*!"); I speak of the communal ("single-body") social life of my African ancestors before the fifteenth-century slave trade, their bodily closeness to the earth. I am Antaeus in this persuasion of the alienated black self's phenomenological pilgrimage to itself, and the whites—flesh-starved invaders, freebooters, buccaneers, seamen who bring syphilis to ancient Africa—are alienated physically from the earth. They see their lost humanity in me. They steal me to take it home. If I am a member of the early Nation of Islam and believe in its mythology of Yacub, the black scientist who created a "white beast" from the black community, I intend the whites as quasi-men "grafted" from the original black-as-body until, by degrees, the Caucasian appears as a pale and pitiful abstraction from myself, ontologically removed several stages from the basic reality which I represent.

Curiously, this persuasion in which stain and the black-as-body are inverted is ahistorical; it must involve a complete reconstitution of cultural meanings with the black body as its foundation: two thousand years of color and symbolism must be recast. Hence, we see the black-as-body in this profile generating new cultural forms: African dress (body extensions), Swahili (what my body speaks), the Nation of Islam and Black Church of Christ (my interiority is black, you see), but behind such a cultural revolution, which I create, is the enigma of the black-as-body in a state of stain. I portray my body to myself as "luscious to the kiss," beautiful, "tropical," soulful, sensuous— as "Fire!" My knowledge is natural, from "Nature" (another vast body) and is called "mother-wit," a form of knowing antithetical to the lifeless thoughts in the upper recesses of the Omnipotent Administrator's brain. I intend the white body as pitifully unstained, stiff, decadent, rigid, unnatural, cerebral, and pasty like something left under my kitchen sink, away from the skin-darkening sun, for too long a time. No attempt to bridge the false dualism of the Supermasculine Menial and the Omnipotent Administrator, between the body and consciousness, is made in these variations.

It should be clear that what is described in Cleaver's "The Primevil Mitosis" is a general human possibility based upon the ability of "embodied consciousness" to be made a problem for itself within a racial caste system. As we have seen, the problem is not diminished by the customary strategies for escaping it. The black body remains an ambiguous object in our society, still susceptible to whatever meanings the white gaze assigns to it.

## Postscript, 1993

This essay, which originally appeared in the Winter 1976 issue of *Ju-Ju: Research Papers in Afro-American Studies*, was written in 1975 as my "style paper" for the Ph.D. program in philosophy at SUNY-Stony Brook. Back then all doctoral candidates were required to submit for the faculty's approval an essay using the methods of one of the three principal schools of twentieth-century philosophy—analytic or British, American philosophy (pragmatism), or phenomenology—and since aesthetics was my field of concentration, I chose the latter. If memory serves, this was easily one of the hardest years of my life. As a graduate student living on a teaching assistantship, I was broke, but that June saw the birth of our son Malik, and the feverish writing of the first draft for *Oxherding Tale*, a novel I would publish seven years later. I remember monkishly retreating into one of the foulest apartment buildings in Port Jefferson, New York (it was all we could afford that summer) and, when I wasn't working on the novel, reading Sartre's *Being and Nothingness*, Heidegger's *Being and Time*, and Merleau-Ponty's *The Phenomenology of Perception* back-to-back in about the space of a month. Out of that context of unemployment and impoverishment and general concerns for my son, and fresh from my immersion in these seminal works of the German and French phenomenological movements, this essay was conjured.

Looking back across eighteen years at this descriptive analysis, I realize that my hope was to examine the black male body as a cultural object and to inquire into how it has been interpreted, manipulated, and given to us, particularly in popular culture. In general, too little has changed in the social world since the essay was first published. Indeed, for a few years things got worse. In the Bush campaign's exploitation of Willie Horton to frighten voters in 1988, in the racial slur about "Gorillas in the Mist" from the policeman who beat Rodney King as he would a dangerous animal, in the television footage of black male destructiveness during the Los Angeles riot, in the rise of the white supremacy movement in the last decade, in Pat Buchanan's attack on NEA for funding a film about gay black men (and ex-Klansman David Duke's startling though brief political success), in the decimation of black communities by AIDS, in the sexual harassment charges against Clarence Thomas, who according to Anita Hill described himself as "Long Dong Silver," in the sexist "gangster" lyrics offered by Ice T and other rap artists, in the gang-banging legions of Crips and Bloods, in the relentless barrage of statistics about murder among young black men and their failure to support their families, and even in the popular novels of several black women authors during the decade of the 1980s, we find that the black male as "Negro beast"—violent, sex-obsessed, irresponsible, and stupid—still has great currency and acceptance in our culture.

However, it's important to point out that none of these cultural meanings cluster around the black *female* body. In an amazing and revolutionary feat of cultural reconstruction, contemporary black women have made dominant the profile of the female body as, first and foremost, *spiritual:* a communal-body of politically progressive, long-suffering women who are responsible, hard-working and compassionate, who support each other in all ways, protect and nurture their children and live meaningful lives without black male assistance. The black female body is, in fact, frequently offered to us as the *original* body of a humankind descended from a black Eve of Africa. Clearly, this profile owes much to both black cultural nationalism of the late 1960s (variation "C" in the essay) and to the embracing of feminism by many black women in the 1980s. Nevertheless, like the Negro Beast stereotype, the Ur-mother profile is a mythology that obscures and one-dimensionalizes our possibilities for experiencing each black person as individual, historical, and so unique that—as in the case of my son or daughter, for example—it must be said that no one like them has ever lived before or will ever live again.

Recently one of my colleagues in African-American Studies said to me that black women have succeeded in culturally "defining" themselves in their own terms and not those of the racial (or gender) Other. If he's right, then we have no choice but to conclude that black males have *not* done this quite as well as their female counterparts. As my friend, a gentle and scholarly man, put it: "People don't know who we are. Even *we* aren't sure who we are."

But isn't that precisely the perennial human dilemma? That we are, after all, beings who must fashion moment by moment what meaning our lives will have, beings in *process* who are subject in a single lifetime to change, transformation, self-contradiction, and constant evolution? In phenomenological terms, one can only achieve adequateness in describing the black male body by employing what some philosophers have called "genetic phenomenology," *i.e.*, by examining an individual as he (or she) exhibits over time a series of profiles or disclosures of being. For a life is process, not product (or pre-given meaning). It more resembles the verb, not the noun.

This, just maybe, explains the current interest of young people in the unusual life of Malcolm X. There is much for critics of culture and philosophers to discuss in Spike Lee's monumental film tribute to this slain leader. Begin with the opening scene when Malcolm Little—a drug-dealer, pimp, and thief—visits a barber shop and has lye combed into his hair, which straightens it so thin another customer says, "It looks white." Go next to Malcolm in solitary confinement at Charlestown State Prison, where he is made to live like a caged animal. Then contrast both of these scenes to Malcolm X on his knees in a temple in Mecca, his hands raised to Allah, an ancient, haunting Muslim prayer sliding from his black throat like song. Here, the black male body is the instrument of the Most High. It is a global body connected to America, Africa, and the Middle East. It is capable of surrender and strength. It is cleansed of drugs, tobacco, and alcohol. It is the temple, the repository, of two millennia of Islamic scholarship, the living vessel for a culture that achieved a remarkably high level of sophistication when Europe was struggling through its Dark Ages—indeed, the culture that preserved Aristotle and transmitted him back to the West. For the first time in motion-picture history, and perhaps in pop culture, the black male body is experienced as the embodiment of intellectual, political, and spiritual ideals.

And yet all these profiles are of *one* life. If Malcolm X had not been slain in 1965, we doubtlessly would have witnessed more, an unfolding of idea and image that, for the phenomenologist, can only suggest the open-ended character of being. If there has been some slim progress since I first published "A Phenomenology of the Black Body," it is of this sort. A gradual accumulation of profiles that expand and qualify our experience of black men: General Colin Powell coolly professional at the center of the Persian Gulf conflict, athlete Arthur Ashe, widely admired for his courage and humanitarianism, astronaut Ron McNair honored for his contributions to the nation and NASA, Seattle mayor Norm Rice laboring, day in day out, to serve an American city that still works. Any accounts we have of black males in the future must, I believe, take these men—and the meanings their lives embody—into consideration.

V

## NOTES

1. Eldridge Cleaver, *Soul on Ice* (New York: Dell, 1968), p. 174.

2. *Ibid.*, p. 169.

3. Cited in Don Ihde, *Hermenutic Phenomenology: The Philosophy of Paul Ricoeur* (Northwestern University Press, 1971), p. 56.

4. Franz Fanon, *Black Skin, White Masks* (New York: Grove Press, 1967), p. 225.

5. Maurice Merleau-Ponty, *The Phenomenology of Perception*, trans. Colin Smith (New York: The Humanities Press, 1970). The discussion of the body is developed in Part One.

6. Rollo May, *Love and Will* (New York: Dell, 1969), p. 229.

7. Merleau-Ponty, *op. cit.*, p. 206.

8. *Ibid.*, p. 146.

9. Cleaver, *op. cit.*, p. 171.

10. Fanon, *op. cit.*, p. 110.

11. Merleau-Ponty, *op. cit.*, p. 167.

12. Fanon, *op. cit.*, p. 138.

13. George Kent, *Blackness and the Adventure of Western Civilization* (Chicago: Third World Press, 1972), p. 173.

14. The term "epidermalization" was first used in a phenomenological sense by Professor Thomas Slaughter, of the Afro-American Studies Department at Rutgers, in his unpublished paper, "Epidermalizing the World."

15. Fanon, *op. cit.*, p. 134.

16. *Ibid.*, p. 110.

17. Merleau-Ponty, *op. cit.*, p. 138.

18. Richard Wright, *The Outsider* (New York: Harper & Row, 1953), p. 159.

# 21 THIRTEEN WAYS OF LOOKING AT A BLACK MAN

HENRY LOUIS GATES, JR.

"Every day, in every way, we are getting meta and meta," the philosopher John Wisdom used to say, venturing a cultural counterpart to Émile Coué's famous mantra of self-improvement. So it made sense that in the aftermath of the Simpson trial the focus of attention was swiftly displaced from the verdict to the reaction to the verdict, and then to the reaction to the reaction to the verdict, and, finally, to the reaction to the reaction to the reaction to the verdict—which is to say, black indignation at white anger at black jubilation at Simpson's acquittal. It was a spiral made possible by the relay circuit of race. Only in America.

An American historian I know registers a widespread sense of bathos when he says, "Who would have imagined that the Simpson trial would be like the Kennedy assassination—that you'd remember where you were when the verdict was announced?" But everyone does, of course. The eminent sociologist William Julius Wilson was in the red-carpet lounge of a United Airlines terminal, the only black in a crowd of white travelers, and found himself as stunned and disturbed as they were. Wynton Marsalis, on tour with his band in California, recalls that "everybody was acting like they were above watching it, but then when it got to be ten o'clock—zoom, we said, 'Put the verdict on!'" Spike Lee was with Jackie Robinson's widow, Rachel, rummaging through a trunk filled with her husband's belongings, in preparation for a bio-pic he's making on the athlete. Jamaica Kincaid was sitting in her car in the parking lot of her local grocery store in Vermont, listening

home, because there are not a lot of relationships that could be put on television that we would think, O.K., that's a good one. I mean, just stop pretending that this is the case." Then, too, she asks, "Isn't it interesting to you that this Faye Resnick person was staying with Nicole Brown Simpson and that she happened to have left on the eighth of June? Does that tell you that maybe there's some awful coincidence here?" The widespread theory about murderous drug dealers Norman finds "perfectly plausible, knowing what drugs do," and she adds, "People are punished for being bad."

There's a sense in which all such accounts can be considered counter-narratives, or fragments of them—subaltern knowledge, if you like. They dispute the tenets of official culture; they do not receive the imprimatur of editorialists or of network broadcasters; they are not seriously entertained on *MacNeil/Lehrer*. And when they do surface they are given consideration primarily for their ethnographic value. An official culture treats their claims as it does those of millenarian cultists in Texas, or Marxist deconstructionists in the academy: as things to be diagnosed, deciphered, given meaning—that is, *another* meaning. Black folk say they believe Simpson is innocent, and then the white gatekeepers of a media culture cajolingly explain what black folk really mean when they say it, offering the explanation from the highest of motives: because the alternative is a population that, by their lights, is not merely counternormative but crazy. Black folk may mean anything at all; just not what they say they mean.

Yet you need nothing so grand as an epistemic rupture to explain why different people weigh the evidence of authority differently. In the words of the cunning Republican campaign slogan, "Who do you trust?" It's a com-monplace that white folks trust the police and black folks don't. Whites recognize this in the abstract, but they're continually surprised at the *depth* of black wariness. They shouldn't be. Norman Podhoretz's soul-searching 1963 essay, "My Negro Problem, and Ours"—one of the frankest accounts we have of liberalism and race resentment—tells of a Brooklyn boyhood spent under the shadow of carefree, cruel Negro assailants, and of the author's residual unease when he passes groups of blacks in his Upper West Side neighborhood. And yet, he notes in a crucial passage, "I know now, as I did not know when I was a child, that power is on my side, that the police are working for me and not for them." That ordinary, unremarkable com-fort—the feeling that "the police are working for me"—continues to elude blacks, even many successful blacks. Thelma Golden, the curator of the Whitney's "Black Male" show, points out that on the very day the verdict was announced a black man in Harlem was killed by the police under disputed circumstances. As older blacks like to repeat, "When white folks say 'justice,' they mean 'just us.'"

Blacks—in particular, black men—swap their experiences of police en-counters like war stories, and there are few who don't have more than one story to tell. "These stories have a ring of cliché about them," Erroll McDon-

counternarrative that has been documented and legitimized, by slow, hard-won scholarship. The "shadowy figures" of American history have long been our own ancestors, both free and enslaved. In any case, fealty to counter-narratives is an index to alienation, not to skin color: witness Representative Helen Chenoweth, of Idaho, and her devoted constituents. With all the appositeness of allegory, the copies of *The Protocols of the Elders of Zion* sold by black venders in New York—who are supplied with them by Lushena Books, a black-nationalist book wholesaler—were published by the white supremacist Angriff Press, in Hollywood. Paranoia knows no color or coast.

Finally, though, it's misleading to view counternarrative as another pathology of disenfranchisement. If the M.I.A. myth, say, is rooted among a largely working-class constituency, there are many myths—one of them known as Reaganism—that hold considerable appeal among the privileged classes. "So many white brothers and sisters are living in a state of denial in terms of how deep white supremacy is seated in their culture and society," the scholar and social critic Cornel West says. "Now we recognize that in a fundamental sense we really do live in different worlds." In that respect, the reaction to the Simpson verdict has been something of an education. The novelist Ishmael Reed talks of "wealthy white male commentators who live in a world where the police don't lie, don't plant evidence—and drug dealers give you unlimited credit." He adds, "Nicole, you know, also dated Mafia hit men."

"I think he's innocent, I really do," West says. "I do think it was linked to some drug subculture of violence. It looks as if both O.J. and Nicole had some connection to drug activity. And the killings themselves were classic examples of that drug culture of violence. It could have to do with money owed—it could have to do with a number of things. And I think that O.J. was quite aware of and fearful of this." On this theory, Simpson may have appeared at the crime scene as a witness. "I think that he had a sense that it was coming down, both on him and on her, and Brother Ron Goldman just happened to be there," West conjectures. "But there's a possibility also that O.J. could have been there, gone over and tried to see what was going on, saw that he couldn't help, split, and just ran away. He might have said, 'I can't stop this thing, and they are coming at me to do the same thing.' He may have actually run for his life."

To believe that Simpson is innocent is to believe that a terrible injustice has been averted, and this is precisely what many black Americans, including many prominent ones, do believe. Thus the soprano Jessye Norman is angry over what she sees as the decision of the media to prejudge Simpson rather than "educate the public as to how we could possibly look at things a bit differently." She says she wishes that the real culprit "would stand up and say, 'I did this and I am sorry I caused so much trouble.'" And while she is sensitive to the issue of spousal abuse, she is skeptical about the way it was enlisted by the prosecution: "You have to stop getting into how they were at

counternarrative that has been documented and legitimized, by slow, hard-won scholarship. The "shadowy figures" of American history have long been our own ancestors, both free and enslaved. In any case, fealty to counter-narratives is an index to alienation, not to skin color: witness Representative Helen Chenoweth, of Idaho, and her devoted constituents. With all the appositeness of allegory, the copies of *The Protocols of the Elders of Zion* sold by black venders in New York—who are supplied with them by Lushena Books, a black-nationalist book wholesaler—were published by the white supremacist Angriff Press, in Hollywood. Paranoia knows no color or coast.

Finally, though, it's misleading to view counternarrative as another pathology of disenfranchisement. If the M.I.A. myth, say, is rooted among a largely working-class constituency, there are many myths—one of them known as Reaganism—that hold considerable appeal among the privileged classes. "So many white brothers and sisters are living in a state of denial in terms of how deep white supremacy is seated in their culture and society," the scholar and social critic Cornel West says. "Now we recognize that in a fundamental sense we really do live in different worlds." In that respect, the reaction to the Simpson verdict has been something of an education. The novelist Ishmael Reed talks of "wealthy white male commentators who live in a world where the police don't lie, don't plant evidence—and drug dealers give you unlimited credit." He adds, "Nicole, you know, also dated Mafia hit men."

"I think he's innocent, I really do," West says. "I do think it was linked to some drug subculture of violence. It looks as if both O.J. and Nicole had some connection to drug activity. And the killings themselves were classic examples of that drug culture of violence. It could have to do with money owed—it could have to do with a number of things. And I think that O.J. was quite aware of and fearful of this." On this theory, Simpson may have appeared at the crime scene as a witness. "I think that he had a sense that it was coming down, both on him and on her, and Brother Ron Goldman just happened to be there," West conjectures. "But there's a possibility also that O.J. could have been there, gone over and tried to see what was going on, saw that he couldn't help, split, and just ran away. He might have said, 'I can't stop this thing, and they are coming at me to do the same thing.' He may have actually run for his life."

To believe that Simpson is innocent is to believe that a terrible injustice has been averted, and this is precisely what many black Americans, including many prominent ones, do believe. Thus the soprano Jessye Norman is angry over what she sees as the decision of the media to prejudge Simpson rather than "educate the public as to how we could possibly look at things a bit differently." She says she wishes that the real culprit "would stand up and say, 'I did this and I am sorry I caused so much trouble.'" And while she is sensitive to the issue of spousal abuse, she is skeptical about the way it was enlisted by the prosecution: "You have to stop getting into how they were at home, because there are not a lot of relationships that could be put on television that we would think, O.K., that's a good one. I mean, just stop pretending that this is the case." Then, too, she asks, "Isn't it interesting to you that this Faye Resnick person was staying with Nicole Brown Simpson and that she happened to have left on the eighth of June? Does that tell you that maybe there's some awful coincidence here?" The widespread theory about murderous drug dealers Norman finds "perfectly plausible, knowing what drugs do," and she adds, "People are punished for being bad."

There's a sense in which all such accounts can be considered counter-narratives, or fragments of them—subaltern knowledge, if you like. They dispute the tenets of official culture; they do not receive the imprimatur of editorialists or of network broadcasters; they are not seriously entertained on *MacNeil/Lehrer*. And when they do surface they are given consideration primarily for their ethnographic value. An official culture treats their claims as it does those of millenarian cultists in Texas, or Marxist deconstructionists in the academy: as things to be diagnosed, deciphered, given meaning—that is, *another* meaning. Black folk say they believe Simpson is innocent, and then the white gatekeepers of a media culture cajolingly explain what black folk really mean when they say it, offering the explanation from the highest of motives: because the alternative is a population that, by their lights, is not merely counternormative but crazy. Black folk may mean anything at all; just not what they say they mean.

Yet you need nothing so grand as an epistemic rupture to explain why different people weigh the evidence of authority differently. In the words of the cunning Republican campaign slogan, "Who do you trust?" It's a commonplace that white folks trust the police and black folks don't. Whites recognize this in the abstract, but they're continually surprised at the *depth* of black wariness. They shouldn't be. Norman Podhoretz's soul-searching 1963 essay, "My Negro Problem, and Ours"—one of the frankest accounts we have of liberalism and race resentment—tells of a Brooklyn boyhood spent under the shadow of carefree, cruel Negro assailants, and of the author's residual unease when he passes groups of blacks in his Upper West Side neighborhood. And yet, he notes in a crucial passage, "I know now, as I did not know when I was a child, that power is on my side, that the police are working for me and not for them." That ordinary, unremarkable comfort—the feeling that "the police are working for me"—continues to elude blacks, even many successful blacks. Thelma Golden, the curator of the Whitney's "Black Male" show, points out that on the very day the verdict was announced a black man in Harlem was killed by the police under disputed circumstances. As older blacks like to repeat, "When white folks say 'justice,' they mean 'just us.'"

Blacks—in particular, black men—swap their experiences of police encounters like war stories, and there are few who don't have more than one story to tell. "These stories have a ring of cliché about them," Erroll McDonald, Pantheon's executive editor and one of the few prominent blacks in publishing, says, "but, as we all know about clichés, they're almost always true." McDonald tells of renting a Jaguar in New Orleans and being stopped by the police—simply "to show cause why I shouldn't be deemed a problematic Negro in a possibly stolen car." Wynton Marsalis says, "Shit, the police slapped me upside the head when I was in high school. I wasn't Wynton Marsalis then. I was just another nigger standing out somewhere on the street whose head could be slapped and did get slapped." The crime novelist Walter Mosley recalls, "When I was a kid in Los Angeles, they used to stop me all the time, beat on me, follow me around, tell me that I was stealing things." Nor does William Julius Wilson—who has a son-in-law on the Chicago police force ("You couldn't find a nicer, more dedicated guy")— wonder why he was stopped near a small New England town by a policeman who wanted to know what he was doing in those parts. There's a moving violation that many African-Americans know as D.W.B.: Driving While Black.

So we all have our stories. In 1968, when I was eighteen, a man who knew me was elected mayor of my West Virginia county, in an upset victory. A few weeks into his term, he passed on something he thought I should know: the county police had made a list of people to be arrested in the event of a serious civil disturbance, and my name was on it. Years of conditioning will tell. Wynton Marsalis says, "My worst fear is to have to go before the criminal-justice system." Absurdly enough, it's mine, too.

Another barrier to interracial comprehension is talk of the "race card"—a phrase that itself infuriates many blacks. Judge Higginbotham, who pronounces himself "not uncomfortable at all" with the verdict, is uncomfortable indeed with charges that Johnnie Cochran played the race card. "This whole point is one hundred percent inaccurate," Higginbotham says. "If you knew that the most important witness had a history of racism and hostility against black people, that should have been a relevant factor of inquiry even if the jury had been all white. If the defendant had been Jewish and the police officer had a long history of expressed anti-Semitism and having planted evidence against innocent persons who were Jewish, I can't believe that anyone would have been saying that defense counsel was playing the anti-Semitism card." Angela Davis finds the very metaphor to be a problem. "Race is not a card," she says firmly. "The whole case was pervaded with issues of race."

Those who share her view were especially outraged at Robert Shapiro's famous post-trial rebuke to Cochran—for not only playing the race card but dealing it "from the bottom of the deck." Ishmael Reed, who is writing a book about the case, regards Shapiro's remarks as sheer opportunism: "He wants to keep his Beverly Hills clients—a perfectly commercial reason." In Judge Higginbotham's view, "Johnnie Cochran established that he was as effective as any lawyer in America, and though whites can tolerate black excellence in singing, dancing, and dunking, there's always been a certain level of discomfort among many whites when you have a one-on-one challenge in terms of intellectual competition. If Edward Bennett Williams, who was one of the most able lawyers in the country, had raised the same issues, half of the complaints would not exist."

By the same token, the display of black prowess in the courtroom was heartening for many black viewers. Cornel West says, "I think part of the problem is that Shapiro—and this is true of certain white brothers—has a profound fear of black-male charisma. And this is true not only in the law but across the professional world. You see, you have so many talented white brothers who deserve to be in the limelight. But one of the reasons they arc not in the limelight is that they are not charismatic. And here comes a black person who's highly talented but also charismatic and therefore able to command center stage. So you get a very real visceral kind of jealousy that has to do with sexual competition as well as professional competition."

Erroll McDonald touches upon another aspect of sexual tension when he says, "The so-called race card has always been the joker. And the joker is the history of sexual racial politics in this country. People forget the singularity of this issue—people forget that less than a century ago black men were routinely lynched for merely glancing at white women or for having been *thought* to have glanced at a white woman." He adds, with mordant irony, "Now we've come to a point in our history where a black man could, potentially, have murdered a white woman and thrown in a white man to boot—and got off. So the country has become far more complex in its discussion of race." This is, as he appreciates, a less than perfectly consoling thought.

"But he's coming for me," a woman muses in Toni Morrison's 1994 novel, *Jazz*, shortly before she is murdered by a jealous ex-lover. "Maybe tomorrow he'll find me. Maybe tonight." Morrison, it happens, is less interested in the grand passions of love and requital than she is in the curious texture of communal amnesty. In the event, the woman's death goes unavenged; the man who killed her is forgiven even by her friends and relatives. Neighbors feel that the man fell victim to her wiles, that he didn't understand "how she liked to push people, men." Or, as one of them says of her, "live the life; pay the price." Even the woman—who refuses to name the culprit as she bleeds to death—seems to accede to the view that she brought it on herself.

It's an odd and disturbing theme, and one with something of a history in black popular culture. An R. & B. hit from 1960, "There's Something on Your Mind," relates the anguish of a man who is driven to kill by his lover's infidelity. The chorus alternates with spoken narrative, which informs us that his first victim is the friend with whom she was unfaithful. But then:

> Just as you make it up in your mind to forgive her, here come another one of your best friends through the door. This really makes you blow your top, and

you go right ahead and shoot her. And realizing what you've done, you say: "Baby, please, speak to me. Forgive me. I'm sorry."

"We are a *forgiving* people," Anita Hill tells me, and she laughs, a little uneasily. We're talking about the support for O. J. Simpson in the black community; at least, I think we are.

A black woman told the *Times* last week, "He has been punished enough." But forgiveness is not all. There is also an element in this of outlaw culture: the tendency—which unites our lumpenproles with our postmodern ironists—to celebrate transgression for its own sake. Spike Lee, who was surprised but "wasn't happy" at the verdict ("I would have bet money that he was going to the slammer"), reached a similar conclusion: "A lot of black folks said, 'Man, O.J. is *bad,* you know. This is the first brother in the history of the world who got away with the murder of white folks, and a blond, blue-eyed woman at that.'"

But then there is the folk wisdom on the question of why Nicole Brown Simpson had to die—the theodicy of the streets. For nothing could be further from the outlaw ethic than the simple and widely shared certainty that, as Jessye Norman says, people are punished for doing wrong. And compounding the sentiment is Morrison's subject—the culturally vexed status of the so-called crime of passion, or what some took to be one, anyway. You play, you pay: it's an attitude that exists on the streets, but not only on the streets, and one that somehow attaches to Nicole, rather than to her ex-husband. Many counternarratives revolve around her putative misbehavior. The black feminist bell hooks notes with dismay that what many people took to be a "narrative of a crime of passion" had as its victim "a woman that many people, white and black, felt was like a whore. Precisely by being a sexually promiscuous woman, by being a woman who used drugs, by being a white woman with a black man, she had already fallen from grace in many people's eyes—there was no way to redeem her." Ishmael Reed, for one, has no interest in redeeming her. "To paint O. J. Simpson as a beast, they had to depict her as a saint," he complains. "Apparently, she had a violent temper. She slapped her Jamaican maid. I'm wondering, the feminists who are giving Simpson such a hard time—do they approve of white women slapping maids?"

Of course, the popular trial of Nicole Brown Simpson—one conducted off camera, in whispers—has further occluded anything recognizable as sexual politics. When Anita Hill heard that O. J. Simpson was going to be part of the Million Man March on Washington, she felt it was entirely in keeping with the occasion: a trial in which she believed that matters of gender had been "bracketed" was going to be succeeded by a march from which women were excluded. And while Minister Louis Farrakhan had told black men that October 16 was to serve as a "day of atonement" for their sins, the murder of Nicole Brown Simpson and Ronald Goldman was obviously not among the sins he had in mind. bell hooks argues, "Both O.J.'s case and the Million Man March confirm that while white men are trying to be sensitive and pretending they're the new man, black men are saying that patriarchy must be upheld at all costs, even if women must die." She sees the march as a congenial arena for Simpson in symbolic terms: "I think he'd like to strut his stuff, as the patriarch. He is the dick that stayed hard longer." ("The surprising thing is that you won't see Clarence Thomas going on that march," Anita Hill remarks of another icon of patriarchy.) Farrakhan himself prefers metaphors of military mobilization, but the exclusionary politics of the event has clearly distracted from its ostensible message of solidarity. "First of all, I wouldn't go to no war and leave half the army home," says Amiri Baraka, the radical poet and playwright who achieved international renown in the sixties as the leading spokesman for the Black Arts movement. "Logistically, that doesn't make sense." He notes that Martin Luther King's 1963 March on Washington was "much more inclusive," and sees Farrakhan's regression as "an absolute duplication of what's happening in the country," from Robert Bly on: the sacralization of masculinity.

Something like that dynamic is what many white feminists saw on display in the Simpson verdict; but it's among women that the racial divide is especially salient. The black legal scholar and activist Patricia Williams says she was "stunned by the intensely personal resentment of some of my white women friends in particular." Stunned but, on reflection, not mystified. "This is Greek drama," she declares. "Two of the most hotly contended aspects of our lives are violence among human beings who happen to be police officers and violence among human beings who happen to be husbands, spouses, lovers." Meanwhile, our attention has been fixated on the rhetorical violence between human beings who happen to disagree about the outcome of the O. J. Simpson trial.

It's a cliché to speak of the Simpson trial as a soap opera — as entertainment, as theater — but it's also true, and in ways that are worth exploring further. For one thing, the trial provides a fitting rejoinder to those who claim that we live in an utterly fragmented culture, bereft of the common narratives that bind a people together. True, Parson Weems has given way to Dan Rather, but public narrative persists. Nor has it escaped notice that the biggest televised legal contests of the last half decade have involved race matters: Anita Hill and Rodney King. So there you have it: the Simpson trial — black entertainment television at its finest. Ralph Ellison's hopeful insistence on the Negro's centrality to American culture finds, at last, a certain tawdry confirmation.

"The media generated in people a feeling of being spectators at a show," the novelist John Edgar Wideman says. "And at the end of a show you applaud. You are happy for the good guy. There is that sense of primal identification and closure." Yet it's a fallacy of "cultural literacy" to equate shared narratives with shared meanings. The fact that American TV shows are rebroadcast across the globe causes many people to wring their hands over the menace of cultural imperialism; seldom do they bother to inquire about the meanings that different people bring to and draw from these shows. When they do make inquiries, the results are often surprising. One researcher talked to Israeli Arabs who had just watched an episode of *Dallas*—an episode in which Sue Ellen takes her baby, leaves her husband, J.R., and moves in with her ex-lover and his father. The Arab viewers placed their own construction on the episode: they were all convinced that Sue Ellen had moved in with her *own* father—something that by their mores at least made sense.

A similar thing happened in America this year: the communal experience afforded by a public narrative (and what narrative more public?) was splintered by the politics of interpretation. As far as the writer Maya Angelou is concerned, the Simpson trial was an exercise in minstrelsy. "Minstrel shows caricatured every aspect of the black man's life, beginning with his sexuality," she says. "They portrayed the black man as devoid of all sensibilities and sensitivities. They minimized and diminished the possibility of familial love. And that is what the trial is about. Not just the prosecution but everybody seemed to want to show him as other than a normal human being. Nobody let us just see a man." But there is, of course, little consensus about what genre would best accommodate the material. Walter Mosley says, "The story plays to large themes, so I'm sure somebody will write about it. But I don't think it's a mystery. I think it's much more like a novel by Zola." What a writer might make of the material is one thing; what the audience has made of it is another.

"Simpson is a B-movie star and people were watching this like a B movie," Patricia Williams says. "And this is *not* the American B-movie ending." Or was it? "From my perspective as an attorney, this trial was much more like a movie than a trial," Kathleen Cleaver, who was once the Black Panthers' Minister for Communication and is now a professor of law at Emory, says. "It had the budget of a movie, it had the casting of a movie, it had the tension of a movie, and the happy ending of a movie." Spike Lee, speaking professionally, is dubious about the trial's cinematic possibilities: "I don't care who makes this movie, it is never going to equal what people have seen in their living rooms and houses for eight or nine months." Or is it grand opera? Jessye Norman considers: "Well, it certainly has all the ingredients. I mean, somebody meets somebody and somebody gets angry with somebody and somebody dies." She laughs. "It sounds like the *Ring* cycle of Wagner—it really does."

"This story has been told any number of times," Angelou says. "The first thing I thought about was Eugene O'Neill's *All God's Chillun.*" Then she considers how the event might be retrieved by an African-American literary tradition. "I think a great writer would have to approach it," she tells me pensively. "James Baldwin could have done it. And Toni Morrison could do it."

What about Maya Angelou?

"I don't like that kind of stuff," she replies.

There are some for whom the question of adaptation is not entirely abstract. The performance artist and playwright Anna Deavere Smith has already worked on the 911 tape and F. Lee Bailey's cross-examination of Mark Fuhrman in the drama classes she teaches at Stanford. Now, with a dramaturge's eye, she identifies what she takes to be the climactic moment: "Just after the verdict was read I will always remember two sounds and one image. I heard Johnnie Cochran go '*Ugh*,' and then I heard the weeping of Kim Goldman. And then I saw the image of O.J.'s son, with one hand going upward on one eye and one hand pointed down, shaking and sobbing. I couldn't do the words right now; if I could find a collaborator, I would do something else. I feel that a choreographer ought to do that thing. Part of the tragedy was the fact of that '*Ugh*' and that crying. Because that '*Ugh*' wasn't even a full sound of victory, really." In "Thirteen Ways of Looking at a Blackbird" Wallace Stevens famously said he didn't know whether he preferred "The beauty of inflections / Or the beauty of innuendoes, / The blackbird whistling / Or just after." American culture has spoken as with one voice: we like it just after.

Just after is when our choices and allegiances are made starkly apparent. Just after is when interpretation can be detached from the thing interpreted. Anita Hill, who saw her own presence at the Clarence Thomas hearings endlessly analyzed and allegorized, finds plenty of significance in the trial's reception, but says the trial itself had none. Naturally, the notion that the trial was sui generis is alien to most commentators. Yet it did not arrive in the world already costumed as a racial drama; it had to be racialized. And those critics—angry whites, indignant blacks—who like to couple this verdict with the Rodney King verdict should consider an elementary circumstance: Rodney King was an unknown and undistinguished black man who was brutalized by the police; the only thing exceptional about that episode was the presence of a video camera. But, as bell hooks asks, "in what other case have we ever had a wealthy black man being tried for murder?" Rodney King was a black man to his captors before he was anything else; O. J. Simpson was, first and foremost, O. J. Simpson. Kathleen Cleaver observes, "A black superhero millionaire is not someone for whom mistreatment is an issue." And Spike Lee acknowledges that the police "don't really bother black people once they are a personality." On this point, I'm reminded of something that Roland Gift, the lead singer of the pop group Fine Young Cannibals, once told a reporter: "I'm not black, I'm famous."

Simpson, too, was famous rather than black; that is, until the African-American community took its lead from the cover of *Time* and, well, blackened him. Some intellectuals are reluctant to go along with the conceit. Angela Davis, whose early-seventies career as a fugitive and a political prisoner provides one model of how to be famous *and* black, speaks of the need

What about Maya Angelou?

"I don't like that kind of stuff," she replies.

There are some for whom the question of adaptation is not entirely abstract. The performance artist and playwright Anna Deavere Smith has already worked on the 911 tape and F. Lee Bailey's cross-examination of Mark Fuhrman in the drama classes she teaches at Stanford. Now, with a dramaturge's eye, she identifies what she takes to be the climactic moment: "Just after the verdict was read I will always remember two sounds and one image. I heard Johnnie Cochran go 'Ugh,' and then I heard the weeping of Kim Goldman. And then I saw the image of O.J.'s son, with one hand going upward on one eye and one hand pointed down, shaking and sobbing. I couldn't do the words right now; if I could find a collaborator, I would do something else. I feel that a choreographer ought to do that thing. Part of the tragedy was the fact of that 'Ugh' and that crying. Because that 'Ugh' wasn't even a full sound of victory, really." In "Thirteen Ways of Looking at a Blackbird" Wallace Stevens famously said he didn't know whether he preferred "The beauty of inflections / Or the beauty of innuendoes, / The blackbird whistling / Or just after." American culture has spoken as with one voice: we like it just after.

Just after is when our choices and allegiances are made starkly apparent. Just after is when interpretation can be detached from the thing interpreted. Anita Hill, who saw her own presence at the Clarence Thomas hearings endlessly analyzed and allegorized, finds plenty of significance in the trial's reception, but says the trial itself had none. Naturally, the notion that the trial was sui generis is alien to most commentators. Yet it did not arrive in the world already costumed as a racial drama; it had to be racialized. And those critics — angry whites, indignant blacks — who like to couple this verdict with the Rodney King verdict should consider an elementary circumstance: Rodney King was an unknown and undistinguished black man who was brutalized by the police; the only thing exceptional about that episode was the presence of a video camera. But, as bell hooks asks, "in what other case have we ever had a wealthy black man being tried for murder?" Rodney King was a black man to his captors before he was anything else; O. J. Simpson was, first and foremost, O. J. Simpson. Kathleen Cleaver observes, "A black superhero millionaire is not someone for whom mistreatment is an issue." And Spike Lee acknowledges that the police "don't really bother black people once they are a personality." On this point, I'm reminded of something that Roland Gift, the lead singer of the pop group Fine Young Cannibals, once told a reporter: "I'm not black, I'm famous."

Simpson, too, was famous rather than black; that is, until the African-American community took its lead from the cover of *Time* and, well, blackened him. Some intellectuals are reluctant to go along with the conceit. Angela Davis, whose early-seventies career as a fugitive and a political prisoner provides one model of how to be famous *and* black, speaks of the need

are rebroadcast across the globe causes many people to wring their hands over the menace of cultural imperialism; seldom do they bother to inquire about the meanings that different people bring to and draw from these shows. When they do make inquiries, the results are often surprising. One researcher talked to Israeli Arabs who had just watched an episode of *Dallas*—an episode in which Sue Ellen takes her baby, leaves her husband, J.R., and moves in with her ex-lover and his father. The Arab viewers placed their own construction on the episode: they were all convinced that Sue Ellen had moved in with her *own* father—something that by their mores at least made sense.

A similar thing happened in America this year: the communal experience afforded by a public narrative (and what narrative more public?) was splintered by the politics of interpretation. As far as the writer Maya Angelou is concerned, the Simpson trial was an exercise in minstrelsy. "Minstrel shows caricatured every aspect of the black man's life, beginning with his sexuality," she says. "They portrayed the black man as devoid of all sensibilities and sensitivities. They minimized and diminished the possibility of familial love. And that is what the trial is about. Not just the prosecution but everybody seemed to want to show him as other than a normal human being. Nobody let us just see a man." But there is, of course, little consensus about what genre would best accommodate the material. Walter Mosley says, "The story plays to large themes, so I'm sure somebody will write about it. But I don't think it's a mystery. I think it's much more like a novel by Zola." What a writer might make of the material is one thing; what the audience has made of it is another.

"Simpson is a B-movie star and people were watching this like a B movie," Patricia Williams says. "And this is *not* the American B-movie ending." Or was it? "From my perspective as an attorney, this trial was much more like a movie than a trial," Kathleen Cleaver, who was once the Black Panthers' Minister for Communication and is now a professor of law at Emory, says. "It had the budget of a movie, it had the casting of a movie, it had the tension of a movie, and the happy ending of a movie." Spike Lee, speaking professionally, is dubious about the trial's cinematic possibilities: "I don't care who makes this movie, it is never going to equal what people have seen in their living rooms and houses for eight or nine months." Or is it grand opera? Jessye Norman considers: "Well, it certainly has all the ingredients. I mean, somebody meets somebody and somebody gets angry with somebody and somebody dies." She laughs. "It sounds like the *Ring* cycle of Wagner—it really does."

"This story has been told any number of times," Angelou says. "The first thing I thought about was Eugene O'Neill's *All God's Chillun.*" Then she considers how the event might be retrieved by an African-American literary tradition. "I think a great writer would have to approach it," she tells me pensively. "James Baldwin could have done it. And Toni Morrison could do it."

cially among subscribers to what might be called the "great event" school of history. And yet Farrakhan's recurrent calls for individual accountability consort oddly with the absolution, both juridical and populist, accorded O. J. Simpson. Simpson has been seen as a symbol for many things, but he is not yet a symbol for taking responsibility for one's actions.

All the same, the task for black America is not to get its symbols in shape: symbolism is one of the few commodities we have in abundance. Meanwhile, Du Bois's century-old question "How does it feel to be a problem?" grows in trenchancy with every new bulletin about crime and poverty. And the Simpson trial spurs us to question everything except the way that the discourse of crime and punishment has enveloped, and suffocated, the analysis of race and poverty in this country. For the debate over the rights and wrongs of the Simpson verdict has meshed all too well with the manner in which we have long talked about race and social justice. The defendant may be free, but we remain captive to a binary discourse of accusation and counteraccusation, of grievance and countergrievance, of victims and victimizers. It is a discourse in which O. J. Simpson is a suitable remedy for Rodney King, and reductions in Medicaid are entertained as a suitable remedy for O. J. Simpson: a discourse in which everyone speaks of payback and nobody is paid. The result is that race politics becomes a court of the imagination wherein blacks seek to punish whites for their misdeeds and whites seek to punish blacks for theirs, and an infinite regress of score-settling ensues—yet another way in which we are daily becoming meta and meta. And so an empty vessel like O. J. Simpson becomes filled with meaning, and more meaning—more meaning than any of us can bear. No doubt it is a far easier thing to assign blame than to render justice. But if the imagery of the court continues to confine the conversation about race, it really will be a crime.

# 22 MIKE'S BRILLIANT CAREER
## Mike Tyson and the Riddle of Black Cool

GERALD EARLY

The poor boy changes clothes and puts on after-shave
To compensate for his ordinary shoes.

—PAUL SIMON

I sincerely believe that only men can develop boys into men.

—JAWANZA KUNJUFU

Mike Tyson. Our future.

—DON KING

When Don King started wooing Mike Tyson in the summer of 1988, the heavyweight champ was close to disaster: though he kept winning fights, he was boxing's most visible and spectacular casualty. Tyson's psychological unraveling was nightly fare on the TV news: Robin Givens, the minor actress he'd married earlier that year, was appearing on tabloids and television talk shows accusing him of spousal abuse; Ruth Roper, her impossibly domineering mother, was egging the media on in an effort to create a scandal. Tyson, who was taking lithium for a misdiagnosed manic-depressive condition, was making regular headlines with ever more bizarre explosions of temper: smashing up the furniture in his house, totaling his expensive cars. But perhaps the most disorienting blow dealt to him was the death of Jim Jacobs, Tyson's long-time and deeply trusted manager, from leukemia—a condition which Jacobs had kept hidden from him. Tyson was crushed, and desperately alone.

Enter Don King, the prince of boxing predators. That Tyson's personal life was in utter chaos, that a prominent black man was playing out the drama of his nervous breakdown before the entire fascinated American public, suited King just fine. The wily promoter invited the champ to his mansion in Orwell, Ohio, and proceeded to work his way into the boxer's trust by cementing a racial solidarity between the two men. Tyson's con-tract—which made Bill Cayton, Jacobs's partner, Tyson's sole manager in the event of Jacobs's death—had been signed by the champ without knowl-edge of Jacobs's terminal illness. King made a point of telling Tyson that Jacobs and Cayton were Jews, and that the Jews were trying to take over boxing. It was a shrewd device, exacerbating what King recognized as the fighter's core insecurity: everyone is against me, so I can trust no one. Tyson did not necessarily trust King: he doesn't appear to like him much, even now. But he had no one else to turn to, no family or friends of any use to him. The comfort of race, however flimsy and unconvincing, was the only refuge left.

Before Tyson left Ohio, King gave him a book that—whether he read it or not—in some ways serves as a key to the life and times of Mike Tyson: Jawanza Kunjufu's *Countering the Conspiracy to Destroy Black Boys.* King keeps more than a dozen copies of the book in his home, for the purpose of winning over reluctant black fighters. *Countering the Conspiracy to Destroy Black Boys* is a very short and easy-to-read piece of racial paranoia—a poorly reasoned, wretchedly researched, badly written book that is enormously popular in Afrocentric circles and among the black reading public generally. (At this writing it has gone through 24 printings.) It argues in almost laugh-ably reductive Freudian terms that whites fear people of color because they (whites) lack color, and so want to rule and destroy them: women have penis envy, whites have melanin envy. Racism is thus a form of hysteria which is perfectly immune to remedy, a kind of genetic disorder.

If *Countering the Conspiracy to Destroy Black Boys* is a preposterous book when considered as an intellectual enterprise, it is less preposterous when considered as an emotional appeal. It is just the sort of book many people take seriously as "truth-telling," not because it proves itself through argu-ment and evidence to be true but because its readers wish it to be so; as the saying goes, for those who like this sort of thing, this is the sort of thing they like. If Tyson read the book, he would have discovered a portrait of him-self—the maladjusted ghetto youth, seasoned by the streets, living by a ma-cho code of honor, confused and misguided after a fatherless childhood. Of course, he had also been spoiled and petted, made into a psychotic brat, and the loving attention that Kunjufu's book bestows on black men is not likely to discredit the concept of spoiling black men—only to suggest that they be spoiled differently, in a more "African" way. Nor is it likely to end the idea that men are special and more important than women. Black men are, after all, "our future," as Afrocentric speakers constantly remind their audiences.

King gives the book to his black fighters not to calm or cure their insecurities, but to worsen them. His encounter with King clearly made Tyson become even more fixated on his status as a *man*, and more self-conscious of the fact that his masculinity was a conundrum to be unpuzzled. He was surely, now, more self-conscious about the fact that his father figures, before King, were white men: Jacobs and Cayton, and his beloved trainer Cus D'Amato. (The major mother figure in his life, D'Amato's common-law wife, Camille Ewald, was also white.) The man who discovered Tyson, Bobby Stewart, and his first two trainers under D'Amato, Kevin Rooney and Teddy Atlas, were white. Tyson had to face the symbolic truth that he was the creation of white men.

◆

When he was growing up in a very tough section of Brooklyn, from 1966 until about 1979, he was teased by the other boys for his lisp, his high-pitched voice, his "fucking eyeglasses," and his weight. Children always ridicule the odd, the helpless, the unfortunate; ghetto children are particularly vicious in this regard. (These rituals of intolerance are, perversely, self-protective: there might be a great many more murders among the poor if not for this technique of bearing one's life by being told how worthless it is.) Mike Tyson comes from an obese family; he weighed over 200 pounds at puberty. He was so big, in fact, that when Cus D'Amato, the man who taught him to fight and who would become his legal guardian, first saw him, he could not believe the boy's age. To be an overweight boy in a poor neighborhood with glasses and a lisp is to be taunted as a weakling, unless one can talk—or fight. On the streets Tyson had been known as "sissy boy." The brand of machismo he created with fury and deliberation was a sissy boy's revenge.

Like other black heavyweight champions—Joe Louis, Sonny Liston, and George Foreman come to mind—Tyson was a moody and skittish, seemingly slow-witted boy, all of which made it difficult to succeed in school. Those who are docile and articulate, or at least glib, and can fit in the desks have a better shot at making it through that pressurized labyrinth of conformity and obedience training. (Louis, Liston, and Foreman could not handle the discipline of schooling either, although they were formidably disciplined men in other realms.) Although a failure at school, Tyson was a success as a fighter on the streets of Brooklyn. He was born to be a fighter in much the way someone with perfect pitch is born to be a musician. He fought so well that the boys left off taunting him and started to respect him, even fear him; José Torres reports in his biography *Fire and Fear* that once the ten-year-old Tyson discovered that he could easily beat up older boys, he enjoyed fighting, "kicking people's asses." In a world where most people are paralyzed by the futility of any kind of normal civic action—of any kind of action, period—Tyson acted decisively, if recklessly and destructively. His reputation proved to be a useful protection for his family, which encouraged his mother and sister to treat him as someone special: in the jungle, it is good to live with the lion.

"If you only knew," Mike Tyson told Torres (himself a former light-heavyweight champion and Cus D'Amato pupil), "I was a spoiled brat. . . . I think it's funny when people talk about me having a hard life." If Mike Tyson was indulged, it was because his pathological behavior made him the perfect denizen of his pathological world: as with some of the great boxers of the past, a life in the ghetto had given him an obsession with forms of honor and contest, with the imposition of will and the ruthless battering down of opposition. The stealing, lying, and violence that eventually led to his institutionalization were similar to the antisocial behavior of Italian fighters like Jake LaMotta and Rocky Graziano, whose boyhood and adolescent lives Tyson's greatly resembles. Had it not been for their fighting skills, the very combination of derring-do, cynicism, and barbarity that guaranteed their survival in the short term would have killed them all as young men. Instead they were channeled into the entertainment industry largely intact.

And yet, in examining the trajectory of his career, his profound insecurity is obvious. There is no sure thing in the ghetto; to rule there is a tenuous proposition. Surely Tyson was aware that his most admired qualities were inherently self-destructive, that he was in some sense both invincible and doomed, supremely powerful and relentlessly, irresistibly sliding toward an early grave. Cus D'Amato was right in his unending philosophizing about fear, for that is what kept Tyson alive — his monumental fear, his fundamental insecurity, and his belief that he could overcome it by winning a place in the mythology of professional boxing.

◆

Tyson has a great consciousness of the history of his sport, its grand masculine pantheon. He has attempted to embrace this history, to acquire both the joy and the anxiety of influence offered by a set of ideal fathers. He is, in short, restlessly searching for what every great artist needs: a tradition. One of Tyson's biographers, Montieth Illingworth, describes the various fables of Tyson's manhood as "Cus and the Kid," "Iron Mike," and "The Public Enemy," to which one might add "The Regenerate Muslim."

The myth of Cus and the Kid was the longest lived. "Cus and the Kid" was invented by Jacobs and Cayton during the early days of Tyson's fighting career, a way to sell him as an amateur fighter despite the fact that in the ring he was mostly an intimidator, a knock-out artist—traits deplored at the amateur level, where scoring points, proper form, and fundamental skill development are doggedly inculcated and highly prized. Here was the sappy story of the black street orphan taken in by a crotchety but good-hearted white boxing trainer, whose only wish was to live long enough to see the kid become a champion. The truth value of this myth remains highly suspect;

D'Amato was loved by literary types because he loved to hear himself talk, which made him much like a literary type, but whether he was a great boxing mind is debatable. Certainly Tyson would have become champion had he been instructed by almost any of the first-rate boxing teachers: Emanuel Steward, the late Ray Arcel, Eddie Futch, Lou Duva, or a score of others. D'Amato had no special knowledge of or insight into Tyson's ability. (The two champions D'Amato had trained before he discovered Tyson—Floyd Patterson and José Torres—were not particularly notable fighters, certainly not great ones.)

In fact, D'Amato indulged his star pupil. He never tried to help Tyson with his problems, his emotional hang-ups and ghetto insecurities, because these were, to D'Amato's mind, at least, the psychological stuffings that made Tyson a good fighter. D'Amato did not care whether Tyson did well in school, or even if he went. He did not care about Tyson's attitudes toward women and sex, which already in his teenage years suggested a tendency toward violence. Tyson knew, too, that D'Amato took an interest in him only because he was a successful fighter. Tyson was often a recalcitrant student. He would disappear from D'Amato's training school for extended periods and was frequently bored by his coach's pontifications, spitting and cursing at him more than once.

Still, despite its manifold flaws, their fictive father-son relationship provided an irresistible formula for a rising boxing star. The sentimentality of racial paternalism is a narcotic of which we Americans, apparently, can never get enough. "Cus and the Kid" was an integrationist riff on the age-old myth of the coach-athlete friendship, that vision of transgenerational male bonding that remains the most celebrated teaching relationship in our culture. "Win one for Cus!"—corny, but effective. The myth presented Tyson to the white public as something more than your typical black fighter, as something more than an escapee from the nearest ghetto. It was an attempt to reinvent Tyson as the new Joe Louis, a black kid worthy to be champion because some whites vouched not only for his ability but for his character. Tyson was from the ghetto, the myth went, but he was not a thug like Liston, or a misanthrope like the young Foreman. If D'Amato, Jacobs, and Kevin Rooney could all love Tyson, why not the whites who watched him fight? Tyson's youth helped; he was under twenty-one when he won his first professional championship. He was also coming up in the wake of Larry Holmes, a very skilled, very capable, but not very popular champion. "Larry Holmes's personality left a lot to be desired," King said recently, and accurately.

Once Tyson became a professional fighter, "Iron Mike" was born. This was Tyson as the austere warrior: coming into the ring crouching and weaving like Jack Dempsey, throwing punches like Henry Armstrong, swaggering like John L. Sullivan, eyeing his prey as scientifically as Joe Gans. His purity of purpose was almost religious. The Iron Mike myth was meant to place Tyson in boxing history by having him self-consciously refer to other great fighters, and to give him a mythic stature that could make him worthy of being compared to the greatest fighters of the past. Tyson named his first son D'Amato Kilrain Tyson after D'Amato and Jake Kilrain, John L. Sullivan's opponent in the last bareknuckle heavyweight championship bout in America—an arcane, but telling, reference. It was never the intention of D'Amato, Jacobs, and Cayton to make Tyson merely a champion, but to have the public recognize him as the greatest heavyweight fighter ever, the heir to a legendary patrimony.

◆

Tyson has had two distinct, if somewhat contradictory, uses for the racialized history of professional boxing. His identification and expropriation of the great white fighters made him a mainstream figure, depoliticizing his masculinity by making him someone who identified with whites, and so someone with whom whites could, on some level, identify. He brought them into the ring with him by wrapping himself in the mantle of great white fighters of the past. But, as Don King knew, Tyson's early self-immersion in the minutiae of boxing history could prove a liability among his own youthful black fans. Identifying with black fighters of the past—or, more precisely, with the street life that produced them—promised to repoliticize Tyson's masculinity and stave off the charges of racial inauthenticity. The "Public Enemy" myth cooked up by Don King was Tyson's most convincing role, if only because it fit so neatly into the roles scripted for young and physically powerful black men in the American mind.

Tyson as "Public Enemy" identified with the black fighters of the past, casting himself as a sort of political and social rebel: the hip-hop bad boy from Brooklyn who could get respect. Like Jack Johnson, the first black man to hold the heavyweight title (1908–15), Tyson has endured a scandalous trial and served time in prison. Johnson, who had numerous white wives and lovers, so infuriated the white public (and the authorities) with his sexual adventures that he was eventually convicted for transporting a woman across state lines for purposes of sexual intercourse under the terms of the 1910 Mann Act—a reform measure meant to stem the tide of poor-girl prostitution—and sentenced to a year and a day in federal prison. Johnson spent several years in forced exile, during which time he lost the title; he then returned to the United States and served his prison term. Like Muhammad Ali, Tyson has endured a three-and-a-half-year break in the prime of his career. Tyson is also ambivalent about the monumental figure of Joe Louis, a black fighter adored by black and white alike, and something of a national hero; like Ali, Tyson, driven by the peculiarities of youthful black honor, wants to be the national hero and the national devil simultaneously.

The "Public Enemy" myth played to black prejudices, as well as white ones. Part of what politicizes Tyson's manhood is simply the fact that he is the champion of a sport that dramatizes male expendability, in an age when the concern with male expendability is, among blacks, almost an obsession. Many blacks believe that "the white power system" is out to destroy Tyson, as it is out to destroy all black men. In this line of reasoning, the most effective weapon in the destruction of the black man is the upwardly mobile black woman who, identifying with whites, tries to emasculate the black man by erasing his blackness. Tyson's disastrous string of relationships dovetails beautifully with this theory. His marriage to Robin Givens (a Sarah Lawrence graduate) lasted all of eight months, during which time she was clearly embarrassed by, and disgusted with, his friends, his taste, his background, and his profession. ("She thinks she's white," Tyson once complained to his homies.) Desiree Washington, the woman who accused him of the rape for which he was convicted in 1992, was a college student and church school teacher, as well as a beauty contestant. His current girlfriend, Monica Turner—the mother of his second child—has been variously described as a pre-med student and a full-fledged pediatrician. Whichever, she is clearly far more educated than Tyson.

Tyson is obviously attracted to middle-class, educated black women, the very women who would not have given him a second look had he not been a successful boxer. Still, Tyson is their unwilling victim, as far as many of his fans are concerned. Most people in the black community, at least most men, feel Desiree Washington was out to get his money, a conviction which ignores strong evidence to the contrary. If she were only a gold digger, why did she turn down a multimillion-dollar settlement offer from Don King—a bribe, in effect, to drop the criminal charges? Why would she risk being cross-examined on the witness stand—risk being exposed as a liar—if the rape never happened? She could have skipped the criminal trial altogether and gone after Tyson in civil court, where a favorable judgment would have been much easier to obtain.

Tyson's defense at the rape trial made him appear out of control. He seemed less and less like a romantic hero and more and more like a pathetic and unbalanced bully. Tyson's lawyers argued, in effect, that he was a sex maniac, and that any woman interested in him would have known this, or should have. The stories of Tyson's marathon sexcapades, many of which are recorded in Torres's biography (a book which angered Tyson deeply, although he did not refute its charges), did little to help his image. One such story, of Tyson reaching climax with twenty-five prostitutes in one night, reeked of particularly desperate braggadocio. (The ironic thing, of course, about this sort of "prowess," which turns sex into the equivalent of a cutting contest or a sparring session, is the terrible sense of inadequacy it masks.) Nor was Tyson helped by his boast, also reported in Torres's book, that the best punch he ever threw was against Robin Givens, when she bounced off of every wall in the room. He seemed depraved.

Tyson is now The Regenerate Muslim, a transformation that took place while he was in prison. Tyson had a Christian conversion when he first joined Don King in 1988, which was either insincere or did not take: after being baptized, he promptly went back to his former debaucheries. This time, things seem to be different. Tyson has politicized his prison experience in much the way Malcolm X did. Indeed, Malcolm seems the paradigm for Tyson: the Muslim conversion, the extraordinary amount of reading, the redemption of his manhood through religion and politics—a black baptism, meant to wash away the years with the whites. But there is also an echo of Muhammad Ali in Tyson's insistence that he was an innocent sent to prison, that the white system tried to break him but could not, in the end.

With his imprisonment and conversion, Tyson may be in a position to enjoy the sort of masculine influence Sugar Ray Robinson exerted on his generation four decades ago. Robinson, the great middleweight champion, was the epitome of cool, the single greatest influence on jazz trumpeter Miles Davis—who made cool an art form of precision, economy of expression, and taste. Robinson, who owned a popular nightclub in Harlem and was a gifted dancer (he made a living at it for two years during his first "retirement" from the ring), is considered the greatest fighter of all time. His conked hair and stylish clothes, his smooth, polished, but deadly ring style, and his gracious composure made him, except for Martin Luther King, the most popular black man of the 1950s. Robinson was the first and only boxer who ever gave the impression of being sophisticated, a cosmopolite—and yet he was unmistakably a black man, perfectly at ease with himself and his blackness. Robinson never needed to reach for the brass ring of respectability, nor did he seem fueled by class resentment. As a result, he made black manhood and boxing into something like a pure aesthetic. Robinson's cool was too apathetic to be appealing to a young black man in that age, but it was this political detachment that ultimately gave Robinson's demeanor its power and its endurance: Robinson's was a black manhood that transcended the need of political contingency or context. He had nothing to prove by being black. He was, therefore, a figure akin to someone like Duke Ellington, a race man whose pride was not dependent on reminding the world at every opportunity that he was a Negro. In the late 1960s, Muhammad Ali thought of himself as the reinvention and revision of Robinson, a heavyweight and a politically engaged black man.

Tyson thinks of himself as a further reinvention of this black masculine cool, the latest in a great masculine tradition, a revision of Muhammad Ali. Like Ali, Tyson is a Muslim and a politically changed black man. But unlike Ali, he does not try to turn his fights into political theater. And while Ali tended to bring out the best in his opponents, Tyson paralyzes his opposition. His challengers can invariably point to their bouts with Tyson as their worst fights. In most cases, they are hardly competitive. But the characteristic which most dramatically sets Tyson off from Ali is his total lack of any sense of humor: like Huckleberry Finn, another archetype of American innocence, Tyson takes himself seriously.

Though Tyson craves stability, a final resting place in the pantheon, does he fully understand the complexity of the tradition (and the tragedy) that characterizes this intersection of attitude and history? Joe Louis, whose most important fight was his 1938 rematch against German heavyweight and former champion Max Schmeling—a fight freighted with large political implications—became an American icon. He died a pauper in Las Vegas, old, sick, and consumed with paranoia. Sonny Liston, whose most important fights were his degrading losses to Muhammad Ali in 1964 and 1965, was a national villain, a convict and mobster who died grotesquely, a needle hanging out of his arm, in 1970. George Foreman was at first an Olympic hero, then a villain, then, in his return to the ring, an avuncular comedian. Even the vaunted Robinson died from Alzheimer's disease, aggravated by the punishment he took from over two hundred professional fights.

Tyson, only thirty years old, has already gone through more avatars than any of these men, and he is likely to go through still more. Today, tattoos of Arthur Ashe and Mao Tse-tung—an odd couple, if ever there was one—line his biceps. The two images are meant to symbolize both his newfound self-control and his revision of black cool: Arthur Ashe, as Tyson admits, was not a man he would have liked personally, but he admires Ashe's literacy, his ability to negotiate the white world, his politics. Mao Tse-tung represents strength and authority, a kind of ideological commitment to the power of transformation itself. Tyson has encased himself with images that represent what is, for him, masculine heroism; the bruiser has scarred himself with men who have qualities that he would have wished for in his own father, but who better serve him not as father figures but rather as icons of mythic liberation and mythic discipline. Mao, the father of a totalitarian nation, and Ashe, the only major black figure in a white-dominated sport: Tyson seeks, through these figures, the piety of manhood.

What Tyson lacks, and what both Robinson and Ali had, is an opponent worthy of him, against whom he can dramatize his manhood. Tyson was beaten only once, by a journeyman fighter who will probably not fight him again; there are no longer fighters capable of challenging him. He has dominated the ring even more thoroughly than Joe Louis did during his reign. Without a ring nemesis, Tyson cannot really evangelize his fights, nor can he give them any greater purpose than to enrich himself and those legions who bet on him.

Tyson is not the sum of his myths; he is the remainder. Myth tries to invest lived experience with greater meanings, but despite the stories that have proliferated around him, Tyson's life can never point to anything larger than itself: his own self-serving actions, his own madness, his own befuddlement and consternation before the revelation of his limitations. Tyson's tragedy, finally, is his solipsism: his biggest drama was and continues to be with himself, for the salvation of himself alone.

# 23

# IT'S RAINING MEN
## Notes on the Million Man March

Robert F. Reid-Pharr

Perhaps the most curious feature of last fall's Million Man March was the way that this massive political demonstration, at least twice the size of the historic 1963 March on Washington, actually worked to reinforce the racial commonsense of the nation. At a political moment when the enemies of black America have consolidated with frightening determination, Minister Louis Farrakhan, his supporters, and even his detractors encouraged the notion that at the root of the difficulties facing African Americans is a certain male lack—an inability, or unwillingness, to take responsibility as *men*, to stand up for community and self.

It was probably an unintended irony that the rhetoric of the march organizers echoed Daniel Patrick Moynihan's infamous 1965 report, "The Negro Family: The Case for National Action," with its diagnosis of pathologies plaguing black families and communities. This resonance, which has gone largely unremarked, is central to the way the march forced so many of us to rehearse the assorted racial, sexual, and political identities by which we define ourselves, and which define us. "Who are you?" the march asked. "Black or not-black? Man or not-man?"

It should be clear to most observers that the way Farrakhan and the other march organizers answered these questions—with appeals to a revitalized patriarchy—worked to reinforce traditional gender norms. What is less obvious is the way that this black spectacle restaged the *racial* commonsense of the nation, the same commonsense that animates much of the conservative rhetoric about issues and policies most directly associated with black communities, especially affirmative action and welfare. In the face of shrinking public resources and an evangelical zeal to "reinvent" (read: dismantle) government, African Americans were once again advised that self-help is the best medicine. The black man was instructed to return home and start providing for kith and kin, to stop making excuses about the scarcity of legitimate, well-paying jobs, and to access his inner manhood, that great and mysterious wellspring of masculinity hidden deep within his psyche, waiting to be harnessed to the project of a beautiful black tomorrow. This all-powerful masculinity was offered as the solution to, and compensation for, the stark curtailments of resources and opportunities that confront African American men (and everyone else) in this country.

In this light, at a celebration of black masculinity predicated on the absence of black women, it is interesting to consider the question of black gay men's participation in the event. For if the real message of the march was that it is going to take a heroic black masculinity to restore order in our various communities, especially poor and working-class communities, then it follows that gay black men are irrelevant, or even dangerous, to that project. And if the march itself was intended to re-create a masculine community of agency and responsibility, through the archetypal figures of father and son, then the surreptitious presence of the *lover* threatened to undo the logic of the event itself.

◆

In the weeks prior to the march, the gay press was full of speculation over the proper stance black gay men should take toward Farrakhan, the other march organizers, and the march itself. The Los Angeles-based Black Gay and Lesbian Leadership Forum vacillated on the question, finally encouraging gay men to attend and to make their presence known. Activists staged a premarch rally and convinced Ben Chavis, the march's executive director, to agree to have an openly gay speaker address the crowd from the podium. (Chavis reneged at the last minute.)

The debate revolved around the question of whether black gay men should support an event so closely identified with Minister Louis Farrakhan, who has made no secret of his homophobia. (In Oakland, California, in 1990 Farrakhan told a crowd, "If God made you for a woman, you can't go with a man. . . . You know what the penalty of this is in the Holy Land? Death.") More to the point, black gay men, even if they stayed home, were again confronted with a rather awkward set of questions. Faced with a celebration of a stable—that is, Afro-centric, bourgeois, and heterosexual—black masculinity, gay men who felt compelled by the march had to decide among a number of plausible responses. They could reject the event itself as "not truly black" because of the homophobia and misogyny in which it trafficked. They could think of the march as representative of a flawed blackness that might be repaired by making a significant black gay presence visible at the event (which many did) or by intervening with the march organizers (which a few attempted). And finally, they could acknowledge the basic logic of Farrakhan's rhetoric. For if the definition of blackness hinges on heterosexuality, then either blackness and homosexuality are incommensurable (and black gays are not really black) or the notion of blackness is untenable, as witnessed by the undeniable existence of large numbers of black gay men.

This last position, of course, is most difficult to accept. It flies directly in the face of much within contemporary black gay and lesbian thought, which most often represents black gays and lesbians as integral, if beleaguered, members of the black family — witness *Brother to Brother, Home Girls, Sister Outsider*, works shepherded by Essex Hemphill, Barbara Smith, and Audre Lorde, respectively. Indeed, the gay response to the march dramatizes the fact that there are remarkably few spaces — even those inhabited by black gays and lesbians — in which one might contest the most basic assumptions that underlie American race and gender identity. Even in the midst of raucous and intense disagreement, the idea of race emerges unscathed. Indeed, blackness has been bolstered, insofar as we all were forced, at least those of us who are black *and* otherwise, to scurry for cover under the great black mantle, to fly our colors, the good old red, black, and green, even as we attempted to resist the homophobic assumptions that structured the event.

◆

More than a political demonstration with concrete political demands, Farrakhan's march was a sort of race spectacle. Following Guy Debord, we should look to locate its meaning not in the striking images it produced or in our individual responses, but in the social relationships constructed by and through these images. Debord doubts that transcendence can be located within the spectacle. For him, spectacles are never progressive events; rather, they represent and reaffirm the larger society. Debord writes, "For what the spectacle expresses is the total practice of one particular economic and social formation; it is, so to speak, that formation's *agenda*. It is also the historical moment by which we happen to be governed."

His point is well taken. Those of us interested in progressive politics need to reconsider the efficacy of the marches, protests, and demonstrations that have convulsed the American public sphere in the last century, as well as the ways in which their themes (civil rights, antiwar, gay pride) are constrained by the nature of the event. Mustering enthusiasm for these events requires a fair dose of ignorance about the contentiousness that invariably surrounds them — disagreements that most often turn on the organizers' unwillingness to push the boundaries of the event. I am reminded here of the successful struggle initiated by Anna Arnold Hedgeman to have women included among the speakers on the platform at the 1963 march, as well as the ease with which civil rights stalwart Bayard Rustin was shut out of the same event because of his homosexuality. That march has become such an important part of the American national memory because it so clearly articulated the rather limited language and values of a liberal America. Indeed, King's "I Have a Dream" speech receives much of its force from the evocation of an ethos that is at once Christian and American nationalist, supporting, in the process, a liberal integrationist agenda that insists upon the expansiveness—and expansion—of the nation.

Mass public spectacles have been a regular means by which changing ideas of race have been disseminated to the American populace. As early as 1895, Booker T. Washington called for black reconciliation with the very whites who were the architects of segregation, disfranchisement, and systematic racist terror, thereby rearticulating the emerging racialist—and segregationist—common sense. Washington's particular genius, evident in his Atlanta Cotton States Exposition speech, was his ability to articulate a conservative racial politics to whites, particularly white southerners, while captivating many blacks with a message that spoke to their basic desire to be admitted as equal participants in American public life. "In all things that are purely social," he argued, "we can be as separate as the fingers, yet one as the hand in all things essential to mutual progress."

It is a compelling irony that the sensibility behind Washington's words should so deeply inform the 1995 rhetoric of Louis Farrakhan. Specifically, both men call for black self-sufficiency, if not self-determination; both swallow, more or less whole, frankly segregationist notions about the proper interaction between the races; and both, oddly enough, subscribe to the myth of America. As Farrakhan argued at the march:

> There's no country like this on Earth. And certainly if I lived in another country, I might never have had the opportunity to speak as I speak today. I probably would have been shot outright, and so would my brother Jesse, and so would Maulauna Karenga, and so would Dr. Ben Chavis and Reverend Al Sharpton and all the wonderful people that are here. But because this is America, you allow me to speak even though you don't like what I may say.

Of all the curiosities uttered by Minister Farrakhan during the march, including the extended numerological analyses, the excoriation of presidents past and present, the religious rhetoric of atonement, and so forth, I was least prepared for this hackneyed bit of American exceptionalism. It was tempting to read this gesture as mere anomaly, the kind of unnecessary bombast that cushions overly long or ambitious speeches. But I suggest we take this piece of Farrakhan's rhetoric seriously—indeed, that we recognize in it the key to his success that day, as he spoke to the assembled masses on the Mall and to the nation.

Minister Farrakhan's particular talent is his ability to sensitize wildly diverse black audiences to their very real oppression while steering them, not simply away from a critique of the political and economic structure of the United States, but toward a reinvestment in the very ideological processes that work to create, and maintain, those structures. It is true that Farrakhan regularly points out the evil of the American enterprise: slavery, segregation, disfranchisement, continued and continual racial degradation. But instead of leading his followers toward radical critique, Farrakhan chooses instead to return again and again to an essentially therapeutic mode, in which he plays the role of the good father come back to set the (national) house in order.

At the Million Man March—"a glimpse of heaven," as the Nation of Islam's newspaper, *The Final Call*, had it—Louis Farrakhan put himself forward as the emblem, the ideal type, if you will, of a newly emergent black masculinity. He appeared as a shining exemplar of a renewed Black Man, striking the posture of the stern—if gentle—father, savior, patriarch, messiah. He scorned our enemies while asking us only to look inward, to find the evil within and cast it out. If we did so, he prophesied, if only we could learn to humble ourselves, we would surely see a new dawn of cleanliness and order, the Black Millennium. He stood, then, as a sort of Emersonian representative man, embodying a masculinity so pure that simply by gazing upon it one could extinguish the fires of ambiguity and uncertainty that rage in the hearts of black men across America.

The agreement on the part of the march's organizers (supported even by progressives like Cornel West) to discourage black women's participation implicitly shored up Farrakhan's myth-making. I never could quite understand *why* a demonstration about the plight of black Americans had to be gendered in the first place. (Wouldn't two Million Black People beat one Million Black Men?) With this strategy—an obvious insult to black women —the march organizers showed themselves to be concerned primarily with lending a certain ontological stability to men whose identities are increasingly complex. The injunction to keep the women at home helped channel public debates about the march into familiar territory, the ongoing "crisis of African American gender relations." In that sense, the sexist rhetoric and the many responses it provoked simply represented (black) business as usual. It was a forceful restatement, à la Moynihan, of the terms we have used to discuss (African) American cultural, political, and economic life since at least the 1960s.

Fundamental changes in American political and economic life are currently being debated, in a conversation largely dominated by the Republican right. What is disconcerting about this is the way rhetorics of blackness (such as Ronald Reagan's "welfare queen" and George Bush's "Willie Horton") have been coupled not simply with critiques of black communities, but with even more blistering attacks on affirmative action, welfare, education, government interventionism, inner-city crime, and so forth. While the march was still in progress, President Clinton made a speech at the University of Texas in which, after distancing himself from Farrakhan, he praised the black men who attended the event for taking responsibility for themselves, and *their* communities. He then went on to make a rather predictable speech on race relations in which he suggested, among other things, that it is not racism that motivates a mother to pull her child close when she passes a black man in a crime-ridden neighborhood.

What is disturbing about this line of argument is not only the crude manner in which it reaffirms the myth of the Dangerous Black Man, but the way that it reiterates the racialist logic that stands at the root of this country's many woes. The idea that there are discrete black communities, beset by black problems, which can and should be solved exclusively by black people taking responsibility for themselves, is precisely the logic of segregation, no matter how empowered individual black people may feel in the process of its articulation. What connects Clinton and Farrakhan, then, is that neither has yet seen his way clear of the pernicious racialism that increasingly dominates American public life.

◆

Despite my reservations about the ideological underpinnings of the march, it would be untrue to say that I do not understand what drew hundreds of thousands of individuals to Washington on that October day. I went, full of skepticism yes, but also expectant, even hopeful. The first thing that struck me was that it was *not* a march, but more of a *happening*. I am accustomed to marches on Washington, with thousands of people—singly or in various more or less well-organized groups—streaming down Pennsylvania Avenue en route to the Mall. Usually the architects of the mass action try to divvy up the crowd into state-based bodies, collectivities of gender and race, various political and social organizations, groups of students, dignitaries, and so forth. The Million Man March, however, had none of this. The few banners and signs that dotted the crowds were largely homemade, expressing local and specific concerns. Moreover, there were surprisingly few individuals who could be clearly identified as members of the Nation of Islam, or even Muslim. The emphasis was on similarity, the incredible and moving oneness we all shared.

I should acknowledge, here, how exciting, titillating even, this oneness actually felt. The beauty of the men was startling. It hung in the air like the smoke of incense, intoxicating us all, calling into existence a fantastic vision of community—a glimpse of heaven, indeed. The entire event, not to mention the debates that framed it, was wholly overdetermined by a kind of black-inflected homoeroticism. It seemed that we men could enact millions of tiny instances of love and desire—a touch, a glance, murmurings of "Pardon me, brother," "Excuse me, sir"—precisely because the women were absent. What remained was a sort of naked masculinity.

A teenage boy comes up to me. I see his baggy clothes, his corn-rowed hair, the cocky lilt in his walk, before I see him. His face is flushed as if he has just witnessed something beautiful and terrible both, like he has just survived a natural disaster or awakened from some horrible fever. He takes my hand, places his other arm around my shoulder, and says, "All this unity, all this love," presses close to me for an instant, then releases me and keeps moving. I am stunned, caught up in the moment. I imagine that I really have seen this boy, that he has seen me. I am no longer afraid, but on the contrary, rather giddy, glad to be here, to have been a part of all this.

At Union station, I buy a disposable camera and begin taking snapshots of other anomalies in the crowd: women, the elaborately dressed, the not-black. In looking back over these pictures, now as then, I think that there is something satisfying about seeing reflected, if only for a brief while and through a deeply flawed lens, an image of an equitable, just, and peaceful community. It felt like freedom, a new beginning. Indeed, for a moment, if only a moment, I felt that I had regained that which was lost, had seen beyond the horizon.

◆

Still, as Paul Gilroy has suggested, it is unsettling that the notion of (black) freedom seems so inevitably dependent on polarities of sex and gender, and accompanied by a certain desperate insistence on black sexual potency. It seems that the idea of freedom has been so overwritten by fantasies of race and gender that it has become nearly impossible to imagine it without reference to these same fantasies. "The Black Man," as the rhetoric of both right and left would have it, is the most *un*free of American citizens. As one-third of the black males in this country languish in prisons or under the stewardship of assorted probation and parole boards; as black men continue to be overrepresented in the drug trade, and among the legions of persons with chronic illnesses—HIV, cancer, heart disease, alcoholism; as we give our lives over to violence or to a certain silent despair, we have become the very emblem of ugliness, bestiality, and barbarism by which the rest of America, particularly white America, can view itself as liberal and free. The image in my mind now is of Rodney King's beating: the endless blows, the irrationality of the white policemen's rage as they labored to drive this black beast deeper into their collective unconscious. It is possible to chart the last several decades of American cultural and political life by lining up our black male martyrs, criminals, and celebrities: Martin Luther King, Malcolm, Medgar Evers, Louis Farrakhan, Clarence Thomas, Mike Tyson, Willie Horton, Yusef Hawkins, O.J. Simpson. The list goes on.

If freedom was truly the ultimate goal of the march, then it was of a discrete, limited kind: freedom from the crushing burden of images—the criminal, the addict, the vengeful lover, and the invalid. Instead we were presented with an ocean of men, orderly, directed, clean-cut, and remark-ably eloquent. Even in their silences. At the march, in the act of rethinking and reenacting our disparate identities, we felt an intimation of some larger notion.

Here, then, despite the regressive racial and gender politics that framed the Million Man March, there were countless improvisational moments of transcendence. The reality of all public spectacles is that the outcome is never certain; no one can confidently predict what its attendees will take away from it, what meanings its many participants will attribute to it. The sad part is that the march organizers evinced so little respect for this wondrously messy and ambiguous process. Once again we were urged to mount the tired horse of black patriarchy. Ministers Farrakhan and Chavis worked to yoke the energy of the event to a simplistic—and segregationist—racial ideology. I still yearn, then, for a vision of the good, for a public dialogue and a civic life that celebrates multiplicity, that prizes ambiguity, and thereby recognizes the play of identity and difference that makes possible community as well as change.

# 24

# DEAR MINISTER FARRAKHAN
## A Letter

MEN STOPPING VIOLENCE

MEN STOPPING VIOLENCE
1020 Dekalb Avenue, #25
Atlanta, Georgia 30307
Voice: (404) 688-1376
Fax: (404) 688-4021

Minister Louis Farrakhan                                    August 24, 1995
c/o Reverend Benjamin Chavis
Million Man March
National Office
145 Kennedy St., NW
Washington, DC 20011-52944

As-salaam-alaikum.

Dear Minister Farrakhan,

We are Black men who are working to end all male violence against women. We warmly greet you with an intense excitement, for we recognize, and share, the profound sense of urgency being expressed by our people in this critical historical period. All across this country, African-Americans are speaking in diverse voices of our undeniable need for a resurgence of social movement for justice. We acknowledge the call for a "Million Man March" as a clear and timely echo of this broad awareness.

We greet you, however, Minister Farrakhan, with extremely grave fears. We believe that Black men do aspire to a profound concern for the health, healing and wholeness of our people. We therefore urge you and your coordinators to reconsider the exclusive nature of this call for one million Black men.

We have been afforded a marvelous opportunity to work with women and other men in order to become more attuned to the realities of women's lives. We intend to become more effective in ending the various abuses they experience from men and male-dominated institutions in this society. What we are learning is that this social order had been constructed from its very foundations as one that is no less sexist than racist. The uniqueness of Black women's experiences is being revealed to us in harrowing terms that belie our learned habits of denying and trivializing what Black women say to us. We have begun to understand how Black women (and Black men) have been struggling and surviving against *multiple forms* of oppression. We are also learning that our particular experiences of race oppression are constantly shaped and reshaped by the impact of other oppressions operating on the basis of gender, class and sexuality. Our definitions of "masculinity" and "femininity," of "manhood" and "womanhood," of "family" and "community," and of "political participation" have all been affected by this oppressive context called "the land of the free." If we are really to atone, to change, to begin a new state in our quest for justice and truth, we must finally admit that we have too often embraced the inequitable notions and behaviors that still dominate this society.

The bitter truth, Minister Farrakhan, is that Black women are being terribly abused by Black men. To be a Black woman is to experience the United States as a dangerous, dehumanizing and deathly place. Black women's bodies are viewed as private property to which Black men are "entitled." Black women are too often seen as mere symbols of our great nation-in-formation—the wombs from which the future issues forth. Black women's intellectual and spiritual capacities are valued only to the extent that they contribute to the agendas defined by men. Spaces that could be called "home" are usually places of unpaid labor, contemptuous control and co-erced sex. They are also places where women are treated like children, while children are brutalized in the name of "order" and "respect." Our religious and civic institutions are equally problematic, for we often "honor" Black women as the backbone, only to try to keep them in the background. In short, we must acknowledge that our struggles for justice have usually been impeded by our own denial of the pervasive influence of sexism in Black life.

Minister Farrakhan, we urge you to consider the physical, mental and spiritual consequences of reinforcing the notion that Black men intend to "take over" the leadership of families which *the conditions of this system* have not allowed us to share. We must not embrace the lies—so viciously trumpeted by the main institutions of this society—that Black men are not responsible, that Black women are dysfunctional parents, or that the current condition of African-Americans has nothing to do with the current structuring of U.S. society.

We realize that plans for the march are moving briskly forward. It is in the spirit of seeking to strengthen this timely movement that we make the following proposals:

1) Open the march to Black women and girls. We need to model the movement we seek to build. Black women have contributed too much to be relegated to the "domestic arena."

2) Choose a Black woman who can adequately speak to Black men about the unique experiences of Black women. Some excellent choices would be bell hooks, Barbara Omolade, Kimberlé Crenshaw, Ashaki Binta, Thandisizwe Chimurenga, Gwen Patton, Pearl Cleage, Connie Tucker or Qiyamah Rahman.

3) Choose a Black man who can speak to Black men about our responsibilities to understand and combat sexist thinking and behavior in our everyday lives. Manning Marable, Cornel West, Dan Aldridge, Mukungu Akinyele, Saladin Muhammad and Sulaiman Nuriddin would be excellent choices.

A word concerning the timing of this letter seems appropriate. Last week Reverend Chavis visited Atlanta for a press conference and town meeting regarding the Million Man March. We are now more aware of opportunities for local input and involvement in the process. We appreciate Rev. Chavis' efforts to expand and deepen the mobilization, and this letter reflects that spirit.

Given your hectic schedule, we ask that you respond in two weeks, so that we can continue our efforts to make this march a pivotal event in the transformation of our people and this society. Our very best hopes and our prayers for you and your family. As-salaam-alaikum.

Respectfully,

cc: Benjamin Chavis
bell hooks
Ava Muhammed
Cornel West

Sulaiman Nuriddin, on behalf of the men of the African-American Initiative of Men Stopping Violence, Inc.:

Stuart Clarke, Ulester Douglas, Thandabantu Iverson and Kwamé-Osagyefo Kalimara

# 25 BLACK MEN IN THE MOVIES
## How Does It Feel to Be a Problem (and an Answer)?

Edward Guerrero

The system-wide, and systematic, devaluation (and simultaneous idolization) of Black men in the nation's movies and popular culture is not a new or, given its pervasiveness, a particularly remarkable phenomenon. Long before the O.J. verdict, the Million Man March, Rodney King, the self-fashioning of Dennis Rodman, the vogueing of RuPaul, the much celebrated retirement of Michael Jordan, or the rise and fall (and rise again) of Joe Jett, for mostly worse, but sometimes better, Black men have been prized media fetishes captured in high print, cinematic, and televisual relief. Moreover, film critics, media scholars, and cultural historians have frequently commented on this paradoxical fascination with the Black male image in all of its incarnations from urban criminal to gangsta rapper to multi-millionaire entertainment or sports icon . . . and beyond. So we must return to rephrase and refocus Du Bois's enduring question on Black men, and ask "How does it feel to be a problem?" . . . while simultaneously that problem's solution? Exploring the society's convoluted psychic desires and media projections, novelist Toni Morrison says it another way through the sardonic voice of her rebel character Sula, when she humorously observes that because of penis envy, rape fantasies, and a ubiquitous attraction/repulsion, "everything in the world loves" the Black man.[1] However, most images of Black men in social memory tend to evoke a nightmare history of barbarism or stereotypic insult: from photos of the mutilated body of man-child Emmett Till to the videotaped police torture of Rodney King or the gladiator Mike Tyson biting off a chunk of Evander Holyfield's ear. Occasionally this melancholy gallery is punctuated with triumphant images like

Tiger Woods's athletics, or Jesse Jackson's negotiated return of U.S. prisoners from Kosovo. Generally though, the construction of the Black male image in commercial cinema follows a paradoxical mix of stereotype and adoration that has taken a convoluted course over cinema history, seemingly driven by a defined yet complexly contradictory formula. While Black men have consistently been held in the lowest social esteem and relentlessly stereotyped as a group, a few have been simultaneously elevated as "exceptions" and worshiped as accomplished individuals, movie stars, and sports icons. This representational gambit has served dominant society well. For through it, the mass of Black males is perceived and fixed in their "place" at the absolute lowest rung of the social order, while an indifferent majority looks on, as Du Bois famously said, "with contempt and pity." Postmodern racism tries hard not to be "personal." Most in that vast consumer audience are personally distanced from social inequality's systemic workings, as they look to high profile Black celebrities for psychic comfort and assurance that the society is making racial progress.

However, a line-up of the "usual suspects" in commercial cinema's historical view convincingly reveals this attraction/repulsion, kiss/kill dynamic. From the inception of the nickelodeon on New York City's Broadway, the spectacle of Black men lynched and swinging from Southern trees was hawked as cheap newsreel entertainment. At minimum, Gus of *Birth of a Nation*, the black and fantastic King Kong clutching his blonde object of desire, or the irrepressible Candyman haunting Chicago's projects with interracial desire, all express powerful, ongoing metaphors for barely contained fears of Black masculinity, sexuality, miscegenation, and perhaps at the bottom of it all, latent political power. And complementing their usual Manichean duties as social and psychic threats to white order and civilization, Black men have long been (and continue to be) cast as minstrels in literature and the cinema. For over two centuries ending only with the resistance of the Civil Rights Movement, "Sambo" was one of America's most popular, and exportable, images.[2] It's not surprising, then, to see echoes of his persona in Eddie Murphy's '80s resurrection of "Buckwheat," or the inept, fumbling tyranny of "Mister" in *The Color Purple* (1985), or in more bluntly throwback caricatures like Jar Jar Binks, the inter-galactic Steppin' Fetchit.

Yet to grasp the social ambivalence and confusion of the dominant love/hate dynamic, we cannot dwell entirely on visions of Black brutes and buffoons. Structured in counterpoint to the beast and fool, commercial cinema has also produced a succession of Black male heroes and idols from Sidney Poitier's "ebony saints," to Melvin Van Peebles's sexual rebel "Sweetback," to Richard Pryor and Eddie Murphy's bi-racial buddies, right up to the more deeply drawn '90s characters played by Lawrence Fishburne, Denzel Washington, Samuel Jackson, Danny Glover, or Will Smith, with the latter cohort almost invariably cast with white co-stars or chaperones to assure a given film's successful "crossover." In any event, one could never miss the box office wisdom of Sylvester Stallone's "loving" symbiotic attachment to Black men while symbolically battling them, with his most successful ventures resulting from epic struggles and/or bonding with Black men in the *Rocky* cycle or his contest with a punked-out dystopian, super-villain played by Wesley Snipes in *Demolition Man* (1993).

Conversely, filmmakers, from the pioneer Black independents Oscar Micheaux and Spencer Williams, to Blaxploitation's Melvin Van Peebles and Gordon Parks, to contemporary directors, including Spike Lee, Rusty Cundieff, Carl Franklin, and Kasi Lemmons have all struggled to define and contextualize Black manhood in broader terms, and against the grain of Hollywood's flattened out, negative/positive binary. Take a scene in Spike Lee's *Do the Right Thing* (1989), depicting the suspicion and antagonism with which dominant society routinely measures Black manhood, as two working-class white cops on patrol pause to exchange hostile stares with a group of Black "corner men." "What a waste," the cops mutter in judgment as they drive off. However, the contempt is mutual. While these cops, as the mediating gaze of dominant society, see idle, wasted lives, the Black corner men also have a perspective and return society's gaze with insight and irony. If the corner men know nothing else, they know that incarceration is a growth business and these cops' jobs are entirely dependent on the Black men trapped in America's ghettos or warehoused in its jails and prisons. Undereducated and unemployed Black men are the throwaway people, the "raw material" that feeds society's burgeoning prison industrial complex as Lee's camera captures an illuminating, counter-hegemonic moment in the popular discourse about the shape and crisis of Black manhood.

Society's bond to its indispensable fetish, is played out daily on our screens, cinematic and televisual, against the backdrop of a media paradox and cruel social mockery. As argued, according to our schizophrenic social vision, the representations of Black men tend to gather at the poles of celebrity and pathology. While we are treated to the grand celebrity spectacle of Black male athletes, movie stars, and pop entertainers conspicuously enjoying the wealth and privilege that fuel the fantasies of the consumer system, we are also subjected to the real time, devastation, and body count of a constant stream of faceless Black males on the nightly news. Besides Black men being the very metaphor of "crime," as an audience we are led into the trap of false perception and reasoning. By following the logic of our screens, the specta-tor arrives at some variation of a reductive query that runs something like "If Bill Cosby or Bryant Gumbel can 'make it' in America, why can't all of those Black men standing on ghetto street corners?" So the social fear of Black men is subtly fed by the adulation of Black celebrity, inviting us to dismiss the vast majority of Black males as suspects, dependents, or victims. Or cine-matically, as the bigoted Pino tells Mookie in *Do the Right Thing*, Prince and Magic Johnson are "exceptions" and the rest are "just niggers."[3]

But we must also factor in the social contradiction, (or, if you prefer, "joke") inflicted on Black men, originating in the very definitions of self-worth and manhood in American society. It has come to be a cruel charade that in a culture where material wealth is the highest measure of self-worth, and that defines "manhood" foremost as the ability to provide economically for one's self and family, the very means of achieving such a narrowly mapped "manhood" (or any measure of self-esteem) are systematically and institutionally kept beyond the reach of all too many Black men. To cite one overdetermining reality out of the entire, grim statistical litany: for over the past two decades Black male unemployment has consistently been kept approximately twice as high as that of white males. Of the Black men between sixteen and sixty-two, 46 percent are not in the labor force.[4] Combine this wanting condition with the Black male's increasingly shrinking educational and social horizons, mix with the hypnotic, electronic flood of images of consumer goods, fantasies of easy money, luxury cars, and romantic tropical vacations that our screens tell us are instantly attainable, and it is not that hard to extrapolate the violent, deadly results that we see daily in the confines of our inner cities.

Sadly and dangerously for us all in an increasingly diverse, multi-racial nation, we have constructed in our films and media, between the love/hate polarities of Tiger Woods and O.J., a vast, empty space in representation. Missing from Hollywood's flat, binary view of Black manhood is the cultural, political, intellectual complexity and humanity of Black men, as well as their invaluable contributions to the culture and progress of the nation. To say this is not to argue simplistically for a wave of insipid, compensatory "positive images" of successful doctors and athletes or happy, middle-class fathers modeled to dominant cultural expectations. Hollywood has given us enough "noble Negroes," de-(or hyper-)sexed comedians, bi-racial buddy combos, and upwardly mobile, Black "exceptions" to fuel several film waves to come, Black or otherwise. Based as it is on the pursuit of short term profit mainly through the "blockbuster" commodification of juvenile fantasy, for the moment (perhaps forever) the Hollywood vision mostly stands at odds with the broader conceptualization and humanization of the Black male in popular culture. Consequently there's much work to be done on an expanded, heterogeneous range of complex portrayals of Black males that transcends the misshapen characters caught within Hollywood's formulaic narratives and habitual strategies for representing Blackness, that is, channeling most Black talent and film production into the genres of comedy or ghetto-action-adventure. We must now work to fill the missing images and gaps with movies about the deeply complicated and brilliant "brothermen"[5] that populate the African American life and its narrative tradition, be that tradition expressed as barbershop ruminations, love or street corner stories, social action, or literary production. Where are the films transposing the illuminating novels of such authors as Ralph Ellison, James Baldwin, Gayl Jones, Richard Wright, John Edgar Wideman, Toni Cade Bambara, Ishmael Reed? At the same time we must jump out of the film industry's genre traps by demanding, making, and consuming a broader range of Black films.

Importantly, we need to fill representation's empty space with many more Black dramas, family films, films with Black men in loving relationships and with broadened sexual identities. But also our genre horizons must include science fiction and horror, and dramatic transcriptions from Black intellectual and political culture.

Black people struggling to define and speak for themselves is the quintessential energy and liberating current in African American cultural production. Accordingly, Black filmmaking, from the Lincoln Motion Picture Company's *Birth of a Race* (1918) to Marlon Riggs's *Tongues Untied* (1991) to Denzel Washington's portrayal of Easy Rawlins in *Devil in a Blue Dress* (1995) and Spike Lee's break with limiting Black directors to a Black focus with *Summer of Sam* (1999), has attempted to challenge and fill the gaps and traps in the dominant film industry's confining expectations of Black men. Whether "mainstream" or "independent," a number of Black-made or Black-focused features have endeavored to define, portray, or diagnose those vital aspects of Black male humanity so often subordinated or missing in dominant cinema. Across a range of brilliant feature films, Black cinema as well as Black performances in the commercial mainstream has struggled against Hollywood's delusions about Black men, attempting to break out of the confines of its master narrative and genre ghettos. Thus it is sadly ironic that while much of the best of Black filmmaking has won worldwide acclaim for its aesthetic innovation, social vision, and dramatic power, the depth and range of this work is hardly known to the mass consumer audience. One can't catch the most profound expressions of Black cinema on late night cable T.V. or at the mall-multiplex, and one can speculate that this might have more than a bit to do with these productions' uncompromising insights about the very real dangers (and pleasures) of being a Black man in this society.

As constricted as the situation has been, a number of feature films have managed to work against the odds, speaking up for the brothers, posing alternatives to their subordination or erasure. Seldom screened masterworks, such as Billy Woodberry's *Bless Their Little Hearts* (1984), Michael Romer's *Nothing But a Man* (1964), or the cinematic adaptation of Lorraine Hansberry's *A Raisin in the Sun* (1961), all meet the issue of Black male survival head on, depicting their protagonists' struggles to achieve manhood and the care of their families against the insult and injury of an unsympathetic world. Duff (Ivan Dixon), in *Nothing But a Man* strives to break a cycle of absent fathers, while painfully rebuilding a family against the political and economic racism of the pre-Civil Rights South. Charlie Banks (Nate Hardman) in *Bless Their Little Hearts,* isn't so lucky. Defeated by institutional forces far beyond his control, unemployed and ghettoized, he drunkenly stumbles off into the emptiness of a weed choked vacant lot that aptly symbolizes his bleak social and economic horizon. Walter (Sidney Poitier) in *A Raisin in the Sun* struggles to recoup his manhood and dreams by standing up to the local housing association that wants to keep its neighborhood "all white." Significantly, all of these seldom seen but brilliant productions situate their Black, male protagonists in the broader contexts of the daunting economic, institutional, or social forces that conspire to marginalize and destroy them. These films tell it from the Black side, in that what happens to one of us, happens to us all, as they refute the Hollywood convention of avoiding serious political engagement by reducing collective consciousness and social struggle to the isolated travails of the individual.

Like rhinoceros horn, poached and smuggled from the "dark continent," Black male sexuality, in all of its variations and identities, is a socially charged and highly prized commodity in Western industrial societies. Making the point humorously in *The Spy Who Shagged Me* (1999), Austin Powers's sexual *mojo*, marked as the essence of Marvin Gaye ("Let's Get It On"), is one recent variation on this endless and vital motif of American psyche and society. Coming from their distinct perspectives, films like Melvin Van Peebles's *Sweet Sweetback's Baadasssss Song* (1971), Wendell Harris's *Chameleon Street* (1989), Isaac Julien's *Looking for Langston* (1989), and Jennie Livingston's *Paris Is Burning* (1990), all explore aspects of Black male sexuality, and as importantly, locate it specifically in the broader context of the outlaw subjectivity and marginality that Black men must endure in the West. Made at the height of the heavily, male-inflected Black Power rebellion and controversial for its depreciated view of Black women, Van Peebles's *Sweet Sweetback's Baadasssss Song* marks a turning point for the Black male image on the commercial screen. *Sweet Sweetback . . .* provided the Black audience with a new paradigm for the Black male: as action movie hero and as a rebuttal to decades of Hollywood's stale "noble Negroes." Drawn on the "bad nigga" archetype of African American oral tradition, the sexual rebel and outlaw Sweetback, fantastically and single-handedly battles the white power structure and wins, thus spawning the wave of ghetto-action sex symbols and flicks like *Shaft* (1971) and *Superfly* (1972), that comprised much of the "Blaxploitation" '70s. Because of its independent "guerilla financing" strategy, and the aesthetic, gender, and political debates that it still inspires, *Sweet Sweetback . . .* stands as a salient marker in the discourse on the construction of Black manhood. Playing on many of the same themes but coming up with different results, William Street in *Chameleon Street* bitterly evokes the invisibility metaphor of Ralph Ellison's legendary novel of the same name. Dissembling and dodging, Street lives on the run, at society's margins, in its shadows, and against the racist protocols that stunt or foreclose so many aspects of Black men's lives. Street (Wendell Harris) masquerades as a doctor, lawyer, and journalist, and thus rebels by infiltrating the exclusive zone of the elite professional caste kept out of the practical reach, and aspirations, of most Black men. Yet, because of hypermasculinist compensations for the dubious sexual role society has assigned him, most of Street's victims are women, from his wife and daughter to his African girlfriend, to the dozens of women he inflicted hysterectomies on as a bogus M.D.

With the '90s Black movie boom, many films, through their oppositional narratives, innovative styles, and the existential resistance of their protagonists, have attempted to directly comment on and broaden the debate about Black male representation and identity. Sustaining the traditional labors of Black protest, *Hollywood Shuffle* (1987) interrogates dominant cinema's ongoing addiction to stereotypes. After examining his conscience, aspiring actor Bobby Taylor (Robert Townsend) ultimately rejects playing Hollywood's standard fare for Black men: criminals, pimps, comics, slaves, and butlers. *Drop Squad* (1994) evolves its resistant stance by questioning the very possibility of a static, cultural, nationalist, *macho* orientation in a world of shifting postmodern identities. Isaac Julien's avant garde *Looking for Langston* (1989), confronts the silences and lacunas of Black literary history and sexual identity in its exploration of poetry, beauty, and desire in the Black gay world. This work is augmented through the features of the late Marlon Riggs's *Tongues Untied* (1991) and *Black Is . . . Black Ain't* (1994). In the stark realism of their "gangsta" noir styles, films like *Juice* (1992), *Menace II Society* (1993), or the more hopefully resolved *South Central* (1992), *Clockers* (1995), and *Belly* (1998), all explore the Black underworld and interrogate its "code of the streets"[6] which narrowly defines manhood while leading so many young Black men to the nihilistic alternatives of prison or the morgue. What is interesting about these two latter currents (films mapping the Black gay world and the urban 'hood), is that they're not as distanced or opposed as one might imagine. As Jennie Livingston's documentary sojourn through the various "houses" of Black men competing at an annual cross-dressing ball in *Paris Is Burning* (1990) points out, in addition to the slings of homophobia, Black gay men suffer from all the limitations, discriminations, and problems of the 'hood-homeboy, and usually on the same turf: the racial and economic ghetto. Moreover, the organization of the "houses" in *Paris Is Burning* (add the gay nightclub in *Looking for Langston*), and the street gangs of the 'hood are not dissimilar in their ultimate purpose: the survival of different social collectivities of Black men facing the varied and sustained attacks of the same discriminatory system.

In all, the dialogue on Black men and their "place" in America, going on in film, literature, drama, painting, dance, and music, is just beginning to gather voices and, once again, take off. Most of the films mentioned here, while they are expressly dramatic narratives, are meant to confront, entertain, and edify with a range of sights and insights about the complex, heterogeneous nature of Black male identity. They are certainly part of that vast cultural project aimed at rearticulating Black male survival and Black manhood in the more relevant and heterogeneous terms of the new millennium. Through these films the brothers speak for themselves, introducing the consumer audience to the issues and stakes in the debate going on, both in Black discourse and mainstream media culture, about the tangled and unresolved fate of Black men (and indeed, Black people) in the nation.

**NOTES**

1. Toni Morrison, *Sula* (New York: Plume, 1973), 103–104.

2. Joseph Boskin, *Sambo* (New York: Oxford University Press, 1986), 3–16.

3. Ed Guerrero, *Framing Blackness: The African American Image in Film* (Philadelphia: Temple University Press, 1993), 157–164.

4. Andrew Hacker, *Two Nations, Black and White, Separate, Hostile, Unequal* (New York: Scribner's, 1992), 3–49. Robert Staples, "The Illusion of Racial Equality," in Gerald Early, ed., *Lure and Loathing: Essays on Race, Identity and the Ambivalence of Assimilation* (New York: Allen Lane, The Penguin Press, 1993), 232.

5. Herb Boyd and Robert L. Allen, eds. *Brotherman: The Odyssey of Black Men in America* (New York: Ballantine Books, 1995).

6. Elijah Anderson, "The Code of the Streets," *The Atlantic Monthly*, 273, no. 5 (May 1994), 80–94. Richard Majors and Janet Mancini Billson, *Cool Pose: The Dilemmas of Black Manhood in America* (New York: Touchstone, 1992).

# PART 4

## BROTHER TO BROTHER
### The Politics of Desire, Sexuality, and Homophobia

# 26

# A LETTER FROM HUEY TO THE REVOLUTIONARY BROTHERS AND SISTERS ABOUT THE WOMEN'S LIBERATION AND GAY LIBERATION MOVEMENTS

HUEY P. NEWTON

During the past few years, strong movements have developed among women and homosexuals seeking their liberation. There has been some uncertainty about how to relate to these movements.

Whatever your personal opinion and your insecurities about homosexuality and the various liberation movements among homosexuals and women (and I speak of the homosexuals and women as oppressed groups) we should try to unite with them in a revolutionary fashion.

I say "whatever your insecurities are" because, as we very well know, sometimes our first instinct is to want to hit a homosexual in the mouth and to want a woman to be quiet. We want to hit the homosexual in the mouth as soon as we see him because we're afraid we might be homosexual and want to hit the woman or shut her up because she might castrate us or take the nuts that we may not have to start with.

We must gain security in ourselves and therefore have respect and feelings for all oppressed people. We must not use the racist-type attitudes like the white racists use against people because they are black and poor. Many times the poorest white person is the most racist because he's afraid that he might lose something or discover something that he doesn't have. You're some kind of threat to him. This kind of psychology is in operation when we view oppressed people and we're angry with them because of their particular kind of behavior or their particular kind of deviation from the established norm.

Remember we haven't established a revolutionary value system; we're only in the process of establishing it. I don't remember us ever constituting any value that said that a revolutionary must say offensive things toward homosexuals or that a revolutionary would make sure that women do not speak out about their own particular kind of oppression.

Matter of fact, it's just the opposite, we say that we recognize the woman's right to be free. We haven't said much about the homosexual at all and we must relate to the homosexual movement because it is a real movement. And I know through reading and through my life experience, my observation, that homosexuals are not given freedom and liberty by anyone in this society. Maybe they might be the most oppressed people in the society.

What made them homosexuals? Perhaps it's a whole phonemena that I don't understand entirely. Some people say that it's the decadence of capitalism — I don't know whether this is the case, I rather doubt it. But whatever the case is, we know that homosexuality is a fact that exists and we must understand it in its purest form; that is, a person should have the freedom to use his body whatever way he wants to.

That's not endorsing things in homosexuality that we wouldn't view as revolutionary. But there is nothing to say that a homosexual can not also be a revolutionary. And maybe I'm now injecting some of my prejudice by saying "even a homosexual can be a revolutionary." Quite the contrary, maybe a homosexual could be the most revolutionary.

When we have revolutionary conferences, rallies and demonstrations, there should be full participation of the Gay Liberation Movement and the Women's Liberation Movement. We understand there are factions within the Women's Liberation Movement. Some groups might be more revolutionary than others. We shouldn't use the actions of a few to say that they're all reactionary or counterrevolutionary because they're not.

We should deal with factions just as we deal with any other group or party that claims to be revolutionary. We should try to judge somehow whether they're operating sincerely in a revolutionary fashion from a really oppressed situation (and we'll grant that if they're women they're probably oppressed.) If they do things that are unrevolutionary or counterrevolutionary, then criticize that action. If we feel that the group in spirit means to be revolutionary in practice but they make mistakes in interpretation of the revolutionary philosophy or they don't understand the dialectics of the social forces in operation, we should criticize that and not criticize them because they are women trying to be free. And the same is true for homosexuals.

We should never say a whole movement is dishonest when in fact they are trying to be honest; they're just making honest mistakes. Friends are allowed to make mistakes. The enemy is not allowed to make mistakes because his whole existance is a mistake and we suffer from it. But the Women's Liberation Front and Gay Liberation Front are our friends, they are our potential allies and we need as many allies as possible.

We should be willing to discuss the insecurities that many people have about homosexuality. When I say, "insecurities" I mean the fear that there is some kind of threat to our manhood. I can understand this fear. Because of the long conditioning process that builds insecurity in the American male, homosexuality might produce certain hangups in us. I have hangups myself about male homosexuality where on the other hand I have no hangups about female homosexuality and that's a phonomena in itself. I think it's probably because that's a threat to me maybe, and the females are no threat. It's just another erotic sexual thing.

We should be careful about using terms which might turn our friends off. The terms "faggot" and "punk" should be deleted from our vocabulary and especially we should not attach names normally designed for homosexuals to men who are enemies of the people such as Nixon or Mitchell. Homosexuals are not enemies of the people.

We should try to form a working coalition with the Gay Liberation and Women's Liberation groups. We must always handle social forces in an appropriate manner and this is really a significant part of the population — both women and the growing number of homosexuals that we have to deal with.

*ALL POWER TO THE PEOPLE!*

Huey P. Newton,
SUPREME COMMANDER,
Black Panther Party

# 27

## BROTHER TO BROTHER
### Words from the Heart

JOSEPH BEAM

. . . what is most important to me must be spoken, made verbal and shared, even at the risk of having it bruised or misunderstood.[1]

> I know the anger that lies inside me like I know the beat of my heart and the taste of my spit. It is easier to be angry than to hurt. Anger is what I do best. It is easier to be furious than to be yearning. Easier to crucify myself in you than to take on the threatening universe of whiteness by admitting that we are worth wanting each other.[2]

I, too, know anger. My body contains as much anger as water. It is the material from which I have built my house: blood red bricks that cry in the rain. It is what pulls my tie and gold chains taut around my neck; fills my penny loafers and my Nikes; molds my Calvins and gray flannels to my torso. It is the face and posture I show the world. It is the way, sometimes the only way, I am granted an audience. It is sometimes the way I show affection. I am angry because of the treatment I am afforded as a Black man. That fiery anger is stoked additionally with the fuels of contempt and despisal shown me by my community because I am gay. *I cannot go home as who I am.*

When I speak of home, I mean not only the familial constellation from which I grew, but the entire Black community: the Black press, the Black church, Black academicians, the Black literati, and the Black left. Where is my reflection? I am most often rendered invisible, perceived as a threat to the family, or am tolerated if I am silent and inconspicuous. I cannot go home as who I am and that hurts me deeply.

Almost every morning I have coffee at the same donut shop. Almost every morning I encounter the same Black man who used to acknowledge me from across the counter. I can only surmise that it is my earrings and earcuffs that have tipped him off that I am gay. He no longer speaks, instead looks disdainfully through me as if I were glass. But glass reflects, so I am not even that. He sees no part of himself in me—not my Blackness nor my maleness. "There's nothing in me that is not in everyone else, and nothing in everyone else that is not in me."[3] Should our glances meet, he is quick to use his *Wall Street Journal* as a shield while I wince and admire the brown of my coffee in my cup.

I do not expect his approval—only his acknowledgement. The struggles of Black people are too perilous and too pervasive for us to dismiss one another, in such cursory fashion, because of perceived differences. Gil Scott-Heron called it "dealing in externals," that is, giving great importance to visual information and ignoring real aspects of commonality. Aren't all hearts and fists and minds needed in this struggle or will this faggot be tossed into the fire? In this very critical time everyone from the corner to the corporation is desperately needed.

> . . . [Brother] the war goes on
> respecting no white flags
> taking no prisoners
> giving no time out for women and children
> to leave the area
> whether we return their fire
> or not
> whether we're busy attacking each other
> or not . . .[4]

If you could put your newspaper aside for a moment, I think you, too, would remember that it has not always been this way between us. I remember. I remember the times before different meant separate, before different meant outsider. I remember Sunday school and backyard barbecues and picnics in the Park and the Avenue and parties in dimly lit basements and skateboards fashioned from two-by-fours and b-ball and . . . I remember. I also recall secretly playing jacks and jumping rope on the back porch, and the dreams I had when I spent the night at your house.

But that was before different meant anything at all, certainly anything substantial. That was prior to considerations such as too light/too dark; or good/bad hair; before college/-army/jail; before working/middle class; before gay/straight. But I am no longer content on the back porch; I want to play with my jacks on the front porch. There is no reason for me to hide. Our differences should promote dialogue rather than erect new obstacles in our paths.

On another day: I am walking down Spruce/Castro/Christopher Street on my way to work. A half block away, walking towards me, is another Black gay man. We have seen each other in the clubs. Side by side, and at the precise moment that our eyes should meet, he studies the intricate detail of a building. I check my white sneakers for scuff marks. What is it that we see in each other that makes us avert our eyes so quickly? Does he see the same thing in me that the brother in the donut shop sees? Do we turn away from each other in order not to see our collective anger and sadness?

*It is my pain I see reflected in your eyes. Our angers ricochet between us like the bullets we fire in battles which are not our own nor with each other.*

The same angry face, donned for safety in the white world, is the same expression I bring to you. I am cool and unemotive, distant from what I need most. "It is easier to be furious than to be yearning. Easier to crucify myself in you . . . " And perhaps easiest to ingest that anger until it threatens to consume me, or apply a salve of substitutes to the wound.

But real anger accepts few substitutes and sneers at sublimation. The anger-hurt I feel cannot be washed down with a Coke (old or new) or a Colt 45; cannot be danced away; cannot be mollified by a white lover, nor lost in the mirror reflections of a Black lover; cannot evaporate like sweat after a Nautilus workout; nor drift away in a cloud of reefer smoke. I cannot leave it in Atlantic City, or Rio, or even Berlin when I vacation. I cannot hope it will be gobbled up by the alligators on my clothing; nor can I lose it in therapeutic catharsis. I cannot offer it to Jesus/Allah/Jah. So, I must mold and direct that fiery cool mass of angry energy — use it before it uses me! *Anger unvented becomes pain, pain unspoken becomes rage, rage released becomes violence.*

Use it to create a Black gay community in which I can build my home surrounded by institutions that reflect and sustain me. Concurrent with that vision is the necessity to repave the road home, widening it, so I can return with all I have created to the home which is my birthright.

## II

Silence is what I hear after the handshake and the slap of five; after the salutations: what's happenin'/what's up/how you feel; after our terms of endearment: homeboy, cuzz, "girlfriend," blood, running buddy, and Miss Thing. I can hear the silence. When talking with a "girlfriend," I am more likely to muse about my latest piece or so-and-so's party at Club She-She than about the anger and hurt I felt that morning when a jeweler refused me entrance to his store because I am Black and male, and we are all perceived as thieves. I will swallow that hurt and should I speak of it, will vocalize only the anger, saying: I have bust out his fuckin' windows! Some of the anger will be exercised [sic], but the hurt, which has not been given voice, prevails and accumulates.

Silence is a way to grin and bear it. A way not to acknowledge how much my life is discounted each day — 100% OFF ALL BLACK MEN TODAY — EVERY DAY! I strive to appear strong and silent. I learn to ingest hatred at a geometric rate and to count (silently) to 10 . . . 10 thousand . . . 10 million. But as I have learned to mute my cries of anguish, so have I learned to squelch my exclamations of joy. What remains is the rap.

My father is a warm brown man of seventy, who was born in Barbados. He is
kind and gentle, and has worked hard for me so that I am able to write these
words. We are not friends: he is my father, I am his son. We are silent when
alone together. I do not ask him about his island childhood or his twelve
years as a janitor or about the restaurant he once owned where he met my
mother. He does not ask me about being gay or why I wish to write about it.
Yet we are connected: his past is my present, our present a foundation for the
future. I have never said to him that his thick calloused hands have led me
this far and given me options he never dreamed of. How difficult it is to speak
of my appreciation, saying: Dad, I love you. *I am here because of you, much
deeper than sperm meeting egg, much deeper than sighs in the night, I am here
because of you.* Our love for each other, though great, may never be spoken.
It is the often unspoken love that Black men give to other Black men in a
world where we are forced to cup our hands over our mouths or suffer under
the lash of imprisonment, unemployment, or even death. But these words,
which fail, are precisely the words that are life-giving and continuing. They
must be given voice. What legacy is to be found in our silence?

Because of the silence among us, each one of us, as Black boys and men
maturing, must all begin the struggle to survive anew. With the incomplete
knowledge of what has gone before, our struggles to endure and maintain,
at best, save us only as individuals. Collectively we falter and stumble, cov-
ering up our experiences in limp aphorisms: Times are hard! Watch out
for the Man! This is the depth of the sage advice we offer each other—at
arm's length. We must begin to speak of our love and concern for each other
as vigorously as we argue party politics or the particular merits of an athletic team.

Daydream: 29 April 1984
Today was the first beautiful day that I have not had to spend at work. Precisely
the kind of day I want to share with a lover: gazing at the blue sky; making love
in the western sunlight on the brown-sheeted bed; massaging each other with
the musk oil that warms on the window sill. We'd shower together, and return
to the bed to dry in the sunlight as we had sweated when we made love.

Today, I think also of Bryan, and of myself as the hopeless romantic that I
sometimes am. How can I be so taken with you, boy-man, who I met only two
weeks ago? Why is it that I want to share all my waking moments with you?
Share my world with you? Protect you? Tell you things no one told me when
I was 22. You are like the little brother I never had; the playmate I was not
supposed to touch. You are the lover who is considerate; the son I will not
issue, eyes bright and inquisitive. I want to hold you the way my father never
held me. I want to know your face, the oily brownness of your skin: its shadows,
the darkness around the elbows and under the buttocks. I daydream of brown-
on-brown-on-brown.

I am at a poetry reading. The brother at the podium is reading a poem about
his running buddy who was killed in Vietnam. At the gravesite of his dead
friend, the poet reminisces about the big fun they'd had, sharing bottles of

wine and hanging on the corner. Only when everyone has gone and he stares at the mound of dirt that covers his homeboy, can he utter: "Man, I really loved you. I really, really loved you."

Why does it take us so long?

I, too, have been there. Two good high school buddies died within a year of our graduation: Chris in a charter plane crash on his way back to college; Steve of a heart attack while playing basketball. We were all nineteen and assumed life would go on. There seemed to be no rush to speak of how we cherished one another's friendship. I was away at college when they were both buried; I will always regret that silence.

We have few traditions like those of Black women. No kitchen tables around which to assemble. No intimate spaces in which to explore our feelings of love and friendship. No books like *The Color Purple*. We gather in public places: barber shops, bars, lodges, fraternities, and street corners, places where bravado rather than intimacy are the rule. We assemble to *do* something rather than *be* with each other. We can talk about the Man, but not about how we must constantly vie with one another for the scant crumbs thrown our way. We can talk about dick and ass and pussy, but not of the fierce competition for too few jobs and scholarships. We can talk about sporting events in amazing detail, but not about how we are pitted, one against the other, as permanent adversaries.

> Dream: 15 February 1984
> We have all gathered in the largest classroom I have ever been in. Black men of all kinds and colors. We sit and talk and listen, telling the stories of our lives. All of the things we have ever wanted to say to each other but did not. There is much laughter but also many tears. Why has it taken us so long? Our silence has hurt us so much.

# III

Dreams are what propel us through life, and allow us to focus above and beyond the hurdles that dot our passage. Medgar, Martin, and Malcolm were dreamers. And they were killed. I dare myself to dream. If I cannot vocalize a dream, which is the first step towards its realization, then I have no dream. It remains a thought, a vision without form. I dare myself to dream that our blood is thicker than difference.

In the fall of 1980, I did not know that one of every four Black men would experience prison in his lifetime. Nor did I know that my motivation for writing to prisoners arose from a deep sense of my captivity as a closeted gay man and an oppressed black man, rather than as an act of righteousness. Finally, I had no idea that such a correspondence would become an integral part of my life and a place for dreaming.

Ombaka and I began writing to each other under unusual circumstances. I had been writing to another prisoner named Morris, who had been transferred or released, but, in any case, had vacated the particular cell, which was to be Ombaka's new home. Ombaka found my last letter to Morris, read it and responded. He apologized profusely in that first letter about how contrary it was to prison etiquette to read someone else's mail and even ruder to respond to it. Almost four years and forty letters later, it seems ironic that this friendship, one of the most important in my life, is the result of such a chance occurrence. More ironic and sadder is that we probably would not have met any other way; we are that different.

I am gay and from the north; he is straight and from the south. I'm an agnostic; he's a Muslim. When I was attending prep school, Ombaka was busily acquiring his street smarts. While I studied in college, he was finishing his stint in the Army. When I was beginning graduate school, he had just begun his prison sentence. Under other circumstances these differences might have separated us. What could have been used as weapons of castigation became tools of sharing.

Our initial letters were filled with the tentative gestures one employs with new friends, the shyness, the formality, and the small talk. We searched for common ground for dialogue and the soft spots to be avoided. We spoke of the advantages and disadvantages of street smarts versus formal education. We talked at length about sexuality and how we became the sexual beings that we are. We discussed our use of language: I greatly admired his rural tongue with its graceful turn of phrase, which seemed more natural than my stilted style, which he respected. He told me of his experiences as a Muslim and as a father; I related tales from college and gay life in the big city. We talked and talked about our differences, but we also gave each other permission to dream and to speak of those dreams. What an exciting yet fearful prospect, dreaming in the open.

Black dreams are dashed as assuredly as Black dreamers are killed. We are allowed to dream of being athletes, entertainers, and lotto winners. These are the dreams which have been dreamt for us to maintain us just where we are. How little support there is, from one another or from society, for dreams borne of personal conviction and desire. I dare myself to dream.

Astronaut Guy Bluford and I grew up on the same block. It was no secret that he dreamed of being an astronaut, but in the early sixties it was difficult for little Black boys to imagine being anything other than what we had seen. And we had seen no Black astronauts nor Black mayors of major U.S. cities. We all thought Bluford was crazy, but his dreams became a reality. We can dream the dark, the seemingly impossible.

Ombaka and I dreamt of being writers. During the course of our correspondence we *became* writers. Several months ago he sent me a 260-page manuscript of his first novel, and I am beginning to work on a major writing project (this anthology). I am extremely happy that our friendship was not lost to anger, or silence, or perceived differences. I dare myself to dream.

I dare myself to dream of us moving from survival to potential, from merely getting by to a positive getting over. I dream of Black men loving and supporting other Black men, and relieving Black women from the role of primary nurturers in our community. I dream, too, that as we receive more of what we want from each other that our special anger reserved for Black women will disappear. For too long have we expected from Black women that which we could only obtain from other men. I dare myself to dream.

I dream of a time when it is not Black men who fill the nation's prisons; when we will not seek solace in a bottle and Top papers; and when the service is not the only viable alternative to high civilian unemployment.

I dare myself to dream of a time when I will pass a group of brothers on the corner, and the words "fuckin' faggot" will not move the air around my ears; and when my gay brother approaches me on the street that we can embrace if we choose.

I dare *us* to dream that we are worth wanting each other.

## IV

Black men loving Black men is the revolutionary act of the eighties.

At eighteen, David could have been a dancer: legs grown strong from daily walks from his remote neighborhood to downtown in search of employment that would free him from his abusive family situation. David, soft-spoken and articulate, could have been a waiter gliding gracefully among the tables of a three-star restaurant. David could have performed numerous jobs, but lacking the connections that come with age and race, the Army seemed a reasonable choice. His grace and demeanor will be of little importance in Nicaragua.

Earl is always a good time. His appearance at parties, whether it's a smart cocktail sip or basement gig, is mandatory. He wakes with coffee and speed, enjoys three-joint lunches, and chases his bedtime Valium with Johnny Walker Red. None of his friends, of which he has many, suggest that he needs help. His substance abuse is ignored by all.

Stacy is a delirious queen, a concoction of current pop stars, bound eclectically in thrift store threads. His sharp and witty tongue can transform the most boring, listless evenings. In private, minus the dangles and bangles, he appears solemn and pensive, and speaks of the paucity of role models, mentors, and possibilities.

Maurice has a propensity for white people, which is more than prefer-ence—it's policy. He dismisses potential Black friendships as quickly as he switches off rap music and discredits progressive movements. He consis-tently votes Republican. At night he dreams of razors cutting away thin slivers of his Black skin.

Bubba and Ray had been lovers for so long that the neighbors presumed them to be brothers or widowers. For decades their socializing had been done among an intimate circle of gay couples, so when Ray died Bubba felt too old to venture the new gay scene. Occassionally he has visitors, an equally old friend or a much younger cousin or nephew. But mostly he sits, weather permitting, on the front porch where with a can of beer over ice, he silently weaves marvelous tales of "the life" in the thirties and forties. Yet there isn't anyone who listens.

Bobbi, a former drag queen, has plenty of time to write poetry. Gone are his makeup and high heels since he began serving his two-to-five year sentence. He had not wanted to kick that bouncer's ass; however, he, not unlike the more macho sissies clad in leather and denim, rightfully deserved admittance to that bar. Although he has had no visitors and just a couple of letters, he maintains a sense of humor typified by the title of a recent set of poems: *Where can a decent drag queen get a decent drink?*

Paul is hospitalized with AIDS. The severity of his illness is not known to his family or friends. They cannot know that he is gay; it is his secret and he will expire with it. Living a lie is one thing, but it is quite another to die within its confines.

Charles is a ventman with beautiful dreads. On days when he is not drinking and is lucid, he will tell you how he winters on the south side of the square and sleeps facing the east so that he wakes with the sun in his eyes. He is only an obstacle to passersby.

Ty and Reggie have been lovers since they met in the service seven years ago. They both perform dull and menial jobs for spiteful employers, but plan to help each other through college. Ty will attend first. Their two-room apartment, which is neither fashionably appointed nor in a fashionable neighborhood, is clearly a respite from the madness that awaits outside their door. They would never imagine themselves as revolutionaries.

Black men loving Black men is the revolutionary act of the eighties, not only because sixties' revolutionaries like Bobby Seale, Huey Newton, and Eldridge Cleaver dare speak our name; but because as Black men we were never meant to be together—not as father and son, brother and brother— and certainly not as lovers.

Black men loving Black men is an autonomous agenda for the eighties, which is not rooted in any particular sexual, political, or class affiliation, but in our mutual survival. The ways in which we manifest that love are as myriad as the issues we must address. Unemployment, substance abuse, self-hatred, and the lack of positive images are but some of the barriers to our loving.

Black men loving Black men is a call to action, an acknowledgement of responsibility. We take care of our own kind when the night grows cold and silent. These days the nights are cold-blooded and the silence echoes with complicity.

### NOTES

1. Lorde, Audre. *The Cancer Journals.* Argyle, N.Y.: Spinster's Ink 1980.

2. Lorde, Audre. *Sister Outsider.* Ithaca, N.Y.: Crossing Press, 1984.

3. Baldwin, James. *Village Voice*, 29, no. 26, p. 14.

4. Blackwomon, Julie. *Revolutionary Blues and Other Fevers* Philadelphia: self-published, 1984. (Distributed by Kitchen Table Women of Color Press, PO Box 908, Latham, N.Y.)

# 28 BLACK MACHO REVISITED
## Reflections of a SNAP! Queen

MARLON RIGGS

Negro faggotry is in fashion.
SNAP!
Turn on your television and camp queens greet you in living color.
SNAP!
Turn to cable and watch America's most bankable modern minstrel expound on getting "fucked in the ass" or his fear of faggots.
SNAP!
Turn off the TV, turn on the radio: Rotund rapper Heavy D, the self-styled "overweight lover MC," expounds on how *his* rap will make you "happy like a faggot in jail." Perhaps to preempt questions about how he would know—you might wonder what kind of "lover" he truly is—Heavy D reassures us that he's just "extremely intellectual, not bisexual."

Jelly-roll SNAP!

Negro faggotry is in vogue. Madonna commodified it into a commercial hit. Mapplethorpe photographed it and art galleries drew fire and record crowds in displaying it. Black macho movie characters dis'—or should we say dish?—their antagonists with unkind references to it. Indeed references to, and representations of, Negro faggotry seem a rite of passage among contemporary black male rappers and filmmakers.

Snap-swish-and-dish divas have truly arrived, giving Beauty Shop drama at center stage, performing the read-and-snap two-step as they sashay across the movie screen, entertaining us in the castles of our homes—like court jesters, like eunuchs—with their double entendres and dead-end lusts, and above all, their relentless hilarity in the face of relentless despair. Negro faggotry is the rage! Black gay men are not. For in the cinematic and television images of and from black America as well as the lyrics and dialogue that now abound and *seem* to address my life as a black gay man, I am struck repeatedly by the determined, unreasoning, often irrational desire to discredit my claim to blackness and hence to black manhood.

In consequence the terrain black gay men navigate in the quest for self and social identity is, to say the least, hostile. What disturbs—no, enrages me, is not so much the obstacles set before me by whites, which history conditions me to expect, but the trap and pitfalls planted by my so-called brothers, who because of the same history should know better.

I am a Negro faggot, if I believe what movies, TV, and rap music say of me. My life is game for play. Because of my sexuality, I cannot be black. A strong, proud, "Afrocentric" black man is resolutely heterosexual, not *even* bisexual. Hence I remain a Negro. My sexual difference is considered of no value; indeed it's a testament to weakness, passivity, the absence of real guts—balls. Hence I remain a sissy, punk, faggot. I cannot be a black gay man because by the tenets of black macho, black gay man is a triple negation. I am consigned, by these tenets, to remain a Negro faggot. And as such I am game for play, to be used, joked about, put down, beaten, slapped, and bashed, not just by illiterate homophobic thugs in the night, but by black American culture's best and brightest.

In a community where the dozens, signifying, dis'ing, and *dishing* are revered as art form, I ask myself: What does this obsession with Negro faggotry signify? What is its significance?

What lies at the heart, I believe, of black America's pervasive cultural homophobia is the desperate need for a convenient Other *within* the community, yet not truly *of* the community, an Other to which blame for the chronic identity crises afflicting the black male psyche can be readily displaced, an indispensable Other which functions as the lowest common denominator of the abject, the base line of transgression beyond which a Black Man is no longer a man, no longer black, an essential Other against which black men and boys maturing, struggling with self-doubt, anxiety, feelings of political, economic, social, and sexual inadequacy—even impotence—can always measure themselves and by comparison seem strong, adept, empowered, superior.

Indeed the representation of Negro faggotry disturbingly parallels and reinforces America's most entrenched racist constructions around African American identity. White icons of the past signifying "Blackness" share with contemporary icons of Negro faggotry a manifest dread of the deviant Other. Behind the Sambo and the SNAP! Queen lies a social psyche in torment, a fragile psyche threatened by deviation from its egocentric/ethnocentric construct of self and society. Such a psyche systematically defines the Other's "deviance" by the essential characteristics which make the Other distinct, then invests those differences with intrinsic defect. Hence: Blacks are inferior because they are not white. Black gays are unnatural because they are not straight. Majority representations of both affirm the view that blackness and gayness constitute a fundamental rupture in the order of things, that our very existence is an affront to nature and humanity.

From black gay men, this burden of (mis)representation is compounded. We are saddled by historic caricatures of the black male, now fused with newer notions of the Negro faggot. The resultant dehumanization is multi-layered, and profound.

What strikes me as most insidious, and paradoxical, is the degree to which popular African American depictions of us as black gay men so keenly resonate American majority depictions of us, as black people. Within the black gay community, for example, the SNAP! contains a multiplicity of coded meanings: as in—SNAP!—"Got your point!" Or—SNAP!—"Don't even try it." Or—SNAP!—"You *fierce!*" Or—SNAP!—"Get out my face." Or—SNAP!—"Girlfriend, *pleeeease.*" The snap can be as emotionally and politically charged as a clenched fist, can punctuate debate and dialogue like an exclamation point, a comma, an ellipse, or altogether negate the need for words among those who are adept at decoding its nuanced meanings.

But the particular appropriation of the snap by Hollywood's Black Pack deflates the gesture into rank caricature. Instead of a symbol of communal expression and, at times, cultural defiance, the snap becomes part of a simplistically reductive Negro faggot identity: It functions as a mere signpost of effeminate, cute, comic homosexuality. Thus robbed of its full political and cultural dimension, the snap, in this appropriation, descends to stereotype.

Is this any different from the motives and consequences associated with the legendary white dramatist T. D. Rice, who more than 150 years ago appropriated the tattered clothes and dance style of an old crippled black man, then went on stage and imitated him, thus shaping in the popular American mind an indelible image of blacks as simplistic and poor yet given, without exception, to "natural" rhythm and happy feet?

A family tree displaying dominant types in the cultural iconography of black men would show, I believe, an unmistakable line of descent from Sambo to the SNAP! Queen, and in parallel lineage, from the Brute Negro to the AIDS-infected Black Homo-Con-Rapist.

What the members of this pantheon share in common is an extreme displacement and distortion of sexuality. In Sambo and the SNAP! Queen sexuality is repressed, arrested. Laughter, levity, and a certain childlike disposition cement their mutual status as comic eunuchs. Their alter egos, the Brute Black and the Homo Con, are but psychosocial projections of an otherwise tamed sexuality run amuck—bestial, promiscuous, pathological.

Contemporary proponents of black macho thus converge with white supremacist D. W. Griffith in their cultural practice, deploying similar devices toward similarly dehumanizing ends. In their constructions of "unnatural" sexual aggression, Griffith's infamous chase scene in *Birth of a Nation*, in which a lusting "Brute Negro" (a white actor in blackface) chases a white Southern virgin to her death, displays a striking aesthetic kinship to the homophobic jail rap—or should I say, attempted rape?—in Reginald and Warrington Hudlin's *House Party*.

The resonances go deeper.

Pseudoscientific discourse fused with popular icons of race in late nineteenth-century America to project a social fantasy of black men, not simply as sexual demons, but significantly, as intrinsically corrupt. Diseased, promiscuous, destructive—of self and others—our fundamental nature, it was widely assumed, would lead us to extinction.

Against this historical backdrop consider the highly popular comedy routines of Eddie Murphy, which unite Negro faggotry, "Herpes Simplex 10"—and AIDS—into an indivisible modern icon of sexual terrorism. Rap artists and music videos resonate this perception, fomenting a social psychology that blames the *victim* for his degradation and death.

The sum total of primetime fag pantomimes, camp queens as culture critics, and the proliferating bit-part swish-and-dish divas who like ubiquitous black maids and butlers in fifties Hollywood films move along the edges of the frame, seldom at the center, manifests the persistent psychosocial impulse toward control, displacement, and marginalization of the black gay Other. This impulse, in many respects, is no different than the phobic, distorted projections which motivated blackface minstrelsy.

This is the irony: There are more black male filmmakers and rap artists than ever, yet their works display a persistently narrow, even monolithic, construction of black male identity.

"You have to understand something," explained Professor Griff of the controversial and highly popular rap group Public Enemy, in an interview. "In knowing and understanding black history, African history, there's not a word in any African language which describes homosexual, y'understand what I'm saying? You would like to make them part of the community, but that's something brand new to black people."

And so black macho appropriates African history, or rather, a deeply reductive, mythologized view of African history, to rationalize homophobia. Pseudoacademic claims of "Afrocentricity" have now become a popular invocation when black macho is pressed to defend its essentialist vision of the race. An inheritance from Black Cultural Nationalism of the late sixties, and Negritude before that, today's Afrocentrism, as popularly theorized, premises an historical narrative which runs thus: Before the white man came, African men were strong, noble, protectors, providers, and warriors for their families and tribes. In precolonial Africa, men were truly men. And women—were women. Nobody was lesbian. Nobody was feminist. Nobody was gay.

This distortion of history, though severe, has its seductions. Given the increasingly besieged state of black men in America, and the nation's historic subversion of an affirming black identity, it is no wonder that a community would turn to pre-Diasporan history for metaphors of empowerment. But the embrace of the African warrior ideal—strong, protective, impassive, patriarchal—has cost us. It has sent us down a perilous road of cultural and spiritual redemption, and distorted or altogether deleted from the historical record the multiplicity of identities around color, gender, sexuality, and class, which inform the African and African American experience.

It is to me supremely revealing that in black macho's popular appropriation of Malcolm X (in movies, music, rap videos), it is consistently Malcolm *before Mecca*—militant, macho, "by any means necessary" Malcolm—who is quoted and idolized, not Malcolm *after* Mecca, when he became more critical of himself and exclusivist Nation of Islam tenets, and embraced a broader, multicultural perspective on nationalist identity.

By the tenets of black macho, true masculinity admits little or no space for self-interrogation or multiple subjectivities around race. Black macho prescribes an inflexible ideal: Strong black men—"Afrocentric" black men—don't flinch, don't weaken, don't take blame or shit, take charge, step-to when challenged, and defend themselves without pause for self-doubt.

Black macho counterpoises this warrior model of masculinity with the emasculated Other: the Other as punk, sissy, Negro faggot, a status with which any man, not just those who in fact are gay, can be, and are, branded should one deviate from rigidly prescribed codes of hypermasculine conduct.

"When I say Gamma, you say Fag. Gamma. Fag. Gamma. Fag." In the conflict between the frat boys and the "fellas" in Spike Lee's *School Daze*, verbal fag-bashing becomes the weapon of choice in the fellas' contest for male domination. In this regard Lee's movie not only resonates a poisonous dynamic in contemporary black male relations but worse, Lee glorifies it.

Spike Lee and others like him count on the complicit silence of those who know better, who know the truth of their own lives as well as the diverse truths which inform the total black experience.

Notice is served. Our silence has ended. SNAP!

# 29

## DOES YOUR MAMA KNOW ABOUT ME?

Essex Hemphill

Throughout the 1980s, many of us grieved the loss of friends, lovers, and relatives who were one moment strong, healthy, and able-bodied, but then in an instant they became thin-framed, emaciated, hacking and wheezing, their bodies wracked with horrible pain. Sometimes brave souls would return to the family roost to disclose their sexuality and ask permission to die in familiar surroundings. Too often, families were discovering for the first time that the dear brother, the favorite uncle, the secretive son was a homosexual, a Black gay man, and the unfortunate victim of the killer virus, AIDS. Some parents had always known and some had never suspected that their son was a Black gay man, a sissy, a queer, a faggot. For some families this shocking discovery and grief expressed itself as shame and anger; it compelled them to disown their flesh and blood, denying dying men the love and support that friends often provided as extended family. In other instances families were very understanding and bravely stood by their brethren through their final days.

Joseph Beam, in his powerful essay "Brother to Brother: Words from the Heart," from *In the Life: A Black Gay Anthology* (Boston: Alyson Publications, 1986), defined *home* as being larger, more complex and encompassing than one's living room:

> When I speak of home, I mean not only the familial constellation from which I grew, but the entire Black community: the Black press, the Black

church, Black academicians, the Black literati, and the Black left. Where is
my reflection? I am most often rendered invisible, perceived as a threat to
the family, or I am tolerated if I am silent and inconspicuous. I cannot go
home as who I am and that hurts me deeply. (p. 231)

Beam articulated one of the primary issues Black gay men are faced with
when our relationships with our families and communities are examined.
We cannot afford to be disconnected from these institutions, yet it would
seem that we are willing to create and accept dysfunctional roles in them,
roles of caricature, silence, and illusion. In truth, we are often forced into
these roles to survive. This critical dilemma causes some of us to engage in
dishonest relationships with our kin. It can foster apathy between us and the
communities of home that we need and that need our presence. The contradictions of "home" are amplified and become more complex when Black
gay men's relationships with the white gay community are also examined.

The post-Stonewall white gay community of the 1980s was not seriously
concerned with the existence of Black gay men except as sexual objects. In
media and art the Black male was given little representation except as a big,
Black dick. This aspect of the white gay sensibility is strikingly revealed in
the photographs of Black males by the late Robert Mapplethorpe. Though
his images may be technically and esthetically well-composed, his work
*artistically* perpetuates racial stereotypes constructed around sexuality and
desire. In many of his images, Black males are only shown as parts of the
anatomy—genitals, chests, buttocks—close up and close cropped to elicit
desire. Mapplethorpe's eye pays special attention to the penis at the expense
of showing us the subject's face, and thus, a whole person. The penis becomes *the* identity of the Black male, which is the classic racist stereotype
recreated and presented as Art in the context of a gay vision.

Mapplethorpe's "Man in a Polyester Suit," for example, presents a Black
man without a head, wearing a business suit, his trousers unzipped, and his
fat, long penis dangling down, a penis that is not erect. It can be assumed that
many viewers who appreciate Mapplethorpe's work, and who construct
sexual fantasies from it, probably wondered *first* how much larger would the
penis become during erection, as opposed to wondering *who* is the man in
the photo or *why* is his head missing? What is insulting and endangering to
Black men is Mapplethorpe's *conscious* determination that the faces, the
heads, and by extension, the minds and experiences of some of his Black
subjects are not as important as close-up shots of their cocks.

It is virtually impossible while viewing Mapplethorpe's photos of Black
males to avoid confronting issues of exploitation and objectification. Additionally, Black gay men are not immune to the desire elicited by his photos. We, too, are drawn to the inherent eroticism. In "True Confessions: A
Discourse on Images of Black Male Sexuality" (*Ten-8*, No. 22, 1986), Isaac
Julien and Kobena Mercer accurately identify this dichotomy when they
observe that Mapplethorpe's images of Black males reiterate "the terms of
colonial fantasy" and "service the expectations of white desire." They then

ask the most critical question of all: "What do [Mapplethorpe's images] say to our wants and desires as Black gay men (p. 6)?"

It has not fully dawned on white gay men that racist conditioning has rendered many of them no different from their heterosexual brothers in the eyes of Black gays and lesbians. Coming out of the closet to confront sexual oppression has not necessarily given white males the motivation or insight to transcend their racist conditioning. This failure (or reluctance) to transcend is costing the gay and lesbian community the opportunity to become a powerful force for creating *real* social changes that reach beyond issues of sexuality. It has fostered much of the distrust that permeates the relations between the Black and white communities. And finally, it erodes the possibility of forming meaningful, powerful coalitions. When Black gay men approached the gay community to participate in the struggle for acceptance and to forge bonds of brotherhood, bonds so loftily proclaimed as *the vision* of the best gay minds of my generation, we discovered that the beautiful rhetoric was empty. The disparity between words and actions was as wide as the Atlantic Ocean and deeper than Dante's hell. There was no "gay" community for Black men to come home to in the 1980s. The community we found was as mythical and distant from the realities of Black men as was Oz from Kansas.

At the baths, certain bars, in bookstores and cruising zones, Black men were welcome because these constructions of pleasure allowed the races to mutually explore sexual fantasies, and, after all, the Black man engaging in such a construction only needed to whip out a penis of almost any size to obtain the rapt attention withheld from him in other social and political structures of the gay community. These sites of pleasure were more tolerant of Black men because they enhanced the sexual ambiance, but that same tolerance did not always continue once the sun began to rise.

Open fraternizing at a level suggesting companionship or love between the races was not tolerated in the light of day. Terms such as "dinge queen," for white men who prefer Black men, and "snow queen," for Black men who prefer white men, were created by a gay community that obviously could not be trusted to believe its own rhetoric concerning brotherhood, fellowship, and dignity. Only an *entire* community's silence, complicity, and racial apathy is capable of reinforcing these conditions.

Some of the best minds of my generation would have us believe that AIDS has brought the gay and lesbian community closer and infused it with a more democratic mandate. That is only a partial truth, which further underscores the fact that the gay community still operates from a one-eyed, one gender, one color perception of *community* that is most likely to recognize blond before Black, but seldom the two together.

Some of the best minds of my generation believe AIDS has made the gay community a more responsible social construction, but what AIDS really manages to do is clearly point out how significant are the cultural and economic differences between us; differences so extreme that Black men suffer a disproportionate number of AIDS deaths in communities with very sophisticated gay health care services.

The best gay minds of my generation believe that we speak as one voice and dream one dream, but we are not monolithic. We are not even respectful of one another's differences. We are a long way from that, Dorothy. I tell you Kansas is closer.

We are communities engaged in a fragile coexistence if we are anything at all. Our most significant coalitions have been created in the realm of sex. What is most clear for Black gay men is this: we have to do for ourselves *now*, and for one another *now*, what no one has ever done for us. We have to be there for one another and trust less the adhesions of kisses and semen to bind us. Our only sure guarantee of survival is that which we construct from our own self-determination. White gay men may only be able to understand and respond to oppression as it relates to their ability to obtain orgasm without intrusion from the church and state. White gay men are only "other" in this society when they choose to come out of the closet. But all Black men are treated as "other" regardless of whether we sleep with men or women — our Black skin automatically marks us as "other."

Look around, brothers. There is rampant killing in *our* communities. Drug addiction and drug trafficking overwhelm us. The blood of young Black men runs curbside in a steady flow. The bodies of Black infants crave crack, not the warmth of a mother's love. The nation's prisons are reservations and shelters for Black men. An entire generation of Black youths is being destroyed before our eyes. We cannot witness this in silence and apathy and claim our hands are bloodless. We are a wandering tribe that needs to go home before home is gone. We should not continue standing in line to be admitted into spaces that don't want us there. We cannot continue to exist without clinics, political organizations, human services, and cultural institutions that *we* create to support, sustain, and affirm us.

Our mothers and fathers are waiting for us. Our sisters and brothers are waiting. Our communities are waiting for us to come home. They need our love, our talents and skills, and we need theirs. They may not understand everything about us, but they will remain ignorant, misinformed, and lonely for us, and we for them, for as long as we stay away, hiding in communities that have never really welcomed us or the gifts we bring.

I ask you brother: Does your mama *really* know about you? Does she *really* know what I am? Does she know I want to love her son, care for him, nurture and celebrate him? Do you think she'll understand? I hope so, because I *am* coming home. There is no place else to go that will be worth so much effort and love.

# 30 BLACK SEXUALITY
## The Taboo Subject

CORNEL WEST

> "Here," she said, "in this here place, we flesh; flesh that weeps,
> laughs; flesh that dances on bare feet in grass. Love it. Love it
> hard. Yonder they do not love your flesh. They despise it. They
> don't love your eyes; they'd just as soon pick em out. No more do
> they love the skin on your back. Yonder they flay it. And O my
> people they do not love your hands. Those they only use, tie,
> bind, chop off and leave empty. Love your hands! Love them.
> Raise them up and kiss them. Touch others with them, pat them
> together, stroke them on your face 'cause they don't love that
> either. You got to love it, You! . . . This is flesh I'm talking about
> here. Flesh that needs to be loved."
>
> —TONI MORRISON, *Beloved* (1987)

Americans are obsessed with sex and fearful of black sexuality. The obsession has to do with a search for stimulation and meaning in a fast-paced,
market-driven culture; the fear is rooted in visceral feelings about black bodies fueled by sexual myths of black women and men. The dominant myths
draw black women and men either as threatening creatures who have the
potential for sexual power over whites, or as harmless, desexed underlings of
a white culture. There is Jezebel (the seductive temptress), Sapphire (the
evil, manipulative bitch), or Aunt Jemima (the sexless, long-suffering nurturer). There is Bigger Thomas (the mad and mean predatory craver of white
women), Jack Johnson, the super performer—be it in athletics, entertainment, or sex—who excels others naturally and prefers women of a lighter

hue), or Uncle Tom (the spineless, sexless—or is it impotent?—sidekick of whites). The myths offer distorted, dehumanized creatures whose bodies—color of skin, shape of nose and lips, type of hair, size of hips—are already distinguished from the white norm of beauty and whose feared sexual activities are deemed disgusting, dirty, or funky and considered less acceptable.

Yet the paradox of the sexual politics of race in America is that, behind closed doors, the dirty, disgusting, and funky sex associated with black people is often perceived to be more intriguing and interesting, while in public spaces talk about black sexuality is virtually taboo. Everyone knows it is virtually impossible to talk candidly about race without talking about sex. Yet most social scientists who examine race relations do so with little or no reference to how sexual perceptions influence racial matters. My thesis is that black sexuality is a taboo subject in white and black America and that a candid dialogue about black sexuality between and within these communities is requisite for healthy race relations in America.

The major cultural impact of the 1960s was not to demystify black sexuality but rather to make black bodies more accessible to white bodies *on an equal basis*. The history of such access up to that time was primarily one of brutal white rape and ugly white abuse. The Afro-Americanization of white youth—given the disproportionate black role in popular music and athletics—has put white kids in closer contact with their own bodies and facilitated more humane interaction with black people. Listening to Motown records in the sixties or dancing to hip hop music in the nineties may not lead one to question the sexual myths of black women and men, but when white and black kids buy the same Billboard hits and laud the same athletic heroes the result is often a shared cultural space where some humane interaction takes place.

This subterranean cultural current of interracial interaction increased during the 1970s and 1980s even as racial polarization deepened on the political front. We miss much of what goes on in the complex development of race relations in America if we focus solely on the racial card played by the Republican Party and overlook the profound multicultural mix of popular culture that has occurred in the past two decades. In fact, one of the reasons Nixon, Reagan, and Bush had to play a racial card, that is, had to code their language about race, rather than simply call a spade a spade, is due to the changed *cultural* climate of race and sex in America. The classic scene of Senator Strom Thurmond—staunch segregationist and longtime opponent of interracial sex and marriage—strongly defending Judge Clarence Thomas—married to a white woman and an alleged avid consumer of white pornography—shows how this change in climate affects even reactionary politicians in America.

Needless to say, many white Americans still view black sexuality with disgust. And some continue to view their own sexuality with disgust. Victorian morality and racist perceptions die hard. But more and more white Americans are willing to interact sexually with black Americans *on an equal basis* — even if the myths still persist. I view this as neither cause for celebration nor reason for lament. Anytime two human beings find genuine pleasure, joy, and love, the stars smile and the universe is enriched. Yet as long as that pleasure, joy, and love is still predicated on myths of black sexuality, the more fundamental challenge of humane interaction remains unmet. Instead, what we have is white access to black bodies on an equal basis — but not yet the demythologizing of black sexuality.

This demythologizing of black sexuality is crucial for black America because much of black self-hatred and self-contempt has to do with the refusal of many black Americans to love their own black bodies — especially their black noses, hips, lips, and hair. Just as many white Americans view black sexuality with disgust, so do many black Americans — but for very different reasons and with very different results. White supremacist ideology is based first and foremost on the degradation of black bodies in order to control them. One of the best ways to instill fear in people is to terrorize them. Yet this fear is best sustained by convincing them that their bodies are ugly, their intellect is inherently underdeveloped, their culture is less civilized, and their future warrants less concern than that of other peoples. Two hundred and forty-four years of slavery and nearly a century of institutionalized terrorism in the form of segregation, lynchings, and second-class citizenship in America were aimed at precisely this devaluation of black people. This white supremacist venture was, in the end, a relative failure — thanks to the courage and creativity of millions of black people and hundreds of exceptional white folk like John Brown, Elijah Lovejoy, Myles Horton, Russell Banks, Anne Braden, and others. Yet this white dehumanizing endeavor has left its toll in the psychic scars and personal wounds now inscribed in the souls of black folk. These scars and wounds are clearly etched on the canvass of black sexuality.

How does one come to accept and affirm a body so despised by one's fellow citizens? What are the ways in which one can rejoice in the intimate moments of black sexuality in a culture that questions the aesthetic beauty of one's body? Can genuine human relationships flourish for black people in a society that assaults black intelligence, black moral character, and black possibility?

These crucial questions were addressed in those black social spaces that affirmed black humanity and warded off white contempt — especially in black families, churches, mosques, schools, fraternities, and sororities. These precious black institutions forged a mighty struggle against the white supremacist bombardment of black people. They empowered black children to learn against the odds and supported damaged black egos so they could keep fighting; they preserved black sanity in an absurd society in which racism ruled unabated; and they provided opportunities for black love to stay alive. But these grand yet flawed black institutions refused to engage one fundamental issue: *black sexuality*. Instead, they ran from it like the plague. And they obsessively condemned those places where black sexuality was flaunted: the streets, the clubs, and the dance-halls.

Why was this so? Primarily because these black institutions put a premium on black survival in America. And black survival required accommodation with and acceptance from white America. Accommodation avoids any sustained association with the subversive and transgressive—be it communism or miscegenation. Did not the courageous yet tragic lives of Paul Robeson and Jack Johnson bear witness to this truth? And acceptance meant that only "good" negroes would thrive—especially those who left black sexuality at the door when they "entered" and "arrived." In short, struggling black institutions made a Faustian pact with white America: avoid any substantive engagement with black sexuality and your survival on the margins of American society is, at least, possible.

White fear of black sexuality is a basic ingredient of white racism. And for whites to admit this deep fear even as they try to instill and sustain fear in blacks is to acknowledge a weakness—a weakness that goes down to the bone. Social scientists have long acknowledged that interracial sex and marriage is the most *perceived* source of white fear of black people—just as the repeated castrations of lynched black men cries out for serious psycho-cultural explanation.

Black sexuality is a taboo subject in America principally because it is a form of black power over which whites have little control—yet its visible manifestations evoke the most visceral of white responses, be it one of seductive obsession or downright disgust. On the one hand, black sexuality among blacks simply does not include whites, nor does it make them a central point of reference. It proceeds as if whites do not exist, as if whites are invisible and simply don't matter. This form of black sexuality puts black agency center stage with no white presence at all. This can be uncomfortable for white people accustomed to being the custodians of power.

On the other hand, black sexuality between blacks and whites proceeds based on underground desires that Americans deny or ignore in public and over which laws have no effective control. In fact, the dominant sexual myths of black women and men portray whites as being "out of control"—seduced, tempted, overcome, overpowered by black bodies. This form of black sexuality makes white passivity the norm—hardly an acceptable self-image for a white-run society.

Of course, neither scenario fully accounts for the complex elements that determine how any particular relationship involving black sexuality *actually* takes place. Yet they do accent the crucial link between black sexuality and black power in America. In this way, to make black sexuality a taboo subject is to silence talk about a particular kind of power black people are perceived to have over whites. On the surface, this "golden" side is one in which black people simply have an upper hand sexually over whites given the dominant myths in our society.

Yet there is a "brazen" side—a side perceived long ago by black people. If black sexuality is a form of black power in which black agency and white passivity are interlinked, then are not black people simply acting out the very roles to which the racist myths of black sexuality confine them? For example, most black churches shunned the streets, clubs, and dance-halls in part because these black spaces seemed to confirm the very racist myths of black sexuality to be rejected. Only by being "respectable" black folk, they reasoned, would white America see their good works and shed its racist skin. For many black church folk, black agency and white passivity in sexual affairs was neither desirable nor tolerable. It simply permitted black people to play the role of the exotic "other"—closer to nature (removed from intelligence and control) and more prone to be guided by base pleasures and biological impulses.

Is there a way out of this Catch-22 situation in which black sexuality either liberates black people from white control in order to imprison them in racist myths or confines blacks to white "respectability" while they make their own sexuality a taboo subject? There indeed are ways out, but there is no one way out for all black people. Or, to put it another way, the ways out for black men differ vastly from those for black women. Yet, neither black men nor black women can make it out unless both get out since the degradation of both are inseparable though not identical.

Black male sexuality differs from black female sexuality because black men have different self-images and strategies of acquiring power in the patriarchal structures of white America and black communities. Similarly, black male heterosexuality differs from black male homosexuality owing to the self-perceptions and means of gaining power in the homophobic institutions of white America and black communities. The dominant myth of black male sexual prowess makes black men desirable sexual partners in a culture obsessed with sex. In addition, the Afro-Americanization of white youth has been more a male than a female affair given the prominence of male athletes and the cultural weight of male pop artists. This process results in white youth—male and female—imitating and emulating black male styles of walking, talking, dressing, and gesticulating in relation to others. One irony of our present moment is that just as young black men are murdered, maimed, and imprisoned in record numbers, their styles have become disproportionately influential in shaping popular culture. For most young black men, power is acquired by stylizing their bodies over space and time in such a way that their bodies reflect their uniqueness and provoke fear in others. To be "bad" is good not simply because it subverts the language of the dominant white culture but also because it imposes a unique kind of order for young black men on their own distinctive chaos and solicits an attention that makes others pull back with some trepidation. This young black male style is a form of self-identification and resistance in a hostile culture; it also is an instance of machismo identity ready for violent encounters. Yet in a patriarchal society, machismo identity is expected and even exalted—as

with Rambo and Reagan. Yet a black machismo style solicits primarily sexual encounters with women and violent encounters with other black men or
aggressive police. In this way, the black male search for power often reinforces the myth of black male sexual prowess—a myth that tends to subordinate black and white women as objects of sexual pleasure. This search for
power also usually results in a direct confrontation with the order-imposing
authorities of the status quo, that is, the police or criminal justice system.
The prevailing cultural crisis of many black men is the limited stylistic options of self-image and resistance in a culture obsessed with sex yet fearful of
black sexuality.

This situation is even bleaker for most black gay men who reject the major
stylistic option of black machismo identity, yet who are marginalized in
white America and penalized in black America for doing so. In their efforts
to be themselves, they are told they are not really "black men," not ma-
chismo-identified. Black gay men are often the brunt of talented black comics like Arsenio Hall and Damon Wayans. Yet behind the laughs lurks a
black tragedy of major proportions: the refusal of white and black America to
entertain seriously new stylistic options for black men caught in the deadly
endeavor of rejecting black machismo identities.

The case of black women is quite different, partly because the dynamics
of white and black patriarchy affect them differently and partly because the
degradation of black female heterosexuality in America makes black female
lesbian sexuality a less frightful jump to make. This does not mean that black
lesbians suffer less than black gays—in fact, they suffer more, principally
owing to their lower economic status. But this does mean that the subculture of black lesbians is fluid and the boundaries are less policed precisely
because black female sexuality in general is more devalued, hence more
marginal in white and black America.

The dominant myth of black female sexual prowess constitutes black
women as desirable sexual partners—yet the central role of the ideology of
white female beauty attenuates the expected conclusion. Instead of black
women being the most sought after "objects of sexual pleasure"—as in the
case of black men—white women tend to occupy this "upgraded," that is,
degraded, position primarily because white beauty plays a weightier role in
sexual desirability for women in racist patriarchal America. The ideal of female beauty in this country puts a premium on lightness and softness mythically associated with white women and downplays the rich stylistic manners
associated with black women. This operation is not simply more racist to
black women than that at work in relation to black men; it also is more de-
valuing of women in general than that at work in relation to men in general.
This means that black women are subject to more multilayered bombard-
ments of racist assaults than black men in addition to the sexist assaults they
receive from black men. Needless to say, most black men—especially professional ones—simply recycle this vulgar operation along the axis of lighter
hues that results in darker black women bearing more of the brunt than their

already devalued lighter sisters. The psychic bouts with self-confidence, the existential agony over genuine desirability, and the social burden of bearing and usually nurturing black children under these circumstances breeds a spiritual strength of black women unbeknownst to most black men and nearly all other Americans.

As long as black sexuality remains a taboo subject, we cannot acknowledge, examine, or engage these tragic psychocultural facts of American life. Furthermore, our refusal to do so limits our ability to confront the overwhelming realities of the AIDS epidemic in America in general and in black America in particular. Although the dynamics of black male sexuality differ from those of black female sexuality, new stylistic options of self-image and resistance can be forged only when black women and men do so together. This is so not because all black people should be heterosexual or with black partners, but rather because all black people—including black children of so-called "mixed" couples—are affected deeply by the prevailing myths of black sexuality. These myths are part of a wider network of white supremacist lies whose authority and legitimacy must be undermined. In the long run, there is simply no way out for all of us other than living out the truths we proclaim about genuine humane interaction in our psychic and sexual lives. Only by living against the grain can we keep alive the possibility that the visceral feelings about black bodies fed by racist myths and promoted by market-driven quests for stimulation do not forever render us obsessed with sexuality and fearful of each other's humanity.

# 31 WHEN YOU DIVIDE BODY AND SOUL, PROBLEMS MULTIPLY
## The Black Church and Sex

MICHAEL ERIC DYSON

> He healed my body, and told me to run on.
>
> —Gospel song, "Can't Nobody Do Me Like Jesus"

> Love . . . gives you a good feeling. Something like sanctified.
>
> —MARVIN GAYE, "Let's Get It On," 1973

> Sexual healing is good for me.
>
> —MARVIN GAYE, "Sexual Healing," 1982

The visiting preacher, a brawny brown man with smooth skin and teeth made of pearl, was coming to the close of his sermon, a ritual moment of climax in the black church. It is the inevitable point to which the entire service builds. Its existence is the only justification for the less dramatic rites of community—greeting visitors, collecting tithes, praying for the sick, reading scripture, and atoning for sins. These rites are a hallway to the sanctuary of zeal and vision formed by the black sermon. The furious splendor of the preacher's rhythmic, almost sung, speech drove the congregation to near madness. His relentless rhetoric stood them on their feet. Their bodies lurched in holy oblivion to space or time. Their hands waved as they shrieked their assent to the gospel lesson he passionately proclaimed. His cadence quickened. Each word swiftly piled on top of the next. The preacher's sweet moan sought to bring to earth the heavenly light of which his words, even at their most brilliant, were but a dim reflection.

"We've got to keep o-o-o-o-on keepin' on," he tunefully admonished. The preceding wisdom of his oration on Christian sexuality, arguing the link between passion and morality, turned this cliché into a sermonic clincher.

"We can't give up," he continued. "Because we've got God, oh yes, we've got Go-o-o-o-d, um-humh, on our side."

"Yes," members of the congregation shouted. The call and response between the pulpit and the pew escalated as each spurred the other on in ever enlarging rounds of emotion.

"We've got a friend who will never forsake us."

"Yes sir, Reverend."

"We've got a God who can make a way outta no way."

"Yes we do."

"He's a heart fixer, and a mind regulator."

"Oh, yes He is."

"I'm here tonight to tell you whatever moral crisis you're facin', God can fix it for you."

"Thank you, Jesus."

"If you're facin' trouble on the job, God can make your boss act better."

"Tell the truth, Reverend."

"If your kids won't act right, God can turn them around."

"Hallelujah!"

"If you're fornicating, and I know some of y'all been fornicatin', God can turn lust to love and give you a healthier relationship with Him."

"Hold your hope! Hold your hope!"

"If you're committin' adultery, and I know some of y'all are doing that, too, God can stop your rovin' eyes and keep you from messin' up. Won't He do it, church?"

"Yes! Yes He will!"

"If your marriage is fallin' apart, and there's no joy—I said there's no jo-oy-oy-oy—at your address, God can do for you what He did for David. David asked God: 'Restore unto me the joy of Thy salvation.' I'm a witness tonight, children. God can do that, church. God can restore your joy. Won't He do it, children?!"

"Yes He will! Thank you, Jesus! Thank you, Jesus!"

"I'm closin' now, but before I go, I just stopped by to let you know that you can't find salvation in things. You can't find salvation in clothes. You can't find salvation in your car. You can't find salvation in your wife or husband. And you certainly can't find salvation in sex. Did y'all hear me? You can't find salvation in sex. You can't find it in sleepin' around, tryin' to fill the empty places of your life with pleasure and loose livin'."

"Thank you, Jesus!"

"You can only find salvation in our Lord and Savior, Jesus Christ! Do y'all hear me? Jesus, that's who you need! Jesus, that's who can save you. Jesus, the author and finisher of our faith. Jesus! Jesus! Jesus!"

"Thank ya! Oh, hallelujah."

The congregation erupted in waves of shouting and hand-clapping as the minister withdrew from the microphone and dramatically spun to his seat. He was thoroughly spent from a 45-minute exercise in edification and enlightenment. As soon as he was done, his fellow ministers on the dais, including me, descended on the preacher's chair to thank him for his thoughtful, thrilling message. Sex, after all, is a difficult subject to treat in the black church, or, for that matter, in any church. This is indeed ironic. After all, the Christian faith is grounded in the Incarnation, the belief that God took on flesh to redeem human beings. That belief is constantly trumped by Christianity's quarrels with the body. Its needs. Its desires. Its sheer materiality. But especially its sexual identity.

I got a glimpse that night, or, I should say, a reminder, of how deeply ambivalent Christians are about sex. I learned, too, how dishonest we're sometimes made by the unresolved disputes between our bodies and our beliefs.

After the service was over, after the worshipers had time to greet and thank the preacher, we ministers, five in all, retired to the pastor's study.

"Doc, you blessed me tonight," beamed the pastor, a middle-aged preacher of no mean talent himself. (Among black ministers and their circle of intimates, "Doc" or "Doctor" is an affectionate term given to preachers. It began, perhaps, as a way of upgrading the minister to the level of respect his gifts deserved, especially at a time when black ministers were prevented from completing their formal education.)

"Thank you, man," the preacher gently replied with a kind of "aw shucks" smile.

"Yeah, Doctor, you were awful, just terrible, boy," a second minister enthused, heaping on the guest the sort of congratulation black preachers often give to one another.

"Revrun, it was judgment in here tonight," another minister chimed in with yet another line of black preacherly praise. "You killed everythang in here. And if it wasn't dead, you put it in intensive care." At that, we all laughed heartily and agreed that the preacher had hit his mark.

As a young minister in my early twenties, I was just glad to be in their number, bonding with ministerial mentors, men standing on the front line of spiritual warfare, or, as the black church memorably refers to it, "standing in the gap": carrying and crying the judgment of the Almighty, opening opportunity for salvation, proclaiming the soul's rescue and the requirements of redemption, and edifying believers with the inscrutable, wholly uncompromising, tell-it-like-it-is, to-be-preached-in-season-and-out-of-season gospel of the living God. I was simply enjoying this magical moment of fraternal friendliness. And it was just that. No women were there. No one thought it odd that they weren't. We never remarked once on their absence, and, indeed, we counted on their absence to say things, manly things, that we couldn't, didn't dare say, in mixed company. Still, I wasn't prepared for what followed.

"Revrun, I need to ask you something," the visiting preacher begged the pastor. His eyebrows were raised, a knowing look was on his face, and his voice affected, if not quite a mock seriousness, then a naughty whisper that clued us that his curiosity was more carnal than cerebral.

"Who is that woman with those big breasts who was sitting on the third aisle to my left?" he eagerly inquired. "Damn, she kept shouting and jiggling so much I almost lost my concentration."

"She *is* a fine woman, now," the pastor let on.

"Well, Doc, do you think you could fix me up with her?" the visiting preacher asked with shameless lust.

"I'll see what I can do, Revrun," the pastor promised.

The married preacher's naked desire shocked me. To my surprise, it also made me secretly envious. The fact that he could seek an affair less than an hour after he had thundered against it offended my naive, literal sense of the Christian faith. I thought immediately of how angry I'd been in the past when I heard preachers justify their moral failings, especially their sexual faults. Such ministers chided their followers with a bit of theological doggerel dressed up as a maxim: "God can hit a straight lick with a crooked stick."

But in ways I didn't yet completely understand, I envied the preacher's sense of sexual confidence. He was able to zoom in on his desire and, to borrow a favorite neo-Pentecostal catchphrase, "to name it and claim it." The preacher — and he was surely aware of it, since he didn't let principle stand in the way of his pleasure — had apparently made his peace, however temporary, with the war between Christian ideals and delights of the flesh. I hadn't.

Still, I'm glad I didn't mount a high horse that night to trample the preacher. I've developed enough failures in the sometimes bloody management of erotic desire. So have many other black Christians. Especially those seeking, like most people of faith, to close the gap between what they believe and how they behave. That night, I was nearly tortured by questions I couldn't answer. Was the preacher's theology off? Did he have a flawed understanding of how a Christian should view the body and its sexual urges? Was his extreme sexual libertarianism just plain out of order? Was he simply a hypocrite? Or was he acting out, however crudely, a confused sense of black Christian sexuality that is, by turns, repressed and excessive? Or all of the above?

The answers to these questions are not as simple as we might believe, despite the rigid certainty of self-anointed arbiters of Christian Truth. And neither are the answers relevant simply for cases, like the one I've described, where everyone can agree that something was wrong. It's much more difficult to figure out how we can have a healthy sense of black Christian sexual identity in a world where being black has been a sin, where black sexuality has been viewed as a pathology, and where the inability to own—and to own up to—our black bodies has led us to devalue our own flesh. We must recover the erotic uses of our bodies from the distortions of white racism and the traps of black exploitation. We must liberate ourselves to embrace the Christian bliss of our black bodies.

At the beginning of the African presence in the New World, black bodies were viewed in largely clinical and capitalist terms. The value of black slave bodies was determined by their use in furthering the reach of Western colonial rule; expanding the market economics of European and American societies; institutionalizing leisure for white cultural elites; deepening the roots of democracy for white property-owning gentry; and providing labor for the material culture that dominates the American landscape. Interestingly, when Christianity poked its nose in, chattel slavery, already a vile and dehumanizing affair, got even uglier.

Christianity insisted there was a need to save the savages from their own cultural deficits. White Christians sought to rescue slaves from perdition by making sure what little soul they had was made suitable for the Kingdom of God. Christianity gave theological legitimacy, and racial justification, to widely held beliefs about black inferiority. It also sanctified the brutal methods deemed necessary to tame the beastly urges of black Africans. White society exploited black labor. White Christianity made it appear that God was behind the whole scheme. Some argued that God used slavery as a tool to bring backward Africans to America. They believed God used white slavers to save black souls by subjugating their bodies. Christian theology shook hands with slavery and sailed off into the sunset of white supremacy.

A key to keeping blacks under white control was the psychological poison pumped into the intellectual diets of slaves. Whites viewed black bodies as ugly, disgusting, and bestial, and blacks were made aware of this. Black bodies were spoken of in the same breath as, say, horses and cows. As if being viewed as an animal wasn't bad enough, blacks were also considered property. Because of Western beliefs about the connection between moral and aesthetic beauty, the belief in the ugliness of black bodies carried over to attitudes about black souls.

Black sexuality sat at the heart of such judgments. If black bodies were demeaned, black sexuality was demonized. Unless, of course, it was linked to breeding black babies for slavery, or, in the case of black women, satisfying the lust of white men. Thus, a central paradox of black sexuality began. Even as whites detested black bodies for their raw animalism, they projected onto those same black bodies their repressed sexual yearnings. Black bodies provided recreational and therapeutic relief for whites. Although that paradox has certainly lessened, it has not entirely disappeared.

For the most part, black sexuality was cloaked in white fantasy and fear. Black women were thought to be hot and ready to be bothered. Black men were believed to have big sexual desires and even bigger organs to realize their lust. White men became obsessed with containing the sexual threat posed by black men. The competition for white women was mostly mythical. It was largely the projection of white men's guilt for raping black women. Even after slavery, white men beat, burned, hung, and often castrated black men in response to the perceived threat black men represented. White men also repressed white female sexuality by elevating a chaste white womanhood above the lustful reach of black men. Well before gangsta rap, the crotch was the crux of black masculine sexual controversy.

During slavery and after emancipation, blacks both resisted and drank in sick white beliefs about black sexuality. Some blacks sought to fulfill the myth of unquenchable black lust. The logic isn't hard to figure out: if white folk think I'm a sexual outlaw, some blacks perhaps thought, I'll prove it. Other blacks behaved in exactly the opposite fashion. They rigidly disciplined their sexual urges to erase stereotypes of excessive black sexuality. During slavery, many black women resisted sexual domination through abortion, abstinence, and infanticide. They interrupted white pleasure and profit one body at a time.

The rise of the black church, first as an invisible institution and then as the visible womb of black culture, provided a means of both absorbing and rejecting the sexual values of white society. Black religion freed the black body from its imprisonment in crude, racist stereotypes. The black church combated as best it could the self-hatred and the hatred of other blacks that white supremacy encouraged with evil efficiency. It fought racist oppression by becoming the headquarters of militant social and political action in black communities. The black church produced leaders who spoke with eloquence and prophetic vigor about the persistence of white racism. It was the educational center of black communities, supporting colleges that trained blacks who became shock troops in the battle for racial equality. Black churches unleashed the repressed forces of cultural creativity and religious passion. The church also redirected black sexual energies into the sheer passion and emotional explosiveness of its worship services.

I'm certainly not saying, as do those who argue that black religion compensates for racial oppression—we can't beat up the white man so we cut up in church—that the displacement of black sexual energy by itself shaped black worship. I'm simply suggesting that the textures, styles, and themes of black worship owe a debt to a complicated sexual history. In sharp contrast to the heat of most black worship experiences, there emerged almost immediately in black churches a conservative theology of sexuality. In part, this theology reflected the traditional teachings of white Christianity. Out of moral necessity, however, black Christians exaggerated white Christianity's version of "p.c."—Puritan Correctness. Later, many black Christians adopted white Christianity's Victorian repression to rebut the myth of black sexuality being out of control.

The contemporary black church still reflects the roots of its unique history. It continues to spawn social action, though not on the same fronts as it once did. The increased secularization of black communities, and the rise of political leadership outside of the black church, has blunted the focus of the church's prophetic ministry. Some things, however, have changed very little. There remains deeply entrenched in black churches a profoundly conservative theology of sexuality. Like all religious institutions where doctrine is questioned, rejected, perhaps even perverted by members, the black church faces a tense theological situation. Unlike, say, the Catholic or Episcopal church where an elaborate and more unyielding hierarchy prevails, historically black churches have a real opportunity to bring lasting change more quickly to their religious bodies. Such change is sorely needed in black communities and churches where issues of sexuality have nearly exploded.

Of course, there are problems that are easily identified but are difficult to solve. Earlier and earlier, black boys and girls are becoming sexually active. Teen pregnancy continues to escalate. Besides these problems, there are all sorts of sexual challenges that black Christians face. The sexual exploitation of black female members by male clergy. The guilt and shame that result from unresolved conflicts about the virtues of black sexuality. The continued rule of black churches by a mainly male leadership. The role of eroticism in a healthy black Christian sexuality. The revulsion to and exploitation of homosexuals. The rise of AIDS in black communities. The sexual and physical abuse of black women and children by black male church members. The resistance to myths of super black sexuality. And the split between mind and body that leads to confusion about a black Christian theology of Incarnation. What should be done?

For starters, the black church should build on a celebration of the body in black culture and worship. Ours, quite simply, is a body-centered culture. Sharp criticism by black intellectuals, including me, of essentialism—the idea that there is such a thing as black culture's essence, and that we get at it by viewing blacks as a monolith, ignoring differences made by region, sexuality, gender, class, and the like—has made many critics reluctant to highlight persistent features of black life. But in many African and black American communities, colorful, creative uses of the body prevail. (Unfortunately, as we have learned with resurgent slavery and genital mutilation of females in Africa, destructive and oppressive uses of the body mark our cultures as well.) Many black folk use vibrant, sometimes flamboyant, styles and colors to adorn their bodies. Johnnie Cochran's purple suit and Dennis Rodman's weirdly exotic hairstyles and body tattoos reveal a flare for outrageous, experimental fashion. Plus, the styling of black bodies for creative expression—Michael Jordan's gravity-rattling acrobatics, singer Anita Baker's endearing tics, Denzel Washington's smoothly sensuous gait, and Janet Jackson's brilliant integration of street and jazz dance—underscores the improvisational uses of black bodies.

The black church, too, is full of beautiful, boisterous, burdened, and brilliant black bodies in various stages of praising, signifying, testifying, shouting, prancing, screaming, musing, praying, meditating, singing, whooping, hollering, prophesying, preaching, dancing, witnessing, crying, faking, marching, forgiving, damning, exorcising, lying, confessing, surrendering, and overcoming. There is a relentless procession, circulation, and movement of black bodies in the black church: the choir gliding in and grooving to the rhythmic sweep of a grinding gospel number; members marching aisle by aisle to plop a portion of their earnings in the collection plate; women sashaying to the podium to deliver the announcements; kids huddling around the teacher for the children's morning message; the faithful standing at service's start to tell how good the Lord's been to them this week; the convicted leaping to their feet to punctuate a preacher's point in spiritual relief or guilt; the deliberate saunter to the altar of the "whosoever wills" to pray for the sick and bereaved, and for themselves; the white-haired, worldly-wise deacon bowing down at his seat to thank God that he was spared from death, that "the walls of my room were not the walls of my grave," his bed "sheet was not my winding sheet," and his bed was not "my cooling board"; the church mother shaking with controlled chaos as the Holy Ghost rips straight through her vocal cords down to her abdomen; the soloist's hands gesturing grandly as she bends each note into a rung on Jacob's ladder to carry the congregation "higher and higher"; the ushers' martial precision as they gracefully guide guests to a spot where they might get a glimpse of glory; the choir director calling for pianissimo with a guileless "shhhh" with one hand as the other directs the appointed soprano to bathe the congregation in her honey-sweet "ha-lay-loo-yuh"; and the preacher, the magnificent center of rhetorical and ritualistic gravity, fighting off disinterest with a "you don't hear me," begging for verbal response by looking to the ceiling and drolly declaring "amen lights," twisting his body to reach for "higher ground," stomping the floor, pounding the pulpit, thumping the Bible, spinning around, jumping pews, walking benches, climbing ladders—yes literally— opening doors, closing windows, discarding robes, throwing bulletins, hoisting chairs, moaning, groaning, sweating, humming, chiding, pricking, and edifying, all to better "tell the story of Jesus and his love." In the black church, it's all about the body: the saved and sanctified body, the fruitful and faithful body, working and waiting for the Lord.

The body, too, is at the center of what Christian theologians have long termed the "scandal of particularity": the very idea that an unlimited, transcendent God would become a human being, time-bound and headed for death, was just too hard for nonbelievers to swallow. That scandal has special relevance for black Christians, who draw courage from a God who would dare sneak into human history as a lowly, suffering servant. From the plantation to the postindustrial city, suffering blacks have readily identified with a God who, they believe, first identified with them.

The black church has helped blacks find a way to overcome pain, to live through it, to get around it, and, finally, to prosper in spite of it. Black religion has often encouraged black folk to triumph over tragedy by believing that undeserved suffering could be turned to good use. That idea sparked the public ministry of Martin Luther King, Jr., a towering son of the black church. The radical identification with Jesus' life and death, which happened, after all, in his body, has permitted black Christians to endure the absurd violence done to their bodies. Through church sacraments, black Christians nurtured and relieved their bodies' suffering memories. On every first Sunday of the month, or whenever they celebrated the Lord's Supper, black Christians broke bread and drank wine, knowing that Jesus' crucified body was their crucified body, and that Jesus' resurrected body could be theirs as well. Every time the words of Holy Communion were repeated, "this do in remembrance of me," black Christians remembered those lost warriors who once fought mightily against oppression but who now slept with the ancestors.

Above all, the Incarnation revealed to black folk a God who, when it came to battling impossible odds, had been there and done that. Because black Christians inevitably had to pass through the "valley of the shadow of death," they could take solace from a God who had faced a host of ills they faced. Divine abandonment. Cruel cursing. Ethnic bigotry. Religious marginalization. Unjust punishment. Spiteful epithets. And most important, vicious death. Just knowing that God had walked this same earth, eaten this same food, tasted this same disappointment, experienced this same rejection, fought this same self-doubt, endured this same betrayal, felt this same isolation, encountered this same opposition, and overcome this same pain often made the difference between black folk living and dying.

It is indeed ironic that, with so much staked on the body, many black Christians continue to punish themselves with the sort of extreme self-denial that has little to do with healthy sexuality. To a large extent, the black church has aimed to rid the black body of lascivious desires and to purge its erotic imagination with "clean" thoughts. All the while, the black worship experience formed the erotic body of black religious belief, with all the rites of religious arousal that accompany sexual union.

Indeed, the story of the visiting minister that begins this chapter portrays the erotic intensity of the black worship experience: the electric call-and-response between minister and congregation; the fervent temper of the preacher's words of wisdom and warning; the extraordinary effort by the minister to seduce the audience onto God's side through verbal solicitation; and the orgasmic eruption of the congregation at the end of the sermon. It requires no large sophistication to tell that something like sexual stimulation was going on.

Perhaps that's because there is a profound kinship between spirituality and sexuality. Great mystics figured that out a long time ago. More recently, so have black singers Marvin Gaye, the artist formerly known as Prince, and R. Kelly. Black Christians are reluctant to admit the connection because we continue to live in Cartesian captivity: the mind-body split thought up by philosopher Descartes flourishes in black theologies of sexuality. Except it is translated as the split between body and soul. Black Christians have taken sexual refuge in the sort of rigid segregation they sought to escape in the social realm—the body and soul in worship are kept one place, the body and soul in heat are kept somewhere else. That's ironic because, as critic Michael Ventura has argued, black culture, especially black music, has healed, indeed transcended, the split between mind and body inherited from Descartes and certain forms of Christian theology. Segments of secular black culture have explored the intimate bond of sexuality and spirituality. The black church has given a great deal to black culture, including the style and passion of much of black pop music. It is time the church accepted a gift in return: the union of body and soul.

The sensuality of our bodies must be embraced in worship. That sensuality should be viewed as a metaphor for the passion of our sexual relations as well. And vice versa. The link between sexuality and spirituality was hinted at when the Bible talked of the church as Christ's bride, and alternately, as the body of Christ. Because Christian belief is rooted in the Incarnation, in the body, Anglican theologian William Temple held that Christianity is literally the most material of all religions. The sheer materiality of our faith is not simply a protection against those versions of Christianity that get high on the soul's salvation and forget about the body's need to eat. It is also a rebuke to those who believe that God is opposed to our sexual pleasure. To twist literary critic Roland Barthes, we should celebrate the pleasure of the text, especially when the text is, literally, our bodies.

Simply put, the black church needs a theology of eroticism. Admittedly, that is a hard sell in an Age of Epidemic, where panic and paranoia, more than liberty and celebration, set our sexual moods. Of course, black sexuality has always thrived or suffered under a permanent sign of suspicion or revulsion. Still, that's no reason to be cavalier about sex when its enjoyment can kill us. A theology of eroticism certainly promotes safe sex. Our definition of safety, however, must include protection against the harmful sexual *and* psychic viruses that drain the life from our desire. Further, a theology of eroticism looks beyond the merely physical to embrace abstinence as a powerful expression of sexuality.

In the main, a theology of eroticism must be developed to free black Christian sexuality from guilty repression or gutless promiscuity. Sermon after sermon counsels black Christians to abstain from loose behavior. To sleep only with our mates. To save sex for permanent love. And to defer sexual gratification until we are married. In black churches, as with most religious institutions, hardly anyone waits for marriage to have sex. People sleep with their neighbor's spouse. Casual sex is more than casually pursued. And because the needs of their bodies make them liars with bad consciences, some drown their demons in a sea of serial monogamies. Little of this is highly pleasurable, but it's pleasurable enough to make us unhappy. Ugh!

What's even more intriguing is that the sermons pretty much stay the same. Black Christians pretty much tell their children and each other that that's how things ought to be. And consistency is seen as a substitute for tradition. But it certainly isn't. Vital, living traditions leave space for people to change bad habits because they have a better understanding of what the tradition should mean. As one wise churchman put it: *tradition* is the living faith of dead people, while the *traditional* is the dead faith of living people. Too often, the latter has ruled black churches. While we may share our forebears' faith, we can certainly leave aspects of their theologies behind.

A theology of eroticism is rooted in simple honesty about black sexuality. While we tell our kids not to have sex, more and more of them do. They are making babies, having babies, and dying from AIDS. The black church should lay off the hard line on teen sexuality. Sure, it must preach abstinence first. It should also preach and teach safe sex, combining condoms and common sense. It should tell kids from ages twelve through seventeen that when it's all said and done, human sexuality is still an enlarging mystery, a metaphor of how life seeks more of itself to sustain itself, of how life, as black theologian Howard Thurman remarked, is itself alive. (Of course, we adults could use a reminder of this as well.) Our sexuality is one way life reminds itself of that lesson. In the hands of groping teens, sex is often little more than bewilderment multiplied by immaturity, despite growing, groaning body parts that seem fit for the job. In an era when music videos, television commercials, daytime soaps, and nighttime cable movies exploit our kids' urges, it's no wonder that they, and indeed, all of us, have sex on the brain. If only we could use *that* organ more in our erotic escapades.

The bottom line, however, is that traditional black church methods of curbing teen sex aren't working. We must make a choice. Either we counsel our kids about how to have sex as safely as they can, or we prepare to bury them before their lives begin. The cruelty of contemporary sex is that the consequences of our kids' mistakes, the same mistakes we made, are often swift and permanent. Most black preachers and parents who tell kids they shouldn't have sex had sex as teens. If not, most of them surely tasted carnal pleasure before they were married. The guilt or embarrassment stirred by their hidden hypocrisy often makes them harsh and unyielding in their views on teen sexuality. The black church's theology of eroticism should place a premium on healthy, mature relations where lust is not mistaken for affection. It must make allowances for our children, however, to learn the difference, and to safely experiment with their bodies in pursuit of genuine erotic health. The black church should pass out condoms on its offering plates. At the least, it should make them available in restrooms or in the offices of clergypersons or other counselors. The days of let's-pretend-the-problems-will-go-away, never-fully-here-anyway, are now most certainly gone.

We must find remedies, too, for angst-ridden black preachers. Many of them stir anxiety in their congregations because of their own conflicted theology of sexuality. The visiting minister I spoke of earlier was bewitched by the erotic double-bind that traps some ministers. He preached a theology of sexuality that satisfied the demands of black church tradition. But he was also moved by erotic desires that are rarely openly discussed in black churches, or in the seminaries that prepare men and women to pastor. The sexual exploitation of black women by black preachers, and the seduction of preachers by female members, rests on just this sort of confusion. (Of course, it also rests on a gender hierarchy in black churches where women do much of the labor but are largely prevented from the highest leadership role: the pastorate. The *ecclesiastical apartheid* of the black church, which is more than 70 percent female, continues to reinforce the sexual inequality of black women.) In many cases, both parties are caught in the thralls of unfocused erotic desire. Such desire doesn't receive reasonable, helpful attention. It is either moralized against or it lands on the wagging tongues of church gossips.

As a very young pastor—I was all of 23 years old—I sometimes participated in the sort of sex play that mocks healthy erotic desire. Once, after assuming the pastorate of a small church in the South, I received a call from a desperate female parishioner.

"Reverend Dyson, I need to see you right away," the soft, teary voice on my phone insisted. "It's an emergency. I can't discuss it on the telephone."

It was seven o'clock at night. Since I lived nearly a hundred miles from the city where my church was located, it would take me at least an hour-and-a-half to reach her home.

"Alright, Ms. Bright (not her real name)," I replied. "I'll be there as soon as I can."

I told my fiancée Brenda, with whom I was living, that a member needed me to come immediately. I tore up the highway in a frantic race to Ms. Bright's home. I was a young, relatively inexperienced pastor, new on the job, and eager to please. When I arrived at Ms. Bright's home, her parents greeted me at the door. Judging by the surprised look on their faces, her parents had no idea of their daughter's distress, or her urgent request to see me. When she appeared a few minutes later, I didn't let on that I'd just zoomed to their house to help relieve their daughter of whatever problem she had. To them, I guess it looked like I had come courting on the sly. After all, neither of us was married, and Ms. Bright was only a few years older than me. Although I was in a committed relationship with Brenda, my members didn't know that we were, as the '70s R&B hit goes, "living together in sin." (Already living in the Bible Belt, perhaps on its buckle, I was caught in the crossfire between sex and soul almost before my career as a pastor began.)

Ms. Bright suggested that we go upstairs to her room to talk. We excused ourselves from pleasant chitchat with her amiable parents. We soon found ourselves alone in her stylish, sweetly scented bedroom. I felt awkward. I'd never spent time alone with her before outside of the few occasions we spoke in church. Besides, I didn't know what signal my presence in her boudoir might send. But I soon found out what was weighing on her heart and mind.

"Reverend Dyson, I think I'm in love with you," she blurted out.

I was genuinely startled. I had never been a Don Juan. And despite the crude stereotypes of ministers as lotharios out to bed every woman within speaking distance, I certainly hadn't been promiscuous. I could count the number of girlfriends I'd had on one hand. And I'd never been led to think of myself as irresistibly handsome. I wasn't a guy, like many I'd known, for whom women seemed to pant and pine. I was just Mike Dyson, the poor kid from Detroit who worked hard, studied long, and mostly lived out his sexual fantasies with a few beautiful women.

"Well, Ms. Bright, I, um, I, well, I'm very flattered," I barely managed. By now my yellow face was flushed and my eyes were boring holes in the floor. "I don't know what to say."

Then it hit me. My pastor, Frederick Sampson, knowing that the advice would one day come in handy, had given me a stern warning.

"Never let a woman down harshly, Mike," Dr. Sampson said. "Always be gentle and considerate." Eureka! Here was my out.

"You know, Ms. Bright, what you've said makes me feel good," I uttered with more conviction. "I'm truly honored that a woman like you would even be interested in me. But you know I'm in love with Brenda."

I saw the disappointment in her eyes. Quickly extending Sampson's rule, I was determined not to make Ms. Bright feel foolish.

"But if I was available, you're the kind of woman I would definitely like to be with."

And I wasn't just blowing smoke, as they say. Ms. Bright was a very intelligent, inquisitive woman, as our few conversations revealed. She was also a beautiful woman; a tall five feet ten inches, she dwarfed my five-foot-nine-inch frame. She had flawless chocolate skin, an incandescent smile, a sensuous voice, and a voluptuous figure.

"Really?" she replied.

In retrospect, I guess that gave her an opening. And despite denying it then, I probably wanted her to find it. Although each of us had been sitting on chairs in her room, Ms. Bright stood up and, well, descended on me. Standing directly above me, she confessed that she'd spent a great deal of time daydreaming about me.

"I just can't get you off my mind," she said. "I really think I'm in love with you, Reverend Dyson. I don't know what I'm going to do."

As the words rolled off her tongue, which I began to notice more and more, she began to run her fingers through my hair. I was embarrassed, ashamed, almost mortified—and extremely turned on.

"Well, I don't know either, Ms. Bright," I muttered. "I guess, well, I don't know, I guess we'll just have to . . . "

Before I could finish, she was kissing me. Before long, we were kissing each other. Our tongues dueled with more energy than we'd been able to devote to resolving her problem. Except now, it was our problem. I wasn't in love with her, but my lust was certainly piqued. Talk about not letting a woman down roughly; I certainly wasn't flunking that test. But I felt bad for cheating on Brenda. I yanked myself free from Ms. Bright's luscious lip-lock and came up for air, reaching as well for a little perspective.

"Look, Ms. Bright, I didn't mean for this to happen," I said through my heavy breathing. "After all, I'm your pastor, and I should be counseling you, not trying to get down with you."

She simply smiled. Then, before I could protest, she was out of her blouse. Next her bra fell to the floor! The queenly, regal pose she struck, part Pam Grier and part British royalty, made me feel like a lowly subject. And gawking at the sheer magnificence of her breasts, I was glad to be in her majesty's service. We groped each other like high-school teens stranded in a hormonal storm. After nearly a half-hour of this pantomimed intimacy, guilt suddenly overtook me. Better yet, the thought of having sex with her parents able to hear the bed creak and groan quenched my erotic fire. I recovered what little pastoral authority I had left—I think it was mixed up with my jacket and tie on the floor—and insisted that we quit. So we fixed up our clothes. Ms. Bright retouched her makeup, and without saying much—what could we say?—we went back downstairs to make small talk with her parents. After fifteen minutes or so, I bid them farewell and drove home far more slowly than I'd driven to my appointment. I was more disappointed at myself than angry at Ms. Bright. Despite what she said—and even she probably didn't really believe it—I didn't think Ms. Bright was in love with me. She simply had a crush, though, admittedly, it was a big one. Plus, she had a healthy dose of sexual desire, a subject we should have been able to talk about, not only in her house but in our church. We should have been able to refer to sex education classes, sermon series, Sunday-school discussions, Sunday-night forums, and a host of other ways that erotic desire might be addressed in the black church. Some churches are doing this, but they are far, far too few in number.

I was flattered that Ms. Bright wanted me. At the same time, I was ashamed that I'd given in to wanting her. I'd come to pray. I'd ended up the prey—the willing prey, as it turned out. Maybe Ms. Bright had seen the desire in my eyes, which failed to be disguised as pastoral concern. Maybe she was simply the first to act on what she knew we both wanted. Maybe she was just more honest.

On my way home, I couldn't help thinking of the visiting preacher. I got a lot more humble. Still, I kept thinking about my erotic encounter with Ms. Bright. Despite trying to feel bad about it, I found myself getting aroused all over again. I hadn't yet figured out that it's alright to enjoy erotic desire—to own up to the fact that you can be horny and holy—as long as you don't live at the mercy of your hormones. But if we can't talk about sex at home, and we can't talk about it at church, black Christians end up lying to ourselves and to the people to whom we're sexually attracted. And too often, we end up being much more destructive because of our erotic dishonesty.

Because so many black Christians have taken up the task of being sexual saviors—of crucifying the myths of black hypersexuality and sexual deviance—we abhor out-of-bounds sexuality. This social conservatism expresses itself as a need to be morally upright. Beyond reproach. (Unsurprisingly, gangsta rappers are high on the list of sinners. If its detractors actually ever listened to more than snippets of gangsta rap lyrics, they'd probably have a lot more grist for their critical mills.) Oh, if it was only that simple. If the black church—for God's sake, if *any* religious institution—was erotically honest, it would admit that the same sexual desire that courses through rappers' veins courses through the veins of its members. If many of the black ministers who wail against the sexual improprieties of hip-hop culture would be erotically honest, they'd admit that the same lust they nail rappers for breaks out in their own ranks. And there aren't too many sermons pointing that out.

The standard religious response has been: "Of course we have the same desires, but we fight them and put them in proper perspective." That's partly true. The desire is certainly fought. Why, you can see the strain of erotic repression on unmade-up faces, in long dresses that hide flesh, and in the desexualized carriage of bodies (notice the burden is largely on the women) in the most theologically rigid of orthodox black churches. But that's just the point: mere repression is not the proper perspective. We've got to find a mean between sexual annihilation and erotic excess. Otherwise, the erotic practices of church members will continue to be stuck in silence and confusion.

Neither are there many sermons that assail ministers for exploiting women. To be sure, there are women who think they were put on earth to please the pastor. For them, embracing his flesh is like embracing a little bit of heaven. Pastors should study their books on transference and help spread light on this fallacy. Of course, there are just as many women who simply get in heat over a man who can talk, especially if they've dealt with men for whom saying hello in the morning is an effort. So let's not romanticize the put-upon, helpless female who's charmed by the wiles of the slick, Elmer Gantry-like, minister-as-omnicompetent-stud-and-stand-in-for-God.

Too often, though, there are women who come to the minister seeking a helping hand who get two instead. Plus some lips, legs, arms—well, you get the picture. The black church is simply running over with brilliant, beautiful black women of every age, hue, and station. Pecan publicists. Ebony lawyers. Caramel doctors. Mocha engineers. Beige clerks. Bronze businesswomen. Brown housewives. Red-bone realtors. Yellow laborers. Coffee teachers. Blueblack administrators. Copper maids. Ivory tellers.

Chocolate judges. Tan students. Often these women are sexually pursued by the church's spiritual head, so to speak.

This fact makes it especially hard to endure the chiding of black preachers, veiled in prophetic language, launched at the sexual outlaws of black pop culture. In reality, the great Martin Luther King, Jr., is the patron saint of the sexual unconscious of many black ministers, but for all the wrong reasons. For most of the time he lived in the glare of international fame, King, as is well known, carried on affairs with many women. He wasn't proud of it. He confessed his guilt. He said he'd try to do better. But he just couldn't give it up. Plus, he was away from home for 28 days of most months. Lest too many critics aiming to bring King down a notch or two for his moral failings get any ideas, bear in mind that he spent that kind of time away from his wife and children, under enormous stress and at great peril to his life, leading the war against racial inequality.

Many black ministers have absorbed King's erotic habits, and those of many white and black ministers before and after him. But they have matched neither his sacrifice nor his achievements. Not that such factors excuse King's behavior. But they do help us understand the social pressures that shaped King's erotic choices. One must remember, too, the ecology of erotic expression for civil rights workers. The wife of a famous civil rights leader once told me civil rights workers often went to towns where their presence reviled whites and upset many complacent blacks. She said it was natural that they sexually fed off of each other within their tight circles of sympathy and like-minded perspective. That squares as well with King's comment that a lot of his philandering was a release from the extraordinary pressures he faced. That's probably a large part of the story, though it can't be the complete story. King's behavior apparently predates his fame. His philandering was a complex matter.

In some senses, King's erotic indiscretions were the expression of a Casanova complex, pure and simple. That complex is especially present in famous men whose success is a gateway to erotic escapades. Indeed, their fame itself is eroticized. Their success is both the capital and the commodity of sex. It procures sexual intimacy and is the gift procured by (female) sexual surrender. Then, too, for black men there is a tug-of-war occurring on the psychosexual battlefield. Black men occupy a symbolic status as studs. That stereotype is one of the few that black men refuse to resist. They embrace it almost in defiance of its obvious falseness, as an inside joke. (How many times did King tell white audiences that blacks wanted to be their brothers, not their brothers-in-law, even as white women flaunted themselves before him? King was even set to marry a white woman when he was in seminary, but she was sent away, and King was warned by a mentor that he would never be able to be a black leader with a white wife.)

There is also a specific psychology of the ministerial Casanova. He believes he merits sexual pleasure because of his sacrificial leadership of the church community. Ironically, he sees the erotic realm as an arena of ful-fillment because it is forbidden, a forbiddance that he makes a living preach-ing to others. (Yes, the cliché is certainly true that "That which is denied becomes popular.") But erotic forbiddance is a trap. The very energy exerted against erotic adventure becomes a measure for ministerial integrity. It be-comes the very force the minister must resist if he is to be erotically honest. Erotic desire both induces guilt in the minister and is his reward for preach-ing passionately about the need for the denial of erotic exploitation! Self-delusion and self-centeredness mingle in this arena of sexual desire.

All of this sets up an erotic gamesmanship between minister and the potential—often willing—object of his erotic desire. One of the rules of the game is, "Let's see if I can get him to fall, to act against what he proclaims as truth." This is more than simply a case of Jezebel out to seduce the minister. It is a case of erotic desire being expressed in a way that reflects the unequal relation between male leaders and female followers.

Many ministers who travel on the revival circuit—delivering sermons and giving a lift to the sagging spirits of churches across the nation—too often settle into comfortable habits of sexual exploitation. Their regimen of erotic enjoyment gets locked in early in their careers. They travel to churches, preach the gospel, meet a woman or women, have sex, return home, go back the next year and do the same. Even ministers who stay in place can roam their congregations, or the congregations of their peers, in search of erotic adventure. What it comes down to is that the Martin Luther King, Jrs., and the Snoop Doggy Doggs of black culture all want the same thing. The Snoops are up front about it. Most of us in the black church aren't.

The same erotic dishonesty applies to another sexual identity: homosexu-ality. The notorious homophobia of the black church just doesn't square with the numerous same-sex unions taking place, from the pulpit to the pew. One of the most painful scenarios of black church life is repeated Sunday after Sunday with little notice or collective outrage. A black minister will preach a sermon railing against sexual ills, especially homosexuality. At the close of the sermon, a soloist, who everybody knows is gay, will rise to perform a moving number, as the preacher extends an invitation to visitors to join the church. The soloist is, in effect, being asked to sing, and to sign, his theological death sentence. His presence at the end of such a sermon symbolizes a silent endorsement of the preacher's message. Ironically, the presence of his gay Christian body at the highest moment of worship also negates the preacher's attempt to censure his presence, to erase his body, to deny his legitimacy as a child of God. Too often, the homosexual dimension of eroticism remains cloaked in taboo or blanketed in theological attack. As a result, the black church, an institution that has been at the heart of black emancipation, refuses to unlock the oppressive closet for gays and lesbians.

One of the most vicious effects of the closet is that some of the loudest protesters against gays and lesbians in the black church are secretly homo-sexual. In fact, many, many preachers who rail against homosexuality are themselves gay. Much like the anti-Semitic Jew, the homophobic gay or lesbian Christian secures his or her legitimacy in the church by denouncing the group of which he or she is a member, in this case an almost universally despised sexual identity. On the surface, such an act of self-hatred is easy. But it comes at a high cost. Homophobic rituals of self-hatred alienate the gay or lesbian believer from his or her body in an ugly version of erotic Cartesianism: splitting the religious mind from the homosexual body as a condition of Christian identity. This erotic Cartesianism is encouraged when Christians mindlessly repeat about gays and lesbians, "we love the sinner but we hate the sin." A rough translation is "we love you but we hate what you do." Well, that mantra worked with racists: we could despise what racist whites did while refusing to despise white folk themselves, or whiteness per se. (Of course, there were many blacks who blurred that distinction and hated white folk as well as they pleased.) But with gay and lesbian identity, to hate what they do is to hate who they are. Gays and lesbians are how they have sex. (I'm certainly not reducing gay or lesbian identity to sexual acts. I'm simply suggesting that the sign of homosexual difference, and hence the basis of their social identification, is tied to the role of the sex act in their lives.)

The black church must develop a theology of homoeroticism, a theology of queerness. (Well, if we want to be absolutely campy, we might term it a theology for *Afriqueermericans*.) After all, if any group understands what it means to be thought of as queer, as strange, as unnatural, as evil, it's black folk. A theology of queerness uses the raw material of black social alienation to build bridges between gay and lesbian and straight black church members. The deeply entrenched cultural and theological bias against gays and lesbians contradicts the love ethic at the heart of black Christianity. Virulent homophobia mars the ministry of the black church by forcing some of our leading lights into secret and often self-destructive sexual habits. James Cleveland, considered the greatest gospel artist of the contemporary black church, died several years ago, it is rumored, from AIDS. Aside from embarrassed whispers and unseemly gossip, the black church still hasn't openly talked about it. Perhaps if gay and lesbian black church members could come out of their closets, they could leave behind as well the destructive erotic habits that threaten their lives.

The black church should affirm the legitimacy of homoerotic desire by sanctioning healthy unions between consenting gay and lesbian adults. After all, promiscuity, not preference, eats away at the fabric of our erotic integrity. Are gays and lesbians who remain faithful to their partners committing a greater sin than married heterosexuals who commit adultery? The ridiculousness of such a proposition calls for a radical rethinking of our black Christian theology of sexuality.

Central to the doctrine of Incarnation in the black church is the belief that God identified with the most despised members of our society by becoming the most despised member of our society. Sunday after Sunday, black ministers invite us to imagine God as, say, a hobo, or a homeless person. Well, imagine God as gay. Imagine God as lesbian. Is the gay or lesbian body of God to be rejected? Better still, isn't God's love capable of redeeming a gay or lesbian person? The traditional black theological answer has been yes, if that person is willing to "give up" his or her sin—in this case, being gay or lesbian—and turn to God. But a more faithful interpretation of a black theology of love and liberation asserts that God takes on the very identity that is despised or scorned—being black, say, or being poor, or being a woman—to prove its worthiness as a vehicle for redemption. We don't have to stop being black to be saved. We don't have to stop being women to be saved. We don't have to stop being poor to be saved. And we don't have to stop being gay or lesbian to be saved. Black Christians, who have been despised and oppressed for much of our existence, should be wary of extending that oppression to our lesbian sisters and gay brothers.

The black church continues to occupy the center of black culture. Although most black folk have never officially joined its ranks, the influence of the black church spreads far beyond its numbers. The black church raised up priests to administer hearing to wounded spirits in slavery. It produced prophets to declare the judgment of God against racial injustice. The black church has been at the forefront of every major social, political, and moral movement in black culture. It remains our most precious institution. It has the opportunity to lead again, by focusing the black erotic body in its loving, liberating lens. A daughter of the black community, Jocelyn Elders, attempted to bring the sharp insight and collective wisdom of our tradition to a nation unwilling to ponder its self-destructive sexual habits. Let's hope that her advice won't be lost on those closer to home. Like Marvin Gaye, black churches and communities need sexual healing. If we get healed, we might just be able to help spread that health beyond our borders.

---

Our youth could use a strong dose of that healing. Too often, though, black nostalgia for how we think things used to be for black folk dries up our compassion and sympathy for our youth. But we've got to find our way back into their heads. And we've got to let them back into our hearts. It will take both old and young hashing out our differences, and reaffirming our similarities, as we embrace across the chasm of age and perception. If we don't, we'll have bigger troubles than the ones we already face.

# 32

# "AIN'T NOTHIN' LIKE THE REAL THING"
## Black Masculinity, Gay Sexuality, and the Jargon of Authenticity

Kendall Thomas

Some years ago I found myself sitting with hundreds of other people in the sanctuary of the Cathedral of St. John the Divine in New York City, just a few blocks away from where I lived and worked in Morningside Heights, on the other side of Harlem. We had gathered to remember and celebrate the life of a writer whose novels, plays, and essays are a powerful record of his historical moment.

During the ceremony, a number of prominent African Americans from the literary world paid tribute to this man whose prophetic pen had given us such pain and pleasure. They all praised James Baldwin as a son of black Harlem who had faithfully borne witness to the suffering and struggle of his people. This, of course, was Jimmy the "bug-eyed griot" (in Amiri Baraka's words), the Baldwin of *Go Tell It on the Mountain*, *The Amen Corner*, and *The Fire Next Time*. Not one of these speakers mentioned the "other" Jimmy, the Baldwin of *Giovanni's Room*, *Another Country*, and *Just Above My Head*, whose stories I had read as a confused teenager in Oroville, California. As I sat in that cold, cavernous cathedral, the silence about this Baldwin cut me to the core, because I knew that while Baldwin may have left America because he was black, he left Harlem, the place he called "home," because he was gay. It was this "other" unacknowledged Jimmy whose stories I had devoured by flashlight under the bedsheets when I was supposed to be asleep. This Jimmy knew that many held him in contempt as an "aging, lonely, sexually dubious . . . unspeakably erratic freak."[1] It was in the words of this Jimmy and in "the heavy grace of God"[2] that I, like so many other confused teenagers, began to understand that those who called me "homo," "punk," or "sissy" did not really know, or care to know, my name. Reading Baldwin, I began to understand that I had another name. Somebody who lived somewhere in the south of France knew that name, and had written with deep insight and aching beauty about the experiences this name so imperfectly expressed. As Baldwin put it in a late interview, he had felt a "special responsibility" to serve as "a kind of witness" to "that phenomenon we call gay."[3]

In the years since Baldwin's death in 1987, his testimony as a witness to gay experience has become the target of a certain revisionist impeachment. One (but by no means the only) representative instance of this tendency is a recent review by Ekweume Michael Thelwell of James Campbell's *Talking at the Gates: A Life of James Baldwin*.[4] Thelwell launches a scathing attack on the Campbell biography by asserting that "certain writers—these days, mostly men and mostly white" find James Baldwin "a source of unending mystery and provocation."[5] Thelwell contrasts the "challenge" Baldwin poses for white readers with his reception among "most of us in the black world," for whom "Baldwin's life and career, though admittedly complex, are neither so ambiguous nor so troubling. . . ." (90). In Thelwell's account, *Talking at the Gates* belongs to a disturbing "new dispensation" of "'major,' 'corrective' new biographies by white men" of figures like Frederick Douglass, Paul Robeson, Martin Luther King, Jr., and Malcolm X, all of which have sought to "supplant the accounts of their lives left by the men themselves" (90). For Thelwell the chief characteristic Campbell's life of Baldwin shares with other recent biographical work on these "luminaries of the Afro-American experience" is its "spirit" of "intellectual appropriation, an assertion of literary and conceptual proprietorship. . . ." (90–91).

Now, there is more than a little irony in all this, since Thelwell betrays the very spirit of appropriation and proprietorship that he finds so objectionable in *Talking at the Gates*. I refer here to Thelwell's treatment of Baldwin's sexuality, to which the review first alludes in discussing the "virtues" of the Campbell biography. It is odd (to say the least) that the sole example Thelwell offers of the "thoughtful clarifications" for which *Talking at the Gates* should be commended is Campbell's observation that "Baldwin was *essentially androgynous* rather than homosexual" (92) (my emphasis). As one progresses through the essay, Thelwell's favorable assessment of this purported "clarification" of Baldwin's biography seems all the more curious. On the very next page of the review, Thelwell mentions the discomfort that Baldwin's "openly admitted sexual orientation" provoked among some of "the more 'established' Negro leaders" (93). The image of Baldwin as androgyne becomes even more perplexing when one comes to Thelwell's assertion (in the final paragraphs of his essay) that "slender, gay James Baldwin taught a generation of us how to be black men in this country, and he gave us a language in which to engage the struggle" (113). Needless to say, these last two remarks about Baldwin's sexuality sit uneasily with Thelwell's earlier insistence on the writer's essential androgyny.

What is at stake here? One could argue that Thelwell has simply failed to say what he means. Perhaps he intends to argue that Baldwin was "essentially bisexual" rather than "essentially androgynous," and unwittingly confuses an expression for gender identity (androgyny) with a reference to sexual orientation (bisexuality). Indeed, this reading of Thelwell would comport with the known facts, at least of Baldwin's early erotic life. Unhappily, Thelwell's utter silence about the substantial body of work Baldwin produced on homoerotic themes (about which Campbell himself has a great deal to say) leads the mind to a less comfortable conclusion. Taken together, Thelwell's equivocations about Baldwin's sexuality and his evident indifference to Baldwin's writings on the subject suggest that something more is involved here than linguistic mistake or conceptual confusion. Stated bluntly, Thelwell's vision of a "neutered" Baldwin betrays a deep and disturbing ideological investment regarding the connections among masculinity, sexuality, and "authentic" black identity.

How is this claim to be understood? The beginnings of an answer to this question might take us to the dictionary. "Androgyne" is a compound noun that consists of the Greek words (respectively) for man and woman. In its "positive" meaning the word refers to an individual who embodies "a mixing of secondary masculine and feminine sexual characteristics";[6] in its "negative" sense, the word refers to someone who is neither a man *nor* a woman. Moreover, the term "androgyny" has historically been the semantic site of a vertiginous slippage. As Francette Pacteau has noted, the "sexually ambiguous" figure of the androgyne simultaneously possesses a "dual sexual identity" *and* a "non-sexual identity."[7]

Both of these "impossible referents"[8] appear to be at work in the Thelwell review, and they suggest two different but equally disturbing understandings of the "androgyny" thesis. To interpret Thelwell's remark as a claim that Baldwin possessed a "dual sexual identity" is to view it as making an underlying, unstated argument about masculinity and male homosexuality. One might infer from Thelwell's remarks that he takes gay identity to be at odds with the very idea of masculinity. In this conception, which has a long pedigree, the male homosexual is deemed to possess "a woman's soul confined by a man's body."[9] The ascription of an ambiguous "dual" sexual identity to Baldwin allows Thelwell to confer a degree of masculinity on the writer to which a homosexual (read "effeminized") man cannot, by definition, lay claim. Needless to say, this understanding of the relationship between masculine identity and gay male sexuality betrays a very narrow vision of both.

A second possible reading of the "androgyny" thesis would take Thelwell's remark as a claim that Baldwin was not "bisexual" but "asexual" in both personality and practice. The implicit assumption here appears to be that sexual identity can be read off from sexual activity. According to this logic, if we want to know who Baldwin was (sexually speaking), we need only determine what (sexually speaking) he did or did not do. Presumably, we are supposed to conclude that because Baldwin did not lead an active sexual life (a fantastication that does not square with the known facts), he could not have been homosexual.[10]

This latter interpretation is in many ways even more distressing than the first, since it does not merely introduce an element of ambiguity regarding Baldwin's erotic affinities, but excludes them altogether. For better or worse, we live in a world in which individual identities are constructed in and through constructs of gendered sexual difference. The very notion of human subjectivity has come to rest on the fictional foundation of a stable, unified sexuality into which we are all inserted at birth. To say in such a world that an individual is androgynous in this second, neutered sense is in effect to deny that s/he exists: the androgyne has no sexual identity, which means that s/he has no identity at all. Nobody can know the androgyne's name, because there is no name by which s/he can be called.

In any event, I am less interested here in what the "androgyny" thesis *means* than in what it *does*. As I have already noted, Thelwell begins his essay by arguing that "most of us in the black world" do not find Baldwin's "admittedly complex" life and literary legacy "ambiguous" or "troubling." Nevertheless, it is clear that Thelwell's review may be read as a cultural brief, which seeks to secure a place for Baldwin in the patriarchal pantheon of "luminaries of the Afro-American experience" (the names of black women are tellingly absent from this list). While "most of us in the black world" may not doubt the significance of James Baldwin's contributions to the struggle against white supremacy in the United States (indeed, throughout the world), the fact remains that some of "us" do: one can point to any number of African Americans for whom Baldwin's sexuality raises an irrebuttable presumption against his inclusion in the annals of black American freedom fighters. Seen in this light, Thelwell's characterization of Baldwin's sexuality serves as a preemptive identificatory strike. Thelwell is surely aware of the ugly homophobic history of Baldwin's reception in certain quarters of black America. Sadly, his defensive insistence that Baldwin was "essentially androgynous" betrays the degree to which the writer's sexuality poses an evidentiary embarrassment for Thelwell himself. In making the case that Baldwin "almost singlehandedly elevated the terms of our discourse on race" (113), Thelwell cannot resist the felt but false necessity to discount, indeed to deny, the sexual dimensions of Baldwin's life. In doing so Thelwell's essay reveals its reliance on the homophobic rule of racial recognition to which his defense of the "androgynous" Baldwin is meant to provide a response. I refer here to the heteronormative logic that conditions the ascription of "authentic" black identity on the repudiation of gay and lesbian sexualities. This jargon of racial authenticity insists, in the words of gangsta-rapper Ice Cube, that "true niggers ain't gay."[11]

Whatever its motivation, Thelwell's awkward answer to those who would "deracinate" Baldwin and reduce the writer to his sexuality is to "desexualize" Baldwin and reduce him to his race. To be sure, these two equally misguided moves are impelled by very different purposes: where Baldwin's detractors remark his sexuality in order to renounce him, Thelwell minimizes Baldwin's sexuality in order to "redeem" him. Ultimately, however, this is a distinction without a difference. For in the final instance, the Thelwell essay stands as yet another example of the symbolic violence that has been inflicted on the name of James Baldwin even by African-American intellectuals who count themselves among the writer's most passionate proponents. The disingenuous disavowal of Baldwin's sexuality implicit in the contention that he was "essentially androgynous" not only deforms the facts of Baldwin's life but dismembers the man himself. Thelwell manages to maneuver his way around the question of Baldwin's sexuality only by engaging in the very "mythmaking, denial and distortion" (93) of which he charges others. To paraphrase Thelwell, there is a "spirit" of "appropriation" and "proprietorship" behind the confident claim that, sexually speaking, James Baldwin was "essentially" not who and what he himself said he was: a man who slept with other men. Baldwin once remarked of his early years, "I did not have any human identity."[12] In divesting the writer's biography of its homoerotic substance, Thelwell dishonors the memory of Baldwin's struggle to resolve what for a time was "the most tormenting thing"[13] in his life: the recognition, as Baldwin put it in his diary, that "I am a homosexual."[14] Seen in this light, Thelwell's "redemption" of Baldwin's name exacts too brutally high a price.

I do not wish my own interest in the case of James Baldwin to be misunderstood. Despite his willingness to talk and write publicly about his sexuality, Baldwin held that, for him, "one's sexual preference is a private matter."[15] Indeed, reading Baldwin's public pronouncements on the subject of sexuality, one cannot help but be struck by their ambivalence. In this respect Baldwin falls short of the achievement of his fellow writer Audre Lorde, whose contemporaneous reflections on gay and lesbian sexualities not only reveal an intellectual rigor but an uncompromising existential confidence regarding the "right and responsibility" of black women "to love where we choose."[16] In the one interview in which he treated the question of gay and lesbian sexualities at some length, Baldwin insisted that his erotic life "had nothing to do with these labels."[17] For Baldwin, the difficulty with the term "gay" was that it "answers a false argument, a false accusation," namely, that "you have no right to be here, that you have to prove your right to be here. I'm saying I have nothing to prove. The world also belongs to me."[18] Moreover, Baldwin's own experience persuaded him that "homosexual" was not a "noun" but a "verb," whose infinitive form is "to love": "I loved a few people and they loved me."[19]

Finally, Baldwin once stated that for black gay men and lesbians "[t]he sexual question comes *after* the question of color: it's simply one more aspect of the danger in which all black people live."[20] "A black person who is a sexual conundrum to society is already, long before the question of sexuality comes into it, menaced and marked because he's black or she's black."[21] At the same time, however, Baldwin remained emphatic about the indivisibility in his life and work of race, on the one hand, and of sexuality, on the other: "The sexual question and the racial question have always been entwined, you know."[22] Baldwin refused to say that sexuality had been "the most important part" of what he was about. "But," he added, "it's indispensable."[23]

My point is this. While I agree with Thelwell that James Baldwin "taught a generation of us how to be black men in this country, and he gave us a language in which to engage the struggle" (113), that was not Baldwin's only lesson. For all its ambivalence, the example of "slender, gay" (113) James Baldwin taught some of us how to be *gay* men in, and of, black America. The life and work of James Baldwin thus give the lie to the notion that black and gay identity are hostile to one another at all points. They show, too, that while "[i]t is difficult to be despised,"[24] black gay men and lesbians must resist the demand (heard in some quarters) that we must choose between these two sources of the self and commit a kind of psychic suicide. Baldwin provides us with an exemplary instance of someone who refused to make this false, and ultimately fatal, choice. We find in James Baldwin a sometimes equivocal, but always articulate, response to the call that gay and lesbian African Americans who want to prove that they are "really" black must renounce their sexuality: "I'm saying I have nothing to prove."

A decade after Baldwin's death it seems clear that the jargon of racial authenticity is alive and well in African-American sexual politics. Indeed, recent events suggest that the jargon has gained a new force, whose effects underscore the continuing relevance and urgency of what James Baldwin tried to teach us about the politics of sexual and racial identity, and its limitations. My project here is to challenge the terms of this jargon and to indicate the direction a critical account of it might take. I believe that the jargon of racial authenticity has had debilitating consequences for black American sexual politics. My hypothesis, in brief, is that the homophobia and virulent masculinism that underwrite the politics of racial authenticity in the current conjuncture are best understood as the displaced expression of internalized racism. I mean to show that the jargon of racial authenticity is an ideological symptom of a sexual anguish and alienation within black America of almost epidemic proportions. I shall argue that the embodied experience of gay, lesbian, and bisexual African Americans stands as a challenge to contemporary antiracist politics to break the grip of an increasingly homophobic black identity politics, and accord the right to black sexual freedom a place on its agenda.

My point of entry here is a moment from *Tongues Untied*,[25] a remarkable video work by one of James Baldwin's most accomplished cultural descendants, the late gay black artist and activist Marlon Riggs. In one of the most

powerful segments of *Tongues Untied*, Riggs offers an extended meditation
on the vexed relation between race and sexuality in black gay experience. At
one point in the narrative, a black nationalist remarks:

> They say, we're all on the same political boat. We should be brothers. But
> before I accept his kinship, political or otherwise, this is what I want to know.
> Where does his loyalty lie? . . . Priorities, that's what I want to know. Come the
> final throwdown, what is he first, black or gay?[26]

Riggs responds to this set of questions with another, which is framed in terms
that warrant some analysis: "How do you choose one eye over another, this
half of the brain over that? Or in words this brother might understand, which
does he value most, his left nut or his right?"[27]

To my mind, the most striking feature of this rejoinder to what Riggs calls
the "absurdity" of the black nationalist demand for a statement of "priorities"
lies in its metaphorical register. Riggs rightly takes this question of politics of
identity all the way down to body. Identity, in this image, is literally *refigured.*
The narrative of *Tongues Untied* shifts the terms of the debate over "authentic" black identity to the flesh-and-blood bodies on which racial (and other)
identities are inscribed. Riggs substitutes a materialist "language of the
body," thus exposing the poverty of the abstract, etiolated language of racial
authenticity that all too many nationalist ideologues have used to mask their
indifference to, and even contempt for, real, actually existing black lives.
*Tongues Untied* draws on the embodied experience of gay black men to insist
that any serious discussion of African-American identity and its attendant
politics must come to grips with the existential fact that "identity is fundamentally about desire and death."[28] The ethical challenge of *Tongues Untied* may thus be read as an aesthetic instance of a position to which Cornel
West has given a more sustained theoretical formulation. As West (drawing
interestingly enough on James Baldwin) so forcefully puts it:

> How you construct your identity is predicated on how you construct desire and
> how you conceive of death: desire for recognition; quest for visibility (Bald-
> win—*No Name in the Street; Nobody Knows My Name*); the sense of being
> acknowledged; a deep desire for association—what Edward Said would call
> affiliation. . . . But identity also has to do with death. We can't talk about
> identity without talking about death. That's what [a gay Puerto Rican] brother
> named Julio Rivera had to come to terms with: the fact that his identity had
> been constructed in such a way that xenophobes would put him to death. Or
> brother Youssef Hawkins in Bensonhurst. Or brother Yankel Rosenbaum in
> Crown Heights. Persons who construct their identities and desires often do it
> in such a way that they're willing to die for it—soldiers in the Middle East, for
> example—or under a national identity, that they're willing to kill others. And
> the rampant sexual violence in the lives of thousands of women who are at-
> tacked by men caught up in vicious patriarchal identities—this speaks to what
> we're talking about.[29]

This recasting of the terms of the identity debate from questions of ideology, identity, and consciousness to material matters of bodies, life, and death

provides a vantage point for critical consideration of issues that have been submerged by the jargon of racial authenticity, and by the obsessive search for black "realness" of which it is a part. One of the most pressing problems in contemporary African-American life is the culture of violence, which has brought devastation to far too many among us. I have argued elsewhere that this threat of violence and death is a continuing thread in gay, lesbian, and African-American experience in this country.[30] Along with African Americans of every sexual orientation, gay, lesbian, bisexual, and transgendered Americans of all colors live with and under the knowledge that at any time, anywhere, we might be attacked for being gay or lesbian or bisexual, for being black, or for being both. Indeed, in the United States, the historical roots of the consistent conjunction of homophobic and racist violence are older than the nation itself.

To take but one example, the 1646 Calendar of Dutch Historical Manuscripts reports the trial, conviction, and sentence on Manhattan Island, New Netherland Colony, of one Jan Creoli, "a negro, [for] sodomy; second offense; this crime being condemned of God (Gen., c. 19; Levit., c. 18:22, 29) as an abomination, the prisoner is sentenced to be conveyed to the place of public execution, and there choked to death, and then burnt to ashes."[31] On the same date the Calendar records the punishment meted out to "Manuel Congo . . . on whom the above abominable crime was committed," who was "to be carried to the place where Creoli is to be executed, tied to a stake, and faggots piled around him, for justice sake, and to be flogged; sentence executed."[32]

I mention the story of Manuel Congo and Jan Creoli not because of some felt necessity to "prove" that gay and lesbian sexualities are part of the black experience in America. I invoke it rather to underscore the political uses to which the history of African-American sexuality has been put. According to the jargon of authenticity, black American history is an essentially heterosexual or, more precisely, heteronormative history. In its more strident cultural nationalist versions, this history holds that gay and lesbian sexuality is alien to the "African tradition" on which the proponents of racial authenticity stake so much of their authority. (We may leave to one side the evidentiary difficulties that the well-documented history of same-sex intimacy in Africa poses for this claim. The asserted absence of homoerotic practices in "traditional" African societies would certainly come as a surprise to the Igbo people in Nigeria, the Basotho in Lesotho, the Kwayama and Ovimbundu in Angola, the Zulu and Bantu in South Africa, the Bakongo in Zaire, the Nandi in Kenya, the Konso and Amhara in Ethiopia, the Ottoro in Nubia, the Fanti in Ghana, the Thonga in Zimbabwe, the Tanala and Bara in Madagascar, the Wolof in Senegal, or the Dinka and Nuer in what is now the Sudan.)[33] In the heteronormative history of the jargon, the bodies of gay and lesbian African Americans are figured (insofar as they figure at all) as the contaminated effect of the encounter between a polluting white supremacy and a once pure (i.e., purely heterosexual) black desire.

One of the most troubling features of the jargon of authenticity lies in its deliberate distortion and denial of the convergent histories of racist and homophobic violence, of which the story of Manuel Congo and Jan Creoli represents but one instance. The heteronormative historical optic of black authenticity has blinded its proponents to the "scaling of bodies"[34] that has consigned black Americans and gay and lesbian Americans to adjoining, and sometimes identical, quarters at the bottom of our social order. The critical point is this. The history of blackness in this country is in large measure a history of degraded bodies and denigrated experience. The suggestion that gay and lesbian sexualities have not been a target of white racism's demonization of black desire is, quite simply, false. As a historical matter, the jargon of authenticity's arrogant insistence that "true niggers ain't gay" belongs less to the history of black sexuality than it does to the history of cynical ignorance and blatant ideological fraud.*

The preceding discussion has focused at some length on the fictive character of the historical account of black sexualities that underwrites the jargon of authenticity. However, my main aim here is not to challenge that jargon's account of our historical past but to make the case for a fresh perspective on our political present. I hope by now to have shown that the richest resource for thinking about the state of black America at the dawn of the twenty-first century is not the metaphysical illusion of an authentic racial identity but a material interest in actual, embodied black existence. In the remaining pages of this essay I want to explore what the move from the politics of black authenticity to a more inclusive body politics might mean in the current conjuncture. My specific concern is to indicate a few of the concrete possibilities that an embodied "politics of location"[35] creates for strategic alliances within as well as across movements against racism and homophobia. I shall proceed by canvassing a number of recent episodes in which a progressive black politics would have been better served by the shift in perspective and practice I am urging here.

The first is the political controversy surrounding the airing of Marlon Riggs's *Tongues Untied*. *Tongues* was produced for broadcast as part of the P.O.V. series of the Public Broadcasting System (PBS). It was the subject of at least two ugly episodes. Some twenty of the fifty PBS stations in the nation's largest markets flatly refused to air the work, and the Federal Communications Commission received a number of formal complaints about the video, filed by conservative media advocacy groups. A few months later *Tongues Untied* became a flashpoint of contention when Pat Buchanan

---

* To avoid misunderstanding, I should make it clear that I in no way mean to imply that violence, death, and degradation (and the often heroic response to them) represent the sum and substance of either black or queer life in the United States. I would say rather that it is precisely in the culture of black joy and queer pleasure that gay, lesbian, and African Americans have found some of the most effective political weapons with which to resist racist and homophobic domination.

produced campaign commercials during his bid for the 1992 Republican
presidential nomination that prominently featured images from the video
depicting men dancing semiclothed. Shortly thereafter, legislation was introduced to abolish the National Endowment for the Arts (NEA), which had
supported production of the video. Buchanan's charge that Bush's NEA had
"glorified homosexuality" also figured in the president's decision to fire John
Frohnmayer, head of the NEA.[36]

During the skirmishes for which *Tongues Untied* served as a site of intersection, African Americans remained largely silent about this cynical political deployment of black cultural representation. This silence stood in striking contrast to the charges of racism leveled by many African Americans
when a series of prosecutions was initiated against the black rap group 2 Live
Crew and individuals who marketed their album *As Nasty as They Wanna
Be* because of its graphic sexual nature.[37] You will recall that in that case the
misogynistic lyrics of 2 Live Crew, which celebrated the mutilation of black
women's bodies, were defended by leading scholars as an example of black
cultural genius. No such cultural defenses were forthcoming for Marlon
Riggs, whose *Tongues Untied* had offered a trenchant critique of the violence directed against black gay and lesbian bodies.

Similarly, few black voices were raised during the campaign to protest the
radio and video airplay of "Boom Bye Bye," in which reggae rapper Buju
Banton warned "Faggots to run / Or get a bullet in the head":

> Homeboys don't condone nasty men
> They must die
> Two men necking
> Lying in a bed
> Hugging each other
> And caressing one another's legs
> Get an automatic or an Uzi instead
> Shoot them now, let us shoot them.[38]

It takes no great insight to see that Banton's murderous melodic call belongs to the same culture of violence that has filled this nation's hospitals,
morgues, and mortuaries with the bullet-ridden bodies of young black men
and women, and populated its prisons with the "homeboys" who have
maimed and killed them. Now, I would like to think that the perspective I
have offered here might well have led greater numbers of African Americans
to engage the issues raised by these episodes. Again, the ground of this engagement would not be an exclusionary identitarian appeal to racial authenticity, but a more inclusive ethical apprehension of the danger the culture of
violence poses to black Americans of whatever sexual orientation, and to gay
and lesbian Americans of all colors.

To understand that antiracist and antihomophobic politics are informed
by a common ethical interest is to create the possibility of coalition across
difference. But that is not all. A politics of embodiment sees homophobic
violence or violence against women as part of the danger "in which all black

people live,"[39] and thus realizes (as Kimberlé Crenshaw has recently argued) that black identity itself represents a process and product of coalition.[40] It is important in this connection to say a word about what for me is perhaps the most disturbing dimension of the jargon of authenticity in the present period. The discourse of authentic black identity has been increasingly accompanied by an authoritarian effort to impose its normative vision. The proponents of authenticity have fashioned a crude racialist litmus test to establish true "blackness," which African Americans for whom the organicist idea of a unitary racial identity is neither a necessary nor desirable predicate for progressive antiracist politics predictably fail to pass. In the name of an imagined unity, the politics of racial authenticity has thus given rise to an aggressive, antidemocratic impulse. This politics has obscured the inflection of, and the antagonisms *within*, racial identity produced by differences of ethnicity, class, gender, religion, sexuality, and the like.

Consider in this connection the policing of racial identity that informed the politics of the recent Million Man March in Washington, D.C. In the months leading up to the October 1995 March, black feminist as well as gay and lesbian activists questioned its militant masculinist thrust. They recalled the long and ugly record of sexist and homophobic statements by the chief organizer of the March, the Nation of Islam's Minister Louis Farrakhan, of which these menacing words from a 1990 speech are a characteristic example:

> Now brothers, in the Holy world you can't switch. [Farrakhan walks across the stage like an effeminate man] No, no no . . . in the Holy world you better hide that stuff 'cause if God made you for a woman, you can't go with a man . . . You know what the penalty of that is in the Holy land? Death . . . They don't play with that . . . [he laughs] Sister get to going with another sister—Both women [are decapitated].[41]

Given this history, critics of the March rightly contended that Farrakhan's call to black men to gather in Washington, D.C., for a demonstration of their "at-one-ment" could not be divorced from his previous homophobic pronouncements. In the matter of sexual diversity, Louis Farrakhan's authoritarian vision of the black public sphere seemed to differ only in its details from the "New Jack-Boot City" depicted in Buju Banton's "Boom Bye Bye."

These concerns about the authoritarian sexual politics behind the Million Man March were compounded when March organizers failed to respond to the reported remarks of one of its spokesmen, the renegade ex-Catholic priest, the Reverend George Stallings, Jr. During a radio program in which a journalist canvassed the objections to Farrakhan's leadership of the March, Stallings offered the following gay-baiting reply: "What kind of leader do you want? A milque-toast? Some sissy-faggot?"[42] Against this backdrop, gay and lesbian African Americans had every reason to view the Million Man March with suspicion.

Our suspicions were not allayed even when as staunch a progressive ally as Cornel West lent his support to the Million Man March. Writing in the *New*

*York Times*, West justified his participation in the March on the grounds that it would "highlight black suffering."[43] "The demonstration," argued West, "is about the general invisibility of, and indifference to, black sadness, sorrow and social misery, and the disrespect and disregard in which blacks are held in America and abroad."[44] What West, Michael Dyson, and other progressive intellectuals never fully addressed was the demonstrated indifference, indeed the morbid delight, that the leader of the march has time and again expressed at the idea of inflicting "black suffering" on the bodies of gay and lesbian African Americans: for us, Louis Farrakhan embodies the very "Politics of Death" against which he had mobilized the million men who came to the Washington Mall. We simply could not ignore the fact that the affirmation of black manhood staged at the Million Man March seemed to *require* the denigration of gay and lesbian African Americans as an enabling condition for its own formation. To many gay and lesbian African Americans the Million Man March was yet another confirmation of our continued invisibility, exclusion, and exile beyond the boundaries of the black public sphere.

Nonetheless, for all its exertions, the rhetorical politics of racial authenticity cannot erase the fact that "blackness" is invariably "lived in the modality"[45] of sexuality and *vice versa*: this is because sexuality is always "racialized" and race always "sexuated." In this respect, the chief lesson I draw from recent work on the construction of racial and sexual identities is that the two depend on one another for their force and form. The search for independent, autonomous racial and sexual identities can never fully or finally succeed. To borrow from Nick Ashford and Valerie Simpson, then, we might say that there "Ain't nothin' *like* the real thing." In their refusal to accept the impossibility of a pure racial identity, the ideologists of black masculinism (not all of whom are men) prove nothing so much as the depths of their own racial and sexual alienation in the signifiers of authenticity. In the retreat to a heterosexist conception of black identity, the jargon of racial authenticity does not repudiate but instead reveals its reliance on the white supremacist logic from which it purports to declare its independence. The homophobic jargon of authenticity simply transposes racism's register into a darker, but no less destructive key. Ironically, the heteronormative vision of a unitary racial identity that would suppress sexual difference among African Americans does not exorcise the specter of white supremacy from the body of black America, but rather reincorporates white racism's phobic conceptions of black sexuality in the denigrated figure of the colored homosexual. In a classic case of strange bedfellows, the homophobic proponents of authenticity thus find themselves embraced in an odd alliance with the racist ideology to which they otherwise claim to be opposed.

Finally, the jargon of racial authenticity forecloses a recognition that what social theorist Benedict Anderson has said about the notion of a "nation" holds true as well for the unitary conception of a "race." That is, it blinds us to the fact that membership in a race, like membership in a national community, is "imagined." Most African Americans "will never know most of their fellow-members, meet them, or even hear of them, yet in the minds of each lives the image of their communion."[46] This is most emphatically not to say that the imagined racial subject comes into being in conditions of its own making. One would be remiss not to point out the institutional and ideological imperatives by which the notion of a racial community takes one form rather than another. It is to suggest that the authentically black self is in significant measure what political theorist William Connolly has called a "branded" or "entrenched" contingency.[47]

What this means, I think, is that the discourse of collective racial identity must, as a political matter, be understood and engaged as a technique or strategy. We may say here of race what James Baldwin once said of sexuality: it is not a noun but a verb. To view "blackness" as a contingent situated strategy is to see that a racial rhetoric that holds out the promise of liberation at one moment may become perilous to our survival down the road. Assertions of black identity that once served as an indispensable tool at one historical moment in the struggle for racial justice may now have become unwitting traps. Gay and lesbian African Americans have borne the heavy costs exacted by the rigid adherence to the illusory ideal of a unitary black identity. The exclusion of black gay men and lesbians from full, equal participation in African-American life has provided an epistemic standpoint for understanding and intervening in the politics of life and death. We know that the obsessive preoccupation with proof of racial authenticity deflects attention and energy away from the need to come to grips with the real, material challenges in whose resolution black Americans of both genders and all sexual identifications have an immediate and urgent interest. In the spirit of James Baldwin, black gay men and lesbians must continue to argue clearly and without compromise that they have nothing to prove. On the contrary, the burden of proof should be shifted onto those who instituted the jargon of authenticity to show its continued relevance to African-American life in the "the Age of Crack"[48] and Uzis and AIDS. Baldwin wrote in *Notes of a Native Son* that because he loved America "more than any other country in the world," he insisted on the right "to criticize her perpetually."[49] Our love for black America demands no less.

## NOTES

A slightly different version of this essay appears in *Representing Black Men*, ed. Marcellus Blount and George P. Cunningham (New York: Routledge, 1996), 55–69.

1. James Baldwin, *No Name in the Street* (New York: Dell, 1972), 18.

2. James Baldwin, *Giovanni's Room* (New York: Dell, 1956), 223.

3. Richard Goldstein, "'Go the Way Your Blood Beats': An Interview with James Baldwin," reprinted in *Lesbians, Gay Men, and the Law*, ed. William B. Rubenstein (New York: New Press, 1993), 41.

4. James Campbell, *Talking at the Gates: A Life of James Baldwin* (New York: Penguin, 1991).

5. Ekwueme Michael Thelwell, "A Profit Is Not Without Honor," *Transition* 58 (1992): 90. All subsequent citations will appear in the text.

6. Francette Pacteau, "The Impossible Referent: Representations of the Androgyne," in *Formations of Fantasy*, ed. Victor Burgin, James Donald, and Cora Kaplan (New York: Methuen, 1986), 62.

7. Ibid.

8. Ibid.

9. David Halperin, *One Hundred Years of Homosexuality and Other Essays on Greek Love* (New York: Routledge, 1990), 23.

10. Or, presumably, heterosexual. It bears remarking that the terms of the opposition Thelwell draws explicitly ignore this logical entailment.

11. O'Shea Jackson (Ice Cube), "Horny Lil' Devil," *Death Certificate* (Priority Records, 1991).

12. Campbell, *Talking at the Gates*, 3.

13. Goldstein, "'Go the Way Your Blood Beats,'" 42.

14. Campbell, *Talking at the Gates*, 33. Although Thelwell does not cite it, the one possible textual warrant for his insistence that Baldwin was "androgynous" is the late essay "Here Be Dragons," which originally appeared in *Playboy* under the title "Freaks and the American Ideal of Manhood." (James Baldwin, "Here Be Dragons," in *The Price of the Ticket* [New York: St. Martin's/Marek, 1985].) Baldwin argues in this essay that "we are all androgynous, not only because we are all born of a woman impregnated by the seed of a man but because each of us, helplessly and forever, contains the other— male in female, female in male . . . " (ibid., 690). Throughout the article, however, Baldwin takes care not to conflate claims regarding gender politics with those about sexual identity and practice. This much is clear from the fact that, alongside the claim that androgyny is a generalized figure of the human condition, "Here Be Dragons" is replete with quite specific references by Baldwin to his sexual experiences with other men and to "how I found myself in the gay world" (ibid., 686). I am grateful to Cora Kaplan for drawing my attention to this text.

15. Goldstein, "'Go the Way Your Blood Beats,'" 44.

16. Audre Lorde, "Scratching the Surface: Some Notes on Barriers to Women and Loving," originally published in *The Black Scholar* 9, no. 7 (1978), reprinted in *Sister Outsider: Essays and Speeches* (Freedom, Calif.: Crossing, 1984), 52.

17. Richard Goldstein, "'Go the Way Your Blood Beats,'" 44.

18. Ibid., 45.

19. Ibid., 44.

20. Ibid., 42.

21. Ibid. As these remarks suggest, Baldwin's argument has to do with the chronology of black gay and lesbian experience, not the priority of black or gay lesbian identity.

22. Ibid.

23. Ibid., 41.

24. Ibid., 44.

25. *Tongues Untied*, prod. and dir. Marlon Riggs, 55 min., color, 1985, videocassette.

26. Ibid.

27. Ibid.

28. Cornel West, "Identity: A Matter of Life and Death," in *Prophetic Reflections: Notes on Race and Power in America* (Monroe, Mass.: Common Courage Press, 1993), 163.

29. Ibid., 163–64.

30. See my "Beyond the Privacy Principle," *Columbia Law Review* 92, no. 6 (October 1992): 1431–1516.

31. Jonathan Ned Katz, *Gay American History: Lesbians and Gay Men in the U.S.A.* (New York: Harper & Row, 1976), 22–23.

32. Ibid., 23. What is more, for reasons that I cannot delineate in detail here, it seems

fairly clear that both homophobic violence and racist violence have a distinctly erotic component. (I might note parenthetically that if you are a black gay man or lesbian, you know, too, that this eroticized violence might come from the hands of someone who looks like your father, uncle, or brother.)

33. A useful summary can be found in William N. Eskridge, Jr., "A History of Same-Sex Marriage," *Virginia Law Review* 79, no. 7 (October 1993): 1419–1513.

34. Iris Marion Young, *Justice and the Politics of Difference* (Princeton, N.J.: Princeton University Press, 1990), 122.

35. The term is Adrienne Rich's. Adrienne Rich, "Notes Toward a Politics of Location," in *Blood, Bread, and Poetry* (New York: Norton: 1986), 210.

36. A useful documentary history of the recounted episodes may be found in Richard Bolton, ed., *Culture Wars: Documents from the Recent Controversies in the Arts* (New York: New Press, 1992).

37. In June 1990, lyrics in 2 Live Crew songs about sodomy and sexual intercourse were adjudged obscene by a federal district court. *Skywalker Records, Inc. v. Navarro*, 739 F. Supp. 578, 596 (S. D. Fla. 1990). A federal circuit court of appeals reversed this conviction in *Luke Records, Inc. v. Navarro*, 960 F. 2d 134 (11th Cir. 1992).

38. From the album *Boom Bye Bye*. Produced by Clifton "Specialist" Dillon and Bobby "Digital" Dixon. Distributed by VP Records (Jamaica, Queens, N.Y.), 1992.

39. Goldstein, "'Go the Way Your Blood Beats,'" 42.

40. Kimberlé Williams Crenshaw, "Mapping the Margins: Intersectionality, Identity Politics, and Violence Against Women of Color," in *Stanford Law Review* 43, no. 6 (1991), 1299.

41. Louis Farrakhan, *The Time and What Must Be Done* (videotape of a speech given on May 20, 1990, in Oakland, California, produced by The Final Call, Inc., Chicago, Illinois). The quoted remarks are taken from Ron Simmons, "Some Thoughts on the Challenges Facing Black Gay Intellectuals," in Essex Hemphill, ed., *Brother to Brother: New Writings by Black Gay Men* (Boston: Alyson Publications, 1991), 222.

42. Kevin McGruder, "Black Men Marching: You Don't Have to Be Loud to Be Strong," *City Sun*, September 13–19, 1995, 29.

43. Cornel West, "Why I'm Marching in Washington," *New York Times*, October 14, 1995.

44. Ibid.

45. Judith Butler, *Bodies That Matter: On the Discursive Limits of "Sex"* (New York: Routledge, 1993), 117.

46. Benedict Anderson, *Imagined Communities: Reflections on the Origin and Spread of Nationalism* (New York: Verso, 1983), 15.

47. William E. Connolly, *Identity/Difference: Democratic Negotiations of Political Paradox* (Ithaca, N.Y.: Cornell University Press, 1991), 176.

48. Eugene Rivers, "On the Responsibility of Intellectuals in the Age of Crack," *Boston Review* 3 (September–October 1992): 3–4.

49. James Baldwin, *Notes of a Native Son* (Boston: Beacon, 1984), 9.

# EPILOGUE
## Reflections on Black Manhood

BEVERLY GUY-SHEFTALL

I am eager to burn
this threadbare masculinity
this perpetual black suit
I have outgrown

—Essex Hemphill

We need to hear from black men who are interrogating sexism,
who are striving to create different and oppositional visions of
masculinity.

—bell hooks

In preparation for the writing of this essay, it was a joy to recall my experiences as a young Black girl growing up in Memphis, Tennessee, with positive male role models within my own family, church, and the segregated schools I attended. I thought, in particular, about my grandfather, Rev. Willie L. Varnado, who was deeply religious, compassionate, sensitive, responsible, reliable, hard-working, non-materialistic, committed to the welfare of Blacks, and respectful of women. As a teenager I considered him to be an almost perfect man, as was my Uncle Frank who had married my mother's older sister, Aunt Doris, and seemed to have been the ideal husband/companion. In fact, as we were growing up, the girls in the family fantasized about marrying someone just like Uncle Frank, though my mother teasingly told us that when God made our uncle, He threw away the pattern! My grandfather certainly defied every stereotype that the dominant culture harbors about southern Black men.[1]

There have been competing notions, to be sure, within African American communities about healthy Black manhood, which can be illustrated in the following oppositional assertions from two influential Black activists. According to Malcolm X, "the true nature of a man is to be strong, and a woman's true nature is to be weak. And while a man must at all times respect his women, at the same time he needs to understand that he must control her if he expects to get her respect."[2] Audre Lorde, on the other hand, contemplates the impact of a White supremacist patriarchal order on Black men: "Raising Black children, female and male, in the mouth of a racist, sexist, suicidal dragon is perilous and chancy. If they cannot love and resist at the same time, they will probably not survive. I wish to raise a Black man who will not be destroyed by nor settle for those corruptions called power by the white fathers who mean his destruction as surely as they mean mine. I wish to raise a Black man who will recognize that the legitimate subjects of his hostility are not women, but the particulars of a structure that programs him to fear and despise women as well as his own Black self."[3]

My own scholarly interest in gender issues and African American men began while I was conducting doctoral research for a study of attitudes toward Black women in the late nineteenth and early twentieth centuries. After reading Rosalyn Terborg-Penn's essay, "Black Male Perspectives on the 19th-Century Woman," I was eager to probe further the nature of progressive gender politics among Black men whose public discourse we would now label "profeminist."[4] Upon completion of the dissertation, *Daughters of Sorrow: Attitudes Toward Black Women*, 1880–1920, whose title was inspired by William E. B. Du Bois's essay "The Damnation of Women," I intended to write an essay on the personal and historical circumstances which produced African American men who were disloyal to patriarchy in their writings and activism, but I soon realized that I had much more work to do.

I was impacted during this period by the work of other Black feminists. As early as 1970, Toni Cade Bambara, whose ground-breaking book, *The Black Woman*, explored gender politics within the African American community at the height of the civil rights and Black nationalist movements, wrote a stunning critique of Black sexism and challenged "revolutionary" brothers to rethink notions of Black manhood which were in fact "counter-revolutionary":

> We profess to be about liberation but behave in a constricting manner; we rap about being correct but ignore the danger of having one half of our population regard the other with such condescension and perhaps fear that that half finds it necessary to "reclaim his manhood" by denying her her peoplehood. . . . We'd better take the time to fashion revolutionary selves, revolutionary lives, revolutionary relationships. . . . Sitting around murder-mouthing incorrect niggers [sic] while your father goes upside your mother's head is not revolutionary. . . . Talking about moving against the Mafia while your nephew takes

off old ladies at the subway stop is not revolutionary. If your house ain't in
order, you ain't in order.[5]

I was also influenced by bell hooks who has written extensively about
masculinity and the need for Black men and women to embrace a revolutionary feminist politics. She argues passionately that "the reconstruction
and transformation of male behavior, of masculinity, is a necessary and
essential part of feminist revolution,"[6] and that women should speak to and
about men in a feminist voice. She is also convinced that despite patriarchy
and sexism, there is a potential among Black men for radical transformation
with respect to their gender attitudes and behavior.

More recently, Barbara Omolade has written about gender politics within the Black community and the need for a "gender agenda which emphasizes the protection and care for Black children; which meets Black teenagers' need for tough love and support; and encourages dialogue and healing
among and between Black men and Black women."[7] She has also written
poignantly, in an autobiographical essay, about her involvement with Black
nationalist and feminist struggles, about the pain she experienced working
in a battered women's shelter in the late 1970s when she learned that cultural nationalist women were "being beaten by the same brothers who had
written poetry about African queens and who were active in Black political
work. I never had time to slip into the illusion that spouse abuse was the
practice of unpolitical Black men, drug addicts or just plain mean men."[8]

My interest in Black feminist theory intensified during graduate school at
Emory University and resulted some years later in the publication of *Words
of Fire* (New Press, 1995), a collection of non-fictional essays which traces
the evolution of feminist thought among African American women from the
1830s to the present. During the course of this project, I also began to collect
profeminist writings by African American men going back to the nineteenth
century which I imagined would result in a companion volume to *Words of
Fire*. I wanted to make the argument that our century-and-a-half-old (at
least) feminist intellectual tradition in this country included brave, transgressive Black men as well. I became convinced that the long process of Black
men becoming disloyal to patriarchy would begin with a different education about their forefathers. It is important for Black boys and men to know
that historically their brothers not only fought for racial equality; they also
fought for gender equality. They needed to be told or reminded that Frederick Douglass and William E. B. Du Bois were relentless women's rights
crusaders; that Douglass was the lone Black at the 1848 Seneca Falls wom-
en's rights convention and had pushed white women toward a more radical
agenda by insisting, along with Elizabeth Cady Stanton, that women's
suffrage be added to their agenda. At the end of his life, when he was reflecting on his accomplishments, Douglass asserted that it wasn't what he
had done for the race that he felt most proud about; it was what he had done
for women. He was proud of the critical role he played at Seneca Falls, and
in 1888 he spoke to the International Council of Women during which he

fondly reminisced: "I have done very little in this world in which to glory, except this one act. . . . When I ran away from slavery it was for my people; but when I stood up for the rights of women self was out of the question, and I found a little nobility in the act." We must rewrite African American history to include the struggles for gender equality within our own backyards. This would include Black nationalist organizations, such as Marcus Garvey's United Negro Improvement Association, particularly the work there of Amy Jacques Garvey. It would include the anti-homophobic writing of Black Panther Party leader Huey P. Newton, and the pro-feminist writing of Bayard Rustin whose recent biography reveals the problems he faced within the civil rights movement because he was gay.[9]

It is important to analyze the personal struggles and evolution of Black activist men, such as that of Malcolm X, who repudiated his sexist past, after he left the Nation of Islam, questioning his earlier problematic gender attitudes. During an interview in Paris three months before he was assassinated, Malcolm X made statements about women which illustrate significant shifts in his views on women:

> One thing that I became aware of in my traveling recently through Africa and the Middle East . . . usually the degree of progress can never be separated from the woman. If you're in a country that's progressive, the woman is progressive. . . . And I frankly am proud of the contributions that our women have made in the struggle for freedom and I'm one person who's for giving them all the leeway possible because they've made a greater contribution than many of us men.[10]

While Haki Madhubuti has sometimes been included in line-ups of sexist Black nationalists because of some of his earlier writings, we must examine his eloquent essay, "Becoming Anti-Rapist," from his new book *Claiming Earth* in which he acknowledges the traps of patriarchal socialization and its negative consequences for the Black community:

> Male acculturation . . . is anti-female, anti-womanist/feminist, and anti-reason when it comes to women's equal measure and place in society. . . . Most men have been taught to treat, respond, listen, and react to women from a male's point of view. Black men are not an exception here. We, too, are imprisoned with an intellectual/spiritual/sexual understanding of women based upon antiquated male culture and sexist orientation (or miseducation). . . . If men can liberate themselves (with the help of women) from the negative aspects of the culture that produced them, maybe a just, fair, good, and liberated society is possible in our lifetime.[11]

Similarly, we can mark the profound changes in Calvin Hernton's writings about women from the publication of his disturbing *Sex and Racism in America* (1965) to his profeminist *The Sexual Mountain and Black Women Writers*, an exposé of sexism within the Black literary establishment, published twenty-two years later:

> Although black and white men stand on opposing sides of the racial mountain in America, they tread on common ground when it comes to the mountain of

sex. . . . The "fathers" and purveyors of black writing have been men. . . . The
male authors have portrayed male heroes and male protagonists almost exclusively, and the complexity and vitality of black female experience have been
fundamentally ignored.[12]

He also chronicles the beginning of a rabid anti-Black feminist writers
backlash within the Black community in the aftermath of the 1976 Broadway production of Ntozake Shange's *For Colored Girls Who Have Considered Suicide When the Rainbow Is Enuf* and the publication four years later
of Michele Wallace's book, *Black Macho and the Myth of the Super Woman.*
The May/June 1979 issue of *Black Scholar* ("The Black Sexism Debate")
came on the heels of the previous issue, which included the hateful, controversial review of *Black Macho* by sociologist Robert Staples, a regular contributor to *Black Scholar* and an apologist for Black men in his numerous
publications about masculinity. It is also important to point out that a year
later the nationalist writer/activist Kalamu ya Salaam (who contributed to
the 1979 issue of *Black Scholar* as well) published a collection of his essays,
*Our Women Keep Our Skies From Falling: Six Essays in Support of the
Struggle to Smash Sexism and Develop Women* (1980), in which there is an
unmistakable profeminist Black male standpoint. Instead of maligning Black
feminism and its advocates, Salaam affirms the value of this new movement
which challenges the hegemony of Black patriarchal praxis. His disloyalty to
heterosexism is also apparent in his affirmations of the work of Black lesbian
writers Cheryl Clarke and Audre Lorde. I also developed while compiling
*Words of Fire* an intense interest in the marriages of public Black political
figures—Ferdinand and Ida Wells Barnett, Robert and Mary Church Terrell,
John and Lugenia Burns Hope, Paul Lawrence Dunbar and Alice Dunbar
Nelson, Paul and Eslanda Robeson—a subject which has received little
scholarly attention. I believe that a serious analysis of the institution of marriage among particular segments of the Black community would help us understand how couples with high-profile political lives negotiate complex
gender issues in their interpersonal relationships. Eventually I hope to complete this project with my friend, colleague, and co-editor, Rudolph P. Byrd.
I also decided that while all of my publishing projects (with the exception of
*Words of Fire*) had been collaborative efforts with other women, it would be
important to engage in this work with profeminist Black men as well. *Traps*
is the first of what I hope will be similar efforts in this regard.

The issue of Black masculinity, which has recently been explored in an
outpouring of publications on the topic, is certainly not a new concern for
Black men which is evident in Calvin Hernton's *Sex and Racism in America*
(1965), Eldridge Cleaver's *Soul on Ice* (1968), William Grier and Price
Cobbs's *Black Rage* (1969), and Robert Staples's *Black Masculinity: The
Black Male's Role in American Society* (1982). What is new and refreshing is
the appearance of gender-progressive, anti-homophobic texts, such as Phillip Harper's *Are We Not Men? Masculine Anxiety and the Problem of African
American Identity* (1996), Keith Boykin's *One More River to Cross: Black and*

*Gay in America* (1996), and Michael Awkward's *Negotiating Difference: Race, Gender, and the Politics of Positionality* (1995), which could be labeled "Black male feminist" texts.[13] There is also a growing number of Black male scholars who employ feminist analytical frameworks, who reject masculinist paradigms, and who struggle to be anti-sexist and anti-homophobic. The scholarly work of Robert Reid-Pharr, Gary Lemons, Kevin K. Gaines, Kendall Thomas, Robin Kelley, Michael Awkward, Luke Charles Harris, Thandabantu Iverson, and Devon Carbado,[14] among others, belongs in this category and suggests that new models of Black manhood are not only possible but already present.

It is also important to remember that Black men's "practices of masculinity," to borrow Awkward's terminology, have always been varied.[15] There is Cheryl Clarke's portrait of her father who was "scarce as hen's teeth." Because he worked nights, his day

> began at 8:00 a.m. with breakfast for my two sisters and me, after which he drove my sisters and me, our various and sundry friends, and some stragglers to our particular schools. While we were in school, he shopped, cleaned the house, did the laundry, raked the leaves, mowed the lawn, and made preparations for our return. . . . He made sure that my sisters and I practiced piano, did homework, played a bit, and ate the dinner he had prepared for us. . . . it was my father who taught me arithmetic, showed me how to print letters, took my sisters and me to the library every week during the summer, monitored our schoolwork. . . .[16]

She would grow up to be a well-known lesbian feminist writer and critic who would describe her father as the nurturer and friend who pushed her "to a larger world and a larger self" (188). Mary Helen Washington's father, David, was the antithesis of Mr. Clarke and she recalls how she both hated and feared him:

> My mother did the grocery shopping for our family on the bus. . . . She got eight children ready for church on Sunday by herself and rode with us on the bus while he drove alone in a new car to his church, passing us on the way to worship God. (82)

Mary Helen grew up to be a well-known feminist literary critic and informs us that not one of her father's eight children grew up to be abusive or cruel or violent.

Rudolph and I hope that *Traps* will provide some useful solutions and cures for what ails us as African Americans where gender and sexuality matters are concerned. We believe that new visions of manhood can be liberating and healing. At the beginning of a new century, Black men and women must struggle for "revolutionary selves, revolutionary lives, revolutionary relationships," which Toni Cade Bambara asserted three decades ago. Rejecting the traps of patriarchy, sexism, and homophobia, African Americans might continue our journey toward freedom in racist America and offer new visions and possibilities for this nation, the world, and generations yet unborn.

## NOTES

1. See Gloria Wade-Gayles, ed., *Father Songs: Testimonies by African-American Sons and Daughters* (Boston: Beacon Press, 1997), for portraits of a variety of Black familial figures, many of whom are not patriarchal, as was the case with my own father who is described in "Confessions: Remembering Walter P.," 310–315.

2. Malcolm X, *The Autobiography of Malcolm X* (New York: Grove Press, 1965), 226.

3. Audre Lorde, "Man Child: A Black Lesbian Feminist's Response," *Sister Outsider: Essays and Speeches* (Freedom, Calif.: Crossing Press, 1984), 74.

4. Sharon Harley and Rosalyn Terborg-Penn, eds., *The Afro-American Woman: Struggles and Images* (Port Washington, N.Y.: Kennikat Press, 1978).

5. Toni Cade, "On the Issue of Roles," *The Black Woman: An Anthology* (New York: Penguin, 1970), 103 and 110. E. Frances White in her pioneering essay, "Africa on My Mind: Gender, Counter Discourse, and African-American Nationalism," *Journal of Women's History* 2 (Spring 1990), 73–97, was one of the first to critique the gender politics of Black nationalism. More recently, Patricia Hill Collins has written an insightful critique of Black nationalist projects such as Afrocentricism by examining its conservative gender ideologies in her recent book *Fighting Words: Black Women and the Search for Justice* (Minneapolis: University of Minnesota Press, 1998).

6. bell hooks, *Talking Back* (Boston: South End Press, 1989), 18

7. "Gender in Black," *The Rising Song of African American Women* (New York: Routledge, 1994), 98.

8. See her essay "Sisterhood in Black and White" in an upcoming book, *Feminist Memoirs*, edited by Rachel Blau Du Plessis and Ann Snitow. See also the work of Beth Ritchie which deals with gender violence in the Black community.

9. See Jervis Anderson's *Bayard Rustin: Troubles I've Seen* (New York: HarperCollins, 1997). See also Eric Brandt's edited collection *Dangerous Liaisons: Blacks, Gays and the Struggle for Equality* (New York: New Press, 1999).

10. George Breitman, ed., *By Any Means Necessary* (New York, 1970), 179.

11. *Claiming Earth* (Chicago: Third World Press, 1994), 112, 123–124.

12. *The Sexual Mountain and Black Women Writers* (New York: Doubleday, 1987), 38–39. See also Deborah E. McDowell's "Reading Family Matters," in *Changing Our Own Words: Essays on Criticism, Theory, and Writing by Black Women*, edited by Cheryl A. Wall (New Brunswick: Rutgers University Press, 1991), for a discussion of the debate within Black male literary circles about Black women writers and their portrayals of Black men.

13. Awkward argues in the introduction that the construct "black male feminist" is not an "oxymoronic formulation" (5).

14. While *Traps* was being readied for mailing to our publisher, Devon Carbado's anthology *Black Men on Race, Gender, and Sexuality: A Critical Reader* (New York, 1999) appeared. While he asserts that his anthology is not "a Black male feminist collection," in his epilogue Carbado urges antiracist men "to embrace and assert a feminist political identity" (417), and in this regard his anthology and ours share a similar progressive ideological stance and include some of the same essays. There are, as well, many differences between these two books. Carbado's epilogue also articulates both the challenges and possibilities of a Black male feminist project and the rewards of "men unbecoming men, the process of men unlearning the patriarchal ways in which they have learned to become men" (425).

15. See his essay "Representing Rape: On Spike, Iron Mike, and the 'Desire Dynamic'," in *Negotiating Difference*, 95.

16. Wade-Gayles, 186–187.

# SELECTED BIBLIOGRAPHY

Alan-Williams, Gregory. *Boys to Men: Maps for the Journey.* New York: Doubleday, 1997.

Allen, L. Robert, and Herbert Boyd, eds. *Brother Man: The Odyssey of Black Men in America.* New York: Ballantine Books, 1995.

Anderson, Jervis. *Bayard Rustin: Troubles I've Seen.* New York: Harper Collins, 1997.

Austin, William Bobby, ed. *Repairing the Breach: Report of the National Task Force on African American Men and Boys.* Dillon, Colo.: Alpine Guild, 1996.

Badinter, Elisabeth. *XY, On Masculine Identity.* New York: Columbia University Press, 1995.

Baker-Fletcher, Garth Kasimu. *Xodus: An African American Male Journey.* Minneapolis: Fortress Press, 1996.

Beam, Joseph, ed. *In the Life: A Black Gay Anthology.* Boston: Alyson Publications, 1986.

Belton, Don, ed. *Speak My Name: Black Men on Masculinity and the American Dream.* Boston: Beacon Press, 1995.

Berger, Maurice, Brian Wallis, and Simon Watson, eds. *Constructing Masculinity.* London: Routledge, 1995.

Blount, Marcellus, and George P. Cunningham, eds. *Representing Black Men.* London: Routledge, 1996.

Bly, Robert. *Iron John: A Book about Men.* New York: Addison-Wesley Publishing Company, 1990.

Bolden, Tonya. *Strong Men Keep Coming: The Book of African American Men.* New York: J. Wiley and Sons, 1999.

Bowser, Benjamin P. *Black Male Adolescents: Parenting and Education in Community Context.* Lanham, Md.: University Press of America, 1991.

Boykin, Keith. *One More River to Cross: Black and Gay in America.* New York: Anchor Books, 1996.

Brandt, Eric, ed. *Dangerous Liaisons: Blacks, Gays and the Struggle for Equality.* New York: New Press, 1999.

Brod, Harry, and Michael Kaufman, eds. *Theorizing Masculinities.* Thousand Oaks, Calif.: Sage Publications, 1994.

Brown, Elaine. *A Taste of Power: A Black Woman's Story.* New York: Anchor Books, 1992.

Carbado, Devon W., ed. *Black Men on Race, Gender and Sexuality: A Critical Reader.* New York: New York University Press, 1999.

Carby, Hazel. *Race Men.* Cambridge: Harvard University Press, 1998.

Carroll, Rebecca, ed. *Swing Low: Black Men Writing.* New York: Crown Publishers, 1995.

Carter, Lawrence C. *Crisis of the African American Male: Dangers and Opportunities.* Silver Spring, Md.: Beckham House, 1993.

Chapman, Mark L. *Christianity on Trial: African-American Religious Thought Before and After Black Power.* New York: Orbis Books, 1996.

Cleage, Pearl. *Mad at Miles.* Southfield, Mich.: Cleage Group, 1990.

Cleaver, Eldridge. *Soul on Ice.* New York: McGraw-Hill, 1968.

Connell, R.W. *Masculinities.* Berkeley: University of California Press, 1995.

Davis, Angela. *Women, Culture and Politics.* New York: Vintage Books, 1990.

———. *Women, Race and Class.* New York: Vintage Books, 1983.

Digby, Tom, ed. *Men Doing Feminism.* New York: Routledge, 1998.

Dyson, Michael Eric. *Making Malcolm: The Myth and Meaning of Malcolm X.* New York: Oxford University Press, 1995.

Early, Gerald. *The Culture of Bruising: Essays on Prizefighting, Literature, and Modern American Culture.* Hopewell, N.J.: Ecco Press, 1994.

Evans, Brenda, and James Whitfield. *Black Males in the United States: An Annotated Bibliography from 1967–1987.* Washington, D.C.: American Psychological Association, 1988.

Franklin, Clyde W. *Men and Society.* Chicago: Nelson-Hall, 1988.

———. *The Changing Definition of Masculinity.* New York: Plenum Press, 1984.

Gary, Lawrence, ed. *Black Men.* Newbury Park, Calif.: Sage, 1981.

Gates, Henry Louis, Jr. *Thirteen Ways of Looking at a Black Man.* New York: Oxford University Press, 1997.

Gibbs, Jewelle Taylor. *Young, Black and Male in America: An Endangered Species.* New York: Auburn House, 1988.

Giddings, Paula. *When and Where I Enter: The Impact of Black Women on Race and Sex in America.* New York: Bantam Books, 1984.

Golden, Thelma, ed. *Black Male: Representations of Masculinity in Contemporary American Art.* New York: Whitney Museum of Art, 1994.

Gomes, Peter. *The Good Book: Reading the Bible with Mind and Heart.* New York: W. Morrow, 1996.

Gordon, Jacob U., and Richard G. Major, eds. *The American Black Male: His Present Status and Future.* Chicago: Nelson-Hall Publishers, 1994.

Guy-Sheftall, Beverly, ed. *Word of Fire: An Anthology of African-American Feminist Thought.* New York: New Press, 1995.

Hare, Nathan, and Julia Hare. *Crisis in Black Sexual Politics.* San Francisco: Black Think Tank Press, 1989.

Harper, Phillip Brian. *Are We Not Men? Masculine Anxiety and the Problem of African American Identity.* New York: Oxford University Press, 1996.

Hearn, Jeff, and David Morgan, eds. *Men, Masculinities and Social Theory.* London: Unwin Hyman, 1990.

Hemphill, Essex. *Ceremonies: Prose and Poetry.* New York: Plume, 1992.

———, ed. *Brother to Brother: New Writings by Black Gay Men.* Boston: Alyson Publications, 1991.

Hernton, Calvin. *The Sexual Mountain and Black Women Writers: Adventures in Sex, Literature and Real Life.* New York: Anchor Press, 1987.

———. *Sex and Racism in America.* Garden City, N.Y.: Doubleday, 1965.

Hine, Darlene Clark. *Speak Truth to Power: Black Professional Class in United States History.* Brooklyn: Carlson Publishing, 1996.

Hine, Darlene Clark, and Earnestine Jenkins, eds. *A Question of Manhood: A Reader in U.S. Black Men's History and Masculinity, Volume 1.* Bloomington: Indiana University Press, 1999.

Hoberman, John. *Darwin's Athletes: How Sports Has Damaged Black America and Preserved the Myth of Race.* New York: Mariner Books, 1997.

Hoch, Paul. *White Hero, Black Beast: Racism, Sexism and the Mask of Masculinity.* London: Pluto Press, 1979.

Holloway, Karla F. C. *Codes of Conduct: Race, Ethics, and the Color of Our Character.* New Brunswick, N.J.: Rutgers University Press, 1995.

Jennings, Robert, ed. *The Status of Black Men in America.* Lawrence, Kans.: National Council of African American Men, 1994.

Johnson, Charles, and John McCluskey, Jr., eds. *Black Men Speaking.* Bloomington: Indiana University Press, 1997.

Jones, Charles E., ed. *The Black Panther Party (Reconsidered).* Baltimore: Black Classic Press, 1998.

Kelley, Robin D.G. *Yo' Mama's DisFunkTional!: Fighting the Culture Wars in Urban America.* Boston: Beacon Press, 1997.

Kunjufu, Jawanza. *Countering the Conspiracy to Destroy Black Boys*. Chicago: African American Images, 1985.

Leibow, Elliot. *Tally's Corner: A Study of Negro Street Corner Men*. Boston: Little, Brown, 1967.

Lemelle, Anthony J., Jr. *Black Male Deviance*. Westport, Conn.: Praeger, 1995.

Lorde, Audre. *Sister Outsider: Essays and Speeches*. New York: Crossing Press, 1984.

Madhubuti, Haki R. *Claiming Earth: Race, Rage, Rape, Redemption*. Chicago: Third World Press, 1994.

———. *Black Men: Obsolete, Single, Dangerous? The African American in Transition: Essays in Discovery, Solution and Hope*. Chicago: Third World Press, 1990.

Majors, R., and Janet Billson. *Cool Pose: The Dilemmas of Black Manhood in America*. New York: Simon and Schuster, 1992.

Mercer, Kobena. *Welcome to the Jungle: New Positions in Black Cultural Studies*. New York: Routledge, 1994.

Morrison, Toni, ed. *Race-ing Justice, En-gendering Power: Essays on Anita Hill, Clarence Thomas, and the Construction of Social Reality*. New York: Pantheon Books, 1992.

Morrow, Bruce, and Charles Rowell, eds. *Shade: An Anthology of Fiction by Gay Men of African Descent*. New York: Avon Books, 1996.

Myrsiades, Kostas, and Linda Myrsiades. *Race-ing Representation: Voice, History and Sexuality*. Lanham, Md.: Rowan and Littlefield Publishers, 1998.

Nelson, Jill. *Straight, No Chaser: How I Became a Grown-Up Black Woman*. New York: G. P. Putnam's Sons, 1997.

Omolade, Barbara. *The Rising Song of African American Women*. New York: Routledge, 1994.

Page, Clarence. *Showing My Color: Impolite Essays on Race and Identity*. New York: Harper Perennial, 1996.

Pettiway, Leon E. *Honey, Honey, Miss Thang: Being Black, Gay and on the Streets*. Philadelphia: Temple University Press, 1996.

Powell, Kevin. *Keepin' It Real: Post-MTV Reflections on Race, Sex and Politics*. New York: One World Books, 1997.

Reid-Pharr, Robert F. *Conjugal Union: The Body, the House, and the Black American*. New York: Oxford University Press, 1999.

Smith, Barbara. *The Truth that Never Hurts: Writings on Race, Gender and Freedom*. New Brunswick, N.J.: Rutgers University Press, 1998.

Smith, J. Michael, ed. *Black Men, White Men: Afro-American Gay Life and Culture*. San Francisco: Gay Sunshine Press, 1999.

Staples, Robert. *Black Masculinity: The Black Male's Role in American Society*. San Francisco: Black Scholar Press, 1982.

Stecopoulos, Harry, and Michael Uebel, eds. *Race and the Subject of Masculinities*. Durham, N.C.: Duke University Press, 1997.

Wade, Gloria Gayles, ed. *Father Songs: Testimonies by African American Sons and Daughters*. Boston: Beacon Press, 1997.

Wallace, Michelle. *Black Macho and the Myth of the Superwoman*. New York: Dial Press, 1979.

Wideman, Daniel J., and Rohan B. Preston, eds. *Soulfire: Young Black Men on Love and Violence*. New York: Penguin Books, 1996.

Wood, Joe, ed. *Malcolm X: In Our Own Image*. New York: St. Martin's Press, 1992.

ya Salaam, Kalamu. *Our Women Keep Our Skies From Falling: Six Essays in Support of the Struggle to Smash Sexism/Develop Women*. New Orleans: Nkombo, 1980.

## Essays and Reviews

Beavers, Herman. "The Cool Pose: Intersectionality, Masculinity and Quiescence in the Comedy and Films of Richard Pryor and Eddie Murphy." In *Race and the Subject of Masculinities*, ed. Harry Stecopoulos and Michael Uebel. Durham: Duke University Press, 1997.

Brown, Claudine K. "Mug Shot: Suspicious Person." In *Picturing Us: African American Identity in Photography*, ed. Deborah Willis. New York: New Press, 1994.

Crouch, Stanley. "Gay Pride, Gay Prejudice." In *Notes of a Hanging Judge: Essays and Reviews, 1979–1989*. New York: Oxford University, 1990.

Delany, Samuel R.. "Aversion/Perversion/Diversion." In *Longer Views: Extended Essays* Hanover: Wesleyan University Press, 1996.

Du Bois, W. E. B. "I Bury My Wife." In *W.E.B. Du Bois: A Reader*, ed. David Levering Lewis. New York: Henry Holt and Company, 1995.

Gates, Henry Louis, Jr. "The Black Man's Burden." In *Black Popular Culture*, ed. Gina Dent. Seattle: Bay Press, 1992.

Harper, Phillip Brian. "Eloquence and Epitaph: Black Nationalism and the Homophobic Response to the Death of Max Robinson." In *Fear of a Queer Planet*, ed. Michael Warner. Minneapolis: University of Minnesota Press, 1993.

Herbert, Bob. "Who Will Help the Black Man?" *The New York Times Magazine* Section 6 (December 4, 1994).

Higginbotham, Evelyn Brooks. "African-American Women's History and the Meta-Language of Race." *Signs* (Winter 1992).

hooks, bell. "Challenging Sexism in Black Life." In *Killing Rage: Ending Racism*. New York: Henry Holt and Company, 1995.

——. "Representations: Feminism and Black Masculinity." In *Yearning: Race, Gender and Cultural Politics*. Boston: South End Press, 1990.

——. "Homophobia in Black Communities." In *Talking Back: Thinking Feminist, Thinking Black*. Boston: South End Press, 1989.

Hurston, Zora Neale. "High John de Conquer." In *The Sanctified Church: The Folklore Writings of Zora Neale Hurston*. Berkeley: Turtle Island Foundation, 1981.

Julien, Isaac. "Black Is, Black Ain't: Notes on De-Essentializing Black Identities." In *Black Popular Culture*, ed. Gina Dent. Seattle: Bay Press, 1992.

Leak, Jeffrey B. "American and European Masculinity: A Transatlantic Dialogue." *American Quarterly* 51, no. 1.

Reid-Pharr, Robert F. "Dinge." In *Boys: Masculinities in Contemporary Culture*, ed. Paul Smith. Boulder, Colo.: Westview Press, 1996.

Riggs, Marlon. "Unleash the Queen." In *Black Popular Culture*, ed. Gina Dent. Seattle: Bay Press, 1992.

Saint-Aubin, Flannigan Arthur. "Testeria: the Dis-ease of Black Men in White Supremacist, Patriarchal Culture." *Callaloo* 17, no. 4.

Wade-Gayles, Gloria Jean. "Fighting My Homophobia: An Essay of Gratitude for My Students." In *Rooted Against the Wind: Personal Essays*. Boston: Beacon Press, 1996.

Walker, Alice. "All the Bearded Irises of Life." In *Living by the Word*. New York: Harcourt Brace Jovanovich, 1988.

——. "What That Day Was Like for Me: The Million Man March." In *Anything We Love Can Be Saved: A Writer's Activism*. New York: Random House, 1997.

## Periodicals

*Challenge: A Journal of Research on African American Men*

*Emerge* 7, no. 2. "Special Issue. Unwanted: The Black Man in America."

*Journal of African American Men*. Publication of the National Council on African American Men.

*Men and Masculinities*

*Sage: A Scholarly Journal on Black Women* IX, no. 1. "Male Kin: A Special Issue."

# BIOGRAPHIES

MICHAEL AWKWARD (1959– ) taught African American Studies and literature for ten years at the University of Michigan and is currently Professor of English at the University of Pennsylvania. He is particularly concerned with the ways in which constructions of race, class, gender, and community impact the representations of African Americans in literature, film, and other expressive cultural forms. His books include *Negotiating Difference: Race, Gender, and the Politics of Positionality* (1995); *Inspiriting Influences: Tradition, Revision and Afro-American Women's Novels* (1989); and *Scenes of Instruction: A Memoir* (1999), which explores the genesis of his relationship to feminism. He also edited *New Essays on "Their Eyes Were Watching God"* (1990). He is completing books on contemporary representations of slavery in African American literature, film, and other popular forms, and a cultural history of Philadelphia International Records, which in the 1970s replaced Motown as the most significant locus of Black popular music.

JAMES BALDWIN (1924–1987), born in Harlem, was one of the most important and prolific African American writers and cultural critics of the twentieth century. His writings include essay collections, novels, short stories, poetry, and dramatic works: *Go Tell It on the Mountain* (1953); *Notes of a Native Son* (1955); *Nobody Knows My Name* (1961); *Another Country*; *The Fire Next Time* (1963); *No Name in the Street*; *Blues for Mister Charlie* (1964); *Jimmy's Blues*; *Giovanni's Room*; *The Amen Corner*; *Going to Meet the Man*; *Tell Me How Long the Train's Been Gone* (1968); and *Just above My Head*. He left his native New York in 1948 to live in Paris where he remained until 1956 when he returned for a while to the United States. A civil rights activist during the 1960s, he died in France in 1987 where he had lived for many years.

JOSEPH BEAM (1954–1988), an important political activist and writer, was the editor of the ground-breaking anthology of Black gay literature, *In the Life* (1986), and prior to his death of AIDS at the age of 33, he began editing *Brother to Brother: New Writings by Black Gay Men*, which was completed by Essex Hemphill and published in 1991 after Beam's death. Remembering Beam at the beginning of the text, Hemphill describes him as an activist "dedicated to ending racism, homophobia, heterosexism, and the debilitating oppressions spawned by patriarchy." He was a board member of the National Coalition of Black Lesbians and Gays and was founding editor of the organization's *Black/Out* magazine. His most enduring legacy has been his unwavering commitment to end the silences surrounding the lives of Black gay men.

DERRICK BELL (1930– ), a visiting professor at New York University School of Law, is the author of *And We Are Not Saved: The Elusive Quest for Racial Justice; Faces at the Bottom of the Well: The Permanence of Racism; Confronting Authority: Reflections of an Ardent Protester; Gospel Choirs: Psalms of Survival in an Alien Land Called Home;* and *Afrolantica Legacies.* He resigned in protest from his tenured post as Weld Professor of Law at Harvard Law School when it refused to hire a woman of color to the law school faculty.

BLACK MEN FOR THE ERADICATION OF SEXISM is an undergraduate organization established at Morehouse College in 1994. Drawing upon Black feminist and womanist scholarship, the membership of BMES places itself in an African American male tradition of profeminist thought and practice that begins with Frederick Douglass. In September 1996, the then leadership of BMES, which included Omar Freilla, Keron Williams, Mark Joseph, Anasa Troutman, and Seitu, organized and hosted a two-day conference at Morehouse College entitled "To Be Black, Male and Feminist/Womanist." Attracting scholars, students, and activists from throughout the region, the conference presenters included Gary Lemons, bell hooks, Rebecca Walker, Robert A. Allen, Trisha Rose, and Beverly Guy-Sheftall.

RUDOLPH P. BYRD (1953– ), educated at Lewis & Clark College and Yale University, is the author and editor of *Jean Toomer's Years with Gurdjieff: Portrait of an Artist* (1990); *Essentials* (1992); *Generations in Black and White: Photographs from the James Weldon Johnson Memorial Collection of Negro Arts and Letters* (1993); and *I Call Myself an Artist: Writings by and about Charles Johnson* (1999). With Beverly Guy-Sheftall, he is the co-founder of the Alice Walker Literary Society. Byrd is Associate Professor of American Studies in the Graduate Institute of the Liberal Arts at Emory University in Atlanta, Georgia.

ALEXANDER CRUMMELL (1819–1898), minister, abolitionist, lecturer, teacher, and missionary, was born free in New York City and became one of the most influential Black scholars of the nineteenth century. In 1839 he graduated from the abolitionist-led Oneida Institute in Whitesboro, New York, and later became a minister of the Protestant Episcopal Church, after having been ordained in 1844. Active in the Negro Convention Movement, he was a close colleague of Frederick Douglass. Attempting to escape American racism, from 1848 to 1853 he lived in England and earned a B.A. from the University of Cambridge in 1853. The following year he became a missionary to Liberia and upon his return to the United States in 1873, he founded St. Luke's Church in Washington, D.C. He taught at Howard University from 1895 to 1897 and was one of the founders of the American Negro Academy in 1897, a year before his death. His publications include *The Relations and Duties of Free Colored Men in America to Africa* (1861); *The Future of Africa* (1862); *Africa and America* (1891); and *The Attitude of the American Mind Toward the Negro Intellect* (1898). His sensitivity to the plight of Black women is apparent in a pamphlet he published and distributed in 1881, entitled "The Black Woman of the South: Her Neglects and Her Needs."

FREDERICK DOUGLASS (1817–1895), one of the most influential Black leaders in U.S. history, was born a slave in Maryland, escaped bondage at the age of 21, and became one of the most important nineteenth-century Black orators, abolitionists, and journalists. His autobiographical narratives include *Narrative of the Life of Frederick Douglass, An American Slave* (1845); *My Bondage and My Freedom* (1855); and *Life and Times of Frederick Douglass* (1881). In 1847 he started an anti-slavery weekly newspaper, *North Star*, in Rochester, New York, the home of a prominent Female Anti-Slavery Society whose members included suffragists Elizabeth Cady Stanton, Susan B. Anthony, and Sojourner Truth. Perhaps less well known is his women's rights activism and advocacy of woman suffrage. He was the lone Black male at the historic 1848 Seneca Falls, New York, women's rights convention and played an active role in the deliberations. Until his death in 1895, he remained a staunch supporter of women's causes and on the day he died, spoke at a meeting of the National Council of Women in Washington, D.C. Phillip S. Foner's *Frederick Douglass on Women's Rights* (1976) is an important collection of Douglass's pro-feminist speeches and writings.

WILLIAM E. B. DU BOIS (1868–1963), probably the most well-known, productive Black intellectual, was born in Great Barrington, Massachusetts. He earned a Ph.D. from Harvard University in 1895. His pioneering book *The Philadelphia Negro* (1899) captured the lives of urban Blacks in America. A professor at Atlanta University from 1897 to 1910, he was a founding member of the Niagara Movement in 1905, which led to the founding of the NAACP in 1910. He also founded and edited *The Crisis*, the official organ of the NAACP. Also known as the father of Pan-Africanism, he helped to organize the first Pan-African Conference in London in 1900. Du Bois renounced his U.S. citizenship in 1963 after moving to Ghana two years earlier at the invitation of President Kwame Nkrumah. His books include *The Souls of Black Folk* (1903); *Darkwater: Voices from Within the Veil*; *Africa: Its Place in Modern History*; and *Dusk of Dawn*. He died in Ghana only a few hours before the beginning of the historic march on Washington in 1963.

MICHAEL ERIC DYSON (1958– ) is the Ida Wells Barnett Professor of Journalism at DePaul University in Chicago, Illinois, and a prolific cultural critic. In addition to teaching, he has pastored several Baptist churches. His books include *Reflecting Black* (1993); *Between God and Gangsta Rap: Bearing Witness to Black Culture*; *Making Malcolm: The Myth and Meaning of Malcolm X*; *Reflecting Black: African-American Cultural Criticism*; *Race Rules: Navigating the Color Line*; and *I May Not Get There with You: The True Martin Luther King, Jr.*

GERALD EARLY (1952– ) is the director of African American Studies at Washington University in St. Louis. His books include *Speech and Power*, an anthology of African American essays; *Daughters: On Fathers and Fatherhood*; *Lure and Loathing: Essays on Race, Identity, and the Ambivalence of Assimilation* (1993), a collection of essays by twenty Black intellectuals addressing Du Bois's concept of double-consciousness among African Americans; *The Culture of Bruising: Essays on Prize Fighting* (1994); and *Tuxedo Junction: Essays on American Culture* (1989). He is currently completing a book about Fisk University.

HENRY LOUIS GATES, JR. (1950– ), is William E. B. Du Bois Professor, chair of Afro-American Studies, and Director of the Du Bois Institute at Harvard University. A prominent literary critic, his books include *Figures in Black: Words, Signs, and the Racial Self*; *The Signifying Monkey: Towards A Theory of Afro-American Literary Criticism*, which won the American Book Award in 1989; *Loose Canons: Notes on the Culture Wars* (1992); and *Colored People*, a memoir. He has edited over twenty books, including *The Schomburg Library of Nineteenth-Century Black Women Writers*. He was a recipient of the prestigious MacArthur Foundation "Genius" Award in 1981. With Kwame Anthony Appiah, he edits *Transition*, and is co-editor with Appiah of *Microsoft En Carta Africana* (1999).

EDWARD GUERRERO (1944– ) is an associate professor of Cinema Studies at New York University and the author of *Framing Blackness: The African American Image in Film* (1992). He has written extensively on Black and Third World film and culture for such journals as *Cineaste*; *Jump Cut*; *Journal of Popular Film and Television*; *Callaloo*; and *Ecrans d'Afrique*. He has curated film programs for institutions such as the Whitney Museum and the Smithsonian Institution's National Museum of American History.

BEVERLY GUY-SHEFTALL (1946– ) is founding director of the Women's Research & Resource Center and Anna Julia Cooper Professor of Women's Studies at Spelman College. She also teaches graduate courses on Black feminisms in the Institute for Women's Studies at Emory University. She is the author of *Daughters of Sorrow: Attitudes toward Black Women, 1880–1920* (1990) and edited *Words of Fire: An Anthology of African-American*

*Feminist Thought* (1995). She is currently completing a book with Johnnetta B. Cole on gender issues within African American communities. She has been involved with the national women's studies movement since its inception and provided the leadership for the establishment of the first women's studies major at a historically Black college. Guy-Sheftall serves on numerous national advisory boards dealing with race and gender issues.

ESSEX HEMPHILL (1956–1995), activist and poet, is the author of *Earth Life* and *Conditions*, and the editor of *Brother to Brother: New Writings by Black Gay Men*. He narrated the Black gay AIDS documentary *Out of the Shadows*, and his poetry appears in the films *Looking for Langston* and *Tongues Untied*.

CALVIN HERNTON (1934– ) is a poet, novelist, writer, critic, and Emeritus Professor of African American Studies at Oberlin College where he taught literature and creative writing. He has published nine books, and numerous essays and poems, including the collection *Medicine Man*. He is the author of *Sex and Racism in America*, which has been in print for more than thirty years and translated into six languages, including Japanese. He is also the author of *The Sexual Mountain and Black Women Writers. The Red Crab Gang and Black River Poems* is his most recent collection of poetry.

CHARLES JOHNSON (1948– ), novelist, essayist, scriptwriter, and cartoonist, is the author of several novels: *Faith and the Good Thing; Oxherding Tale; Middle Passage*, which won the 1990 National Book Award; and *Dreamer*. He also wrote *The Sorcerer's Apprentice*, a collection of short stories, and a book of criticism, *Being and Race: Black Writing since 1970*. With Robert Adelman, he is the author of *King & the Photography of Martin Luther King, Jr.* In 1998 he was the recipient of a prestigious MacArthur Foundation "Genius" award. He is presently the S. Wilson and Grace M. Pollock Endowed Professor of Writing at the University of Washington in Seattle.

GARY L. LEMONS (1950– ) is Associate Professor at Eugene Lang College at the New School for Social Research in New York City where he teaches English and women's studies. He self-identifies as a Black male feminist and is the author of several essays, including "To Be Black, Male, and Feminist: Making Womanist Space for Black Men" in the *International Journal of Sociology and Social Policy*. He is presently conducting research on the history of Black women in U.S. fashion design.

HAKI R. MADHUBUTI, formerly Don L. Lee (1942– ), is a poet, essayist, lecturer, community activist, and cultural critic. He is founder of Third World Press (1967) and the Institute of Positive Education in Chicago (1969). He is currently Professor of English and founding director of the

Gwendolyn Brooks Center for Creative Writing at Chicago State University. His publications include *Think Black* (1967), his first volume of poetry and several collections of essays, which include *Black Men: Obsolete, Single, Dangerous?* (1990) and *Claiming Earth: Race, Rage, Rape, Redemption* (1994).

MANNING MARABLE (1950– ), a historian, writer, lecturer, and activist, who self-defines as a Marxist, is Professor of History and Political Science and founding director of the Institute for Research in African-American Studies at Columbia University where he also edits *Souls: A Critical Journal of Black Politics, Culture, and Society.* His books include *Blackwater: Historical Studies in Race, Class Consciousness, and Revolution* (1981); *How Capitalism Underdeveloped Black America* (1983); *Race, Reform and Rebellion* (1984 [1991]); *The Crisis of Color and Democracy* (1992); *Beyond Black and White* (1995); *Black Liberation in Conservative America* (1997); *Black Leadership* (1998); and *Speaking Truth to Power* (1996). His commentary series, "Along the Color Line," appears in more than 325 newspapers in the United States and abroad.

BENJAMIN ELIJAH MAYS (1895–1984), trained as a theologian, was the legendary president of Morehouse College from 1940 to 1967. He was dean of Howard University's School of Religion in 1934. His books include *The Negro's God as Reflected in His Literature* (1938), one of the first scholarly works on African American religion, and his autobiography, *Born to Rebel.* Following his retirement from the Morehouse presidency, he was active on the Atlanta Board of Education and an outspoken civil rights advocate.

NATHAN McCALL (1955– ) is a writer who grew up in Portsmouth, Virginia. After serving three years in prison, he studied journalism at Norfolk State University. He is the author of the best-selling autobiography, *Makes Me Wanna Holler: A Young Black Man in America* (1994), and a collection of personal essays, *What's Going On* (1997). Currently, he teaches in the Journalism Program of Emory University.

MEN STOPPING VIOLENCE (MSV) is a social change organization dedicated to ending men's violence against women. It works locally and nationally to dismantle sexist belief systems, social structures, and institutional practices which oppress women and children and dehumanize men themselves. In the early 1980s, two white men in Atlanta, therapists with a history of involvement in progressive social change, decided to work with men who batter. Independently, two other men, Dick Bathrick and Gus Kaufman, Jr., having been impacted by the battered women's movement, inquired locally about the advisability of conducting a program for batterers and approached Susan May, then Executive Director of the Coalition for Battered Women, who encouraged them to continue. Shortly after they launched their first batterers' group, Kathleen Carlin, then Executive Director of the Cobb County YWCA, hired them to run a group for court-mandated batterers. In 1982, Carlin left the shelter to become the founding executive director of Men Stopping Violence. Five years later, Sulaiman Nuriddin joined MSV and is now Batterers' Intervention Program Team Manager, and coordinates the African-American Initiative, which serves in an advisory capacity to MSV with respect to concerns in the Black community. Ulester Douglas joined in 1994 and is now Co-executive Director for Programs.

HUEY P. NEWTON (1942–1989), co-founder of the Black Panther Party (BPP), with Bobby Seale, is perhaps the most well-known revolutionary figure of the Black liberation struggle of the 1960s. The BPP's advocacy of armed self-defense, Black nationalism and self-determination, and revolutionary politics made it a target for a broad range of repressive tactics, including arrests, detention, and electronic surveillance, by the federal government (especially the FBI and its counterintelligence initiative, COINTELPRO) and local and state police. In 1968, the high-profile murder trial of Newton, who was accused of killing a police officer, began in Oakland, California, which resulted in the international Free Huey Movement. Newton completed a doctorate in the history of consciousness at the University of California at Santa Cruz, and wrote a dissertation entitled "War against the Panthers: A Study of Repression in America," which was published posthumously in 1996. His other books include his autobiography, *Revolutionary Suicide*, and his collection of BPP writings, *To Die for the People*. Chief theoretician of the BPP, Newton wrote a number of position papers in which he articulated the Party's radical platform and philosophy. He also envisioned a revolutionary liberation movement in which racism, sexism, and homophobia would be eliminated, a stance which would distinguish the BPP from other civil rights organizations of the period.

KEVIN POWELL (1966– ) is a poet, journalist, cultural critic, essayist, editor, college lecturer, and activist based in Brooklyn, New York. He is the author of *recognize*, a volume of poetry, and a collection of personal essays, *Keepin' It Real—Post-MTV Reflections on Race, Sex, and Politics*; and he edited, with Ras Baraka, *In the Tradition: An Anthology of Young Black Writers*. Additionally, his essays, articles, and reviews have appeared in *The Washington Post, Vibe, Rolling Stone, Essence, The New York Times, George, Ms.*, and *Code*, the new Black men's magazine for which he is presently a columnist. Powell has lectured on the music, the culture, and the politics of his generation at dozens of colleges and universities across America, and is a frequent commentator on television, radio, and the Internet. A noted hiphop journalist, he is completing a biography of the late Tupac Shakur. He is also completing a memoir, *homeboy alone*.

ROBERT F. REID-PHARR (1965– ) is a writer, scholar, and activist who is presently a professor of English at Johns Hopkins University and director of the Program in Comparative American Cultures. He is the author of *Conjugal Union: The Body, the House, and the Black American* (1999).

MARLON RIGGS (1957–1994) was an award-winning documentary filmmaker. He was the producer, director, and writer of the documentary *Ethnic Notions*, which received an Emmy award, and its sequel, *Color Adjustment*. He also produced, directed, and edited the documentary *Tongues Untied*, a film about Black gays. Prior to his death he was a member of the faculty at the Graduate School of Journalism at the University of California/Berkeley.

ARTHUR J. ROBINSON, JR. (1936– ), is employed at the Center for Disease Control in Atlanta, Georgia, where he resides with his wife, Dr. Johnnetta B. Cole, President Emerita of Spelman College. Prior to moving to Atlanta, he was the Equal Employment Opportunity Officer for the National Library of Medicine at the National Institutes of Health in Bethesda, Maryland. He received a B.A. in biology from Lincoln University and a M.A. in Library and Information Studies at Clark Atlanta University. His community service activities include having served on the Board of Directors for the Atlanta/Fulton County Public Library, the Board of Directors of Planned Parenthood of Atlanta, and the Atlanta Opera. He has also volunteered at the Cascade House, a shelter for homeless mothers and their children.

BAYARD RUSTIN (1912–1987), civil rights strategist/activist, socialist, and pacifist, is perhaps best known for having organized the 1963 March on Washington in the nation's capital, August 28, 1963. He also helped organize the Montgomery bus boycott of 1955–1956, and was a close associate of Dr. Martin Luther King, Jr. A member of the Communist Party, which he left in 1941, Rustin remained committed to socialist principles. He was cofounder and field secretary of the Congress of Racial Equality (CORE) and cofounder of the Southern Christian Leadership Conference (SCLC) in the aftermath of the successful Montgomery bus boycott, of which Dr. King assumed leadership in 1957. From 1964 to 1979 he was director of the A. Philip Randolph Institute in New York City. His writings include *Down the Line: The Collected Writings of Bayard Rustin* (1971) and *Strategies for Freedom: The Changing Patterns of Black Protest* (1976). Jervis Anderson's biography *Bayard Rustin: Troubles I've Seen* (1997) reveals the difficulties Rustin experienced with the civil rights establishment because he was gay.

KENDALL THOMAS (1957– ), a graduate of Yale College and Yale Law School, is Professor of Law at Columbia University in New York City, where he has taught constitutional law, communications law, legal philosophy, feminist legal theory, critical race theory, and law and sexuality. In 1998 he was a Berlin Prize Inaugural Fellow at the American Academy in Berlin,

Germany. His writings have appeared in several law journals; the *Village Voice*; *GLO: A Journal of Lesbian and Gay Studies*; *Assemblage: A Critical Journal of Architecture and Design Culture*; and *Race-ing Justice, Engendering Power: Essays on Anita Hill, Clarence Thomas, and the Construction of Social Reality*, edited by Toni Morrison. He is co-editor of *Critical Race Theory: The Key Writings that Founded the Movement* (1996). He is currently engaged in book-length projects on Clarence Thomas and on sexual democracy in the United States.

CORNEL WEST (1953– ) is a philosopher, theologian, lecturer, and social critic. He is presently Professor of African American Studies at Harvard University. He is the author of *Prophetic Fragments, Prophecy Deliverance: An Afro-American Revolutionary Christianity; The American Evasion of Philosophy; Race Matters; Keeping Faith: Philosophy and Race in America; The Evasion of Philosophy: A Genealogy of Pragmatism;* and *Breaking Bread*, a dialogue with bell hooks.

KALAMU YA SALAAM (1947– ) is a writer and activist and former executive director of the New Orleans Jazz and Heritage Foundation of New Orleans. He was associated with Ahidiana, a Pan-African nationalist organization from 1973 to 1983, and was a founding member and editor of *Black Collegian Magazine* for thirteen years. The author of eight plays, his most recent work is *What Is Life?: Reclaiming the Black Blues Self* (1994), a collection of his poetry and essays. He is also the producer and scriptwriter for Crescent City Sounds, a nationally syndicated weekly radio program in New Orleans. His pro-feminist pamphlet, *Our Women Keep Our Skies from Falling* (1980), was a refreshing collection of essays from a committed Black nationalist who understood the connections between racism and sexism. In *What Is Life?*, his anti-patriarchal stance continues. He celebrates the much-maligned work of contemporary Black women writers (such as Ntozake Shange, Alice Walker, and Audre Lorde), and rejects the idea that their male characters are negative. He also condemns male violence against women; explains why he reads *Out/Look*, a gay magazine, and opposes homophobia, including among Blacks; and questions outmoded notions of Black masculinity.

# INDEX

INDEX

367

eroticism, theology and, 317–318
*Essence* magazine, 131
Ethiopianism, 88n.6
Eve of Africa, 233
*Evening News* (Atlanta), 108
"Exoduster," 127
exploitation, 117

Fabio, Sarah Webster, 151–152n.92
families
economics and, 68–69
effect of slavery on, 121
Fanon, Frantz, 224, 227–228, 229
farming, 95–98
Farrakhan, Louis
Bill Clinton and, 263–264
on birth control, 131
homophobia of, 19, 260–261, 337–338
influences on, 262–263
Million Man March, 15, 237, 243–244,
248–249, 259–266
patriarchalism, 82, 266
sexism, 267–269, 337–338
fatherhood, 80, 199
Fauset, Jesse Redmond, 128
Federal Bureau of Investigation (FBI), 238
Federal Communications Commission
(FCC), 335–336
feminism
African American tradition of, xiv
black feminism, 144, 181–184, 190–191
capitalism and, 152n.98
"Feminism and Equality," **111–112**
feminist black men, 85
male feminism, 81–82, 86–87, 178–184,
190–191
Huey P. Newton and, 345
patriarchalism and, 190–191
racism and, 84
socialist politics in, 152n.98
"Feminism and Equality" (Rustin), **111–112**
*Feminist Theory: From Margin to Center* (bell
hooks), 83–84
Ferguson, Kate, 65, 80
Feudal system, 49
Fifteenth Amendment, 126, 153
film and cinema
*Birth of a Nation*, 112
*Birth of a Race*, 274
*Black Is . . . Black Ain't*, 276
*Bless Their Little Hearts*, 274
*Chameleon Street*, 275
*Childhood of Maxim Gorky*, 211
*Clockers*, 276
*Demolition Man*, 272
*Devil in a Blue Dress*, 274

*Do the Right Thing*, 272
*Drop Squad*, 276
*Hollywood Shuffle*, 276
*House Party*, 295
*Juice*, 276
*La Bête Humaine*, 211
*Looking for Langston*, 275, 276
*The Lower Depths*, 211
*Menace II Society*, 276
*Nothing but a Man*, 274
*Paris Is Burning*, 275, 276
*A Raisin in the Sun*, 274–275
*Rocky*, 272
*School Daze*, 296
*Shaft*, 275
*South Central*, 276
*The Spy Who Shagged Me*, 275
*Summer of Sam*, 274
*Superfly*, 275
*Sweet Sweetback's Baadasssss Song*, 275
*Tongues Untied*, 274, 276, 332–333, 335–
336
X (Malcolm X documentary), 296
*Final Call, The* (newspaper), 262–263
*Fire and Fear* (Torres), 252–253
*Fire Next Time, The* (Baldwin), 327
Fishburne, Lawrence, 271
*Fisk Herald*, 129
folklore, 1–22, 223–224
Foner, Eric, xv
Foner, Phillip, xiv
*For Colored Girls Who Have Considered
Suicide When the Rainbow Is Enuf*
(Shange), 13, 135–136, 346
"For Some Black Men" (Rogers), 134
Foreman, George, 252, 254, 258
Fortune, T. Thomas, 125
Foster, Frances Smith, xviii
Fourteenth Amendment, 153
Fox, Margaret, 36n.13
Franklin, Carl, 272
Franklin, John Hope, 121
Frazier, E. Franklin, 109
Freaknik, 204
"Freaks and the American Ideal of Manhood"
(Baldwin), 207, 340n.14
*Frederick Douglass on Women's Rights*
(Foner), xv
*Free Speech and Headlight*, 128
*Freedom's Journal*, 125
Freetown, Sierra Leone, 53
Freilla, Omar, xix
Freyre, Gilbert, 122
Frohnmayer, John, 336
Fuhrman, Mark, 238, 246
Fuller, Emma, 58